VOLKSWAGEN
WATER-COOLED, FRONT-DRIVE
Performance Handbook

Greg Raven

Motorbooks International
Publishers & Wholesalers Inc
Osceola, Wisconsin 54020, USA ®

First published in 1987 by Motorbooks
International Publishers & Wholesalers Inc,
PO Box 2, 729 Prospect Avenue, Osceola,
WI 54020 USA

Printed and bound in the United States of
America

Library of Congress Cataloging-in-Publication Data
Raven, Greg.
   Volkswagen watercooled/front drive performance
handbook.

   Includes index.
   1. Golf automobile—Performance—Handbooks, manuals,
etc. 2. Rabbit automobile—Performance—Handbooks,
manuals, etc. 3. Jetta automobile—Performance—Handbooks, manuals, etc. 4. Scirocco automobile—Performance
—Handbooks, manuals, etc. I. Title.
TL215.G65R38 1987   629.2'222   87-18656
ISBN 0-87938-268-6 (pbk.)

Both cover photographs were shot by C. Van
Tune. On the front is Autotech's supercharged
with nitrous Golf; on the back is the Bob Hen-
derson/Alistair Oag 16V Scirocco three-
wheeling at Sebring in early 1987.

Contents

About the author

Greg Raven is one of the nation's foremost authorities on Volkswagens, both air- and water-cooled varieties. In addition to the many years he worked on them at various repair shops, Greg also writes about them each month in the pages of *VW&PORSCHE Magazine*. This is a man who lives and breathes VWs; the perfect person to write such a book.

C. Van Tune
Executive Editor,
Autotech
1987

Acknowledgments

The author would like to thank the following people for their many contributions, both small and large, to this book:

James Sly, whose cooking got me involved in the Volkswagen aftermarket, and whose technical knowledge and enthusiasm kept me hooked.

Les Martin of Eurorace, who has been in the Volkswagen aftermarket seemingly forever, and who gave me the run of his stockroom, machine shop, equipment and employees. Les was able to provide all the stuff that everybody else had heard about but never seen, along with the story behind it.

Darrell Vittone of Techtonics, who provided a truly rare commodity, dyno test results. Different people have different ideas about what works and what does not, and separating fact from fiction when dealing with hearsay can be just about impossible. As Darrell is fond of saying, "One test is worth more than 1,000 expert opinions."

Jay Jones, who helped enormously by sharing his years of accumulated knowledge with me.

Randy Michel and Jeff Jardine at Stuttgart Automotive, who gave me unlimited use of the hoists and other equipment at their Porsche/Audi/Mercedes repair shop.

Jim Fuller, vice-president of operations at Volkswagen, who is the ultimate Volkswagen enthusiast. Listening to him talk about his special-project vehicles, I wonder when he has time to drive their stock counterparts.

Gerhard Delf, in charge of powerplant and drivetrain development for Volkswagen in the United States, who not only talks about balancing different aspects of a car but has the technical brilliance to achieve it.

It is rare to come across men like Fuller and Delf. I'm sure Volkswagen's products would be much more boring (and much less successful) without them. The example they set in their lives is a constant inspiration to me. Thanks, too, to their staffs, who bore the brunt of my sometimes incessant telephone calls.

C. Van Tune, who, while serving as editor and editorial director for four magazines, spent many of his own precious spare hours to look over my shoulder and give me guidance.

Preface

What is it about Volkswagens? First they make history with the revolutionary "people's car," the Beetle, and next they start the whole trend toward small, front-wheel-drive cars with the Rabbit. Although these two cars could hardly be more different from one another, they both have the mystical power to inspire their owners to personalize them in one way or another.

As it did with the Beetle, in the Rabbit Volkswagen has provided us with a great day-to-day vehicle. Good looks, good mileage, and a solid and dependable design all add up to a car that can deliver year after year of basic transportation.

And, as with the Beetle, this "basic transportation" is also an incredible platform for high performance. The Rabbit chassis is light but strong, the suspension is simple and fairly easy to tune, and the powerplant seems nearly limitless in terms of what it can be made to do.

With each passing year, the new Volkswagens become more and more capable and sophisticated—and expensive. However, those of us with older Volkswagens, and a little time and money, can easily build up our own personalized "pocket rocket," a phenomenon first envisioned by the appearance of the GTI in Europe in 1976.

The aftermarket for the water-cooled Volkswagen is fast approaching a point at which just about any type of high-performance part is available. And where the Beetle of yore was pumped up to do battle with the so-called muscle cars, today's Volkswagen can easily be injected with enough performance to keep it door-handle-to-door-handle with the latest and greatest of the new high-tech offerings from any continent.

Driving around southern California, meeting the aftermarket parts suppliers and talking with Volkswagen enthusiasts, it becomes apparent that most enthusiasts want to build up their cars for better performance without losing streetability. For them, their hot rods are also their daily drivers. Most of the information in this book is aimed at this type of enthusiast.

On the other hand, it is hard to ignore the people who are putting thousands of dollars and hundreds of hours into making their cars the ultimate machines. Therefore, I have tried to include as much of the "no-limits" information as I could get my hands on. I may not be able to promise you a win at the Longest Day at Nelson Ledges, but I can at least get you thinking about some of the things you will need to consider.

To all of you, I hope that getting there will be half the fun, and that when you get your car set up just the way you have always wanted it, it is as sweet as you always knew it would be.

Philosophy

This book concerns hot rodding your Volkswagen. Because there is so much information and so little room to squeeze it into, I have purposely left out some of the things (such as hands-on procedures) that you will find in a shop manual.

The best shop manuals I have found are those published by the Robert Bentley Company, and I highly recommend that you purchase the one for your model and year car. Used alongside this book, it will provide a very complete picture of what is happening with your car. The new Bentley manuals are laid out completely differently than the old ones, and either can prove to be a little difficult to work with. The information is there, however; all you have to do is find it.

Shop manuals are valuable for another reason, and that is to keep you in touch with the basics. Before you go hot rodding, you owe it to yourself to understand at least some of the basics about what you are changing.

For example, suppose you have a burnt valve in your engine. The easiest thing in the world is to blame that darned old fuel injection (which you really do not understand, so it must be the problem), instead of performing some simple tests to get at the root of the poor running. If you throw away your fuel injection and install carburetors without addressing the true problem, the car will still run poorly.

To take another example, if your suspension is out of alignment, your car will handle badly and the tires will wear out more quickly. Buying expensive tires will not improve the handling, and they will be that much more costly to replace when they wear out prematurely.

No matter how extreme your car gets, pay attention to the basics. Even when you are *sure* you have guessed exactly what is causing some mysterious problem, go through the well-established diagnostic steps rather than jump to a conclusion and miss the fault entirely.

One difficulty in producing a book such as this is that the subject is still growing and evolving. Even setting aside for a moment the fact that in a couple years Volkswagen may have a supercharged, intercooled V-6 engine in its top-performing cars, an author still must try to address the needs of both the nearly penniless teenager for whom a 1975 Rabbit is the living end, and the upwardly mobile young executive who could have bought a BMW but chose instead to purchase a new Golf, spend a few thousand customizing it and pocket the difference. As much as possible I have attempted to cover both extremes, and the variations in between as well.

One area I let slide a little was that of the all-out racer. There are several reasons for that.

First, I have not done much racing, and it would be misleading for me to tell you what to do without personally trying the modifications out.

Second, just about all the basics you need to start racing can be found in one of Carroll Smith's books that cover the race car exclusively.

Third, racing tends to evolve so quickly that even if we could get all the latest up-to-date tricks written down, by the time the book came back from the printer there would be a whole new load of tricks—or rules outlawing the tricks.

Fourth, Volkswagen racers now have access to parts and technical advice through VW Sport (a separate branch of Volkswagen of America). As this is being written, VW Sport is brand-new, but it is the best source for up-to-the-minute go-fast trivia.

Finally, if you are racing and you are even mildly successful, you are going to stay that way only because you are out there discovering what works and what does not work in your specific application. Successful racers are constantly searching for any advantage; if it could be found in a book, librarians would win every race.

I have tried to incorporate a blend of basics, specifics and theory in this book. The basics I hope will keep you out of trouble, and the specifics will reduce the amount of experimentation necessary during any type of change. The theory will help you evaluate new developments in the field that are not covered in this edition, and provide food for thought.

The best way to keep up with what is happening now is to subscribe to magazines that cover this field and to stay on the aftermarket suppliers' mailing lists. It is no secret that advertising is designed to portray products in the best light, but it is surprising how much good information you can glean from reading advertisements and catalogs.

Compromise

Everything ever designed involves compromise. A case in point is the car you drive. If your goal is to eliminate all compromise from your car, you will be disappointed. At virtually every turn you will be confronted with a choice, a trade-off, that involves compromising one factor for another.

Do you want the ultimate fifteen-inch wheel and tire combination, or do you want something that will not rattle your teeth out on the frost heaves and potholes of the turnpike? Do you want the highest amount of horsepower per cubic centimeter, or do you want to be able to use pump gas?

Hot rodding involves more than mere maintenance, and thus can be expensive. There are no limits on the amount of money you can spend on your car. The first performance upgrades may be inexpensive, but as you get further and further from stock you will also find it takes more and more money to proceed. High performance costs money. The limiting factor is more often your wallet than the engineering or labor involved to get there.

One trap that can be difficult to avoid is the "For $100 More" syndrome. This usually grips you after you have everything apart; as you are preparing for reassembly, you find out that "For $100 More" you can have your crankshaft spiffed up, or your gears specially treated or whatever. You will be able to tell when you have fallen prey to this syndrome when your car is taking forever to put back together because you are forever waiting for parts, yet you need more parts still and have stopped balancing your checkbook because you are afraid to look at how much money has been funneled into your project. Forewarned is forearmed.

This book was not conceived to eliminate all compromise, merely to help you examine some of the options you have should you choose a different set of criteria for your vehicle than it comes with from the factory.

Caveat emptor

Everything that involves getting out of bed in the morning can be dangerous. In particular, the car you drive off the showroom floor has a tremendous potential for havoc, personal injury and tragedy. If you want to get into trouble with your car, you do not need to make it into a hot rod first—it is ready when you are.

The aim of this book is to make the car more responsive to the wishes of the driver. A more responsive car is usually a safer car, whether we are talking about the brakes, the handling or the acceleration.

However, having a high-performance car is not a license (or a demand) for its driver to behave irresponsibly. Surface streets are there to help people get to and from their destinations; they are not race courses in disguise. If you need to get the Call of the Wild out of your system, join a car club and rent a race track for a weekend. Maybe attend a high-performance driving school. Above all, consider the consequences of your actions. It is not only your life and health and your car that are at stake, it is the life, health and property of innocent people.

Introduction

About your warranty

If your car is still new enough to have part or all of its warranty in force, consider the consequences of modifying your car if doing so will make it impossible to make a warranty claim. Even though it may seem ridiculous that the warranty will be voided by something as sensible as using a long-drain-interval motor oil, those provisos are there for your protection.

About air pollution, laws and inspections

Air pollution is the dark side of automobile use. Fortunately, auto makers have made impressive strides in reducing auto-related air pollution through oxygen sensors, catalytic converters and vapor recovery systems. Even the basic CIS (continuous injection system) fuel injection that most Volkswagen products are fitted with runs fairly cleanly without any help at all.

In the early days, the words "air pollution control equipment" were irrevocably linked with the image of "low-performance automobiles." This image was due primarily to the way American car manufacturers approached air pollution controls, leading to a lot of "tuning tips" that involved disconnecting the pollution control equipment. With only a couple exceptions, Volkswagen has not had the problems with pollution control equipment that the American car makers have had. In fact, disconnecting your Lambda probe can actually lose you power (and it is illegal).

Whether or not you leave everything connected, if your fuel-injected car is running dirty there is a good chance you have missed something somewhere; you should not have to be a polluter to make horsepower. If you are running carburetors, it can be more difficult to get your motor "clean," but your car can often make just as much or more power running clean as dirty, and a clean engine will usually last longer as well.

To ensure that people are not tampering with their cars, many states have instituted vehicle inspections. Some states use only the sniff test, while others conduct a visual inspection as well. Many states also have established lists of aftermarket parts and products that may be used legally, making anything not on the list illegal to use. Aftermarket suppliers are bound to print warnings along the lines of "certain parts may not be legal for sale or use on pollution-controlled motor vehicles," or "for off-road use only on vehicles that will never be operated on the highway." If you ask an aftermarket firm to install "off-road" parts, it may require you to sign a statement that the car will never be used on the highway. This protects the firm from the massive penalties some states levy against anyone who tampers with pollution control devices. Before you make radical modifications, find out what the procedure is in the state where you will be licensing your car.

There are some things you can do with your motor that will not change its appearance even though they double your horsepower. Even a larger throttle body can be blended into the manifold well enough to pass just about anybody's inspection. Turbochargers and superchargers are different matters entirely. If you have your heart set on one of those, make sure it has been certified for use where you will be licensing your car.

Many aspects of engine hot rodding are antithetical to air pollution laws. However, it is not the intent of this book to encourage anyone to modify his or her vehicle to the detriment of air quality, whether or not the modifications or the emissions are against the law. After all, everyone breathes the same air.

About dynamometer numbers

The dynamometer (chassis or engine) can be a wonderful help in the search for

more horsepower. You can test your theories and new products, and find out if they make more power or not—or whether they can take the abuse of wide-open throttle operation. And some things, like carburetor jetting, are almost impossible to do correctly without one.

But dynos are expensive, and few people have one. Even if you have your own dyno, setting up for a dyno run can take a long time, and a thorough test of a new product can run into days.

In addition, not all dynos read the same, with each other *or* with themselves. You can imagine what can happen when similar yet different engines are tested on different dynos. This difference is compounded when dyno testing does not take into account ambient temperature and humidity. The dyno is a measuring tool. And, as you would not use a ruler that arbitrarily expanded and shrank, you should not depend on dyno numbers that do not incorporate correction factors.

Sometimes companies guess at their horsepower figures based on past experience, instead of spending money on a series of dyno runs. Other companies that spend the time dyno testing may come up with different numbers than a competitor just across town. Still others may hear about the results of someone else's dyno testing and "borrow" the figures for themselves. This means that you should be cautious when buying parts—that you are not just buying a horsepower figure.

From time to time this book gives horsepower figures. These are supplied not to show absolute numbers so much as to show comparative numbers; for example, how much gain you get from a camshaft and an exhaust system.

If you need to buy the most horsepower you can get, find a shop that tests its products on a calibrated dyno, following established dyno procedures. You may not get a number that will beat every other number around, but at least you will know that the money you have spent has gone into making more horsepower, and not into inflating an imaginary figure.

Both engine dynos and chassis dynos work pretty much the same way. The difference is that on an engine dyno, the resistive load is connected to the fly-wheel. On a chassis dyno, the resistive load is applied to the drive wheels. Because a chassis dyno gives you a better idea how the motor will perform as installed (it accounts for just about everything except aerodynamic drag), it is in some ways more accurate. It is certainly easier to use, as you simply drive the car onto the rollers and let it go. An engine dyno, by eliminating external factors, makes it easier to detect more subtle differences without worrying about trans-

mission anomalies or about whether the tires are slipping, as they can on the chassis dyno rollers.

A dyno measures the engine's ability to push against a resistive load, expressing this ability as either horsepower or torque. Dyno runs are all performed at full throttle, with the resistive load being increased or decreased to bring the engine to the rpm range that the dyno tester wants to measure. By performing a number of runs with different loads, the dyno tester can get a complete picture of the power curve of the engine.

If you have your engine dyno tested on an engine dyno, and then install it in your car and retest it with a chassis dyno, you will get two completely different sets of numbers. This is because on the chassis dyno the engine power must be transmitted to the dyno through the transmission and drivetrain, resulting in approximately twenty-five percent lower

engine power figures. Because of the differences among drivetrains, there is no universal correction factor for calculating engine power based on chassis power, or vice versa.

Therefore, when your 102 hp GTI shows only 77 hp on the chassis dyno, do not panic. Use whatever number you get as a base line, and work off that for all future modifications.

About hot rodding

When it comes right down to it, hot rodding your car means making it quicker, or faster, or both. Whether you are talking about quarter-mile speed or time through a slalom, hot rodding your car makes it perform that operation better than it did when you started.

C. Van Tune, editor of *Autotech*, can climb into a car he has never driven before and, at the end of a 0-60 accelera-

tion test, guess within a couple of tenths of a second what the car ran. Most people cannot do that, which is one reason stopwatches were invented. Lord Kelvin once said, "When you can measure what you are speaking about, and express it in numbers, you know something about it; but when you can not measure it, when you can not express it in numbers, your can not express it in numbers, your knowledge is of a meager and unsatisfactory kind: It may be the beginning of knowledge, but you have scarcely, in your thoughts, advanced to the stage of science."

Beyond the stopwatch, there are also available devices such as the Vericom and the G-analyst that use accelerometers to quantify performance. These are useful tools for the enthusiast, although the price for either is a little steep. If you have a car club or a group of enthusiast friends, you may want to pool your resources. I prefer the Vericom, but the G-analyst will give you better information at a road course track. (Both of these tools are discussed in chapter 13.)

If you are serious about hot rodding your Volkswagen, try to get some numbers before and after each modification. Before-and-after testing (whether with a stopwatch or on the dyno) lets you know when you have made a wrong turn or when you have overlooked something. And it helps you to be able to go back to your mechanic or parts supplier with solid evidence that whatever was recommended did not work.

While you are doing your testing, keep in mind that you are usually going to be dealing with incremental improvements. In other words, there will not be one part that, once bolted on, gives you all the horsepower or handling you need. Often you will get a little from one modi-

fication, then a little more from another. It is the sum of all these little gains that gives you the total performance you are looking for.

About those who do the work

This book was written under the assumption that you will be doing at least some of the work on your own car. Whether you are or not, it helps to have a good relationship with your mechanic or tuner. And developing that relationship can be just about as difficult as developing the skills to be a mechanic!

If you do not have the skills of a mechanic and do not yet have a mechanic you trust, the best way to check out a shop is to have it perform some routine maintenance for you. An oil change is a good, inexpensive way to audition an unfamiliar shop. While you are there, you can find out if the shop is interested in doing custom work. Some have found it difficult to put up with temperamental hot rodders, and will not touch such work. Others have the pioneer spirit, are just plain curious or maybe have a hot rod Volkswagen themselves, and will welcome the opportunity to do a little exploration.

Whatever you do, do not beg someone to perform custom work for you. The chances are good that neither of you will be satisfied with the results.

About your budget

The number 1 question in the minds of enthusiasts seems to be, "What should I do to my car if I only have $_____ to spend?" You can fill in the blank with whatever figure you want. The common denominator is that no one has an infinitely large amount of money to spend on his or her car, so somewhere the line has to be drawn.

What is different is that all people have different sets of priorities about what they want out of their cars. Some think the handling is fine but the power is lousy, and some think just the opposite. Clearly, no one set of recommendations will suit everyone.

But that is no reason not to try.

First, enthusiasts can be divided into two groups: those who are satisfied with the way they drive, and those who are not. It is no shame to admit that you could be a better driver, and many times the better driver in a worse car will beat the poorer driver in the better car.

If you have never participated in a high-performance driving school such as those listed in the appendix, and you suspect that your skills could be honed beyond what you have already learned, the first thing you should do is sign up for driver's school. When you graduate you will have a significantly better understanding of your abilities, your car's abilities, how the car should be set up and what needs to be done on the car next—if anything.

If, on the other hand, you are satisfied with your driving abilities (or you have already attended driver's school), I can make some recommendations for what to do with a limited budget.

To start, it is a lot less expensive to let something wear out before you replace it. If you use a super motor oil and change your dual-filter setup every 1,500 miles, you may not want to wait until you wear out your motor before you get big-bore pistons, but you get the idea. There is not much point in wasting seventy-five percent of the life of a set of brake pads

Like the Audi before it, the VW Fox has the engine mounted longitudinally, but many of the modifications discussed in this book will work the same as on a Rabbit.

or shock absorbers or tires unless you are really upset about the way they are performing. If you feel you just have to take near-new parts off your car, save them for later when you want to sell the car but keep your trick parts.

Something else to keep in mind is that it will be less expensive in the long run if you have an idea about what your goal is before you start hanging parts on your car. For example, there is not much point in spending the time and money required to bolt in the latest rage in radical camshafts, and then a couple of months later bolting on that supercharger you have been saving up for.

You may have to remind yourself of your goal from time to time, especially when you bolt on a big throttle valve and a camshaft, and see only modest improvements. But you will find your patience has been rewarded when you finally get a free-flow exhaust, letting the other parts fully work for you for the first time.

Suspension upgrades are the first priority for many of the leading aftermarket tuning firms. Keep in mind, however, that an experienced driver with a stock suspension will beat an inexperienced driver using a high-performance suspension every time.

Assuming that you want more hardware instead of more driving lessons, your first choice for a pre-1985 vehicle would be a lower stress bar, followed by antiroll bars, then an upper stress bar. Chassis and suspension changes in 1985 made stress bars far less necessary, and in the GTI the suspension is pretty good as it sits.

If your shocks are showing wear, do those next. A good set of Tokico low-pressure gas shocks will make those old springs seem much better then they did before. To keep the engine from seeming too sleepy, you can install an exhaust system as a start toward whatever your ultimate horsepower setup will be. (Suspension work is covered in chapter 8; exhausts are covered in chapter 5.)

The next step is a tossup between further suspension work and starting in on the engine modifications. Depending on the condition of the roads where you live, the importance you place on ride quality, and the tires and wheels your car came with, you may choose more power instead of lower but stiffer springs, and tires with a better grip but harsher ride. If you have a GTI, the fourteen-inch rims may be as much as you are willing to give up in terms of ride comfort to get better handling. (If you just have to have different wheels and tires, see chapter 9. Bolt-on horsepower tips can be found in chapter 1.)

Another consideration at this step is engine longevity. Even though an oil cooler and a different fan switch do not make your car any faster, they can make your motor last longer if you live in a temperate or tropical zone. (Oil and water cooling are both covered in chapter 6.)

It is getting close to the moment of truth. How far do you plan to go in your search for high performance? With the suspension taken care of, you can start on your motor. But first you have to decide if you are going to swap for a bigger motor, or maximize the displacement you have. Are you going to try forced induction, or are you going to go for porting and polishing? (Engine work is covered in chapter 2.)

And if you are going for a really big jump in horsepower, are your brakes going to be able to stop you safely? If your car has solid rotors up front, factor in the cost of new brakes to offset the

higher engine output. (Brake upgrades are discussed in chapter 10.)

In summary: Make sure you can drive first; go for chassis and suspension modifications second; make wheel, tire, engine longevity and bolt-on horsepower changes third; and do the engine and brakes together last. Creature comfort and appearance items can come any time you need them. After all, what good is a great-handling car if the seat is so uncomfortable you cannot enjoy driving it?

About safety

There are a few things to be aware of when working on or around cars. Some of them are trivial almost to the point of being nuisances, but some can kill you if you do not keep your wits about you.

When working under the car, always use jacks stands *and* a floor jack. The floor jack serves as a safety in case the car is accidentally pushed sideways and the jack stands flop over. (Note: Always work on level ground.)

If you have the use of a hoist, keep in mind that nearly sixty percent of the weight of the water-cooled Volkswagen is in the front of the car. If you remove the engine while the car is up on the hoist, the weight balance will be immediately and radically transferred toward the rear end of the vehicle.

Do not run the motor in an enclosed space unless you have an exhaust line connected to the tailpipe. The red blood cells in your lungs will bond with carbon monoxide much more readily than they will with oxygen. Because of this preference, carbon monoxide will continue to displace oxygen in your bloodstream even after you step outside for a breath of fresh air. Therefore, it takes quite a while before your lungs return to normal. It is better to not have to deal with it in the first place.

Be conscious of the fact that one gallon of gasoline is powerful enough to propel you, three friends, their luggage and 2,000 pounds of car nearly thirty miles. When working around gasoline, make certain there are no open flames (water heaters, for example), electrical heaters, electric motors, burning cigarettes and so on. It is also a good idea to have a fire extinguisher available. The models with Halon are the best, although they are more expensive, too. Make sure you buy a large one.

If you have to drain gasoline from your fuel tank, store it safely in a sealed container. When you loosen a fuel line on a fuel-injected car, remember that the fuel can be under nearly 92 psi of pressure. It tends to spray out and can get in your face. Also, when spraying out under that much pressure the fuel is atomized, making it *much* more susceptible to ignition.

Speaking of explosions, your battery is a potential bomb as well. Inside the case, the chemical action that stores electrical energy also makes hydrogen gas. Remember the Hindenburg? Same stuff.

When working on the car, disconnect the ground strap first. (This may be a hassle but it is very important.) If you disconnect the positive terminal first and your wrench touches metal, you will create an arc that will do its best to ignite the hydrogen in and around the battery. It is also not a good idea to smoke around a battery, or check the electrolyte level with a match. Be especially cautious around batteries that are charging, or that have just finished charging; that is when they make the most gas.

The same goes for jump-starting a car. Do not connect both ends of the jumper cable to the battery; connect the negative end to the chassis or engine block, away from the battery, in case it arcs across.

For maximum safety, wear safety goggles when working with a battery that is charging or when jump-starting a car. If the battery blows up, it sends hydrochloric acid everywhere. If you get acid on yourself or on your clothes, wash

15

it off immediately. Your clothes will probably be ruined anyway, but you can save your skin if you move fast.

When the motor is running, keep your fingers, hair, test equipment leads, tools, shoelaces, worry beads, shop rags and everything else out of the mechanism. If you get something caught between a belt and a pulley, you may be surprised how fast things happen.

MacPherson struts like those found in the front suspension of your Volkswagen must be taken apart using a spring compressor. Even when the strut assembly is out of the car, the spring is under enough compression to give it a pretty good launch if you undo the retaining nut at the end of the shock absorber piston rod without first clamping the spring.

Carburetor cleaner, brake parts cleaner, hot tank solutions and many other solvents found around cars should be kept off your bare skin. Otherwise, they will soak in through the skin and attack your central nervous system. This is not something you notice right away, but over a period of years it all adds up. Once it gets into your body, it does not leave. These solutions are also not kind to paint, so avoid contact between these solvents and your car's finish.

Another toxic compound that can move in for keeps is asbestos. This is most often found in brake pads and clutch discs, and thus in brake dust and clutch dust. Do not blow asbestos dust around the shop with an air hose. If you are going to be working around asbestos dust a lot, invest in a box of inexpensive breathing filters, the kind that painters use.

Brake fluid is toxic, too, but most people do not attempt to bleed their brakes orally. Brake fluid will, however, strip paint right down to the metal.

If you find yourself facing a fastener that will not budge, be patient. Make sure that you will be under control of the wrench if it slips off the fastener (cracking your knuckle open is no fun). Spray some penetrating oil on the reluctant fastener, tap it with a small hammer to set up a vibration and then try a slow, steady application of torque.

If you change your own oil, gear lube, antifreeze or brake fluid, dispose of the waste liquid properly. Many garages and service stations recycle oil. *Never* dump waste oil on the ground, into a body of water, down the drain or anywhere else where it will not be recycled. The toxins in even a small amount of waste oil are enough to pollute thousands of gallons of otherwise pure water.

There are two additional common chemicals you should handle with care: Freon and silicone spray. Freon 12 (dichlorodifluoromethane) is a mildly dangerous fluorocarbon even before you let it enter the air intake of a running motor. By the time it reaches the end of your tailpipe it can turn into phosgene gas, a chemical warfare agent. If you do get Freon into the intake, shut off the engine and get some air immediately.

If you are not handling Freon around a running motor, caution is still advised. First, if it sprays on your skin you can get frostbite within a few seconds.

Second, if you hook up the recharging system to the air conditioner the wrong way, the bottle of Freon can explode. Wear safety goggles.

Finally, Freon has been linked to the deterioration of the ozone layer. It is true that millions of pounds of Freon are released every year into the atmosphere, but it does not hurt to do everything you can to keep from adding to this pollution.

Silicone spray is not quite as dangerous, but it can be costly when misused around cars that have Lambda sensors. The silicone spray bonds with the sensing surface of the Lambda probe, rendering it worthless. (Even though it is not silicone-based, antiseize compound can ruin a Lamba sensor, too.)

Pike's Peak dual-engine Golf. Su Kemper

Bolt-on engine performance

1

A surprising boost in horsepower can be gained through the use of bolt-on components—parts that do not require taking the entire motor apart to install. But it is also surprising how much money you can waste on parts that do not do you a bit of good. One way to avoid wasting money is to have a plan for what you ultimately want to do with your car. Another is to use only parts that have proven their worth on the dyno.

The term *bolt-on* also implies that you do not have to be an engineer to install the part. Most people can tackle the installation chores on a recurved distributor, a camshaft or adjustable cam sprocket, a larger throttle body or an exhaust system. Most suspension pieces also fall into the bolt-on category.

Some consider a reworked head to be a bolt-on item because you can unbolt the stock unit and bolt on the high-performance unit. However, this book considers a head swap to be more than a bolt-on upgrade for price and other reasons.

For now, consider some of the quick and simple things you can do to improve the performance of your engine, usually in just a few hours' time.

Tune-up

Yes, the lowly tune-up. A tune-up not only optimizes the performance of your car as it sits, but it also puts you in touch with the basics. Without getting the basics right you are wasting your money on high-performance parts. A common example of this is when people replace their fuel injection with carburetors because the car is not running right, only to find that the car runs worse with the carburetors because they never diagnosed the original problem. You must understand the basics before you charge off into the great unknown world of high performance.

In addition to setting the timing (including points, if you have them), adjusting the valves, installing new Bosch platinum plugs and replacing all filters, do not forget to check the plug wires and replace them if necessary. Stock plug wires work great in just about all applications. The so-called high-performance wires can help a little, but they are not strictly necessary. Also check the air sensor plate height, and center and adjust it if necessary before setting the mixture. Tune-up and adjustment procedures can all be found in the Bentley manual for your car.

Recently, Sun has been working to perfect a diagnostic analyzer for automobiles. The current version of its machine is called the Interrogator 2, and considering the thoroughness with which it can examine the motor's operation, you owe it to yourself to have your car checked out at least once by someone who has one. In the hands of a skilled

This is a perfect example of an all-out motor. Note the twin camshafts, mechanical fuel injection, combination dry-sump and fuel pumps (lower left), crank-fired magneto trigger (bottom), and block-off plate for the intermediate shaft hole. Drake Engineering

An engine dyno tests the engine out of the car by applying a load against which the engine must work. Techtonics

operator, the Interrogator 2 can tell you virtually anything you might need to know about the condition of your motor, the fuel injection and the ignition system.

Exhaust

Depending on the year of the car and how much of the exhaust system you are willing to replace, you can find between 5 and 15 hp with a free-flow exhaust. For this reason, and because a high-performance camshaft will show little gain without improving the exhaust, the exhaust is first on my performance bolt-on list.

For years it was argued that on some 1983–and–later cars, replacing the catalytic converter with a straight pipe would cause a *loss* of horsepower. Subsequent tests have shown this *not* to be the case, but I would not recommend removing or disabling the converter. Not only is removal illegal in many states, but the converter helps reduce pollution. The 1983 and 1984 GTIs do have an incredibly restrictive header, however, and replacing it is a big step in the right direction.

On all cars with catalytic converters, if you remove the converter you may have to replace it with a resonator pipe to return the exhaust system to the state of tune at which it will work best. If your state conducts visual smog equipment

inspection or a catalytic converter test, there is no resonator pipe that looks close enough to pass.

There are no real tricks to replacing an exhaust system, but there are several types you can consider. The various offerings are discussed in chapter 5.

Recurved distributor

Recurving the distributor brings in more advance sooner, which you would think would bring in more horsepower as well. And it does, but do not be surprised if you run across someone who claims that a recurved distributor is a waste of money. He or she may have dyno tested a recurved distributor and found that it makes no additional horsepower.

This does not mean you should not buy a recurved distributor. The methodology of dyno testing is not well suited to showing what a recurved distributor does. Where the recurved distributor will help is under partial-load conditions, as opposed to the maximum-load conditions encountered on the dyno. This will give you a seat-of-the-pants difference, and one that can be measured with a stopwatch, but not one that can be detected on the dyno.

Both breaker and breakerless distributors can be recurved. The installation procedure can be found in chapter 12.

Mild cam

For the sake of this discussion, a *mild camshaft* is defined as a camshaft for which it is not necessary to change the valve springs. Everybody has a different opinion on how big a camshaft the stock valve springs will tolerate, but most people agree that the stock springs are not good for much over 0.425 inch of lift. Once you get up to 0.430 inch of lift, you might run out of room.

The problem is that the stock springs vary widely in terms of how soon they go into coil bind (when the coils of the valve spring touch each other, prohibiting further compression). If you have valve springs that will not allow a high-lift camshaft, you must replace the valve springs to avoid broken springs or a ruined camshaft. Replacing the valve springs is also a bolt-on operation, but it requires some special tools, a little talent and patience.

Your choices are to install a camshaft that is only slightly improved over the stock camshaft, install the camshaft you want and let the valve springs worry about themselves, or pull out all the valve springs and have them checked. The odds are with you if you decide to bolt in the big camshaft and pray that the valve springs will be okay. Lots of people have done it, and lots of people have gotten away with it.

If you decide you do not care to chance it, read the section on valve

A chassis dyno tests the engine in the car. Load is applied to the road wheels through rollers. APS

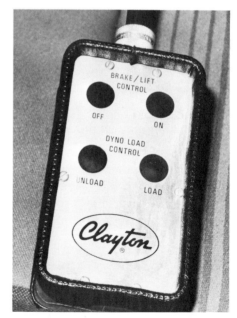

The chassis dyno controls allow the operator to engage or disengage the rollers and to vary the load so that the entire rpm range can be tested. APS

springs in chapter 2 *before* you order that set of ultratrick springs for your street motor.

Staying with nothing more than a mild camshaft, you can expect roughly an additional 5 hp over the gains possible with an exhaust system. Because of the interaction between these two items, do not install a camshaft without a free-flow exhaust.

Adjustable cam sprocket

An adjustable cam sprocket allows you to vary the overall timing of the camshaft relative to the rotation of the crankshaft, and is a perfect example of compromise in high performance. By advancing the camshaft, you move the torque peak lower in the rpm range; by retarding the camshaft, you move the torque peak higher in the rpm range. You get about the same amount of horsepower, but the adjustable cam sprocket allows you to move it around: When you advance the camshaft, you will show a gain of 4 or 5 hp up to 4500 rpm (with a matching loss at the high end), and 5 hp or more from 4000 to 6500 rpm in the retard position (with a corresponding loss on the low end).

In spite of the big horsepower numbers that are casually talked about on cars that need to be wound out to 8500 rpm to work, most people find that they drive their cars under 4500 rpm most of the time. Therefore, advancing the camshaft would provide a better feel and better drivability around town.

In addition to the normal adjustable cam sprocket, there is also an automatic cam sprocket that changes the amount of retard in relationship to the speed of the engine. This is the perfect bolt-on power maker for someone with a $40,000 engine. If you are wondering where that figure came from, consider this: On the dyno, the automatic cam sprocket shows an improvement of 1 hp over the stock sprocket. If you bought one of these, you paid $400 for that 1 hp. If you had paid the same amount for your stock 100 hp engine, it would have cost you $40,000. If you *did* pay that much for a 100 hp engine, this cam sprocket will make perfect sense for you. If not, you may want to spend your money on something else.

Installation and setup of camshafts, valve springs and adjustable cam sprockets are covered in chapter 2.

Throttle body

Installing a monster throttle body seems like a great first step to more horse-

Horsepower needed to attain ¼ mile speed

Speed at the end of ¼ mile	1900 lb	2000 lb	2100 lb	2200 lb	2300 lb	2400 lb
80	89	94	99	104	109	114
85	105	113	118	124	130	136
90	108	134	140	146	152	158
95	149	157	165	173	181	189
100	172	182	191	201	210	220
105	204	215	226	237	248	259
110	238	250	263	276	288	300

Although no substitute for dyno testing, this chart is remarkably accurate at guesstimating peak horsepower based on vehicle weight and quarter-mile speed at the drag strip.

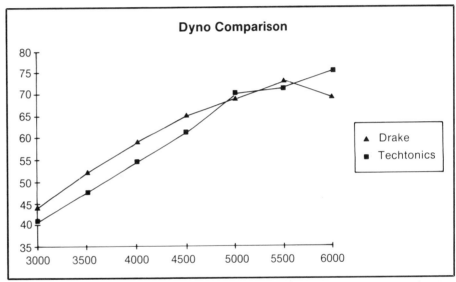

This is why you can get into trouble buying parts based solely on a claimed horsepower number. These two lines show the results of two nearly identical engines run on two different engine dynos using two different procedures. For best accuracy, a calibrated dyno using atmospheric correction factors is the way to go.

The read-out on a chassis dyno is simple: the display shows miles per hour and horsepower. It is up to the operator to determine coolant and oil temperature and any other factors of interest. APS

power, especially if you have an early car with the restrictor venturi that creates the vacuum needed by the EGR (exhaust gas recirculation) system to work properly. In 1985, Volkswagen even went to a large throttle body (compared with the small dimensions of the earlier throttle bodies). Unfortunately, the throttle body is one of the last bolt-on pieces to buy, and only after you have freed up the rest of your engine's breathing.

The throttle body is *not* the restriction in the intake tract; that honor falls to the intake manifold. For maximum benefit from the throttle body, you will need to match port the intake manifold at the throttle body end, and port the intake manifold runners. Even then you will find that a bigger throttle body works best on large, modified motors.

There are two styles of throttle body: the single-butterfly style (as exemplified by the Weber Big Throat) and the progressive style (as exemplified by the Audi 5000). Most suppliers now recommend and sell progressive throttle bodies.

The Weber Big Throat throttle body is not only hard to drive, it also flows no more air on the flow bench than the stock body, mostly because of the adapter plate that is required to make it mate with the intake manifold. All in all, this is a poor choice for any application.

A more complete discussion of the throttle body can be found in chapter 3.

Lambda Power

The Lambda Power allows you to increase the duty cycle in oxygen sensor

fuel injection systems. This works only on the pre-1983 cars, but it can mean up to 1.5 seconds less in 0–60 time. The Lambda-equipped GTIs have a similar function built into the stock fuel injection, so you will not see much gain there. If you are running a force-inducted motor, the Lambda Power can boost low-end response, but it is tricky to set up.

Carburetors

Should you install a set of trick carburetors on your car? Yes and no. Yes if you have a 1975 or 1976 Volkswagen with the stock carburetors. They are difficult to live with and should be replaced early in the hot rodding process.

No if you have fuel injection. Volkswagen fuel injection is incredibly nice. Not only is the drivability of the stock fuel injection better than that of a carburetor, but it will automatically compensate for lots of engine modifications without a squeak of protest. If you have CIS injection on your car, hang onto it.

If you have to have a carburetor for whatever reason, see chapter 3.

Unplugging the Lambda sensor

The Lambda sensor is viewed with suspicion by some, but unless you have been diddling with the adjustments and as a result your car is running the same way a gasoline engine runs when the attendant fills the tank with diesel, the

Lambda sensor is a great watchdog that makes sure your motor is getting the right amount of fuel. If you unplug it, you will lose horsepower and mileage.

The only reason you should ever defeat the Lambda sensor is if you need to run leaded gas, at which time you must remove it and the catalytic converter to avoid damaging those components.

Breakerless ignition

If your distributor has points, consider a breakerless ignition. Breakerless ignitions can deliver a hotter spark than points can, and you have to adjust them only once. Although in some cases you can find more horsepower with a breakerless ignition, I install them more for the convenience than anything else.

One area in which a breakerless ignition gives more horsepower than a points ignition is consistent timing. As points wear, the timing will change and you will lose horsepower gradually. With a breakerless ignition there is no wear and no timing change, so your ignition runs at peak performance always.

There are a couple of good units on the market, including the Allison and the Perlux. Installation procedures can be found in chapter 12.

Coils

Coils make only a very slight difference in the way the car performs, and they almost never go bad. The stock coil is fine for most high-performance applications.

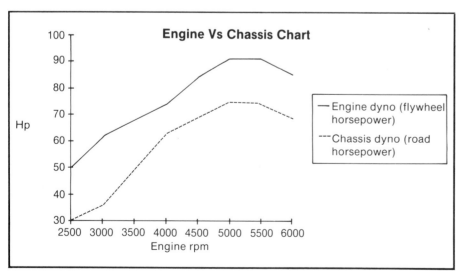

The difference is even greater when comparing engine dynos with chassis dynos. Because of power losses through the transmission, the drivetrain and tire slip, the chassis dyno will always read lower.

Techtonics Tuning Dyno Test

Engine	Fuel	Induction	Ignition	Conditions
Bore ____ Stroke ____ Disp. ____ C. R. ____ Cam ____ Cam Timing ____	☐ Pump Gas ☐ Race Gas ☐ Alcohol	☐ Carb(s) ☐ Fuel Injection ☐ Turbo ☐ Supercharger Valve Sizes ____	☐ Conventional ☐ Electronic ☐ Magneto ☐ With Knock Sensor Ignition timing ____	Date ____ Temp. (°F) ____ Humidity ____ Bar. Press. ____

RPM	Scale in Lbs.	Re-Test	BHP	BHP (corr.)
2500				
3000				
3500				
4000				
4500				
5000				
5500				
6000				
6500				
7000				
7500				
8000				

As above except for the following: _____

RPM	Scale in Lbs.	Re-Test	BHP	BHP (corr.)
2500				
3000				
3500				
4000				
4500				
5000				
5500				
6000				
6500				
7000				
7500				
8000				

The more things you take into consideration when testing, the more accurate your results will be. This sample dyno sheet allows you to accurately compare results attained over a period of time without having to remember all the little details yourself.

The engine

2

In many cars, the quickest way to get more horsepower is through an engine swap, typically using a big American V-8 in place of a smaller engine. This is next to impossible with the Volkswagen. The Volkswagen powerplant is very versatile, however, and it is a strong basis for performance modifications. Even though it cannot be built up to the same displacement as a big V-8, it can be made considerably larger with a combination of added bore and stroke. When you are all done, you will have a very reliable motor because you do not have to solve basic engineering problems that were left unaddressed by the manufacturer. In many cases, it seems as if

Volkswagen is encouraging us to explore the limits of performance with the tremendous little engine it has given us.

Engine swaps are still possible, provided you stay with the Volkswagen block. Even with the vast differences between a 1975 Rabbit and a 1987 Scirocco 16V, it is still possible to fit any engine and transmission in any chassis, although sometimes you will have to work at it a little. The biggest change came with the 1985 cars, when Volkswagen started using a subframe to hold the engine and transmission, changing the motor mounts in the process. The 1985–and–later motors also have the fuel distributor on the right side of the

engine bay, with the exception of the Scirocco, which still has the fuel distributor where you expect it to be.

It would be very difficult to mount a subframe in an early car, or to do without a subframe in a later car, but there are pieces available to make engine swaps possible.

As you look through the pages of magazines, you will notice that many firms sell complete engines. Two terms commonly used in connection with these motors are short-block and long-block. A *short-block* is the block with a crankshaft, an intermediate shaft, an oil pump, pistons and connecting rods. In other words, it will include everything below

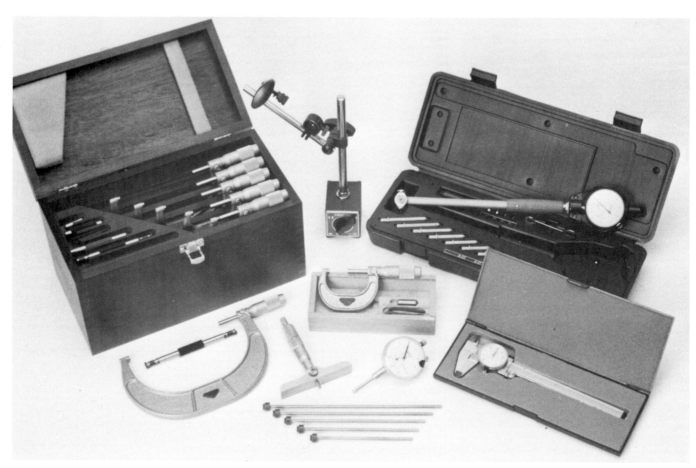

A micrometer set, inside mikes and depth mikes can put a big dent in your budget. Start off with some dial calipers and Plasti-

gauge and add more pieces as you need them. BHJ Products

the cylinder head, with the possible exception of the oil pan. A *long-block* will have all of these items, plus the cylinder head (with valves, seats, springs and so on), camshaft and cam belt. If you are short on time, patience or mechanical ability, buying a short- or long-block is one way of getting your car on the road with a minimum of fuss.

Tools and techniques

You have seen the ads for the long-blocks, but this time you want to build your own. Now it is time to get serious about putting together the motor. One of the most important things you can do when preparing your engine for assembly is to keep everything clean. Not so the parts look clean at twenty feet, but really clean. The cleaner you keep everything during the assembly process, the longer your engine will last once you get it together. Once you get the parts clean, store them in plastic bags until you are ready to install them.

In looking over the steps outlined here, especially the steps on cleanliness, you might feel overwhelmed by the details involved in building a true high-performance machine. Keep in mind that the procedures mentioned are for a worst-case situation. In other words, you can usually get away without doing some of them. But the more you follow the recommendations, the better off you will be, especially if your previous motor died a horrible death or if you are planning on going all out with the motor you are building.

Two terms that are used a lot are balancing and blueprinting. *Balancing* is the process of making all reciprocating and rotating parts weigh the same so the engine will spin as smoothly as possible. *Blueprinting* refers to the process of machining the various engine components to match the "perfect" dimensions called for in the blueprint when the part was designed.

Blueprinting is necessary because not all parts are manufactured precisely as they were intended. When Paul and Karl Hacker bought a pair of Scirocco 16Vs for the Firestone Firehawk series, for example, a teardown revealed that one of the rod journals was larger than the specifications allowed. Had they attempted to race with that crankshaft, they would have had a tough time winning—or even finishing. Blueprinting will not always show up flaws this serious, but for maximum performance you want to have

everything as close to perfect as you can make it.

In addition to the normal tools, there are some special tools called for to adjust the valves on cars with solid lifters. The first of these tools is not really that special, but if you have the right one the job will go much faster. I am talking about a feeler gauge. The one I use is from Snap-On, and is a feeler blade holder that holds a different blade on either end. By having a 0.008-0.012 inch go/no-go gauge on one side and a 0.016-0.020 inch go/no-go gauge on the other, I can quickly and easily check all the clearances without fumbling around for a feeler gauge.

If you are going to be measuring everything, you are going to need tools to measure with. After you purchase a machinists rule and a couple of microm-

eters, however, your passion for acquiring more measuring instruments will probably be somewhat dampened. After all, this is money you could be spending on parts!

A good example of a tool you probably will *not* buy right away is a set of inside micrometers. These are expensive and can be difficult to use properly. If you have a good set of outside micrometers and a good feel for measuring things, you can get by with a set of snap gauges, but there is something even less expensive that seems to work just about as well: Plastigauge.

Plastigauge is the brand name of a soft, round material that comes in several different sizes and can be used for checking inner clearances, such as between crankshaft journals and rod bearings. The Plastigauge itself is a precise

Bore vs stroke

	Stock bore and stroke	Stock stroke with 1 mm larger bore	Stock bore with 1 mm larger stroke	Stock bore with realistic stroker crank
Bore	79.50	81.50	79.50	79.50
Stroke	86.40	86.40	87.40	90.50
Displacement	1715.53	1802.93	1735.38	1796.94

By plugging different bores and strokes into the formula, you can quickly see that engine size goes up much faster as the bore is increased than when the stroke is increased.

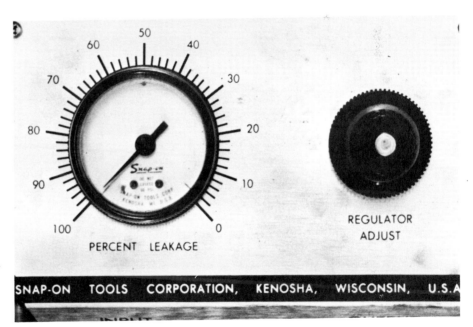

A leakdown test is the next step beyond the compression test. A cylinder-leak detector such as this Snap-On unit is required, however.

This two-liter engine has hundreds of hours of labor in it and covers the quarter-mile in 14.73 seconds at 93.75 mph, but it still looks almost totally stock from the outside. Techtonics

With these components and a little head work you can have one screaming two-liter motor. Techtonics

diameter, so that when it is crushed flat the width of the crushed Plastigauge can be predicted, and used to determine the amount of clearance.

Different sizes of Plastigauge are different colors, and each package has markings on the outside to help you determine the measurement you are seeking.

When using Plastigauge, never place it in such a position that the weight of a component will be resting on it, or you will get a false reading. For example, do not put the Plastigauge over the crankshaft bearing shell and then lay the crankshaft on top of the Plastigauge. Lay the crankshaft in first, then lay the Plastigauge on the journal, then carefully install and torque down the bearing cap.

Never move a part or use oil around the Plastigauge, as the reading will be distorted.

For engine diagnostic work, another valuable tool is the leakdown tester. The leakdown tester helps you determine the integrity of the combustion chamber by pressurizing the chamber and then telling you how much of that pressure is leaking out. Low leakdown means that the rings, valves and head gasket are sealing properly, and that there are no cracks between the combustion chamber and the block or head. A leakage figure in the middle range (ten to twenty percent) indicates that something is wrong. A leakdown figure above twenty percent means it is time to tear down the motor and fix whatever is wrong.

Leakdown testers are specially built, so you cannot use a compression gauge to duplicate the results of a leakdown tester. If you do use a leakdown tester and find that you are getting an unacceptable leakdown reading, try to locate the source of the problem before you pull down the engine. Intake valve leaks will

be audible through the intake manifold. Exhaust valve leaks can sometimes be heard through the tailpipe. Head gasket leaks and cracks in the head or block will show up as bubbles in the coolant, so remove the radiator cap before you pressurize the cylinder. Bad rings will produce audible leaking sounds through the oil filler cap.

Alway check leakdown with the engine at TDC (top dead center) for the cylinder you are checking. Remember that when you pressurize the cylinder, the engine is going to want to spin if the piston is not exactly at TDC, so any wrench you have on the end of the crankshaft to turn the motor is going to go flying. If you have the transmission in gear and the wheels

The 1987 VW GTI 16V.

The 1987 VW Scirocco 16V. Note that its fuel distributor is in the "old" location, unlike the GTI version.

This adapter, flywheel and pressure plate let you bolt a Rabbit engine to a Beetle transmission. Eurorace

25

are touching the ground, the car is going to want to move. In short, observe all the common safety precautions.

Not as useful as a leakdown tester for diagnostic work, but much easier to use, is the compression tester. When using a compression tester, remember to disconnect the ignition so you do not get a shock. Also keep in mind that compression readings are dependent on the speed at which the engine cranks over, so if the starter or battery is not in good shape or the motor oil is frozen, you will get low compression readings.

If you perform a compression test along with your normal maintenance schedule, you will be able to catch downward performance trends before they become bigger problems. Also watch the reading of the very first compression stroke. If it is in the neighborhood of 80 to 90 psi, there is a good chance that the leakdown percentage will be low. If the first compression stroke gives a low reading that then builds up to a normal reading, you may have some leakage.

When inspecting a car for purchase, at least do a compression test. Try to perform a leakdown test, too, to get a clearer picture of the condition of the engine.

Increasing engine size

Bigger engines make more horsepower. Although forced induction (examined later in chapter 4) can make a smaller engine act more like a bigger engine, in most cases the straightforward approach to enhanced performance comes from more cubic centimeters in the motor.

In the search for more cubes, you can increase the bore, or increase the stroke, or both. The difference between these alternatives can be seen in the formula for calculating engine displacement:

$$\text{Displacement} = \frac{\pi \times B \times B \times S \times C}{4 \times 1000}$$

In this formula, B equals the bore in millimeters, S equals the stroke in millimeters and C is the number of cylinders. Every increase in the bore increases the displacement by the square of the increase divided by 4 (the 1000 is there to convert the answer to cubic centimeters). An increase in the stroke increases the displacement only by the amount of the increase divided by 4.

A 1 mm increase in the bore will yield more of an increase in displacement than will a 4.1 mm increase in the stroke. It would also be less expensive to bore the block for the larger pistons than it would be to buy the long-stroke crankshaft and pistons to match. Furthermore, larger bores have more room for the combustion chamber and bigger valves, allowing better breathing. Therefore, if you are in search of a larger-displacement engine bigger-bore pistons are a less expensive way to go.

This is not to say that longer strokes are not very nice. The Volkswagen block will allow only about 3 mm of overbore before you start running out of room. If you are still looking for more displacement, you can get it with a long-stroke crankshaft. In a turbocharged application, a radical overbore is not the best idea because you run into cooling problems, so again the answer is to lengthen the stroke.

This Bertil Racing 1800 features dual-sidedraft Weber 34s, 13:1 compression, Bosch crank-triggered ignition and solid lifters to make 180 hp for the Champion Spark Plug Challenge series. Note the boxed strut towers and the alternator drive off the camshaft. The transmission is a custom-built crashbox.

Here's one way of doubling your displacement: adding an engine in the rear. Su Kemper

As the stroke becomes longer (relative to the connecting rod), the engine makes more torque lower in the rpm range, which is one of the reasons the late 86.4 mm crankshaft with 144 mm rods is more drivable than the early 80 mm crankshaft with 136 mm rods. Even though the later rods are 8 mm longer, the rod/stroke ratio is 1.67 as opposed to the early motor's 1.7 ratio.

In theory, any of these combinations (and others, as well) is possible. In practice, some of these combinations are more common than others. Unless you have a pressing need to hit a specific displacement, stick with the common combinations. They are a lot less expensive.

Factory motors

The factory has given us seven combinations of major interest (a listing of the various cars and their displacements can be found in the appendixes). Chronologically, they are as follows.

1471 cc, 76.5 mm × 80 mm

For the Volkswagen, this was the first engine size. With the head off, the block can be easily identified because there are no steam holes between the cylinders, as in all later blocks. The later motors also have siamesed cylinder bores for greater strength, something missing from this block. With the reduced cylinder wall clearance, this block cannot be honed to more than 79.5 mm. This is a fine motor to sell to someone else who is not interested in hot rodding.

1588 cc, 79.5 mm × 80 mm

This motor (commonly referred to as the 1600) is what helped Volkswagen gain its reputation. The motor is strong and has all the basics necessary for performance tuning. Super Vees use a variation of this engine and get over 170 hp, albeit at very high rpm.

European 1588cc, 79.5mm x 80 mm

In Europe, the 1600 cc motor (as found in the GTI) made 100 hp running 9.5:1 compression. To get the increased compression ratio, the GTI motor uses dished pistons and a flat head surface, so instead of the combustion chamber being in the head it is in the piston. On an early car, you too can bolt on twenty-eight percent more horsepower by swapping your flat-top pistons for the dished pistons and your head for the Heron type of the Euro GTI.

At the time these engines came out they were considered the best. Lately the

The back side of the 1.8 block. Note the larger oil return hole at the center front of the block, and the additional oil return hole on the right front. Techtonics

The back side of a 1.6 liter block. Techtonics

The back side of a 1.7 liter VW block (the Chrysler blocks say "1.7"). Techtonics

trend has been more toward motors that make their power lower in the rpm range.

1457 cc, 79.5 mm × 73.4 mm

This is what happens when you combine a fuel crunch with strict emissions standards. The crankshaft was changed from the forged unit to a cast piece that was not fully counterweighted. If you are shopping for a core motor, be aware that the stamping on the back of the block still reads "1.6." Pull the pan before you plunk down your money.

1715 cc, 79.5 mm × 86.4 mm

The 1700 motor continued the tradition of the 1600 engine, and the after-market jumped all over it as well. The increase in stroke makes this the best choice of the early motors for hot rodding. The 1700 block has the letter H stamped on the back. If you come across a block that has 1.7 stamped on the back, you have a block out of a Chrysler Omni or Horizon.

Volkswagen sold motors to Chrysler for a couple of years, and if you are buying a motor from a junkyard you may be offered one of them. The Omni block can be used in any build-up, with two caveats. First, it does not have the drilled and tapped pads for mounting the air conditioner bracket, so you cannot use this block in any application that requires air conditioning. Second, the Chrysler products came with carburetors only, so to run fuel injection you will need to switch heads.

1781 cc, 81 mm × 86.4 mm

The 1800 engine showed up in the first American incarnation of the GTI in 1983. The rods are 144 mm in center-to-center length compared with the 136 mm length of the rods in the early cars, the wrist pin is smaller at 20 mm and the rod journal is larger (all this even though the stroke is the same as that of the earlier crankshafts). The valves are spaced a little farther apart than in the earlier motors, and there is an additional oil return drain to complement the larger drain located front and center.

The heads from this motor can be made to work on the earlier blocks, but some modification is required. The blocks are marked 1.8. These blocks have enough internal clearance to accept a 91 mm crankshaft as a bolt-in.

1595 cc, 81 mm × 77.4 mm

This engine appears only in Europe in a version of the Jetta that runs carburetors and 9.0:1 compression. It uses the cylinder head from the 1800 motor, along with the rods and block.

Metal preparation

This section often refers to different types of metal preparation. Brief explanations of the different techniques follow.

Magnafluxing

Magnafluxing is a method of detecting flaws in metal components that would not otherwise be visible to the naked eye. It works only on ferrous materials such as steel and cast iron.

The component to be Magnafluxed is placed in a very strong magnetic field while it is being bathed in a special fluo-

For best results, all boring and honing must be done with a torque plate on top of the block and with the main caps bolted on. Techtonics

Displacement

				Stroke				
Bore	73.4	77.4	80	84.6	88	90.5	91	94.5
76.5	1349.5	1423.0	**1470.8**	1588.5	1617.9	1663.9	1673.1	1737.4
79.5	**1457.4**	1536.8	**1588.5**	**1715.5**	1747.3	1796.9	1806.9	1876.4
80.5	1494.3	1575.7	**1628.7**	**1759.0**	1791.5	1842.4	1852.6	1923.9
81.0	1512.9	**1595.4**	1649.0	**1780.9**	1813.9	**1865.4**	**1875.7**	**1947.8**
82.5	1569.5	1655.0	1710.6	**1847.4**	1881.7	**1935.1**	1945.8	**2020.6**

This chart shows displacement in cubic centimeters for all the combinations of bore and stroke. Common combinations are shown in boldface.

rescent solution. Under an ultraviolet lamp, the trained operator can tell by the way the fluorescent solution forms patterns on the metal where the flaws are.

Everything from stress risers to subsurface cracks can be detected this way, often saving a lot of money and hard work that would otherwise go into further preparation of the component (a crankshaft, for example), to say nothing about the cost of the damage that would be done when the part breaks, or of the cost of losing a race.

Nitriding

Nitriding involves heating a piece of ferrous metal in a salt bath. The salt attaches to the surface of the metal, making it much more resistant to scratches and other damage.

Tuftriding is a special version of the nitriding chemical and heat-treating process. It uses molten cyanide salts and 1,000-plus-degree-Fahrenheit temperatures to reduce surface friction, increase wear resistance and increase component strength. After being Tuftrided, the top few thousandths of an inch of the part has an iron carbide outer surface, beneath which is an intermediate diffusion zone. Under the diffusion zone, the metal is unchanged.

Shot peening

Metal that is shot peened is bombarded by thousands of pieces of cast-steel or cast-iron shot of various sizes and hardnesses, depending on the end result required. When a piece of shot hits the surface of the metal, the upper layer of the metal (0.005 to 0.010 inch deep)

is stretched slightly. This causes a compressive stress in the surface of the metal that can be much higher than the normal tensile stress found within the part. The two stresses offset each other, resulting in increased fatigue and crack resistance.

The ability of shot peening to change residual tensile stress to beneficial compressive stress is particularly good on machined or ground surfaces. Areas of concentrated tensile stress, such as notches and fillets in crankshafts and gears, also can be made stronger using shot peening.

After shot peening, the metal surface is usually not processed any further, except for the application of a coating of oil to prevent corrosion. Heat treatments of any sort, for example, reduce or eliminate the effectiveness of shot peening.

Moly impregnation

Moly impregnation is *not* done by adding a can of liquid molybdenum to your oil. Moly impregnation is done after the parts have been painstakingly cleaned and the surface prepared to accept the moly. So-called dry moly (molybdenum disulphite, or MOS_2) is used, going deep into the pores of the metal. In this compound, the molybdenum is bonded to the metal by the sulphur. Sulphur also has a high affinity for hot metal, so if you lose lubrication, even on a microscopic area, the sulphur will bond to it, carrying the moly with it.

Molybdenum construction is similar to that of a deck of cards. If you place a deck of cards on the table and press down hard, you can still slide the cards relative to each other. The molybdenum disulphite fills in all the dips and valleys in the metal, presenting a smooth and low-friction surface to other moving parts.

Moly impregnation is a multifunction coating in that it not only aids lubrication, it also helps dissipate and radiate heat. In the combustion chamber, for example, this means that less of the heat will soak into the head, block and piston. What heat does soak in is quickly and evenly spread out to reduce detonation-causing hot spots. Simultaneously, the soaked-in heat is being transferred to the coolant (in the head and block) and into the oil (from the underside of the piston). The lubricity of the moly even retards carbon build-up.

Treated parts come out black from the excess of moly that is applied, but after a running-in period the excess will rub off, leaving the part looking similar to an untreated part. The moly is still in the pores of the metal working, however. Moly impregnation does not change tolerances, although with the increased lubricity of the metal, tolerances can be reduced if desired.

Gun Kote

Gun Kote is the name of the process developed by Kalgard to coat metal with

Removing casting flash and making room for a stroker crank. Note the tape protecting the bearings. James Sly

Techtonics uses an intermediate shaft that has been sawn in half to check the intermediate shaft bearings.

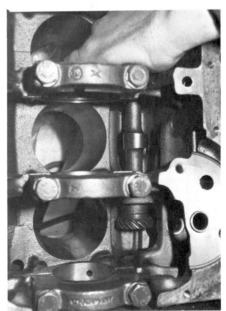

a phenolic resin that contains molybdenum disulphite and other ingredients for the purpose of promoting cooling. The difference between Gun Kote and moly impregnation (which is also a Kalgard process) is that the Gun Kote is not used in areas of friction. The molybdenum does work in a similar fashion to disperse and radiate heat quickly.

Zirconium oxide coating

Zirconium oxide was developed for the space industry. When applied to aluminum it reduces heat transfer, as a result of the lower heat conduction of zirconium oxide (0.53 BTU/hr/ft) compared with the heat conduction of aluminum (139 BTU/hr/ft). The coating is applied using a special process that mixes powdered zirconium oxide with superheated plasma gas that is sprayed onto the aluminum. The coating is three layers thick, adding a substantial 0.015 to 0.018 inch to the surface.

If you are way under budget on your engine work, Turbokoting is for you. Pistons cost about fifty dollars apiece to coat, and the cylinder head will run around $300. For this reason, I recommend this only for highly stressed turbo motors, and then only if the coating is properly applied.

So far there have been no real problems with the coating flaking off and destroying the turbo (although any coating of this type has the potential for doing so), but it is a good idea to take some 220 or 320 grit sandpaper and lightly scuff the finished coating.

Another reason that this does not get an unqualified okay is that it does not remove or reduce the heat of combustion, it just keeps it from soaking into the coated surface. This heat still has to go somewhere. In a turbo motor, if you can get it all going out the exhaust port you will have better turbo efficiency and better throttle response. The problem is that some of the heat also gets to the rings, the cylinder walls, the valves and so on.

For less than an all-out motor, you probably will not want to get involved in the research and development it would take to discover the pros and cons of using this coating in your application.

The block

Differences among blocks

Undecided between building up your old block and buying a complete short- or long-block that promises all new parts? For some parts the newer they are the better. However, in this case a seasoned block has the advantage over a brand-new casting. Because of the metallurgy and construction of a block, things tend to shift around a bit as the block settles in dimensionally. If you need to replace a motor that is completely worn-out, you may not have a choice. Otherwise, go with a good used block.

Preparation

Preparation involves many diverse activities, such as making sure you have all the parts you will need, having all the proper tools, getting all the machine work done in the right order, having the right information available and so on. Read through all the following steps even if you do not plan on performing them on your engine. Any engine would benefit from all these steps, but not everyone has all the time and money needed to complete them. If you are going to take short cuts, at least be aware of what you are missing.

Clearancing the block (and other pieces) for a big crankshaft will be another step in the preparation for some of you. That step is covered later in this chapter in the section on crankshafts.

Initial cleaning and inspection

The very first thing to do with any block, new or used, is to give it a thorough cleaning with soap and water. Many coin car-washes have an engine-cleaning area that is good for jobs like this. If you are really dedicated, you can take out the oil galley plugs and clean the galleys, too.

If the counterweights don't tip you off, a forged crankshaft can be identified by the forging seam that runs through the centerline. Eurorace

The manufacturing process of a cast crankshaft creates no seam. Eurorace

A comparison of the VW and Chrysler crankshafts. Chrysler's longitudinal mounting necessitated a slightly different pilot shaft bearing (right). Techtonics

It is not necessary to hot tank the block. If you feel better with a hot-tanked block, be aware that you will need to replace the intermediate shaft bearings when you are through. Intermediate shaft bearings come both finished and unfinished. Get the finished ones and save yourself having to hone the bearings to size.

Once the block is clean you can perform a visual inspection to see if everything looks good enough to proceed. If you are going to be subjecting the engine to lots of stress, have the block Magnafluxed at this point, as well.

Freeze plugs

You can take out the freeze plugs for the cleaning process, but the factory freeze plugs are better than any available aftermarket plugs, so this is not recommended unless your freeze plugs are rusting out. Use brass freeze plugs if you need replacements.

If you plan to be doing hard racing where everything gets knocked about, you have probably thought about drilling and tapping the freeze plug holes for threaded plugs. That is one way of doing it, but it takes forever to do, and the time is much better spent doing something else. Instead, use a punch to stake the freeze plugs in place. They will stay put, and you can use all your "extra" time to measure everything once more.

Stress relieving

To stress relieve the block, the main caps are bolted up and torqued to spec. Then the block is heated to 1,050 degrees Fahrenheit and baked for two hours. Next the temperature is reduced in 200

degree steps, letting the block bake for one hour at each step. Once it reaches 500 degrees, the block can be air-cooled. After stress relieving, you will need to buy new main bearing cap bolts; do not use the ones that were baked with the engine. This procedure is not usually performed on Volkswagen motors.

Deburring

Deburring is done with a hand grinder, and the goal is to eliminate all casting flash, small pockets of sand (from the casting procedure) and roughness from the block. Some engine builders overdo this, making the entire inside of the engine as smooth as a used bar of soap. This much grinding creates stress risers all over the block, necessitating shot peening, heat-treating or some other step to neutralize it. Unless you want to go to this much trouble, all you need to do is get rid of all the loose stuff

Align the drill with the oil galley. Eurorace

The stock oil galley plugs rarely fall out, but they must be removed for proper cleaning. Centerpunch the old galley plug before drilling. Eurorace

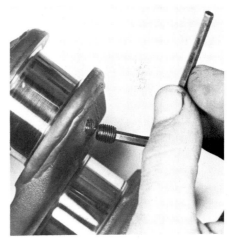

Although it means more work, pipe plugs are the better way to seal off the oil galley holes. Techtonics

An inexpensive way of closing off the oil galleys after cleaning the crankshaft is with aluminum plugs. Eurorace

When you have finished, the end of the plug should be recessed slightly below the surface of the crank. Eurorace

Install one of the aluminum oil galley plugs. Eurorace.

that might float out of, or away from, the block while the motor is running. However, a shot-peened block would be very durable, and would earn you the admiration of those who know.

A little deburring is a great idea, however, and it is a good way to spend your idle moments while you are waiting for your long-ago-promised high-performance parts to arrive . . . you know, the ones that you were supposed to receive last month at the very latest.

While you are going over the block, you should also chase all the threads with a tap lubricated with light oil to make sure they are clean. After the block has been decked (if necessary), chamfer all threaded holes, especially the head bolt holes. Chamfering the bolt holes removes the top thread so it will not be pulled above the surface of the block when you torque the bolt.

With only four counterweights, the factory cast crankshaft is easy to identify. Eurorace

The late-model crank nose (right) is much sturdier than the early version. Techtonics

Align boring

For most uses, it is sufficient to install the crankshaft in the block and see if it turns easily. If you have any doubts about the integrity of your block, or if you are going to be racing with this engine, you should next align bore the crankshaft mains. Align boring removes all doubt about whether or not the crankshaft bore is true and straight . . . as long as the machine shop does the job right.

Once you are satisfied that the crankshaft bore is straight, you can check the deck height of the block to see that the block is square.

Truing

Two things that must be checked on your block are that the top of the block is parallel to the centerline of the crankshaft, and that the cylinder bores line up with the centerline of the crankshaft. If the top of the block is not parallel to the crank centerline, each piston will come up to a different level in the cylinder bore, which will make each combustion chamber a different size and compression ratio. If the cylinder bores are not lined up, the pistons will not apply force against the crankshaft in the most efficient manner.

Before you can check for squareness, you must have already sized your piston rods, and all your pistons must be identical (see the sections on pistons and rods in this chapter).

To check for squareness, measure the distance between the centerline of the crankshaft and the top sealing surface of the block. This can be difficult, but if you can get (or fabricate) a large set of dividers, you can get pretty close.

If the block needs to be machined to bring it into square, make sure that the gasket surface is not polished too smooth. The head gasket will seal better if there is some surface roughness.

For stock purposes, the factory head gasket works fine. For big-bore applications, use a big-bore head gasket. Most tuners who sell big-bore kits also sell a head gasket to match.

If you are running a turbo motor with a lot of boost and you find yourself blowing out head gaskets no matter what, you may be tempted to consider O-rings instead of head gaskets. This involves cutting O-ring grooves around every opening in both sealing surfaces of the head and the block (water passages, bolt holes, cylinder bores and so on), and installing metal O-rings. As you might guess, the work required for this is substantial, and it is almost never necessary on a properly prepared block running less than an insane amount of compression. Before you decide to install O-rings, check everything else one more time, including your exhaust gas temperature. It is extremely rare to find a Volkswagen engine application that requires O-rings.

Checking to see that your cylinder bores are aligned with the crankshaft axis is more difficult. Typically, this checking (and any needed adjustment) is performed by the shop that does the cylinder honing.

Cylinder honing

Honing the piston bores is necessary when the bore is worn from use and must be made round again, or when you are increasing the piston size to gain displacement. If you are not sure of the proper method for measuring the cylinder bore, refer to the Bentley shop manual. Honing is probably not a procedure you will tackle by yourself, but the more you know about it the better able you will be to discuss the matter with the machine shop that does it.

When honing the cylinder bores, it is important to install the main bearing caps and to use a torque plate on the cylinder head mating surface. The torque plate is a heavy piece of steel with holes in it that correspond to the cylinder bores and the head bolts. It bolts to the top of the block and is tightened to the same torque as the head would be.

By installing both the main bearing caps and the torque plate, the block will be placed under approximately the same stresses as it will see in use. Thus, when the cylinder bores are honed they will be much closer to round than if they were honed without taking these preliminary steps.

When opening up the cylinder bores for larger pistons, the rough hone should be done to within 0.0025 inch. To finish hone the cylinder bores, use a 625 stone if you are going to be using chrome rings, and an 820 stone if you are going to be using moly rings.

Always hone each bore to match the piston that will be used in that hole. Measure each piston carefully, and number it to correspond with the bore it will be run in to prevent mix-ups.

Once the bores are honed to size, check the piston ring gap while the torque plate is still bolted up. Do not file the ring gap with the ring in the cylinder bore. After removing the torque plate, use fine sandpaper to chamfer the top of the cylinder bore. Work carefully so you do not wind up sanding on your newly honed cylinder bore.

Final cleaning

After you have done all the machining and before you begin to assemble the motor, do one final cleaning of the block. Start with solvent and finish with detergent and warm water. Scrub everything, especially the inside of the cylinder bores, and blow the block dry with compressed air or wipe it dry with paper towels. Compressed air is better than paper towels because the towels can shred, leaving little scraps behind. If you do not have access to an air compressor, however, you can use paper towels if you are careful. Cloth towels leave behind lint, and should be avoided.

All threaded holes should be chased with a tap to clean out the garbage that gets into them. If your tap cuts into the metal while you are cleaning the threads, the tap is too big—do not use it. A good investment is to buy some undersize taps, such as those that come three-to-a-pack for cutting threads precisely (finish tap, first undersize, rough cut). They are not available at every hardware store, but they can be purchased at industrial supply houses that cater to machinists.

You are not done yet, however. The honing process imbeds metal particles deep in the pores of the metal, and neither the solvent nor the soap and water got it all out. Take cheesecloth and SAE 10 oil, and clean the cylinder bores as if they were gun bores. The first few times, the patches will come out dirty. Persevere. Eventually they will come out clean.

Also go to a gun shop or a sporting goods store and buy two bore bristles and two cleaning rods, one each for a 410 shotgun and a .22 rifle. Get a couple boxes of patches in both of these sizes, too. These will allow you to clean the oil galleys thoroughly. Again, clean them as if they were gun bores. Do not quit until the patches come out clean.

After the final cleaning, coat the entire block with a light preservative such as WD-40, and wrap it in a large trash bag to keep out dirt and moisture. At this point, you can either send the block out for moly impregnation and water jacket

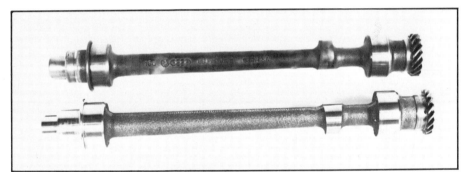

When using a stroker crankshaft, the stock intermediate shaft (top) must be clearanced at the distributor drive to allow the crankshaft to swing by. Techtonics

Offset grinding on this welded stroker created a weak point, with predictable results. Eurorace

The stock three-piece bearings are a trick way to go, but if you can't find replacements the standard one-piece bearings will work. Techtonics

treatment, or just set it aside until it is time to assemble the motor.

Crankcase oil jets

These are common on turbo motors, and the 16V motor has them as well. Small squirters are mounted in the block, pointing up at the bottom of the piston. When the engine oil pressure reaches approximately 30 psi, oil is sprayed on the underside of the pistons to help transfer some of the heat away.

Apparently no one has yet retrofitted these to a non-16V block, although the oil galley that feeds the oil squirters is there waiting to be tapped into. Machine shops have been doing this same service for high-performance Beetle and Porsche motors for years. If you fit these to your block, you will also need to upgrade your oil pump to feed them.

The crankshaft

There are two types of crankshafts: forged and cast. Forged crankshafts can be much stronger than cast crankshafts, and for years were the only crank to consider for serious high-performance use.

The cast crank is making a comeback, however. It first appeared in the 1978 Volkswagen and 1979 Rabbit, and although it is not fully counterweighted, it is fine for most hot street machines—unless you need a longer stroke for more cubic inches. Techtonics has also found that some of its customers who have broken welded crankshafts have not been able to break a cast crankshaft.

How can a cast crankshaft be stronger than a forged crank? With a welded crankshaft, the offset grinding can sometimes cut to within a couple of millimeters of the oil hole. This creates a very weak area in the crankshaft, on the side of the journal that takes a lot of stress at the bottom of the stroke. The cast crankshaft does not have the inherent strength of a forging, but at least its oil holes are in the right place.

Volkswagens are famous for *not* having crankshaft problems, as the lower end of the block is very sturdy and prevents crank flex. A cast crankshaft might well fit into your budget better than a welded one (or than a true forged crankshaft!).

If you choose a cast crankshaft for your high-performance application, have it shot peened or Tuftrided. Shot peening can increase the fatigue strength of a cast crankshaft by as much as fifty per-cent, and Tuftriding can improve strength by up to eighty-eight percent. In many cases this additional strength permits a cast crank to be used where it would not otherwise work.

But don't forget forged and welded crankshafts. Many engine builders use welded cranks in some pretty high stress applications, where they seem to live just fine. The Oettinger 94.5 mm forged crankshaft is superb, and it is very similar to the factory-forged crankshafts in terms of metallurgy and manufacture. The care that goes into the Oettinger is reflected in the price tag, however. In addition, it carries no warranty, unlike the better welded crankshafts. This leaves most of us using welded cranks, and so far the results have been positive.

Differences among crankshafts

In addition to metallurgy and stroke, there are two other differences among crankshafts that you should be aware of. First, the rod journals on 1.6 liter and 1.7 liter crankshafts are smaller at 46 mm than those on diesel and 1.8 liter crankshafts, which are 47.758 mm. When you buy an aftermarket crankshaft, be sure to

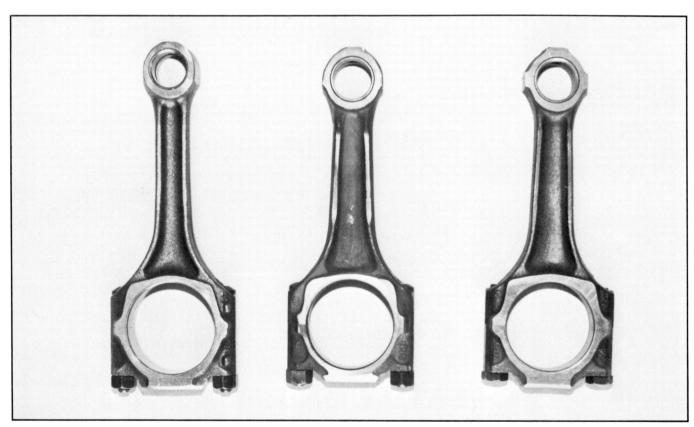

From left to right: a 1.8 rod, a 1.6 rod and an Audi rod. Techtonics

find out what rods you have to use with it.

Volkswagen also introduced a 1.7 liter crankshaft in 1983. The cam belt drive sprocket no longer is indexed to the crankshaft with a Woodruff key, instead using a different crankshaft snout and cam belt drive gear. It can be very irritating to get everything put together to that point, only to find that no dealership for miles around has the new-style gear (they never break, so why stock 'em, right?). Get this detail taken care of at the same time you get the crankshaft.

If you vote for a 90.5 cast crank and are using the 136 mm connecting rods, you will have to clearance the underside of the pistons to allow the counterweights to swing by. In the 1.8 liter blocks, the 91 mm cast crank works just fine with the 144 mm rods—no clearancing is required.

Preparation

There are many steps to preparing a crankshaft, although not all of them will be needed in all cases. The following are descriptions of all the steps that can be done to a crankshaft. Some are important any time you have the crankshaft out of the car, others can be classified as solutions for problems that may exist.

Measuring the crankshaft

Much time, effort and money can be spent on a crankshaft to make it better, so make sure before you start that the crankshaft you have is worth all the hard work. The first step is to measure all the journals to make sure that the crankshaft is the right size and that the journals are round. Remember to measure each journal twice, the second time at ninety degrees from the first measurement. Be very gentle with the crankshaft and the micrometers. The last thing you want to do is nick a journal with the sharp edge of a micrometer.

Magnafluxing

This is the second step after making sure that the crankshaft is worthy of your attention. Note that a marginally cracked crankshaft can still ring like a bell, so the sound test is not really a test at all but merely an indication of whether to Magnaflux the crankshaft or throw it away. (Note: Because of the stress risers induced by welding, no welded crankshaft will pass Magnaflux inspection.)

Indexing

On V-8 crankshafts, the rough crankshaft blank is stamped out or cast, then it is heated and twisted so that the throws are lined up the way they are supposed to point. Manufacturing tolerances being what they are, the throws might not be in the right place on every crankshaft.

The Volkswagen crank is a "flat" crankshaft requiring no such abuse during the manufacturing process. As a result, the indexing is very rarely off. It would not hurt to check, but if you choose not to, you need not lose any sleep over it.

Cross-drilling

Cross-drilling is something that started with the big American V-8s to ensure positive lubrication of the main and rod journals through 360 degrees of crankshaft rotation. By cross-drilling the cranks, manufacturers were able to use flat-faced lower bearings instead of bearings that incorporated an oil groove. The elimination of the oil groove provided more surface area on the bearing to take the pounding of the crankshaft.

There must be something to it. The stock Volkswagen crankshaft comes cross-drilled, as should any aftermarket crankshaft you buy.

Stroking

Stroking refers to changing the distance between the centerline of the crankshaft and the centerline of the connecting rod journal. Although it usually refers to an increase in this distance, it can also refer to a decrease, or a de-stroking.

There are two main ways to stroke a crankshaft. The first is to offset grind the existing journals and use connecting

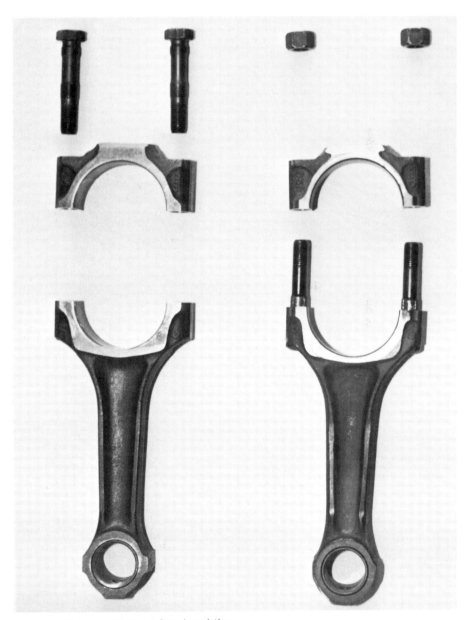

An exploded view of the 1.6 rod and the Audi rod. Techtonics

rods with smaller big ends. The second is to weld extra material to the journal before offset grinding for the stock big-end-diameter connecting rods. For the Volkswagen, this second method is by far the most popular.

Welding the extra metal onto a journal tends to warp the crankshaft. Fortunately, there are two journals on each side of the crankshaft, so there should be two equal pulls on each side of the crankshaft. Just to be on the safe side, however, a welded crankshaft should always be checked for straightness.

Whenever the stroke of the crankshaft is changed, the connecting rods, the pistons or both must be changed. If, for example, the stroke is increased, using the same rods and pistons could result in the top of the piston protruding above the top of the engine block. To bring the top of the piston down, you must use shorter rods and/or pistons, with the piston pin located closer to the top of the piston. Different-length rods will be difficult (and expensive) to come by, but there are many pistons available with the correct pin height for long-stroke crankshafts.

The stroke of a diesel crankshaft is 80 mm. If you have one of these, you could offset grind the rod journals to 46 mm to gain an 81.5 mm stroke and pick up a little displacement. You will then have to use the 1.6 or 1.7 liter rods, and you will need to either deck your pistons or live with the increased compression. You could do the same on an 86.4 mm crankshaft, taking it out to 88 mm and then changing to the early rods and decking the pistons to match.

Checking for straightness

It does not take much of a bend to make the crank whip around pretty good at 7000 rpm. To check for straightness, place the crankshaft in the bearings and check each main bearing surface with a dial indicator. Any reading of more than 0.001 inch means the crankshaft should be straightened. Straightening is done by a special hammering process; bending it straight creates stress risers. Darrell Vittone of Techtonics says that if the crankshaft turns easily when the main caps are bolted down, it is probably straight enough to run with.

Nitriding

Nitriding (or Tuftriding) can extend the life of a crankshaft by up to five times owing to the wear resistance it imparts to the bearing surfaces. In addition, Tuftriding can almost double the strength of the crankshaft, and friction over a Tuft-rided surface is cut nearly in half. Just as important, the crankshaft is not made brittle by this process. Before Tuftriding, all sharp edges should be radiused and smoothed down.

Shot peening

Because shot peening leaves a slightly rough surface, the journals and thrust surfaces must be masked off so the shot peening does not ruin them. Masking tape does not work for this purpose; shot peening requires adhesive-backed rubber to repel the steel shot from sensitive areas. When taking a crankshaft in for shot peening, be sure to specify which surfaces are to be treated and which surfaces are to be left as is.

In addition to the throws, the fillets (where the journal joins the throw) are also shot peened, as this is a high-risk area for breakage.

Before shot peening, all sharp edges should be radiused and smoothed down. Only limited polishing can be performed on shot-peened surfaces.

Balancing

Balancing is not something that happens only to crankshafts. For proper balance, all reciprocating and rotating weights attached to the crankshaft must be balanced, too. Reciprocating weights include the pistons, the piston pins, the piston rings and the small end of the connecting rod. Rotating weights include the big end of the rod, the rod bearings, the flywheel, the pressure plate and the front pulley or pulleys.

In a stock motor, the components are balanced exceptionally well compared with other production line motors. If you are building a race engine or changing any of the components, take these parts out to be balanced before assembling your motor. Record all balance weights in case you must later replace a component. Knowing the existing weights will make it unnecessary to rebalance the entire motor just to accommodate one changed component.

Cleaning

Cleaning the outside of the crankshaft is no problem, but cleaning the inside of the oil galleys can be a real chore. You will need to drill out the existing plugs, and then either replace them with aluminum plugs or drill and tap the holes for threaded plugs.

Do not by-pass this step. Removing the plugs makes it possible to get into the oil galley for a thorough cleaning that is just about impossible any other way. This is vitally important with a used or reground crankshaft because centrif-ugal force packs grime into the outer ends of the oilways (behind the plugs), and the only way to get it out is to remove the plugs. On engines that were not well cared for, baked-on oil residue will have narrowed the oil galleys (kind of like hardening of the arteries). On a reground crankshaft abrasive compound can be hiding anywhere, and can be removed only by taking out the oilway plugs or installing the dirty crankshaft in your engine, at which time the stuff will float out and get into everything. On a new crankshaft the odds are better that the oil galleys will be clean, but it does not take very long to run a brush through the galleys, and it is better to be safe.

The easier of the two methods is with the aluminum plugs. Centerpunch the existing plug and drill it out with a 6 mm drill. Run your bore bristle and patches through all the oil galleys until the patches come out clean.

Insert the aluminum plugs pointed-end first, and hammer them in with a ball peen hammer until the top of the plug is flush with the surface of the crankshaft. To finish off, take a punch with a rounded end or a rod with a small-diameter ball bearing welded to it, and keep hammering until the plug is slightly concave. If you follow this procedure, you should never have to worry about the plug coming loose.

If you plan on frequent crankshaft cleaning or you do not trust hammered-in plugs, you can drill and tap the oil galleys for $\frac{1}{16}$ inch pipe plugs. Make sure to Loc-tite the plugs in after cleaning!

Whatever you do with the oil galley plugs, double-check them before buttoning up the motor. Pressed-in plugs may come out in operation, resulting in a puzzling lack of oil pressure.

Chrome plating

One trick for making a very smooth and very tough journal is to chrome plate it. The plating adds metal and increases the diameter of the bearing surfaces, so the journals must be ground with that in mind before sending the crankshaft to the platers.

Another consideration with chrome plating is that plating cracks can propagate into the base metal in a process known as hydrogen embrittlement. These cracks reduce the strength of the part and can cause failure unless the part is properly prepared for chroming.

For crankshafts, the hard compressive surface left by shot peening has proved to be very resistant to cracking. Before sending any highly stressed part out to have chrome plating, electroless nickel plating or cadmium plating applied, have the part shot peened.

With the inherent durability of the Volkswagen crankshaft, chrome plating is not needed.

Moly impregnation

In a perfect world you would never need to moly coat crankshaft journals, because the journal is supposed to ride on a soft carpet of oil—never touching the bearings.

Every time you turn off the motor, however, the oil coating goes away and the crankshaft settles downward, eventually resting against the bottom bearing surface. When the starter motor is engaged, those first few seconds can be tough on a crankshaft while it turns in the bearings waiting for lubrication. This is where moly impregnation comes in handy. Theoretically, it would also help if there were ever a strong enough load to push the oil film aside, such as might happen if the engine detonated heavily.

Because of the nature of molybdenum, impregnation can be of benefit to untreated, polished or chromed crankshafts.

Bearings

There is nothing trick to know about the bearings, although there is something to watch out for if your main journals have been ground undersize. The Kolbenschmidt main thrust bearings come 0.1 mm too thick, and must be dressed down to set the end play. A flat piece of glass or marble with 600 grit wet-or-dry sandpaper on it works well for this. After you get the size right (0.07 to 0.17 mm), make certain that you have a mirror finish on the thrust surface.

If this sounds like a lot of work, specify Brazilian bearings instead of the Kolbenschmidts. The Brazilian bearings come properly sized.

No matter what bearings you use, *always* set the end play on any motor you put together.

Rod bolts

Type	Shank	Threads	Nut
136 mm factory rod bolt	8.26 mm	8.90 mm	14 mm
144 mm factory rod bolt	7.30 mm	7.90 mm	14 mm
⅜" SPS bolt	9.53 mm	10.00 mm	½" 12-point

As you can see from this chart, the bolts found in the 136 mm factory rods are more than strong enough for most applications.

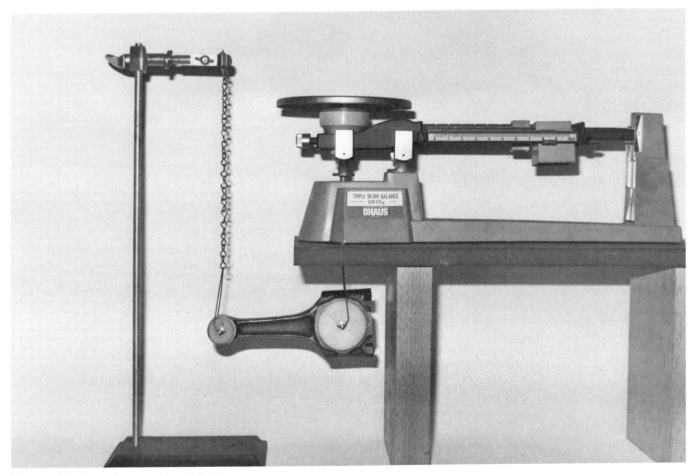

Use a triple-beam balance to weigh the rods end-for-end. Techtonics

The flywheel

When your car is all apart, you can mark the true TDC on the flywheel so you will have no trouble finding it in the future.

To find the true TDC, you must first dead-stop the motor. To do this, you must have the crankshaft bolted into the block, with the connecting rod and piston for cylinder number 1 installed. Bolt a piece of metal (the dead-stop) across the top of the number 1 cylinder bore so that it interferes with the piston at the very top of the stroke.

Now rotate the engine in one direction until the piston touches the dead-stop. Make a temporary mark on the flywheel corresponding to the factory mark on the transmission housing. Now rotate the engine back the other way until it again touches the dead-stop. Make another mark on the flywheel opposite your same point of reference. Halfway between these two points of reference is the TDC for your motor. If the factory's TDC mark is off from the TDC of your motor, mark the true TDC with a chisel or a centerpunch, and then fill the mark with white paint so it will show up when you illuminate it with the timing light.

Having an accurate TDC mark will become critical later on when you time the camshaft and set the ignition timing.

For a street car, there is not much else you will need to do to the flywheel unless it is damaged or out of balance. It is not a good idea to lighten the flywheel because the car will not idle as nicely and the flywheel helps dampen vibrations that develop in the motor. You will also get a better launch off the line with a heavier flywheel because it stores energy better than a light flywheel. Without the flywheel there to smooth things out, broken crankshafts and worn-out bearings become more commonplace.

American cars have had harmonic dampers for years. Even on the Beetles, the hot tip is to add a harmonic damper at the end of the crankshaft opposite the flywheel. This helps offset crankshaft twist, and even makes for better launches off the line because there is more energy stored in the motor when you drop the clutch.

I have not seen an aftermarket front pulley damper for the Volkswagen yet, but again, the Volkswagen block is much stronger than the Beetle case, so the crankshaft does not need as much help. Those of you with air conditioning have a built-in damper in the form of the air conditioner pulley, although with the added weight of the air conditioning components and the extra drag the belt exerts on the crankshaft, you will not detect much of a benefit.

If you are racing a lightweight car in short races where power is everything, you will want to lighten the flywheel so the engine does not have as much mass to spin up when you press on the accelerator pedal. The tradeoff will show up in engine longevity, but that is racing. Take the weight off the outer rim of the flywheel, but leave enough metal there to soak up the heat generated when the clutch slips. If you do not have enough metal there, the flywheel will develop hot spots, reducing its effectiveness. Compared with the stock flywheel at 7.8 kilograms, a lightened flywheel will be about 5.3 kilograms.

For motors that will see extreme duty, the flywheel can be dowel-pinned to the crankshaft, just as is done with the Type 1 motors. And, as with the Type 1, dowels are placed between the flywheel holes, for a total of six dowels. You want the dowels to take the torsional stress instead of the flywheel bolts, so make the holes a 0.0015 inch interference fit on the dowels.

The rods

Choices

By varying the ratio between the rod length and the crankshaft stroke, you can determine some of the characteristics of the motor. This ratio is calculated by dividing the center-to-center length of the connecting rod by the diameter of the crankshaft stroke.

Generally, you want the ratio to be between 1.5:1 and 1.9:1. As the ratio gets closer to 1.5:1, the engine will produce torque lower in the rpm range with a flatter overall curve. As the ratio gets closer to 1.9:1, the engine will produce torque higher in the rpm range and a much peakier torque curve. With a high-ratio motor you can get more area under the curve, but the drivability will be nicer with the low-ratio motor (especially in conjunction with a short camshaft).

Because of the geometry of the rod swinging around on the end of the crankshaft journal, the piston in a long-rod (high-ratio) engine will linger a split second longer at TDC and BDC (bottom dead center), with faster piston speed in between. The faster speed creates more suction over a shorter period of time, making valve timing less critical.

With a short-rod (low-ratio) engine, valve timing is more critical because the piston accelerates and decelerates more evenly to and from TDC and BDC. The benefit is that the piston does not spend as much time near peak velocity as it does in the long-rod engine.

If you are having a problem with piston speed being too high, using a shorter rod will not help; you need a shorter stroke or a lower rpm limit. It is doubtful that you will ever have to consider any of this when putting together your engine.

The Volkswagen motor has had two different-length rods. The 1.5, 1.6 and 1.7 liter motors all use a 136 mm rod with a 22 mm piston pin, and the 1.8 liter motor uses a 144 mm rod with a 20 mm piston pin. The diesel uses the 136 mm rod with a 24 mm piston pin. If your dream is to play around with offset bushings on a short rod, here is your golden opportunity.

Audi rods come in the same length as the Volkswagen rods, but are of a different construction. Instead of a nut and bolt holding the cap on (with the nut at the bottom), the Audi rod has a bolt that threads up from the bottom. This leaves more metal in the beam of the rod (and a reduced area for stress risers), and makes clearancing the block for long-stroke crankshafts less of a chore. If you cannot find a set in a junkyard, there is no need to panic. Super Vee racers use reworked Volkswagen rods without problems, and they run their engines up to 9000 rpm. The Audi rods are beautiful, but they are not necessary.

As you consider using a crankshaft with a stroke bigger than 86.4 mm, watch your rod ratios. Even with the 144 mm rod, a 94.5 mm crankshaft will give you a ratio of 1.52, which is a little low. With the long rod and the long throw, you start running out of room on the piston to put the connecting rod, which is why Darrell Vittone is considering putting together a motor with a 94.5 mm crankshaft and the 136 mm rods. The resulting 1.44 ratio should prove to be very interesting.

One alternative is, of course, to use custom-length rods such as those available from Carillo. These are expensive, however, and they also bring up the question of what to do with the piston. The longer the rod, the farther up in the cylinder the piston will be at TDC. This means more compression, at the very least. This might be desirable in some circumstances, but if you need to lose compression you will then need to mill the top of the piston or find a piston with a higher pin height. (Both of these alternatives are explored in the piston section later in this chapter.) Another feature of the longer rods is that the Volkswagen engine runs smoother with them than with the shorter rods.

Preparation

It is the job of the connecting rods to transfer the movement of the piston to the crankshaft, and in a high-output motor they are asked to do a lot. The more you ask of your engine, the more important it becomes to condition the rods.

Magnafluxing

Magnafluxing the rods can be done at either one of two times, depending on how much preparation you are planning. If you are leaving the rods basically stock, Magnaflux them after the initial cleaning. If you are going all the way, Magnaflux them after grinding and polishing but before squaring, balancing or shot peening.

Checking the length (center-to-center) and squaring

Both of these operations are best carried out by a machine shop that has the proper tools for measuring and correcting any problems. The center-to-center length must be the same for all rods so that the compression ratio and deck height will be the same from one end of the block to the other. Squaring prevents side loads on the rod, crankshaft and wrist pin. Even a small amount of out-of-squareness will lead to side motion in the rod—enough in some cases to hammer the wrist pin clip right out of the piston.

If you have either too much or too little deck height with your combination of stroke, rod length and piston pin height, the center-to-center length can be adjusted by offset honing the small-end bushing. This is good for only a millimeter or so, but it is there if you need it. It is better to plan out your motor ahead of time to avoid problems like this.

Grooving small-end bushings

The 1.8 liter bushing has a groove that earlier bushings did not have. The groove is located at the top of the bushing in such a way that oil that enters the pin oiling hole is distributed almost halfway down both sides of the piston pin.

This would be difficult to machine by hand, but it could be duplicated in a mill. I have seen few problems caused by insufficient piston pin oiling, but Volkswagen does not include extra-cost items like this unless it has found a benefit.

Lightening

The Volkswagen rod is a stout piece and can stand to lose some weight without sacrificing strength. If you are using a very light piston assembly, the rod can be lightened still further. For Super Vee racing with piston assemblies weighing 425 grams (as opposed to the stock 550 gram weight), the early 136 mm rods can be lightened by up to 68 grams without a problem. A lot of the weight will come off the small end, although you do not want to remove so much metal that you endanger the strength of the rod. Unless you do this for a living, by happy with balancing the rod and let someone else find out how much metal is too much to take off the rod.

Polishing

All Volkswagen rods come with a seam that runs along the side of the beam. This seam is created during the forging process. Although it is not necessary, this seam can be ground down while you are rounding off all the other sharp edges on the rod.

Always grind in the same direction as the length of the rod, never crosswise. Your final grinding should be fairly smooth, and final polishing should be done with 400 grit sandpaper.

Because grinding creates a lot of tensile stress on the surface of the metal, all ground and polished rods must be shot

1.8 liter connecting rod small-end bushings are relieved across the top for better pin oiling. Eurorace

A variable-length rod like this comes in mighty handy. Techtonics

Rod length in mm

Stroke	136	144
73.4	1.85	1.96
77.4	1.76	1.86
80.0	1.70	1.80
86.4	1.57	1.67
88.0	1.55	1.64
90.5	1.50	1.59
94.5	1.44	1.52

This chart is an excellent reference source for comparing rod ratios.

Always grind rods lengthwise. Shot peen afterward to relieve grinding stress. James Sly

peened. If you cannot afford shot peening, do not waste your time polishing the connecting rods. A rough forged connecting rod is stronger than a polished but unpeened rod. If you can afford shot peening but are in no mood to polish your connecting rods, shot peening the rough forging will provide you with a stronger rod than stock.

Balancing

Balancing is done after lightening and polishing, after the bushings have been replaced and sized, after the big end has been sized, and after any other operation that adds weight to or removes it from the rod. The purpose of balancing the rod is to get the center of mass at the same place for all four rods.

You will need a weighing scale that is capable of reading to a gram. For best accuracy, the rod must be hung as close to horizontal as possible. This means fabricating a set of jigs, one for the big end of the rod and one for the small end. The weight of the jigs is not critical because you are only comparing small ends with small ends, and big ends with big ends; at this point you are not con-

The Audi rods (left) have more metal in the area at the base of the beam. Techtonics

40

cerned with the overall weight of the rod itself. Of more importance is making all the small ends weigh the same, and all the big ends weigh the same.

You can only take metal away, so the trick is to find the lightest rod ends and grind the others to match. First weigh all the rods end for end, noting the weights on a piece of paper. You now have eight numbers. Compare the small-end weights only with the other small-end weights, and the big-end weights only with the big-end weights.

Once you have picked out the lightest small end and the lightest big end, grind the other small ends to match the weight of the lightest small end, and then grind the big ends to match the weight of the lightest big end. All grinding should be done off the pads at the top and bottom of the rod. If you go too far with one, make that your new "lightest" rod and grind the others to match.

As a bonus, when you are done the overall weights of all your rods will be the same.

Shot peening

Shot peening is done only after all the metal has been removed by the grinding, polishing and balancing operations. Do not have the insides of the holes, or the rod bolts and nuts, shot peened, just the outside of the rod itself. You can shot peen rough rods, and you must shot peen polished rods. An untreated polished rod is actually weaker than a stock (rough) rod.

Rod bolts

Super Vee motors use the stock rod bolts to 9000 rpm, so your motor will probably get by with the stock bolts, too. For extreme duty, the rods can be modified to run ⅜ inch SPS bolts. These are costly, however, and required only in applications such as off-road vehicles, where the drive wheels may leave the ground with the motor at full throttle, and then land with the throttle full-on as well.

If you are worried about your rod bolts you can have them Magnafluxed, but check the price first to see if it would be less expensive to simply buy a new set of bolts.

The pistons

There are two basic types of pistons: cast and forged. The stock pistons are cast, as are many of the better replacement pistons for normal and hot street uses.

Then why use forged pistons? In some high-stress applications, such as in full-race engines or engines with a turbocharger, it can be difficult to control the thermal expansion of a cast piston. A forged piston will give you greater strength without a weight penalty.

The drawback is that a forged piston expands much more than a cast piston, so it must have more clearance when installed. The more clearance there is between the cylinder wall and the piston, the more the piston can rock from side to side, upsetting the seal between the ring and the cylinder wall. When forged pistons are run loose, they are noisier and can use more oil than cast pistons.

Piston-to-wall clearance for a cast piston is 0.001 inch. You can run a forged piston as tight as 0.0015 inch, although 0.002 through 0.005 inch are more common clearances. The spec for Mahle and Kolbenschmidt forged pistons is 0.0025 inch; TRW pistons are often run at 0.0045 to 0.0055 inch. At 0.0015 inch you will not get appreciably more noise than with properly set up cast pistons, but you have to know what you are doing to run them that tight.

Choices

The American Volkswagens used pistons that were nearly flat on top, incorporating only a shallow dish. The European Volkswagens used a piston with a deep dish on top. These differences were due to the differences in cylinder head design, and are explained in the next section on cylinder heads. You can get either-style top in both cast and forged pistons.

In choosing new pistons, you can opt for pistons that directly replace the stock ones, pistons that raise the compression ratio but leave the displacement the same, pistons that increase the displacement but leave the compression ratio the same, or pistons that increase both the displacement and the compression ratio.

Bigger-bore piston do more than increase the displacement, they also have more room available for unshrouding the valves. The third benefit, as mentioned earlier in the section on techniques, is that installing bigger-bore pistons is a less expensive way of increasing displacement than going to a longer-stroke crankshaft.

Piston pins

Everything at the end of the piston rod (piston, piston rod, pin clips, rod end and rings) is part of the reciprocating assembly. Therefore, the lighter the

assembly is, the lower the acceleration and deceleration forces will have to be when the assembly changes directions at TDC and BDC.

For street use, piston pins must not be too light because of the need for durability in this high-stress area. However, very high rpm race engines can benefit from lightened pins. Because of their lighter weight and greater strength, forged pistons can use lighter pins than can comparable cast pistons. The strength of the forged piston also allows the use of shorter (and hence lighter still) piston pins. In turbo applications, it is better to stick with heavier piston pins for durability.

For most street machines, the stock wrist pin clips work fine. For heavier-duty use the Spiralok clips are better, but they are also much more difficult to remove. If your desert racer keeps hammering out the clips no matter what type you try, there are always Teflon buttons, although the block is stiff enough that they are rarely needed.

Compression ratio

There is a reason everybody is always trying to get as much compression as possible. The higher the compression ratio, the better the thermal efficiency; hence, the better the engine output and the lower the fuel consumption.

This is due to the smaller volume of the combustion chamber:

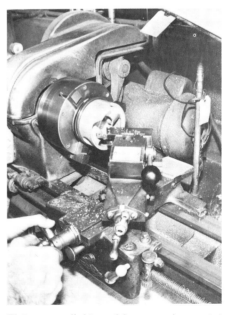

Pistons are lightened by removing metal from the pads underneath the crown. For a street engine, you would only do this to balance the pistons, as heavier pistons will last longer.

• During the exhaust stroke, the cylinder is evacuated more effectively; the fresh cylinder charge thus has fewer noncombustible residual gases.

• During the compression stroke, the fuel and air particles are more densely compressed, they get hotter and fuel droplet atomization is increased, thus permitting more rapid and complete combustion.

• During the power stroke, both the pressure of the hot gases and their temperature are reduced; the cooler exhaust gases dissipate less heat.

The smaller volume of the combustion chamber in turn has a smaller cooling surface, so heat losses through the cylinder walls and head are correspondingly less.

For each point of extra compression, you get increased power output and better fuel economy, up to about 15.0:1, although by that time you have long since stopped using pump gas. After 15.0:1, you start to lose more in pumping losses than you gain in efficiency. Raising the compression ratio does not increase horsepower in a linear relationship. Instead, a little less horsepower is gained with each additional point of compression.

The negative sides of compression are that when the compression gets too high, you run into motor-destroying detonation, and you generate more oxides of nitrogen (NO_x).

Checking your compression ratio

If all you do when you rebuild your motor is freshen things up, you should not need to check your compression ratio. However, if you surface the head or the block, reshape the combustion chambers, change the height of the valve head in the combustion chamber or install a set of big-bore pistons, you need to check to ensure that you are getting the compression ratio you want.

Most people can understand why the compression ratio has to be checked when they add or take away metal in the combustion chamber, but many do not realize that an increased compression ratio also results from increasing the piston bore.

The formula for calculating the compression ratio is

$$\text{Compression ratio} = \frac{CD + PV + HV + HGV}{PV + HV + HGV}$$

In this equation, CD equals cylinder displacement (the swept volume of the cylinder), HV equals head volume, HGV equals head gasket volume and PV equals piston volume. Therefore, before you can calculate your compression ratio, you need to know the bore, the stroke, the volume of the head, the volume of the piston and the compressed thickness of the head gasket.

I assume you know the bore and stroke of your motor; the formula for calculating cylinder displacement is

$$\text{Cylinder displacement} = \frac{\text{bore} \times \text{bore} \times \text{stroke} \times 0.0031416}{4}$$

Plugging in the bore and stroke numbers from a stock engine gives

$$\text{Cylinder displacement} = \frac{79.5 \times 79.5 \times 86.4 \times 0.0031416}{4} = \frac{1715.53}{4} = 428.88 \text{ cc}$$

Now you need to determine the piston volume, or the amount of space in the cylinder when the piston is at the top of its stroke. Lower the piston in the cylinder and smear a *light* coat of white

The upper ring is thinner for less flutter at high rpm. The 82.5 mm piston weighs less than the factory piston for the 1600 engine. James Sly

The raised edge around the center dish creates a squish area in the combustion chamber to boost turbulence and promote air/fuel mixing. James Sly

The Techtonics Big Bore pistons are well-made, less-expensive versions of famous German Volkswagen pistons. The piston on the right has a bigger dish area to lower the compression ratio. As with the factory pistons, the alloys, shape and construction of the Techtonics piston are such that the

effects of thermal expansion are minimized, so tighter piston-to-wall clearances can be used. This means rings will seal better and there will be less piston slap. There is a steel skirt insert. Techtonics, James Sly

grease around the top of the cylinder. Turn the crankshaft until the piston comes up to TDC for the piston you are checking. If necessary, rock the crankshaft back and forth slightly to be sure you have TDC. As the piston rises in the cylinder, the white grease will seal the rings against the cylinder wall, making the cylinder liquid-tight. Wipe away any excess grease from the top of the piston.

You now need a piece of Plexiglass with a small hole in the center, and a graduated burette.

Apply the white grease to the surface of the head surrounding the cylinder you wish to measure. Place the Plexiglass over the cylinder so the hole is over the piston. The white grease must completely seal the Plexiglass to the top of the block.

Fill the burette with light oil and note the volume of the oil. Now decant the oil through the hole in the Plexiglass until the cylinder is filled and there are no air bubbles underneath the Plexiglass. Note the volume of oil in the burette, and subtract the second reading from the first reading. This is the volume of the piston.

Again using the piece of Plexiglass, the burette, the oil and the white grease, it is time to measure the volume of the combustion chamber. Before you fill the combustion chamber with oil, however, do a test run to see that the valves are liquid-tight. If not, open the valve enough to smear some white grease on the mating surface. Then install a spark plug before proceeding.

With the sealing surface of the head horizontal, place the Plexiglass on the head using the white grease as a sealant, and decant the oil into the combustion chamber until there are no bubbles beneath the Plexiglass. Note the difference in readings in the burette, and cal-

culate the combustion chamber volume.

Because you already know the head gasket compressed thickness, the next step is to calculate head gasket thickness displacement. The formula for this is

Head gasket displacement =

$$\frac{bore \times bore \times thickness \times 0.0031416}{4}$$

If the compressed thickness of the head gasket is 1.75 mm, then the volume of the head gasket is 8.7 cc.

Plugging the figures you have obtained into the formula, this is what you get: Compression ratio =

$$\frac{428.88 + 26 + 27 + 8.7}{26 + 27 + 8.7} = \frac{490.58}{61.7} = 7.95{:}1$$

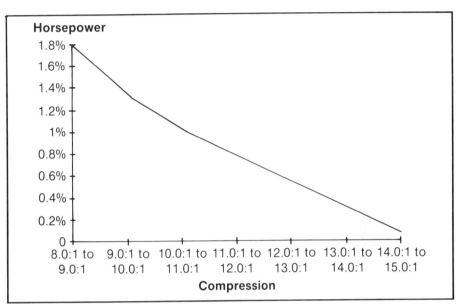

The lower your compression ratio is to start with, the bigger the gain you will get by going to higher compression. After a point, however, it just isn't worth it.

These special pistons with sodium-filled pins are used in ITB (Improved Touring, Class B) racing. Abt

Just when you thought you had "squish" and "quench" all figured out, the factory comes up with these pistons for the 16V.

The design of the combustion chamber allows these pistons to work. Techtonics

43

Compression ratios should be checked on both stock and nonstock motors to ensure longevity and avoid detonation.

Clearances

With big valves and reduced deck height, you need to check the piston-to-valve clearance before assembling the motor. Modeling clay works well for this. Put a piece of the clay on top of the piston, and turn the motor over with the head bolted down (with the head gasket), and with the cam belt and cam timing set as you are going to run the motor. For checking purposes, set the valves to the tight end of the specification to give yourself a little leeway. The closest point should be on the exhaust stroke just before TDC, when the intake valve begins to open.

Remove the clay and note where the valve made an impression. Carefully cut through the thinnest point of the impression and measure the thickness of the clay. This is your piston-to-valve clearance.

You are looking for 0.125 inch of clearance at the minimum point. If you have less, you should have the valve pockets cut. You can either turn the whole thing over to a machine shop, or you can take out your valves, temporarily replace the head and mark the centerline of the valve stem on the piston by inserting a long, thin punch down through the valve guide. The pistons can then be removed and machined.

Coatings

The pistons can take a lot of heat from the combustion process, especially in race and turbo applications. One way to cut down the heat and the possibility of detonation is by coating the tops of the pistons with zirconium oxide or impregnating them with molybdenum.

Zirconium oxide coating and moly impregnation differ slightly in where the material is applied and in how they work. Zirconium oxide is applied only to the top of the piston to reflect heat. Moly is applied to the entire piston to reduce friction, even-out temperature across the surface of the component and reflect heat away from the part.

Temperature flow is a property of moly that reduces hot spots by transferring heat quickly from high-temperature areas to low-temperature areas. But the moly also reflects heat away from the part, so there is less heat to transfer across the surface of the part. In a piston, this would mean a lot of the heat from the combustion process would be kept from soaking into the piston in the first place. What heat did soak in would be evenly distributed across the surface of the piston. This lower amount of heat would then be quickly radiated into the oil by the moly applied to the underside of the piston. There would also be less frictional heat in the piston because the skirts are treated.

One other benefit of moly impregnation is that the moly tends to shed carbon, so carbon build-up in the combustion chamber will be reduced.

Remember, if you treat one component in the combustion chamber, you should treat all the components to avoid heat overload of any untreated components.

For most people, coatings are too expensive to justify in all but the most high performance applications.

Rings

For normal applications, the standard thicknesses of rings are fine. If you are building a very high rpm motor, you will need to use thinner rings. The thinner the ring is the less well it wears, but at high rpm a thin ring does not have as much momentum as a thick ring, so it can change direction easier. A thin ring also has less friction against the cylinder

Forged pistons. Eurorace

The 1.7 pistons (left) can be replaced with Euro 1.6 Heron pistons for higher compression. Autotech

wall, so less power is lost. If you are experiencing a lot of blow-by with a high-rpm, high-compression motor, try using a thinner ring to reduce ring flutter.

Eurorace's forged pistons, for example, use 1.5 mm top rings, 1.5 mm second rings and 4.0 mm oil control rings, compared with the stock GTI rings at 1.5 mm, 1.75 mm and 5.0 mm. Mahle pistons for Super Vee racing use 1.2 mm, 1.2 mm and 4 mm rings, and even rings as thin as 1.0 mm, 1.0 mm and 3.0 mm. In general, as engine performance increases, the rings get thinner.

Any time you have your motor apart you should check the ring end gap. The gap is checked with a feeler gauge after the ring is placed 15 mm from the bottom of the cylinder bore. Use the bottom instead of the top of the bore, because the bottom gets less wear and is the point in the stroke where the ring ends are most likely to touch if the gap is too small. Make certain that the ring is exactly perpendicular to the axis of the bore before you measure. One way of ensuring this is to use a piston with no rings on it to push the ring into position at the bottom of the bore.

If you need to increase the gap, remove the ring from the bore. Clamp a file in a vise and file the ring from the outside in, *never* the other way around. Make sure you file the ends at right angles to the top and bottom ring surface. When the gap is right, dress the ends of the rings with 400 grit sandpaper.

For street use, the stock ring gap settings are fine. Compression rings must have 0.30 to 0.45 mm of end gap; oil scraper rings must have 0.25 to 0.45 mm of end gap. For racing use, stay toward the upper limit of the ring gap specification.

Before sliding the pistons and rings into the bores, position the ring end gaps as follows: Line up the expander ring of the oil control ring set with the axis of the wrist pin. Position the top and bottom oil control ring rails one inch to either side of the axis of the wrist pin. Then align the second ring gap with the gap in the top oil control ring rail, and align the top ring gap with the gap in the bottom oil control ring rail. Do not line up the ring end gaps, as this will cause a loss of compression and an increase in oil consumption.

The head

The head plays a dominant role in the performance of the motor. Every bit of air and fuel that your engine needs to make horsepower flows through the head at least twice, and the better it flows the more horsepower you will make.

The standard two-valve head on the Volkswagen is a single-port-face design, meaning the intake manifold is on the same side as the exhaust manifold. This is not ideal for performance—in fact, some typical high-performance tricks will not work on this head. The four-valve head is a cross-flow design, and has other things going for it as well.

Two-valve heads

The Volkswagen comes with six different styles of two-valve head. All the two-valve heads have the intake manifold and the exhaust manifold on the same side.

Carbureted

The head for the carbureted Volkswagen looks very similar to the early fuel-injected head in most respects, except that there are no holes for the injectors. The combustion chamber is in the head. You cannot modify a carbureted head for a fuel-injected application.

Early fuel injected

As it appeared on the 1.6 liter motors, this head differs from the carbureted head in that there are threaded openings above each intake port into which the fuel injector fits. The combustion chamber is in the head.

In flow-bench testing done by Greg Brown for Autotech SportTuning, it was discovered that the stock port started losing airflow after 0.330 inch of valve lift. The stock camshaft at that time offered 0.406 inch of lift, so going to a still larger camshaft without head work is not the hot tip. Gains from switching camshafts in this head are the result of different lobe profiles and lobe centers.

As it sits, this head is good for making 85 to 90 hp with bolt-on accessories.

Heron

As previously mentioned, the European GTIs used this flat-bottom head in combination with deep-dished pistons. This head is very distinctive, and you should not have any difficulty identifying it. The combustion chamber is in the piston. There are threaded openings for the fuel injector nozzles.

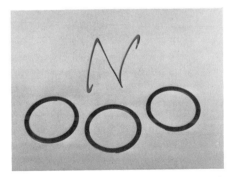

Spiralok wrist pin clips are unnecessary in all but the most high performance motors. Eurorace

It takes a lot of skill and a flow bench to come up with ports such as these. James Sly

45

In most cases, the pistons that mate with this head cannot be interchanged with those from an American head without changing the head, too. The exception is that the pistons from the 1.6 liter GTI bolt into the 1.7 liter motor, raising the compression ratio to 9.2:1. Other than this, you will normally use flat-top (or shallow-dished) pistons with American-style heads, and the deep-dished pistons with the Heron heads.

GTI

All the preceding heads share a common valve spacing. When Volkswagen made the bore bigger in 1983, it made good use of the extra room in the cylinder by spacing the valves 1 mm farther apart.

This is a great head right out of the box, with big valves, straight ports and good valve spacing, so for most applications you can use it as is. You can see gains from bigger valves and porting, but you will pay a lot and not get much in return.

These heads have an additional oil return hole at the front of the head between cylinders 3 and 4 (you can see the bump from the outside of the head), and the original front oil return hole was enlarged. To make this head work in cars with earlier blocks, the additional oil return hole must be filled in, and the enlarged front oil return hole must be welded up and then drilled to match the smaller-size hole of the earlier heads.

GTI with air-shrouded injectors

This head is similar to the GTI head, with the addition of a passage that feeds air in around the injector for better atomization. For maximum value, this head must be used with the air-shrouded injector assemblies. It would be very difficult to modify a non-air-shroud head to work with air-shrouded injectors.

The injectors for this head also have a brass insert instead of plastic. The injector itself has a plastic shroud, a directional shield and an additional circlip to hold the sealing O-ring in position.

Hydraulic

In 1985, Volkswagen added hydraulic lifters to its already great cylinder head. These heads are easily identified by the number 4 cam bearing cap, which was removed to make room for an oil squirter, and by the oil feed hole in the lifter bore to feed the hydraulic lifter. The addition of the oil squirter makes it mandatory to use the plastic splash guard, which made its first appearance in this engine. A hydraulic follower is easy to identify as such by putting your thumb inside the follower and your finger on the top, and squeezing. If it is a hydraulic cam follower, it will compress.

If you are looking for maximum performance from your head, be aware that not all Volkswagen heads are of the same quality. Some early Mexican heads have reduced port flow, shrouded valves and poor alignment of the valve stem center-lines. More recent Mexican heads have been improving, and they should soon be every bit as good as other Volkswagen heads.

No matter where it comes from, check your cylinder head for flow, valve shrouding and valve centerline before you invest time and money in it. If it is too far off, purchase a good used head and start with that.

If you are racing your car in a class that does not allow changes outside of blueprinting, you can gain 0.5 point of compression by shaving the head to its lowest limit. This is no good for street motors, because if you ever need to mill the gasket surface there will be no more metal left and you will have to replace the head. Remember that shaving the head retards the camshaft timing.

Four-valve heads

Consider for a moment what happens inside the engine when it is operating. When the intake valve is open the intake air column rushes into the cylinder, drawn by the low pressure created in the wake of the receding piston. So far so good. Then the valve closes. The air column tends to want to stay in motion, but with the valve shut it has nowhere to go, so it stops. By the time the intake valve begins to open again, the air column is out of the mood and wants to stay where it is.

Even if it were still in the mood, the air column would have precious little opportunity to express itself for the first few degrees of crankshaft rotation. At the beginning of the intake cycle, the camshaft is able to open the valve only a small amount. No matter how strong the

The factory camshaft splash guard for the later cars fits the early cars, too, and works just as well.

This special valve guide installer is a must when manually inserting valve guides. The tool is designed to apply pressure to the thicker shoulder area of the valve guide to eliminate distortion of the guide wall. *Schley Tools*

airflow of the head is when the valve is fully open, what counts is what happens the rest of the time—when the valve is only partially open. And when the valve is just beginning to open, there is not much room for the intake air column to get by the head of the intake valve.

This problem is addressed by using two smaller intake valves for each of the bigger valves. The greater circumference of these four small valves compared with the two big ones not only helps breathing, it gives more surface area on the valve seat for the valves to cool off.

The flow is what you are after, however. For example, look at what happens in two heads when the valves are 1 mm off the seats. The first head will have one intake valve, and the second head will have two intake valves.

Using a 40 mm valve in the single-valve head, the curtain area (the opening through which the air can flow) is 1.26 mm². Using two 34 mm valves to do the same job results in a curtain area of 1.82 mm², over forty-four percent larger. This shows that the critical low- and partial-lift figures will be much higher with a four-valve head than with a two-valve head.

The tradeoff comes in a loss of air velocity. At high rpm this is not a problem, but the normal response curve of a four-valve engine shows that low-end torque suffers relative to high-end torque. This is one of the reasons Volkswagen went to such extraordinary lengths in the design of its intake manifold for the 16V.

A four-valve motor has two other benefits not yet mentioned: reduced valve component weight, and less need for a radical camshaft. Even though there are more valves, springs and retainers to actuate, the weight of each individual assembly is lighter than that of its larger counterpart in a two-valve head. This reduced weight makes it much easier to control valve movements, thus making it possible to hit higher rpm without suffering from valve float. This is further helped by the fact that less valve movement is needed, so a tamer camshaft can be used and still get the proper amount of air into the cylinder. Because the valves are lighter, however, the valvetrain will tolerate a more radical camshaft, if desired. The best of both worlds.

There are three four-valve heads for the Volkswagen, all of cross-flow design.

16V

The 16V head from Volkswagen has two intake and two exhaust valves per cylinder, exotically shaped intake ports, siamesed exhaust ports and room for two camshafts. Inside the head are five camshaft bearings for each camshaft, plus an oil squirter. Because there are twice as many cam followers, the followers from adjacent cylinders nearly touch, leaving no room for the lower half of the camshaft bearing. These bearings narrow down to a knife-edge at the very bottom, but all the load is in an upward direction so this is not a problem. Because of the number of valves, the spark plug is in the middle of the cylinder head. The camshaft belt drives the exhaust cam; the intake camshaft is driven by a chain at the opposite end of the camshaft from the belt drive. The 16V head is a one-piece casting.

Oettinger

The Oettinger four-valve head was available for some time before Volkswagen introduced its, and it is a nice piece. Aside from the same number of valves, spark plugs in the center of the combustion chamber and a cross-flow design, there are few similarities between the details on this head and the details on the Volkswagen head. The camshafts are gear driven, with a vernier adjustment for intercam timing adjustment. A separate camshaft carrier bolts into the trough of the main head cast, which also holds the combustion chamber.

Drake

The Drake four-valve head is different still. This head is in two pieces like the Oettinger, although Drake divides up the castings differently. Drake drives the distributor rotor off the exhaust cam, as does Volkswagen, but it uses a crank-fired ignition as opposed to the knock-sensor ignition in the Volkswagen.

Currently, the Drake head is a race-only piece. There is a good possibility, however, that John Drake soon will be working on a street version to be used first in one of James Sly's hot street machines.

Porting and polishing
Using a flow bench

A flow bench allows the engine builder to isolate the head from the rest of the motor to see just what contribution it is making. By sucking air through intake

The VW four-valve head is very different from the Oettinger head. The squish area is built into the combustion chamber in the head instead of into the piston. Techtonics

The combustion chamber of the Oettinger four-valve head led John Drake to comment, "It looks like the perfect setup if you are running square pistons." Techtonics

ports and blowing air through exhaust ports with the valve at various distances off the valve seat, the engine builder can experiment with different port shapes and dimensions without having to assemble the entire motor and run it on the dyno. A probe inserted into the port shows where there are areas of fast-moving air (low pressure) and areas of relatively dead air (high pressure).

Through careful shaping of the port, the flow can be improved by eliminating or reducing discontinuities in the air path. By measuring the differential between the air pressure entering the head and the air pressure exiting the head, the overall efficiency of the port can be determined. As a rule of thumb, for every additional cubic foot per minute (cfm) of airflow through the port, you should realize an additional 0.4 hp per cylinder. On a 1600 cylinder head, porting increases the airflow by nearly 10 cfm on top of the 14.6 cfm gained by utilizing GTI valves. This translates to a theoretical potential of 124 to 129 hp, compared with the stock theoretical potential of 85 to 90 hp.

There are many different ways to port a head for more power. The optimum port is the smallest port that will flow the most air; *small* so the velocity is high, and *flow* so the air gets into the combustion chamber where it will do some good. Although no set formulas or procedures work on all heads and all ports, the more a tuner uses a flow bench, the better he or she may understand what the head needs to work right.

Be careful. You can easily grind through into the water jacket, or otherwise damage the head if you are inexperienced. Practice before you try to port your only cylinder head, and use a flow bench.

The flow bench gives calculated numbers that indicate what the head should do. It is very helpful, but in the final analysis the only thing that matters is how much horsepower the head makes when it is in the car.

Unshrouding the valves

If you have your head ported and polished, part of the procedure is to unshroud the valves. On a stock valve job, for the first few thousandths of an inch of valve lift, the airflow past the head of the valve is obscured by the ledge of metal that runs around the valve seat. Unshrouding the valves involves removing this lip so the air can flow unimpeded into (and out of) the cylinder.

Valves
Sizing

There is a formula that can help you figure out what is best for your application, and it works by matching the valve size to the engine displacement. First you figure out the intake valve size, and from that you calculate the exhaust valve size.

$$\text{Diameter (in inches)} = \sqrt{\frac{\text{rpm} \times S \times B \times B}{2,286,000}}$$

In this equation, S equals the stroke in mm and B equals the bore in mm.

To see how this works, consider a 1588 cc motor. The bore is 79.5 mm, and the stroke is 80 mm. You expect to rev the engine to 6000 rpm. This gives you

$$\sqrt{\frac{6000 \times 79.5 \times 79.5 \times 80}{2,286,000}} = 36.4 \text{ mm}$$

Thus, the theoretical intake valve is 36.4 mm in diameter. This is 2.5 mm

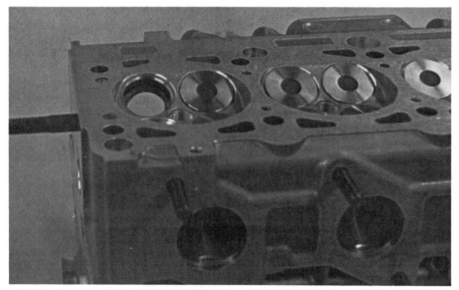

The view through the intake port on the VW four-valve head. The port is much straighter than on the Oettinger. Techtonics

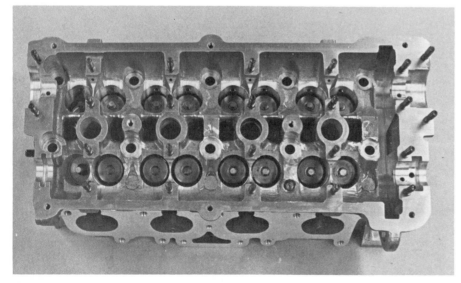

The view from above the VW four-valve head. Note the knife-edges on the camshaft bearing surfaces. Techtonics

larger than the stock valve. The theoretical exhaust valve is eighty-five percent of the size of the intake valve, or about 31 mm.

In dyno tests with various-size engines, this formula seems valid for most high-performance street applications.

Selecting

With the introduction of the GTI motor in 1983, the stock factory steel valves (40 mm intake, 33 mm exhaust) have become very popular. Not only are they the right size, the right length, the right material and long lasting, they are also available through most dealerships, as well as from many aftermarket suppliers. These valves are highly recommended for all street applications.

These steel valves are even good in the early 1600 heads, where the additional flow bumps the performance capabilities of the head up to 100 to 115 hp without any other modifications to the ports.

In some applications, however, you might need a valve that is a different diameter or length than this (or any other) stock valve. If so, you can buy either steel valves, which do many things very nicely, or stainless steel forged valves.

Stainless steel valves (when made properly) are stronger than steel valves. All stainless steel valves are one-piece valves, because the metallurgy involved is not conducive to making two-piece valves. The factory steel valves are all one-piece as well, but not all aftermarket steel valves are. Stainless steel is more elastic than steel, so it can take more of a bend without breaking or taking a set. Those of you with turbo motors will be glad to hear that stainless steel valves seem to be more burn resistant, too.

They are not perfect, unfortunately. Stainless steel valves are more expensive than steel valves, and are slightly softer, so they will require refacing and replacement more often. It is also possible for the chrome plating to come off poorly made stainless steel valves, at which point the valve guide takes a real beating.

The stainless steel valves that are commonly available are slightly longer than a stock-length valve. If you need a stock-length valve, you will have to machine down the end of the stem to match the distance between the valve seat and the cam follower (assuming the stainless steel valve has been made with enough material above the keeper groove to allow machining).

Some people install special matching seats that stick out into the combustion chamber by the same amount that the

valve stems are too long. This would allow you to unshroud the valves without having to port and polish the head or rework the combustion chamber. However, this not only increases your compression ratio and reduces your piston-to-valve clearance, it also creates hot spots in the combustion chamber—which can lead to preignition.

The Flying Dutchman markets a tool called the Pad Saver that is designed specifically to set the valve length before you proceed with the final cylinder head

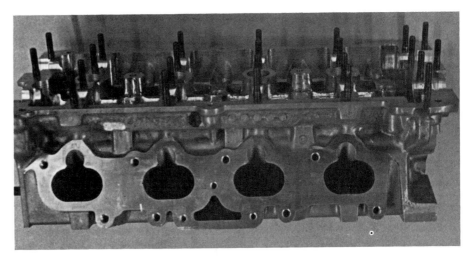

The intake ports of a VW four-valve head. Techtonics

assembly. It is called the Pad Saver because it lets you set up the valve length to work with valve-adjusting shims from the middle range (3.70 to 3.75 mm).

The Pad Saver comes with a specification tag to let you take measurements directly. Because I sometimes work with camshafts that have reduced base circles (as discussed in the section on camshafts), I prefer to zero the Pad Saver using an upper cam bearing shell, then calculate the measurement by adding together the valve lash and the difference

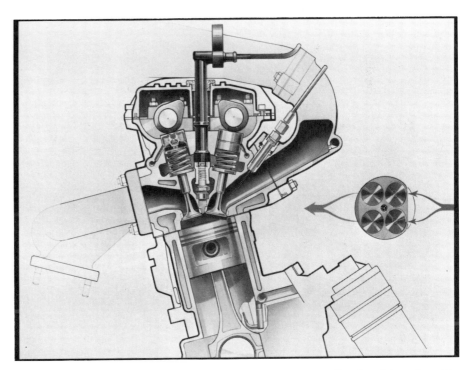

This cut-away view of the VW four-valve engine clearly shows the port design, the 25-degree intake valve angle and the squish area, as well as the piston oil squirters down below. Volkswagen

between the base circle and the OD (outside diameter) of the camshaft bearing.

Once you get the measurement, the valve stem tip is ground down on a valve grinder until the Pad Saver gets the reading you are after. This eliminates the need to completely assemble the head, install the camshaft, attempt to adjust the valves, measure the lash on any valves that will not adjust, remove the camshaft, disassemble the valvetrain, dress the valve stem tip on the grinder and then start the whole procedure over again, hoping you did the math right.

Horsepower	Airflow
1	0.69
2	1.39
3	2.08
4	2.78
5	3.47
6	4.16
7	4.86
8	5.55
9	6.25
10	6.94
11	7.63
12	8.33
13	9.02
14	9.72
15	10.41
16	11.10
17	11.80
18	12.49
19	13.19
20	13.88
21	14.57
22	15.27
23	15.96
24	16.66
25	17.35
26	18.04
27	18.74
28	19.43
29	20.13
30	20.82
31	21.51
32	22.21
33	22.90
34	23.60
35	24.29
36	24.98
37	25.68
38	26.37
39	27.07
40	27.76
41	28.45
42	29.15
43	29.84
44	30.54
45	31.23

When evaluating add-ons it can be helpful to estimate current and promised airflow. This chart works for complete motors as well as add-ons. For example, a stock 1600 cc motor in a good state of tune requires only about 54 cfm. An add-on exhaust, camshaft or throttle body that promises ten percent more power (7 hp) is really promising to increase the flow almost 5 cfm.

Either way you use it, the Pad Saver not only makes it easy to get your valve shims in the middle of the range, it greatly reduces the amount of time it takes to set up a head.

Warning: Sodium-filled valves must be treated with special handling because the sodium is under high pressure. Do not grind or break the stem of a sodium-filled valve. Do not dispose of a sodium-filled valve with the rest of the scrap metal, as doing so will then present a danger to others.

Cutting valve angles

The proper angle for the valve face is forty-five degrees, as shown in the Bentley manual. Flow-bench testing shows that even with the 33 mm valves and extensive head work, low-lift flow on the exhaust port is not as high as we would like it. This could be improved by performing an additional sixty-degree cut on the *margin* of the valve (the area between the stem and the seat face), but it would come at the expense of longevity. Stick with a single cut at forty-five degrees for street motors.

Valve seats

As with some of the other procedures in this book, working with valve seats is not something you should tackle on your own unless you plan on making a living at it. Valve seats can be tricky to work with, and if you make a mistake your engine will not run right, at the least. The worst that can happen is that the seats will fall out of the head while the motor is running, ruining your whole day.

Although anybody can have a seat come out of the head, it is more prevalent with the "high-performance" heads you see advertised at "too-good-to-be-true" prices. The low prices can be enticing, but head work is so important to the overall performance of the motor that you will be money ahead getting a good-quality head and passing up the bargains.

Valve seats have an ID (internal diameter) measurement and an OD measurement (valves have an OD measurement only). The ID measurement gives you an idea how much air will flow through the seat. The OD measurement gives you an idea how much trouble it is going to be to fit the seat in your head.

One reason Volkswagen went to the different valve spacing on later heads was to fit more valve. The 1600 cc heads will not fit much more than a 40 mm intake seat. Even at that you can hit the water jacket in the center cylinders, which can crack the head. These cracks will ooze

coolant into the combustion chamber after you shut the car off, and if extreme enough will allow combustion gases into the coolant.

If your 1600 with big valves runs rough after one hour of sitting, it may not be the fuel injection. Pull the radiator cap off and run the motor to see if the cooling system is building up unusual pressure when cold. Let the motor warm up, then pull a spark plug and check for coolant in the cylinders. If you see a little green puddle, head for the store and pick up some Alumiseal. If that does not work, consider upgrading to an 1800 cc head modified to work on your block. Not only are the stock valves the size you want them, but the ports are far superior right out of the box.

Cutting valve seat angles

The way the valve seat is cut is as important as the way the port is shaped, because it has to let air past smoothly, it has to provide a sealing surface for the valve and it has to act as a heat sink, as well.

	CFM	Theoretical hp
Stock	54.9	85-90
GTI valves	69.5	108-113
Porting	79.4	124-129

Airflow and hp at .462 lift
1600 cc head

Blueprinting, balancing and so on are nice, but you must get the engine to breathe, which means head work on the early heads, as shown by these results of flow-bench tests by Greg Brown for Autotech Sport-Tuning.

Valve size	Curtain area of single valve	Curtain area of double valve
40	1.26	2.51
39	1.19	2.39
38	1.13	2.27
37	1.08	2.15
36	1.02	2.04
35	0.96	1.92
34	0.91	1.82
33	0.86	1.71
32	0.80	1.61
31	0.75	1.51
30	0.71	1.41
29	0.66	1.32
28	0.62	1.23
27	0.57	1.15
26	0.53	1.06
25	0.49	0.98

As you can see from this chart, the much larger curtain area of two small valves compared with one big valve allows the engine to breathe much better; calculated at 1 mm lift off the valve seat.

To accomplish all these tasks, the valve seat has three different angles ground into it. The first angle blends the seat into the port. It is called the bottom cut, and must be sixty degrees.

The seat, where the valve touches, must have the same angle as the valve face, or forty-five degrees. On the intake valve, the width of the seat contact area is 2 mm. On an exhaust valve, the seat contact area is 2.4 mm wide.

The width of the contact area is critical. If it is too thick, there will be too many square millimeters of seat against which the valve face will ride. Unless you are changing valve springs, too, the valve spring pressure will be spread out over a greater surface area. The valve spring will not be able to pull the valve closed tightly enough to seal, and eventually the valve will burn.

To blend the airflow over the seat into the combustion chamber, one final cut must be made at thirty degrees.

If you are going to be porting and polishing your head after installing new valve seats, the new seat must be rough cut to 0.25 mm smaller than the finished diameter.

Lapping the valves

Some machinists will tell you that with the new valves and valve seat cutters available, you no longer have to hand-lap your valves. It is tempting to believe this because hand-lapping can be a lot of work.

The trouble is that many machine shops are not as careful as they should be, and you may wind up with a valve that does not sit on the seat quite right. This results in small leaks that start out by simply robbing you of horsepower, but that can progress to the point where the valve will burn and you must do the job over again.

If you are after professional results, take a few minutes and hand-lap your valves. After all, it is your engine, and you want it to live for a long, long time. Lapping the valves is also important in racing classes where you cannot do anything to the motor other than blueprinting.

Valve guides

The best-wearing and longest-lasting valve guides are made of silicon-bronze

In the hydraulic heads, the number 4 cam bearing has been replaced with an oil squirter. Eurorace

Polishing is done to the combustion chamber. At the same time, the combustion chamber volumes are all made equal. Precision Porsche

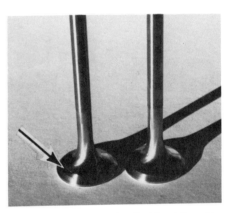

This extra cut on the back side of the valve allows better airflow but reduces longevity. Precision Porsche

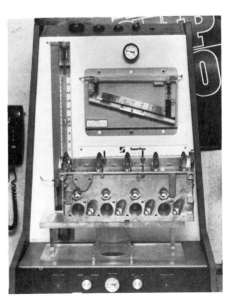

Flow-bench testing, while not always indicative of final performance, does show the engine builder things that can't be separated out with a dyno. Precision Porsche

alloy. These are readily available from most automotive supply houses. The valve guides in the Volkswagen motor are relatively short, so they should be checked carefully for wear when you have the head apart. A tight fit is necessary to help cool the valve and to make sure the valve closes properly on the seat each time it comes down.

After installing new guides, always run a guide reamer through them for good measure.

Selecting a high-performance head

When buying a head, here are some questions to ask:

• What valves are used?
• What springs are used? How much lift will they accept?
• What seats are used, and what size are they?
• Are the valves set up for a stock-base-circle camshaft?

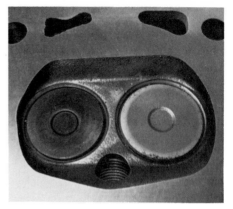

Stock 1600 combustion chamber showing the valve shrouding. Eurorace

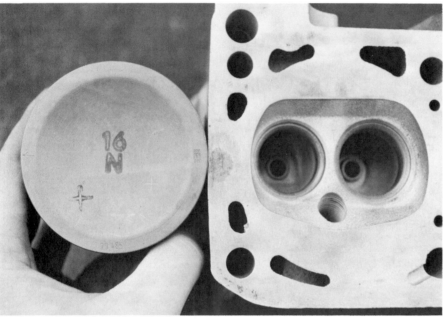

US-style head with matching pistons. The combustion chamber is in the head. Abt

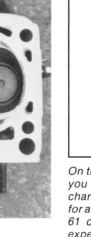

Hydraulic head, showing the two front oil return holes. Eurorace

Airflow (cfm)	Horsepower
1	1.4
2	2.9
3	4.3
4	5.8
5	7.2
6	8.6
7	10.1
8	11.5
9	13.0
10	14.4
11	15.8
12	17.3
13	18.7
14	20.2
15	21.6
16	23.0
17	24.5
18	25.9
19	27.4
20	28.8
21	30.2
22	31.7
23	33.1
24	34.6
25	36.0
26	37.4
27	38.9
28	40.3
29	41.8
30	43.2
31	44.6
32	46.1
33	47.5
34	49.0
35	50.4
36	51.8
37	53.3
38	54.7
39	56.2
40	57.6
41	59.0
42	60.5
43	61.9
44	63.4
45	64.8

On the other hand, if you know the airflow, you can estimate the horsepower. This chart works for complete motors as well as for add-ons. A stock 1600 head flows about 61 cfm. Therefore, the most you could expect with bolt-on modifications would be about 88 hp.

- Is the head flow tested? How much would it cost to flow test the head?
- Is the installed height of the valve spring checked?
- Is a camshaft included?
- Do the seats have a three-angle cut?

Miscellaneous tips and techniques

Valve cover studs

One of the best things you can do for early heads is to upgrade the valve cover gasket studs. This goes double if you have a very early head that uses bolts to hold the valve cover on. The new-style studs have a shoulder in the middle. After removing the old studs (or bolts), Loc-tite the new studs in. Between the shoulder and the Loc-tite, you can crank on them to make them stay.

With the new-style studs, you can use the new-style gaskets that have larger holes. These seal better than the early-style gaskets because the shoulder prevents the valve cover nuts from being tightened down so far that the gasket is flattened. This does not increase the performance of the motor, but it does keep it cleaner and make it nicer to work on.

Oil splash/blow-by guard

Another easy modification for the early cars comes straight from Volkswagen. Starting in 1985, the company began installing a black plastic splash guard that sits atop the camshaft bearing studs, under the valve cover. This simple device cuts down the amount of oil splash that can cause valve cover gasket and oil fill cap leaks, and it also helps separate out the oil in the blow-by.

If your air filter is getting saturated with motor oil, you should install one of these. It even seems to help the performance of aftermarket valve covers in this respect, although none of the aftermarket valve covers I have ever seen seal, handle blow-by, provide oil cooling or fit as well

as the stock valve cover. An aluminum valve cover may look good, but the stock unit does everything a valve cover needs to do.

Preventive maintenance

The only problem with the camshaft splash guard is that it obscures the view of the intake and exhaust lobes for cylinder 1. This makes it impossible to quickly check the position of the cam (or the condition of the inside of the head) by removing the oil fill cap.

If you do not have a camshaft splash guard, check the inside of the head any time you have your valve cover or oil fill

cap off. Are the surfaces clean and shiny, with a light coat of oil? Or are they caked with black or dark brown sludge? If the inside of the head is not clean down to the bare metal, you are doing something drastically wrong, and your engine is going to get revenge someday.

That caked-on gunk is oxidized oil. Oil oxidizes either because it is old and abused, or because it has been overheated. Either way, you have to do something about it before your engine dies a horrible death.

Go to the auto parts store and get some oil and an oil filter. While you are

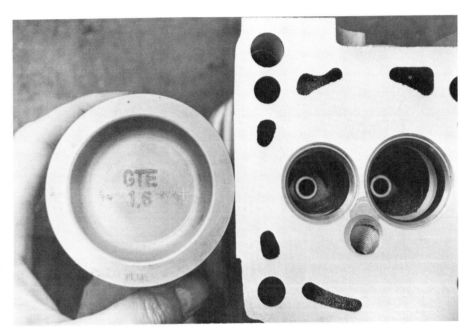

European-style head with matching pistons. The combustion chamber is in the crown of the piston. Abt

The air port for the air-shrouded injectors on a 1984 GTI head. Techtonics

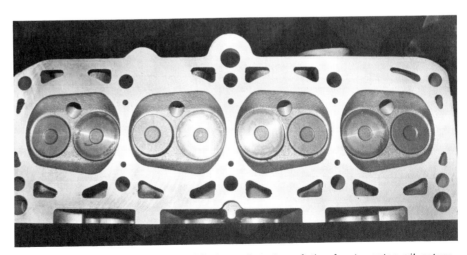

This late-model head has been modified to work on an early block by welding up the right front oil return and reducing the diameter of the front center oil return. Techtonics

there, pick up a can of carburetor cleaner. Berryman's Chem-Tool is a good product, but keep it away from your paint.

Take some old rags and the carb cleaner, and clean off as much of the gunk from the inside of the head as you can, taking care not to let too much of the carb cleaner get into the oil drain-back holes. When you are finished, drain the oil, change the filter and pour in the new oil.

Repeat this procedure every 1,000 to 1,500 miles until the head is clean inside. Your car will run much cooler, and your oil will protect your engine longer when it no longer has to fight the existing oil sludge from the minute you pour it in the crankcase.

Camshaft bearing problems

Another problem I hope you never have to deal with is that of bad camshaft bearings. The Volkswagen engine has no bearing shells for the camshaft to ride in; it spins directly in the head material itself.

Normally the camshaft bearings should last well over 100,000 miles. If the oil gets very dirty they can become scored, however. Camshaft bearings will also be turned into hamburger if you reassemble the engine with the head gasket on upside-down, or if you torque the bearing caps on backward.

If the bearings are damaged, they can be surfaced and the camshaft bore rehoned to size. If there is greater damage, the camshaft bearing saddles will have to be machined for bearing inserts. Rimco is the place to get this done, and it

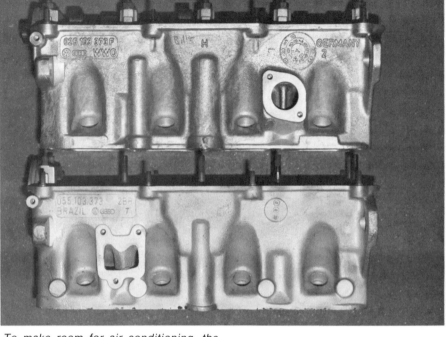

To make room for air conditioning, the water return port was moved from the right side of the head (bottom) to the left. Techtonics

Measuring the volume of the piston. Techtonics

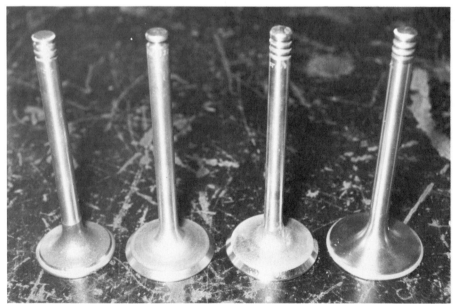

Intake valves from left to right: 34 mm (1600 and 1700), 38 mm (Mexican 1800), 40 mm (GTI) and 41 mm (Oettinger 2021 kit). Techtonics

Measuring the head volume. Techtonics

is also the place to buy the camshaft bearing shells if you need them.

Moly impregnation

As described at the end of the section on engine tools and techniques, moly impregnation can help a camshaft, crankshaft, cylinder bore or piston skirt. But the inside of the head?

According to the people who do this sort of thing, it works, and works well. By coating the inside of the head, heat flow is improved across the surface of the combustion chamber, helping eliminate hot spots and thus cutting down on preignition. Used in combination with coated pistons, moly impregnation keeps more heat in the combustion chamber and out of the motor.

As nice as this all sounds, it is not something everyone will want to do. The Volkswagen motor runs fine without it, so this is another technique that is relegated to the race-only category.

Camshafts

As with many aspects of the Volkswagen motor, the stock camshaft is very well thought out, providing a good example of what to look for in an aftermarket camshaft. The stock profile integrates all the design parameters you expect in a camshaft while paying heed to emissions requirements, and it does a good job of balancing performance against pollution. There is a lot more performance to be had from other camshaft profiles, however.

Theory

In an *ideal* world, the camshaft would open the intake valve fully and instantaneously the moment the piston reached top dead center. As the piston then started toward bottom dead center, the fresh air/fuel mixture would be pulled in by the resulting vacuum to fully fill the cylinder. When the piston reached BDC, the camshaft would instantaneously close the intake valve. The piston would then move toward TDC, compressing the air/fuel mixture. When the piston reached TDC, the spark plug would ignite the air/fuel mixture, and the push of the expanding gases would force the piston back to BDC. After the spark-ignited mixture had forced the piston to BDC again, the camshaft would instantaneously open the exhaust valve, which would stay open until the piston reached TDC. With the piston again at TDC, the camshaft would instantaneously close the exhaust valve and open the intake valve.

The real world operates quite differently and is far more complicated, making the camshaft that much more important.

The combustion chamber of the Drake four-valve. James Sly

Camshaft operating parameters

A vast number of characteristics are embodied in camshaft design. And every single aspect of the camshaft must be taken into consideration if you are to get the most from your engine.

The Pad Saver allows you to set up the head without having to install the camshaft.

There are two main parameters that determine cam performance (not counting the effects of intake and exhaust efficiency): *when* the valves open and close, and *how much* they open. These two main parameters can be broken down into nine separate categories, each of which interrelates with the next. To these nine categories I have appended three additional categories specific to the Volkswagen engine.

Intake opening and closing

Of the four cam-controlled events mentioned earlier, it is widely acknowledged that intake valve closing is the most important. The sooner the valve is closed the sooner cylinder pressure will begin building up, thus boosting low-end torque.

Intake opening is set by the operating rpm of the engine. The sooner you can open the intake valve (up to a point), the more time the engine will have to fill the cylinder with the fresh air/fuel mixture. At low rpm, opening the intake too early results in a rough idle and poor off-idle response because the air/fuel mixture mixes with the exhaust gases that are still trying to get out of the cylinder. At higher rpm, the exiting exhaust gases will actually pull the air/fuel mixture into the cylinder, and the engine will breathe better.

Exhaust opening and closing

After the spark plug ignites the air/fuel mixture, the piston is forced downward by the expanding gases. This is called the power stroke, and it ends when the exhaust valve opens. The sooner the exhaust valve opens, the shorter the power stroke. On the other hand, you do not want to delay opening the exhaust valve for too long, because after a point there is not enough energy left in the expanding gases to continue to create meaningful force against the piston, but there is enough residual force to help flow the spent gases out the exhaust port. By opening the exhaust valve at just the right time, you can take advantage of this residual energy to help evacuate the cylinder. Because the exhaust valve is usually left closed until long after the point at which the combustion gases are contributing to the power output, the exhaust valve opening has the least effect on torque of the three main valve events (intake closing, intake opening and exhaust opening).

The exhaust valve usually does not close until after the intake valve has begun to open. This promotes intake breathing to some extent, and the cooler temperature of the intake charge helps take some of the heat out of the exhaust valve to keep it from burning.

In conjunction with the intake opening parameter, the exhaust closing parameter allows you to calculate valve overlap.

Duration

Duration is the measurement in crankshaft degrees between when the valve

This is the proper way to remove the cam sprocket bolt with the motor in the car. To avoid marring the cam lobe you might want to use a rag between the crescent wrench and the camshaft. Autotech

Because this is a permanent fixture, it makes sense to go to the extra effort to adapt a Beetle degree pulley. But if you plan to do only one or two camshafts, this would be too much trouble. Eurorace

Here is the custom setup I use to degree camshafts, making use of a junked head. Eurorace

opens and when it closes. For example, if the intake valve opens at seven degrees BTDC (before top dead center) and closes at forty-nine degrees ABDC (after bottom dead center), you add the number of degrees between the opening of the valve and TDC (seven degrees) to the number of degrees between TDC and BDC (180) and the number of degrees between BDC and the closing of the valve (forty-nine).

Intake open to TDC + TDC to BDC + BDC to intake closed = duration

$$7 + 180 + 49 = 236$$

In this case, the duration is 236 degrees. What is not so obvious is why the duration is often measured at 1 mm, instead of directly off the surface of the camshaft lobe, or off the follower or valve face with the valve clearance properly set.

There are three reasons for this: One, Volkswagen measures its camshafts at 1 mm. Two, for the purposes of engine builders, there is not much airflow past the valve at low lifts (when the valve is just starting to open or almost completely closed). And three, the transition area on the cam lobe between when the valve is closed and when the valve is being forced open is called the clearance ramp.

At running tolerance, these ramps are critical for proper valve and lifter control. For setting up an engine, they are worse than worthless, because they might not have anything to do with the working profile of the cam. Therefore, to make calculations based on a duration

that is not 100 percent usable is misleading. By measuring duration at the cam at a figure such as 1 mm, however, you can predict the performance of an installed cam in an engine after all the tolerances are taken up and the valve is open enough to allow meaningful airflow.

When either valve is open, the engine cannot make any compression, so long-duration camshafts are found only in engines that see high rpm and need to

breathe more than they need dynamic compression. This type of motor would usually be built with lots of static compression, so there would be some compression left when the engine was running.

Lobe centers

The lobe center is the number of camshaft degrees between the centerline of the intake lobe and the centerline of the exhaust lobe. The lobe centerlines are

If you look closely you will be able to see that there is a flat spot ground into the bearing surface of the camshaft. This allows a little oil to squirt out onto the cam follower for better lubrication. This is not needed except in very high performance applications. Eurorace

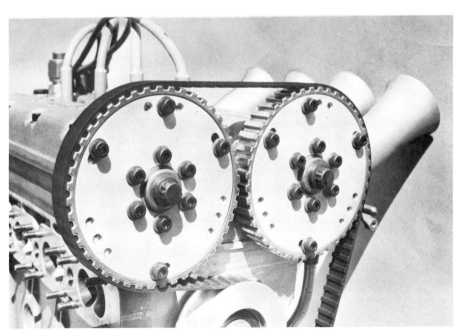

This is an example of an adjustable cam sprocket. Note the wide range of adjustment available. Eurorace

Adjustable cam sprockets are a necessity on a twin-cam motor, both for setting cam timing and for setting overlap. Drake Engineering

imaginary lines through the axis of the cam that bisect the cam lobes at their point of highest lift.

If you know the opening and closing times of both the intake and exhaust valves, you have all the information you need to calculate lobe centerlines and lobe centers. Taking numbers from the sample camshaft, remember that the intake opened at seven degrees BTDC and closed at forty-nine degrees ABDC. When you added these two numbers to the 180 degrees there are between TDC and BDC, you got

$$7 + 180 + 49 = 236$$

This is the total time the intake is open. Assuming the lobe is symmetrical

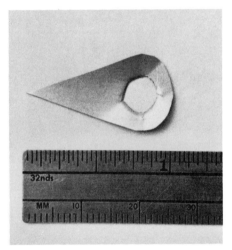

With a pair of scissors and an aluminum can you can make a pointer for the cam sprocket.

The pointer eliminates erroneous readings when dialing in the camshaft.

(see the later section on lobe profile), you can divide this number by 2 to get the exact midpoint of the lobe, or the lobe centerline.

$$236 \div 2 = 118$$

This is the number of crankshaft degrees between the lobe centerline and the opening (or closing) of the valve. To find out where this lies in relation to TDC, subtract the number of degrees that the valve is open BTDC from the lobe centerline value.

$$118 - 7 = 111$$

This gives the number of crankshaft degrees between TDC and the lobe centerline. Running the numbers for the exhaust lobe, you will find the lobe centerline value to be

$$\frac{9 + 180 + 47}{2} - 9 = 109$$

Now that you have the lobe centerlines in crankshaft degrees, you can calculate the lobe centers, which are always expressed in camshaft degrees. Add the two centerline values together and divide by 2 (because the crankshaft turns twice for each time the camshaft turns once). This gives

$$\frac{111 + 109}{2} = 110$$

The lobe center for this camshaft is 110 degrees (at the camshaft).

As discussed earlier, the lobe center determines how much time the intake and exhaust valves will be open at the same time. The closer together the lobe centers are, the longer the two valves will be open simultaneously, all other factors being equal.

Valve overlap

Overlap is the time (expressed in degress of crankshaft rotation) that both the intake and exhaust valves are simultaneously open in the same cylinder. Overlap is a function of the lobe centers and camshaft duration:

$$D - 2L = O$$

D represents the duration, L represents the lobe center and O represents the overlap. Therefore, the sample camshaft with 236 degrees of duration and 110 degrees of lobe center has sixteen crankshaft degrees of overlap.

As the lobe centers are spread farther apart, overlap is reduced. Engine power

range is narrowed, becoming concentrated toward the upper end of the rpm curve. This is because of the later closing of the intake valve.

Moving the lobe centers closer together increases the overlap and increases cylinder pressure (because the intake valve is closing earlier), but it also increases exhaust scavenging. Too much overlap will lead to increasing portions of the incoming air/fuel mixture being scavenged (pushed out the exhaust without being burnt), which negatively affects the brake-specific fuel curve.

Engines run with a lot of cam overlap usually have more static compression built into them to compensate. In a CIS-injected motor, the proper amount of valve overlap for all-around performance is found in camshafts with about 108 to 110 degrees of lobe center. Any more overlap (less lobe center) than that will create a rough idle as pressure pulses from the exhaust cycle affect the intake tract, causing the air sensor plate to flutter. As the rpm increase this ceases to be a problem, and advancing the camshaft (either by grinding advance into the camshaft or with the use of an adjustable cam sprocket) can mitigate air sensor plate flutter. Early carbureted Golfs used 114-degree-lobe-center camshafts, and Super Vees with mechanical (not CIS) injection used 100-degree-lobe-center camshafts.

In all cars, the greater the overlap, the less vacuum the engine will pull at idle.

Cam timing

There are two ways to alter cam timing. The first is to grind the amount of advance or retard into the cam itself. The figures that are important in calculating camshaft advance or retard are the intake valve opening and exhaust valve closing specifications. If the intake duration is the same as the exhaust duration, and the intake opening figure is the same as the exhaust closing figure, then there is no advance or retard ground into the cam, and it is said to have a split overlap.

To determine the amount of advance or retard ground into a cam with equal intake and exhaust duration but unequal intake opening and exhaust closing figures, subtract the smaller of the two figures from the larger of the two figures, and divide by 2. This gives you the amount of advance or retard in crankshaft degrees. If the intake opening figure is larger, the cam is retarded. If the exhaust closing figure is larger, the cam is advanced.

The sample camshaft is one illustration of this. It begins opening the intake at seven degrees BTDC and closes the exhaust at nine degrees ATDC. From this you can immediately see that the cam is ground with a slight amount of retard in it. How much?

$$\frac{7-9}{2} = -1$$

This camshaft is ground with one crankshaft degree of retard.

Sometimes the intake duration and the exhaust duration are unequal. In that case, subtract the smaller duration from the larger duration and divide by 2. Then subtract this figure from each end (opening and closing) of the larger figure. You will have one adjusted duration and one unadjusted duration. You can then determine the amount of advance or retard as outlined earlier. This gives you an approximate figure, at which time you will need to put in some time on the dyno to accurately evaluate whether or not the cam will work in your application.

Lobe profile

Each cam lobe has two sides. One opens the valve and one closes it. Normally, it is sufficient if the shapes or profiles of both sides are the same. Also, it is normally sufficient if the profiles of the intake lobes are the same as those for the exhaust lobes. However, that is not the only way to do it.

Asymmetric cams are ground with different profiles for opening the valve than for closing it. This is normally done to allow the cam to pop the valve open at a maximum rate and then allow for a more leisurely closing to prevent valve float (uncontrolled or false motion in the valvetrain).

A dual-pattern cam, on the other hand, is one in which the profile of the intake lobe is different than that of the exhaust lobe. A dual-pattern cam is a special-duty design, and most applications work well without going to dual-patterns.

Lift

Lift is measured at the cam, and is defined as the difference between the cam base circle and the highest part of the toe or nose. Because the lift of the camshaft is measured at the nose of the camshaft, there is no need to worry about the 1 mm checking height that is so important when talking about duration and timing.

Lift determines how much the camshaft will open the valve. The stock cam is pretty mild, and the Volkswagen motor will accept a much higher lift cam than the factory puts in. However, the factory valve springs will accept only a certain amount of lift before the coils of the spring start touching each other, or go into coil bind (see the following section on valve springs).

You can check the lift on a solid-lifter camshaft yourself. You need some way of measuring the camshaft accurately (a set of outside micrometers or a dial caliper will do the trick). On hydraulic camshafts (and some full-race camshafts), the ramps extend down to the point where you will be measuring, which will throw the numbers off. To measure these, put the camshaft between centers and use a dial indicator to check the lift.

The first measurement to take is from the nose (high point) of one of the camshaft lobes to the opposite side of the cam. Write this number down. The next measurement must be taken at ninety degrees from your first measurement. Subtract your second measurement from the first to get the lift of the cam. For example, if the first measurement is 1.925 inches and the base circle is 1.5 inches, the lift of your camshaft is 0.425 inch.

Area under the curve

Although this might remind you of the calculus class you took in high school, you are not going to have to work out first derivatives and integrations. Picture instead two camshafts that both open and close the intake valve at the same crankshaft degrees. If one camshaft has a lift of 0.410 inch and the other has a lift of 0.425 inch, the second camshaft will have a great deal more area under the curve than the first, even though the durations are the same.

If the cam grinder so desired, he or she could reduce the duration on the second cam by some extent, and still have more area under the curve than with the lower-lift cam. In theory, whenever the area under the curve is increased, the engine's ability to breathe should improve.

Base circle

One thing that prevents a camshaft from interchanging directly with the stock unit is the base circle. It is possible

Measure from the straightedge to both the front and rear sealing surfaces. The distances must be identical.

A quick-and-dirty method for setting the camshaft to TDC utilizes a straightedge.

(sometimes even desirable) to grind the cam on a different base circle than the factory cam's. On a replacement cam with a smaller base circle, the valve stem will need to come up higher toward the camshaft (by being longer or by having the valve sunk deeper into the head), all the adjustment shims will need to be thicker to compensate, or you will need to use lash caps between the end of the valve stem and the cam bucket.

When people were first starting to do high-performance work on Volkswagens, there were no high-performance camshafts or valves available. If you wanted a hot camshaft, you reground the one you had. Grinding reduced the base circle of the camshaft, requiring different valves or the use of lash caps.

A reduced-base-circle camshaft has one advantage over the stock-base-circle camshaft. By reducing the base circle and leaving the nose of the camshaft alone, you get much more lift than is possible with a stock base circle. With this extra lift, however, comes the necessity of changing the valves, followers and springs, in addition to machining the head to make the followers and springs work. None of this will be required for any reasonable street machine, and only the most radical race engines need make use of it.

Thus, for most of us, a stock-base-circle camshaft is the only way to go. In fact, the hot setup is to use stock GTI valves and a stock-base-circle camshaft. This combination will give you a lot of performance in a street machine, and you will have the peace of mind that comes from knowing that if anything goes wrong, you will be able to get parts no matter where you are.

What might go wrong? Your car may not break down, but what happens when your state passes smog inspection legislation and you have had your entire head set up to run a nonstock-base-circle cam? With stock-length valves you can slide your old stock camshaft right back in there (you did save it, didn't you?).

A stock-base-circle solid-lifter camshaft will measure about 1.5 inches. A stock-base-circle hydraulic camshaft will measure about 1.34 inches.

Billets

There seems to be quite a bit of consternation about the source of billets used in the manufacture of camshafts. Some companies tout the fact that their camshafts are "German chill-hardened" for the ultimate in wear resistance. A chill-hardened camshaft is cast in a special mold that chills the hot metal quickly on the outside, causing the carbon in the metal to form a tough surface facing while the inside is still hot. This combination makes for a very good cam billet. The allegation is that the American billets are not chill-hardened and are therefore junk. There are two problems with this argument.

First, there are few sources for German chill-hardened billets. Many of the so-called German billets are in fact made in Mexico or Brazil. They are still chill-hardened, and they are still good, but they are not German.

Second, the American billets are not made of the same material as the factory billets. If they were, and they were not chill-hardened, they would indeed have problems. The American billets are cast from a material called Proferal (short for Process Ferrous Alloy). Proferal is cast using more traditional sand-casting, which is less labor intensive and thus less expensive than chill-hardening.

The controversy arises because the early Proferal formulation gave spotty results in some applications. It takes only a couple of camshafts going flat to start the word around, and that is what happened. The Proferal formulation now has more chrome for increased wear resistance, making it good for Volkswagen camshafts.

Valve center spacing

Valve center spacing changed from the early heads with the mechanical adjustment to the GTI heads. At first, it was claimed that the camshafts would have to be different. As it turned out, the valve spacing proved not to be a problem. Although a different camshaft lobe

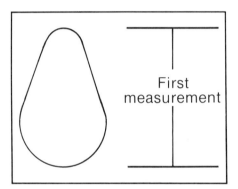

When trying to determine the lift of your camshaft, use your dial caliper to measure this distance first.

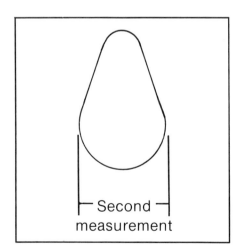

Next, measure the base circle as shown here. If you have a hydraulic or high-performance camshaft, the ramp will already be starting here so your calculated lift figure will be off by a couple of thousandths on the low side.

Cam lift in mm

mm	inches	mm	inches	mm	inches
9.00	0.354	11.25	0.443	13.60	0.535
9.05	0.356	11.30	0.445	13.65	0.537
9.10	0.358	11.35	0.447	13.70	0.539
9.15	0.360	11.40	0.449	13.75	0.541
9.20	0.362	11.45	0.451	13.80	0.543
9.25	0.364	11.50	0.453	13.85	0.545
9.30	0.366	11.55	0.455	13.90	0.547
9.35	0.368	11.60	0.457	13.95	0.549
9.40	0.370	11.65	0.459	14.00	0.551
9.45	0.372	11.70	0.461	14.05	0.553
9.50	0.374	11.75	0.463	14.10	0.555
9.55	0.376	11.80	0.465	14.15	0.557
9.60	0.378	11.85	0.467	14.20	0.559
9.65	0.380	11.90	0.469	14.25	0.561
9.70	0.382	11.95	0.470	14.30	0.563
9.75	0.384	12.00	0.472	14.35	0.565
9.80	0.386	12.05	0.474	14.40	0.567
9.85	0.388	12.10	0.476	14.45	0.569
9.90	0.390	12.15	0.478	14.50	0.571
9.95	0.392	12.20	0.480	14.55	0.573
10.00	0.394	12.25	0.482	14.60	0.575
10.05	0.396	12.30	0.484	14.65	0.577
10.10	0.398	12.35	0.486	14.70	0.579
10.15	0.400	12.40	0.488	14.75	0.581
10.20	0.402	12.45	0.490	14.80	0.583
10.25	0.404	12.50	0.492	14.85	0.585
10.30	0.406	12.55	0.494	14.90	0.587
10.35	0.407	12.60	0.496	14.95	0.589
10.40	0.409	12.65	0.498	15.00	0.591
10.45	0.411	12.70	0.500	15.05	0.593
10.50	0.413	12.75	0.502	15.10	0.594
10.55	0.415	12.80	0.504	15.15	0.596
10.60	0.417	12.85	0.506	15.20	0.598
10.65	0.419	12.90	0.508	15.25	0.600
10.70	0.421	12.95	0.510	15.30	0.602
10.75	0.423	13.00	0.512	15.35	0.604
10.80	0.425	13.05	0.514	15.40	0.606
10.85	0.427	13.10	0.516	15.45	0.608
10.90	0.429	13.15	0.518	15.50	0.610
10.95	0.431	13.20	0.520	15.55	0.612
11.00	0.433	13.25	0.522	15.60	0.614
11.05	0.435	13.30	0.524	15.65	0.616
11.10	0.437	13.35	0.526	15.70	0.618
11.15	0.439	13.40	0.528	15.75	0.620
11.20	0.441	13.45	0.530	15.80	0.622

Use this chart to translate metric cam specs to inches and vice versa.

spacing would have been nice, cars with the new heads run with old camshafts just fine.

Selecting a camshaft
Fuel-injected camshafts

If you have a normally aspirated CIS fuel-injected car, selecting a camshaft is fairly easy. Be conservative in your selection, and if possible drive a car fitted with the camshaft you have your eye on before you buy. If others tell you a certain camshaft is not very good for street use, believe them. There are definite limits to what the CIS motor will accept.

I find that more of my driving time is spent with the car at idle than at redline. Therefore, a camshaft with good idle characteristics is more important than a camshaft that gives me 5 hp more above 6500 rpm. You must also free up the exhaust flow before a hot camshaft will do you much good.

The most camshaft you can run in a 1.6 or 1.7 engine with stock springs and CIS measures about 0.425 inch of lift with a 108 to 110 degree lobe center. The 1.8 engines have been known to run 0.435 inch of lift. Use too much lift, and you run into problems with valve springs; more overlap than that, and the back pulse in the intake manifold will cause the airflow sensor in the fuel distributor housing to flutter, destroying horsepower.

Several aftermarket camshafts are available that are designed for cars with hydraulic heads. People are still experimenting with hydraulic camshafts, however, and the next couple of years should prove interesting. The biggest difference with the hydraulic-lifter camshafts is that the ramps start very early, presumably to preload the lifter so it will be locked up by the time the flank of the camshaft comes around.

For those lucky few with 16V motors, the 130 hp of the European version of this car is available by changing the exhaust camshaft (in conjunction with the Euro 16V exhaust). There is also a matched set of Group A racing camshafts available for those who will be racing and can use all the horsepower on the big end. (For even more big-end horsepower, see the discussion of intake manifolds in chapter 3.)

Carburetor camshafts

If you have a carbureted motor, the first thing to remember when selecting a camshaft is do not overcam—just as with a fuel-injected motor, but for slightly different reasons. Overcamming kills bottom-end power and will result in poor idling. Unless you are racing, most of your daily driving is done at relatively low rpm, so you want to preserve or improve the low-end torque as much as possible.

You can check for possible overcamming by loosening the valve adjustment 0.010 to 0.015 inch. If your engine runs better with more valve lash, you have too much cam for the rest of your engine in your application. When running a single carburetor, one of the CIS-style camshafts would be a good choice. With two or more carburetors you can get more radical.

Second, measure your cam at 1 mm. The reasons behind this are covered earlier. Many cams are advertised with measurements taken at the valve, or at a 0.004 inch clearance or whatever. Do not trust these claims. Measure everything at a clearance of 1 mm so you know you are comparing apples with apples. Then, before you install the cam you have selected, double-check the measurements to ensure the figures you were quoted are right.

Third, the more overlap you use, the more static compression the engine will need to make horsepower. This is because no compression is being built up during the overlap period, so all compression must come from that part of the piston travel remaining after both valves finally close. (Also remember that moving the lobes closer together is better for high-rpm applications, and that spreading the lobe centers boosts low-end performance.)

Fourth, the more carburetor, head work and exhaust efficiency you have, the more camshaft you can run. Just

Camshaft pulley degree equivalents

Teeth	Degrees	Teeth	Degrees	Teeth	Degrees
0.5	4.09	15.5	126.82	30.5	249.55
1.0	8.18	16.0	130.91	31.0	253.64
1.5	12.27	16.5	135.00	31.5	257.73
2.0	16.36	17.0	139.09	32.0	261.82
2.5	20.45	17.5	143.18	32.5	265.91
3.0	24.55	18.0	147.27	33.0	270.00
3.5	28.64	18.5	151.36	33.5	274.09
4.0	32.73	19.0	155.45	34.0	278.18
4.5	36.82	19.5	159.55	34.5	282.27
5.0	40.91	20.0	163.64	35.0	286.36
5.5	45.00	20.5	167.73	35.5	290.45
6.0	49.09	21.0	171.82	36.0	294.55
6.5	53.18	21.5	175.91	36.5	298.64
7.0	57.27	22.0	180.00	37.0	302.73
7.5	61.36	22.5	184.09	37.5	306.82
8.0	65.45	23.0	188.18	38.0	310.91
8.5	69.55	23.5	192.27	38.5	315.00
9.0	73.64	24.0	196.36	39.0	319.09
9.5	77.73	24.5	200.45	39.5	323.18
10.0	81.82	25.0	204.55	40.0	327.27
10.5	85.91	25.5	208.64	40.5	331.36
11.0	90.00	26.0	212.73	41.0	335.45
11.5	94.09	26.5	216.82	41.5	339.55
12.0	98.18	27.0	220.91	42.0	343.64
12.5	102.27	27.5	225.00	42.5	347.73
13.0	106.36	28.0	229.09	43.0	351.82
13.5	110.45	28.5	233.18	43.5	355.91
14.0	114.55	29.0	237.27	44.0	360.00
14.5	118.64	29.5	241.36		
15.0	122.73	30.0	245.45		

By using this chart you can get to within a couple of degrees when measuring or degreeing your camshaft.

remember to match the camshaft to the other components after you have decided on the other components. In the Volkswagen motor, it is a lot easier to change camshafts to match your other components than it is to port the heads to allow the camshaft to work properly. A stock exhaust will diminish any benefit from a camshaft change. Change your exhaust first.

Fifth, if you have a choice between two cams that each make about the same horsepower, but one is noisier than the other, choose the quieter one. Popping the valve open quickly usually results in more power, but you pay for it in engine longevity. Unfortunately, most people find out which cams are noisy the hard way—they install one. Also beware of any camshaft that requires a different clearance than the stock camshaft's when used for hot street performance.

In any case, the camshafts for a water-cooled Volkswagen may not be less expensive than those for a Chevy or Beetle, but you do not have to take the motor apart to try one out.

Supercharger camshafts

For a supercharger, studies done by Volkswagen for its G-lader show that the best combination of power and emissions can be had with minus seven crankshaft degrees of overlap. In other words, the exhaust valve is almost completely closed when the intake valve starts opening. This reduces the tendency of the blower to force the incoming air/fuel mixture right out the exhaust port.

Volkswagen also shortened the intake valve closing time to twenty-six degrees ABDC, splitting the difference between the maximum torque point at 1300 rpm and the maximum power point at 6000 rpm. Closing the intake valve earlier

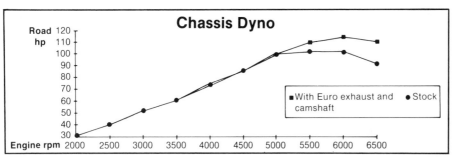

16V horsepower improvements are all on the big end when adding the Euro exhaust and exhaust camshaft. Porting the intake manifold would increase the horsepower peak further, but at the expense of low-end torque and drivability.

Checking height	Intake open	Intake close	Duration
.001	58	98	336
.010	40	77	297
.020	22	58	260
.030	13	50	243
.040	9	46	235
.050	6	42	228

This table shows how checking the camshaft at different heights changes the camshaft specifications, using a Eurorace S1 camshaft as an example. Because of variations in camshaft design, these same relationships will not necessarily hold true for other camshafts.

Cam Specs

Designation	Base circle	Intake opens at	Intake closes at	Exhaust opens at	Exhaust closes at	Intake lift	Exhaust lift	Intake Duration	Exhaust duration	Lobe Center	Overlap	Advance or retard
Drake 426	1.500	7	48	45	9	0.425	0.425	235	234	109	16.50	-1.00
Drake Sport	1.500	14	58	52	19	0.409	0.409	252	251	109	33.50	-2.50
Eurorace B	1.500	8.5	47.5	46.5	7.5	0.423	0.423	236	234	110	17.00	0.50
Eurorace P	1.500	17	50	51	14	0.433	0.433	247	245	108	32.00	1.50
Eurorace S	1.500	7	48	45	9	0.423	0.423	235	234	109	16.50	-1.00
Eurorace S1	1.500	9	46	44	11	0.410	0.410	235	235	108	20.00	-1.00
Eurorace S2	1.340	17	50	50	15	0.433	0.433	247	245	107	33.00	1.00
Eurorace S3	1.465	12	47	49	10	0.479	0.473	239	239	109	22.00	1.00
Eurorace S4	1.500	14	49.5	50.5	13	0.450	0.447	244	244	108	27.00	0.50
Eurorace T	1.500	21	57	63.5	20	0.433	0.433	258	264	110	38.25	0.50
Eurorace U	1.500	28	52	54	30	0.453	0.453	260	264	102	56.00	-1.00
Eurorace V	1.500	22	64	60	27	0.460	0.465	266	267	109	48.50	-2.50
Eurorace W	1.400	34	63	61	36	0.502	0.502	277	277	104	70.00	-1.00
Eurorace X	1.400	44	74	74	44	0.472	0.472	298	298	105	88.00	0.00
Eurorace Y	1.276	52	73	74	51	0.575	0.575	305	305	101	103.00	0.50
Neuspeed	1.500	7	48	45	9	0.423	0.423	235	234	109	16.50	-1.00
VW 1300	1.500	6	32	42	0	0.354	0.354	218	222	107	4.00	3.00
VW 1500	1.500	3	37	43	7	0.394	0.394	220	230	108	5.00	-2.00
VW 1600	1.500	2	48	42	8	0.406	0.406	230	230	110	10.00	-3.00
VW G grind	1.500	7	48	45	9	0.423	0.423	235	234	109	16.50	-1.00
VW N grind	1.500	3	44.5	46	8	0.406	0.425	228	234	110	7.75	-2.50
VW 1300 Polo	Unk.	3	45	48	0	Unk.	Unk.	228	228	113	3.00	1.50
VW G-lader	Unk.	-7	26	48	0	Unk.	Unk.	199	228	110	-21.50	-3.50
Hydraulic cams												
Drake	1.300	6.5	43	43.5	5	0.427	0.427	230	229	109	12.00	0.75
Neuspeed	1.340	2	47.5	45.5	4	0.413	0.412	230	230	112	6.00	-1.00
Oettinger	1.340	-13	69.5	26	30	0.434	0.437	237	236	110	17.25	-21.50
VW GTI 1985	1.340	2.5	38	42	2	0.401	0.402	221	224	109	2.75	0.25

All cams checked at 1 mm valve lift (.3927 inches)

Positive numbers indicate advance, negative numbers indicate retard.

would have picked up the bottom-end torque only about one percent, and a later intake valve closing would have improved maximum power even less. Tests show that the short intake duration is more than made up for by the cylinder charging of the supercharger. That is what you call a good compromise. The negative overlap reduced hydrocarbon emissions by over fifty percent, compared with emissions at three crankshaft degrees of overlap.

Cam sprockets

At this point, you may be wondering about cam sprockets, adjustable and otherwise. Adjustable cam sprockets allow you to move the torque curve of the engine around by altering the timing of valve events. Advancing the timing of valve events means that the intake valve opens sooner and the exhaust valve closes sooner, helping low-end torque. Retarding the cam does just the opposite and helps move the torque toward the big end.

If you have trimmed your head down and decked the block, the centerline of the camshaft will be that much closer to the centerline of the crankshaft, retarding your cam timing. An adjustable cam sprocket will help you recover the relationship between the cam and the crank, or to run the camshaft slightly advanced for better low-end torque.

An adjustable cam sprocket is also handy on a big-cam, small-lobe-center motor and on an automatic transmission Rabbit. Advancing the small-lobe-center camshaft allows you to recover some smoothness at idle, and advancing the automatic camshaft helps fill in that flat spot off idle.

Some adjustable cam sprockets come with four degrees of adjustment on either side, some with six or more. The more adjustment there is, the easier it will be to set up your cam timing, but you only need four degrees because each tooth on the cam sprocket is worth a little over eight degrees. By skipping teeth and setting the cam sprocket, you can come up with just about any combination of advance or retard you need (whether or not it runs).

If you are going to play around with cam timing, just remember that you are only rarely going to detect less than two degrees of difference.

As helpful as an adjustable cam sprocket is in degreeing the camshaft, the Volkswagen SOHC (single overhead cam) motor is very difficult to set up for checking the phase relationship between the camshaft and the crankshaft. The DOHC (double overhead cam) motor is a different story, because you can drop the dial indicator down through the spark plug hole. The procedures for checking camshaft specifications and for degreeing the camshaft to the crankshaft are explained later.

If you decide to stick with the stock cam sprocket, be aware that not all of them are perfectly marked when they come out of the factory. They may have the TDC dimple off to one side or another, relative to the sprocket tooth. The section on checking the camshaft specifications also explains how to check the TDC mark on your camshaft.

Cam belts

The cogged cam belt Volkswagen uses is a surprisingly rugged component. Neglectful owners have seen many thousands of miles pass beneath their oil pans without the belt needing replacement or service of any kind. For a high-performance motor, *especially* in a big-valve motor where the valves can contact the pistons when the belt breaks, changing the belt is inexpensive insurance. The stock belt is fine, but for that extra margin of safety, Drake markets a heavy-duty belt.

The following directions will work for changing a belt with or without the installation of an adjustable cam sprocket.

Installing an adjustable cam sprocket

Remove the upper portion of the cam belt cover. Remove the oil cap so you can see the camshaft. Now turn the motor so that it is at top dead center for the number 1 cylinder. The easiest way to do this is to find an area of level ground, then put the car in top gear, let off the brake, and push or pull the car until both lobes on the camshaft for the number 1 cylinder are sticking up where you can see them. You will also be able to see the following:
• The little dimple on the outer rim of the cam gear lines up with the top edge of the head.
• The zero mark on the flywheel falls under the timing mark on the transmission housing.
• The distributor rotor points toward the mark on the side of the distributor housing.

Remember this alignment; you will need to duplicate it later. Once you have everything the way you want it, reapply the parking brake, leaving the transmission in gear. This helps hold the crankshaft in the right place.

Remove the alternator belt, the air conditioner belt, and any other belt or contraption that stands in the way of getting the lower portion of the cam belt cover off, and remove the cam belt cover. This allows you to see the timing marks on the crankshaft pulley that line up with the dimple on the intermediate shaft pulley. This alignment is hard to see from above without the use of a mirror and a flashlight. Everything should be lined up, but it does not hurt to double-check.

A word of caution: Never try to turn over the motor by putting a wrench on the camshaft pulley bolt. The cam belt was not meant to put up with that, and it probably won't.

Locate the idler pulley that is used for adjusting the tension on the cam belt. Before you loosen the clamping nut, make sure you have something to grab the idler pulley adjustment nut with when the time comes to retension the cam belt. Early cars require a 27 mm wrench or an adjustable-end wrench of suitable size. Cars from 1986 on require a special spanner wrench. Schley Tools makes one that is sold by many of the aftermarket suppliers. If you are properly equipped, loosen the idler pulley and pull the belt off the cam sprocket.

You can remove the cam sprocket whenever you wish, but it is easiest to do it while the camshaft is still held down by the cam bearing caps. The best way to do this is to hold one of the camshaft lobes with an adjustable-end wrench. Wrap the lobe with a rag first, and make sure that the faces of the wrench jaws do not have any dings in them that could damage the camshaft lobe. Then use a 19 mm box-end wrench to loosen and remove the camshaft sprocket pulley bolt. Do not expect the cam belt to hold the pulley while you are breaking the bolt free.

Wiggle the cam sprocket off the end of the camshaft. If you are going to replace the camshaft at this time, go to the section on installing a camshaft and follow the procedure there.

As you are sliding the sprocket onto the camshaft, watch behind the sprocket to make sure that the Woodruff key is not being pushed out of the keyway. If it is, reseat it and lower the front end of it a little to prevent the sprocket groove from catching on it. If this still does not work, you may have to remove the Woodruff key and dress it down with a file until there are no burrs on it. Replace the camshaft sprocket bolt and, holding

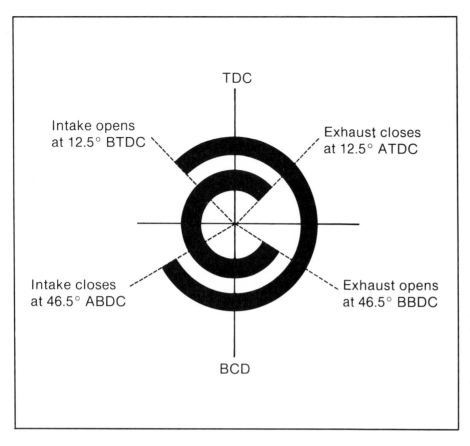

TDC

Intake opens
at 12.5° BTDC

Exhaust closes
at 12.5° ATDC

Intake closes
at 46.5° ABDC

Exhaust opens
at 46.5° BBDC

BCD

This is the way camshaft events are typically depicted. In this cam, the duration is 239 degrees at 0.050 inch and the lobe center is 107 degrees. Although you cannot tell from this chart, the lift of this particular camshaft is 0.432 inch.

To relate this chart to the four engine cycles, start at the point labeled "Intake opens." As you follow around clockwise, the cylinder starts taking in the fresh air/fuel mixture soon after the heavy line representing the intake valve crosses the thin vertical line labeled TDC. Notice that the intake valve opens before the motor actually starts taking in air and fuel, and that the intake valve does not close until after the piston has passed BDC. Leaving the intake valve open these few extra degrees allows the engine to make use of the momentum of the incoming air/fuel charge.

After the intake valve finally does close at "Intake closed," the compression stroke starts. Neither valve is open at this point, and you must follow around the circle clockwise past TDC again until you get to the point labeled "Exhaust opens." Notice that once again this happens before the piston has reached BDC. By opening the exhaust valve early, the motor can take advantage of the weak but still expanding gases to evacuate the cylinder. The exhaust valve stays open past TDC, again making use of the momentum of the outgoing air.

It is time to start the cycle again, but wait! We need the intake valve open. Fortunately it has already started opening before waiting for the exhaust valve to close. Both valves open at the same time is called the overlap.

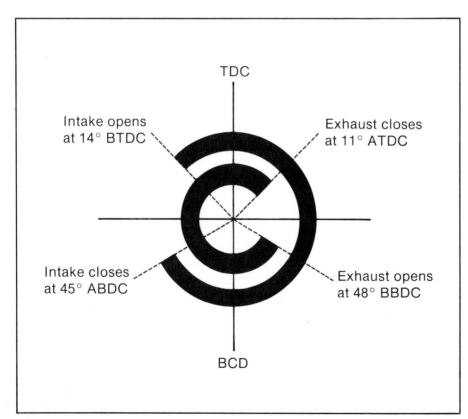

TDC

Intake opens
at 14° BTDC

Exhaust closes
at 11° ATDC

Intake closes
at 45° ABDC

Exhaust opens
at 48° BBDC

BCD

a lobe with an adjustable-end wrench as before, tighten it to 58 lb-ft.

The next task is to reinstall the cam belt. If your belt has many miles on it, this is a good time to replace it with a new one.

Unless something unusual has happened, the crankshaft should be in the same place as before. Chances are that the intermediate shaft has turned, however, and the camshaft needs to be set back in place. To set the camshaft, align the dimple in the sprocket with the top gasket surface of the cylinder head where the valve cover sits. If you are replacing the stock sprocket and you cannot locate the dimple on the sprocket, check to see if you have installed it wrong-side out. If you have, the sprocket will be too close to the valve cover, and it will rub when the motor is started.

Aligning the crankshaft and the intermediate shaft is done with a mirror, as previously explained. It is impossible to align these sprockets and then put on the belt. Put the belt on and see how close

Although the duration is still 239 degrees at 0.050 inch for both the intake and the exhaust, and the lobe center is still 107 degrees, the intake valve is being opened 1.5 degrees (crankshaft) advanced. Because the intake valve is closing earlier, the compression stroke starts sooner, and the torque curve is moved lower in the rpm range.

you are. It usually takes a couple tries to get these sprockets all lined up.

Once the sprockets are in line, loop the belt up to the camshaft sprocket. The tension side of the belt is the side closest to the front of the car, so work from that side. Have your 19 mm wrench handy to jiggle the cam pulley bolt to line up the teeth on the belt with those on the sprocket.

After you get the cam belt on, turn the motor over twice and recheck all your settings. You may need to make a couple tries before you get it right. Use the idler pulley to tension the cam belt, as described in the Bentley manual.

Installing a camshaft

For a bolt-on application, this section assumes that you do not want to change the valve springs. If you do, the procedure for changing springs can be found in a later section.

Remove the cam sprocket, as described earlier in the section on installing an adjustable cam sprocket. After you have the sprocket removed, remove the valve cover and save the gaskets for later. Stuff rags into the oil return holes to make it more difficult to drop things into the motor.

The cam sprocket is held from turning on the end of the camshaft by the Woodruff key, a small half-moon-shaped piece of metal that fits in a cutout in the camshaft and in a groove in the camshaft pulley. Remove the Woodruff key, taking care not to damage it because you are going to reuse it.

If you cannot grab the Woodruff key with pliers or a pair of sidecutters, take a small punch and tap down on one end of the Woodruff key. The back side is rounded, so it will scoot right out. Do whatever it takes to keep track of the Woodruff key, as finding a replacement for it can be a long and wearisome task.

It is now time to remove the camshaft.

Five camshaft bearings are used to hold the camshaft in (four in a hydraulic head). You will notice that some of the camshaft lobes are pointing up and some are pointing to the sides or down. The ones pointed down are pressing against the valve springs, which are pressing back. If you loosen the bearings one at a time and pull them off, the force of the valve spring pressing against the cam lobe can be enough to snap the camshaft in two.

Make sure the camshaft is still at TDC. If you are working on a solid-lifter head, remove bearing cap 5, bearing cam 1 and bearing cap 3, in that order. On a head, remove bearing cap 5, bearing cap 1 and bearing cap 3, in that order. On a hydraulic head, remove bearing caps 1 and 3. With the remaining bearing caps (2 and 4 on a solid-lifter head, 2 and 5 on a hydraulic head), you want to gradually loosen the four nuts a little at a time, using a diagonal pattern to maintain even pressure on the camshaft. It takes a little while to do it this way. If you find yourself getting impatient, step back, take a deep breath and when you have calmed down continue on.

Check to see that the bearing shells are coming up as you loosen the nuts. Sometimes the bearing shell will get cocked on the studs, so that you can take the nuts all the way off and the bearing shell will still be tight against the head. If you see a bearing shell that is not moving, stop loosening the bolts. Grab the bearing shell with a big pair of pliers and rock it gently until it gets straightened out before proceeding.

Once all the cam bearing nuts have been removed and the shells lifted off, the camshaft can be lifted out. Keep the bearing shells in order and facing the right way. You may want to mark them in some way so that you can tell which shell goes where and in what direction it points.

Remaining in the head are the cam follower buckets, with a shim atop each one. The valve springs are hiding beneath the cam followers. If you are going to change the valve springs, see the later section on valve spring replacement.

If any dirt or grime got into the works while you were wrestling with the camshaft, clean it up now. Smear cam lube on the shims and coat the cam bearings with clean motor oil. Do not put cam lube on the cam bearings.

Clean your new camshaft thoroughly. Wipe the camshaft seal sealing surface with clean motor oil, and carefully slip the camshaft seal on. If the camshaft seal looks worn or has tens of thousands of miles on it, you might want to replace it at this time. It generally does not leak, but a new one is not very expensive and you have already done all the labor to get to it, so why not?

Coat all exposed surfaces of the camshaft lobe with cam lube. Any camshaft you buy should be sold with cam lube. If not, do not proceed until you have acquired some. It is critically important that the camshaft be properly lubricated the first time it is run. Wipe the cam bearing journals with clean motor oil, and set the camshaft in the head with the lobes for the number 1 cylinder pointing up.

Because of the downward-pointing lobes, the camshaft is not going to want to sit squarely in the bearings. You still should be able to install the cam seal in the proper place, however, if you have

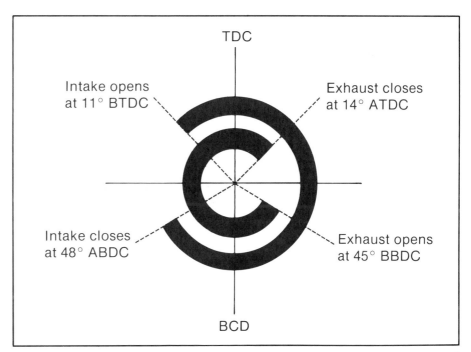

Here is the same camshaft again, only now the intake valve is being opened 1.5 degrees (crankshaft) retarded and the intake valve is closing later. Retarding the camshaft moves the torque higher in the rpm range.

the lobes for the number 1 cylinder pointing up. Place the cam bearing shells in their proper positions.

Note that the bearing shells will go on backward, but only just. If you manage to hammer them on the wrong way, the cam will be pinched in the bearing, and the bearing misalignment will form a lip that will scrape lubricant off the cam bearing journal as the camshaft turns. The results will be disastrous. If you find you have to force something, check to make sure you are installing it the right way.

Also because of the downward-pointing lobes, not all of the bearing shells will seat down far enough to get a nut started. Start the ones you can and tighten them enough so the others can be started, then tighten all the nuts evenly, just as you loosened them. Torque the nuts to 14 lb-ft.

Install the Woodruff key in the keyway. Tap it all the way down into the keyway, and align the top of the Woodruff key parallel to the axis of the crankshaft.

The camshaft sprocket can now be reinstalled. The procedure for doing this is described in the previous section on installing an adjustable cam sprocket. After you have reinstalled the cam sprocket and belt, you need to check the valve adjustment.

With the engine cold, the intake valves should be adjusted to 0.006 to 0.010 inch, and the exhaust should be adjusted to 0.014 to 0.018 inch. Try not to scrape all the cam lube off the lobes, and touch up any areas that look barren before you put the valve cover back on. If you can, reuse the old gasket and seal for now. They only need to last another half-hour.

Replace the alternator belt, but do not reinstall the lower cam belt cover just yet. You are going to run the motor for a few minutes and then recheck the adjustment of the valves, so you do not need to have everything in place now. Snap the distributor cap back on, and tighten

down anything else you loosened up, or that is flopping around and could cause a problem once the engine is running.

The most critical time in a camshaft's life is the first few minutes. The cam lube is there to help a little, but with the pressure of the valve springs, the cam really needs to run for a few minutes until all the rough edges are knocked off. Ideally the motor would start immediately instead of being cranked over for long seconds or even minutes.

Once started, the motor should be run at high idle (2000 rpm) for twenty minutes. Have someone else hold open the throttle so you can check out the cam belt adjustment. If the adjustment is too loose the belt will be flopping around, and if it is too tight the idler pulley will be making a complaining noise. If you are very careful, you can get in there with your wrenches and adjust the belt tension while the motor is running, but this is dangerous. Work cautiously.

While this is happening the motor will also be growing nice and warm. After the break-in period, you can remove the valve cover and adjust the valves to their hot running specifications: intakes at 0.008 to 0.012 inch and exhausts at 0.016 to 0.020 inch. Double-check that the cam is timed properly to the crankshaft and the intermediate shaft.

When everything is okay, put back *both* cam belt covers, all V-belts and the valve cover with the new gaskets you bought just for this occasion. Now comes the fun part, when you get to take your stopwatch out and see how much improvement you picked up. Whatever the result, be sure to recheck the valve adjustment at 500 miles.

Checking camshaft specifications

Any cam you buy should come with a cam card that will tell you all the vital information about the cam (except how it will run in your motor!). For hot street performance you may not need any of this information, but if you are looking for every last bit of horsepower in your engine, you are not only going to have to understand the figures, you are going to have to know how to ensure that the figures on the card relate to the camshaft you are installing. This means checking the cam.

One problem you will run into when checking out cams is that not everybody uses the 1 mm clearance in measuring camshafts. It can be very frustrating trying to determine the actual difference between two cams when different clear-

Dead-stop made from a spark plug housing.

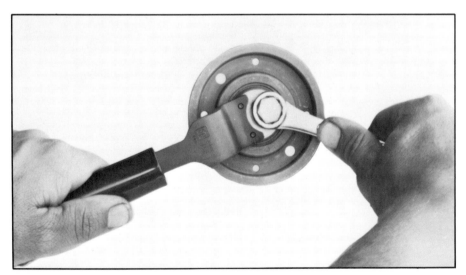

If you have a later-model car you will need this special tool to adjust the cam belt tension. Schley Tools

ances are used in specification sheets, and there is no easy formula for translating one to the other. The solution to this problem is to measure the camshaft yourself.

Darrell Vittone has made up a special dial indicator that allows him to check the camshafts without taking them out of the head. This works very well with the hydraulic lifters because the lifter is always pushing up to touch the camshaft. With a solid lifter, he has to replace the valve springs with lighter units from a hardware store (to avoid damaging the valve springs through a coil bind), and insert an extra shim to take up the clearance between the camshaft and the lifter, but this is simple compared with having a head set up specially to check camshafts (or taking off the head).

The setup I used was a specially modified cylinder head out of a junkyard, but any cylinder head will do as long as you can bolt in the camshaft you want to check. For this setup, remove all the intake and exhaust valves, and reinstall the followers for cylinder number 1 with light-gauge springs underneath them so they will still track the camshaft lobe. Only solid lifters will work for this checking procedure.

With either of these methods you need a degree wheel to bolt to the end of the camshaft. Because no one makes a degree wheel for this application, you will either have to modify a Type 1 crankshaft pulley, or get a one-size-fits-all stick-on degree wheel. Your choice will in part dictate the construction of the pointer needed to show where on the degree wheel the camshaft is. I made my pointers out of a soft drink can. It took about five minutes, and I "drilled" the hole with a centerpunch.

You can also use a stock pulley. It will be aggravating to use and not quite as accurate, and you will have to be careful with your counting and math, but if you are only doing one or two camshafts it might be easier than rigging up a custom degree wheel.

The trick with the stock pulley is that it has forty-four teeth, meaning that each tooth is worth 8.182 degrees. It does not matter if you count from the center of a tooth or from the edge, as long as you are consistent. Most of the time you are going to have to guess at degree values that fall between teeth.

Install the camshaft and degree wheel, taking care not to cock the followers in their bores. Stand the cylinder head on its side (or stand it on its end, if that is easier), and mount your dial indicator holder so you can put the shaft of the indicator through the valve guide until it rests against the bottom of the follower. Note that you cannot indicate off the head of the valve, because with the valve installed the follower does not press up against the camshaft. You are trying to eliminate all clearance between the follower and the camshaft lobe.

Whichever measuring device you choose (degree wheel or sprocket), you will have to zero it relative to the pointer. There are two zero positions for every pair of intake and exhaust lobes on any camshaft. One zero position is somewhere on the heel of both camshafts; the point where both heels are touching the followers simultaneously. In this position the lobes will be facing away from the followers in a V shape.

The second zero position is 180 camshaft degrees from this position (more or less). On camshafts with equal duration for both intake and exhaust, this zero can be found using either one of the following two methods.

Method 1

Put a dial indicator on both the intake and exhaust cam followers, zeroing them on the heels of their respective lobes, then turning the camshaft so the leading flank of the exhaust lobe and the trailing flank of the intake lobe are touching the followers.

Watch both dial indicators as you turn the camshaft slowly back and forth. You will see that there is one point at which the lift on both followers is the same. This is the second zero position. Note the degree reading or place a light mark on your sprocket.

Now remove the sprocket or degree wheel and install it backward. Find the zero position again and note the degree reading. If it is not exactly 180 degrees opposite your first mark, add 180 to your second reading, and then split the difference between your first reading and your second reading. This calculated figure is the TDC point for that pair of cam lobes. If you used the lobes for cylinder number 1, you will more easily

Check the cam adjustment mark to ensure it is in the center of the tooth. Eurorace

For 1985, Volkswagen ground the backs of the camshafts this way, then changed back to the standard cam heel in 1986, so it apparently makes no difference. Abt

be able to time the camshaft to the crankshaft, as described later.

Method 2

Turn the engine over until the lobes for cylinder 1 are visually close to TDC. Lay a straightedge across the lobes for cylinder 1 and, using a dial caliper, measure from the straightedge to the gasket sealing surface on the top of the head. If the distance from the straightedge to the front sealing surface is the same as the distance from the straightedge to the back sealing surface, the camshaft is at TDC. You can now set up your degree wheel and pointers.

The camshaft chart shows that not all the numbers come out nice and even. Some variations are due to the grind of the camshaft and some are due to slight differences in manufacturing tolerances. This chart is not the last word on camshaft specifications, but it does provide an indication of what to expect from some of the available grinds. If it shows a couple thousandths of an inch more or less lift, or is off a degree or two here or there, do not be concerned. The important measurements are the ones on the camshaft you are installing.

Timing the camshaft to the engine

Degreeing the camshaft is nothing more than making sure that the camshaft opens when you think it is opening, relative to the pistons. This procedure is carried out with the cylinder head bolted up to the block just the way it will be when the car is running, with the cylinder head gasket and everything. You want the distance from the centerline of the crankshaft to the centerline of the camshaft to be set before you start, or you will have to redo your work later on.

If you have not yet dead-stopped the number 1 piston and marked the flywheel as described in the sections on crankshaft and flywheels, do so now.

You will need to make a special tool. This will require an old spark plug, and either a bolt and matching tap or some unthreaded rod and a welder. Knock the porcelain and both electrodes out of the threaded base of the spark plug, and insert either the rod or the threaded bolt (after preparing the base by cutting threads with the tap). I prefer the bolt because my welding is not so good, and the movable dead-stop is more versatile.

Bring your engine up close to TDC and screw in the dead-stop tool. Thread the bolt down until you feel it touching the top of the piston. Turn the motor up gently until it stops, and lightly mark the flywheel relative to some easy-to-remember point on the transmission housing. Now turn the motor back the other way until the piston again gently touches the dead-stop. Lightly mark the flywheel again opposite that same point on the transmission housing. Half the distance between these two points is the true TDC of the engine.

You now have both your engine TDC and your camshaft specifications. Remove the dead-stop and turn the engine to TDC. If the timing belt is not installed, install it now. Check your camshaft degree wheel and see where the camshaft is relative to the crankshaft. You can now adjust this relationship. Remember, when looking at the adjustable camshaft sprocket, turning the center of the sprocket counterclockwise relative to the belt advances the camshaft timing, and turning the center of the sprocket clockwise retards the camshaft timing.

Valvetrain

Valve springs

The stock valve springs are fine up to 7200 rpm in motors up to 1982 (somewhat less in the GTIs), and even can be used in some high-performance applications. The more you intend to ask of the valve spring, however, the more desirable it is to check it, or to replace it with a heavier-duty spring.

The one problem you are most likely to come up against is running the valve spring into coil bind. Coil bind occurs when the valve spring is compressed so tightly that the coils touch each other. This is very fatiguing for the spring, and will result in early failure. Worse, beyond a point the spring will not compress any more because the coils are solidly up against one another, and the camshaft will have a tough time swinging over the nose. When this happens you can get accelerated wear on the camshaft nose, a motor that will not turn over or a broken camshaft.

The problem is that the stock valve springs are very close to their operating limit when used with a camshaft with 0.425 inch of lift. *Very* close. Often you can install a 0.425 or 0.430 lift camshaft on top of your stock springs and drive the car for years. Sometimes, though, your valve springs will be binding up and you may not know it until something wears out, refuses to turn over or breaks.

If you do not want to take a chance, have the springs checked on a spring

Here is a cam nose starting to go flat. Techtonics

The auto-advance cam sprocket: $400 for 1 hp. Techtonics

tester. Avoid installing sport valve springs if at all possible, not only because of the money involved but because the extra tension in the spring costs 1.5 hp at 6000 rpm, and the camshaft will wear more quickly.

The reason that the high-performance springs work where the stock springs do not is that they have fewer coils, with more space between each coil. This allows room for the spring to be collapsed farther, but it is also harder on the spring. Fewer coils mean a stiffer spring, and the coils must be able to flex deeper than those in a spring with more coils. The combination of extra stiffness and more flex fatigues the valve springs, so they can fail earlier. In a street application this is nothing to worry about, but in a race motor you should definitely check your spring tension often until you get an idea about how long your springs will hold tension—or hold together without breaking.

Valve spring preparation

For the last forty-five years or so, valve springs have been shot peened by automobile manufacturers even for stock applications. Just about any valve spring that you buy should be shot peened by the time you get it. The only other thing you may want to do is give the valve springs a moly impregnation treatment. This reduces the operating temperature and greatly extends their life. You may not see the benefits in a mild street rod motor, but in an all-out motor this would be a real plus.

It is very nice to have access to a valve spring compressor to check your valve springs. The first check is to see that the valve springs will produce the proper seat pressure when installed at the specified height.

The second check is to see that there will still be 0.010 inch of clearance (checked with a feeler gauge) between the coils at full lift of whatever camshaft you have chosen.

The third check is to match the inner springs with the outer springs to balance out the total spring pressure. For example, an outer spring with less tension than the other outer springs would be matched up with an inner spring with more tension than the other inners.

Never compress a valve spring to the point of coil bind, either in the valve spring checker or in the cylinder head. This weakens the spring and will hasten the onset of failure.

Replacing valve springs in the car

Although it sounds as if it would be more difficult to replace the valve springs with the head in the car, it can actually be easier. When the head is off the car, you have to find some way of holding it down while you wrestle with the valve springs. When the head is on the car, the head bolts and the block usually keep the head from wandering around.

The high-performance inner and outer valve springs on the right have fewer coils than the stock springs, but must flex more in operation, causing greater fatigue. Eurorace

Oettinger parts are expensive, but pieces such as these rifle-drilled camshafts aren't available anywhere else. Techtonics

Intercam timing on the Oettinger heads is handled the same way Porsche 911 cam timing is set. Techtonics

You will need a valve spring compressor either way. If you plan to do the job in the car, you will also need an adapter that will allow you to pressurize the combustion chamber while you work, and an air compressor to supply the air.

Remove the camshaft as described previously. You should now be confronted with the camshaft followers sitting in their bores. Lift out each camshaft follower, and store the followers out of the way in the same order they sit in the head. You now will be able to see the top of the valve stem and the spring retainer.

Remove all the spark plugs. Install the cylinder pressurizer adapter into the spark plug hole for cylinder number 1 (that is the cylinder you should have at TDC). If the car is on the ground and not on a hoist or jack stands, make sure the transmission is in high gear with the parking brake on. Connect the air supply to the cylinder pressurizer adapter. If the cylinder you are pressurizing is not exactly at TDC, the air pressure will try to turn the engine (and move the car).

The air pressure pushing on the underside of the valve will keep it against its seat while you work above. For this

reason, you can work on only one cylinder at a time.

Warning: If you take off the valve spring retainer without pressurizing the cylinder, the valve will drop into the cylinder, and you may have to take off the cylinder head to retrieve it. If the force of the air pressure turns the motor, the piston will be at bottom dead center. If you then remove the air pressure without securing the valve, the valve will slip into the cylinder. If the transmission is in gear and the wheels are on the ground, the force of the air pressure might be enough to move the car. Make sure the parking brake is applied.

Bolt the fulcrum bar of the valve spring tool to the top of the head. Use the valve spring tool to push down on the spring retainer so you can remove the split keeper.

In a perfect world you would push down on the valve spring tool and the retainer would cleanly move away from the keeper, allowing you to fish the keepers out with a magnet. Life being what it is, however, the retainer and the keepers will often be stuck to one another. If you find this to be the case, you will need to jar them apart.

Apply a 19 mm impact socket on a six-inch extension to the valve retainer, and tap on the end of the extension with a soft-face hammer. The shock will usually separate the retainer from the keeper. Do not pound too hard; it does not take a lot. By the way, the loud popping sound you hear each time you hit the retainer is air escaping from the cylinder through the slight opening in the valve. Once you have jarred the retainer apart

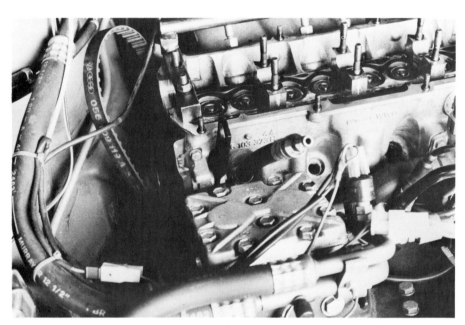

With the camshaft removed, the air pressure hose is screwed into the spark plug hole to keep the valves closed after the keepers are removed.

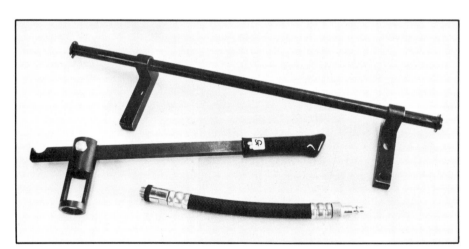

Schley Tools makes the crossbar and the lever; the air presure adapter is out of a Snap-On compression tester kit. James Sly

After jarring the keeper loose from the retainer, the lever is used to push down on the spring so the keepers can be removed.

from the keepers, you can proceed with the valve spring tool.

Unless you have very tiny fingers, you will find that a magnet is quite helpful in fishing out the keepers once you have depressed the valve spring retainer enough so that you can get the keepers out. With the retainers and the keepers out of the way, you can remove the stock springs and install the springs you want. Put the retainer back, and using the valve spring compressor, push down on the retainer and slip the keepers back into place. Use long, thin needle-nose pliers for this job, because space is tight and the keepers can be slippery.

Now you have finished cylinder 1, which is still at TDC. The piston for cylinder 4 is also at the top of its stroke. This makes it quite easy to replace the springs for cylinder 4 next. Do not forget to completely install the springs for one cylinder before moving on to the next cylinder, and do not forget to pressurize the cylinder before removing the retainer and keepers.

After finishing cylinders 1 and 4, if you turn the engine exactly 180 degrees, cylinders 2 and 3 will be at the tops of their strokes (one on the power stroke and one on the exhaust stroke, as before). Do both of them together, and then turn the engine back the opposite way 180 degrees to get back to TDC for piston number 1. Check by looking at the timing mark through the hole in the bellhousing. If you keep track of TDC, it will be much easier to retime the motor.

Once you have replaced all the valve springs, coat the skirts of the camshaft followers with oil and slip them back into the bores they came out of. Do not coat them with grease. Oil allows them to rotate so they will not wear prematurely.

Valve spring installed height

If you have done a valve job on your head, are using different-length valves or have gone for a different valve spring, check the valve spring installed height. Any of these factors can affect the distance between the valve spring seat and the valve spring retainer.

If the valve springs have been checked with a spring tester, installing them at the correct height will ensure that the distance is small enough (compressing the spring enough) to get the right seat pressure when the valve is closed, and large enough to keep the spring out of coil bind when it is all the way open.

Owing to the construction of the Volkswagen head, checking the valve spring installed height can be more trouble than it should be. One easy way to check is to use an old valve spring retainer with a piece cut out of it. Assemble the valve, retainer and keepers using a supersoft spring (which you can buy at a hardware store). It is then a simple matter to measure from the top of the retainer to the valve spring seat and subtract the width of the retainer to arrive at the installed height. If you buy a set of high-performance springs, be sure to get the installed height measurement as well.

If the installed height is smaller than spec, you will have to machine the head or use thinner valve spring seats. If it is bigger, you will need to use shims to reduce the distance. Shims are readily available at many parts houses and machine shops. They come in different thicknesses, and the ones you want measure 1¼ inches OD and ⅞ inch ID.

Measuring the spring to get the proper seat pressure is a short cut. A better way to do this would involve even more special tools. After assembling the valve with the spring and retainer, one tool would press down on the tip of the valve, giving a read-out of the amount of pressure being exerted. A dial indicator on the head of the valve would show the precise moment the valve came off the seat. This would give you the installed height spring pressure directly. Apparently there is a tool expressly for this purpose, but measuring the springs has worked well for decades.

Once you have everything measured, you can assemble the head with the valve springs, and double-check your work.

Valve guide seals

Early on, Volkswagens had a problem with valve guide seals. The original valve guide seals would become hard as a result of heat, and would then allow up to a quart of oil to be sucked into the engine every 250 miles. The motor would run fine and the plugs never seemed to foul, but there was always the danger of running out of oil and ruining the motor. Volkswagen eventually issued a recall and replaced all the problem valve guide seals, but this is something to remember in case you come up against a motor that is using oil and you cannot figure out where it is going.

When oil gets past the valve guide seals (or piston rings), you lose horsepower. This is because oil lowers the octane rating of gasoline, taking between ten and fifteen percent off the

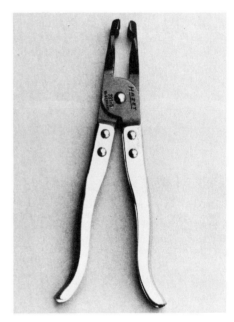

Special pliers such as these are extremely valuable when removing valve guide seals.

These tongs reach around the camshaft to grab the valve adjusting shim.

peak horsepower. Between losing horsepower and putting your engine at risk, you can do without faulty valve guide seals. If yours are leaking, replace them as soon as you can.

There are three types of valve guide seals. The first is the original type made of rubber; even if you wanted these, you probably could not find any. There are some black rubber seals floating around that are supposed to be the new, improved version of the old-style stem seal, but they are to be avoided. The second type is a Teflon seal, easily spotted because it is white with a silver metal control ring wrapped around it. The third type is called Viton, which is green and feels like a very supple rubber seal. Viton seals are made by the Goetze (pronounced "gutsa") company in Germany.

Both the Teflon and Viton seals are effective at reducing oil flow down the valve guides. The Teflon seals, in fact, may be too effective; excessive wear shows up on the valve stem and valve guide, probably as a result of the great sealing job the Teflon seals can do.

The Viton seals will take nearly as much heat as the Teflon seals, but allow some oil to remain on the valve stem for lubrication. If heat is destroying your valve guide seals, you have other problems that need to be fixed as well.

If you find you must use the Teflon seals for whatever reason, be very careful when installing them not to scratch the inner sealing surface. The Teflon will flow around small sharp edges, but if you scratch the inner surface too deeply you will have to replace the seal again or put up with oil consumption.

The only other thing you might want to check with valve seals will only apply when you run a camshaft with more than 0.430 inch of lift. With a high-lift camshaft like this, the valve spring retainer can sometimes run into the valve stem seal. If you anticipate this problem, you can buy special shortened versions of the valve stem seals.

Changing valve stem seals in the car involves doing everything already discussed for changing the valve springs, with the additional step of removing the old valve stem seal and installing the new one. To remove the old seal you will need a pair of special pliers that are made just for this task. To replace them you can use a special valve stem seal installer, but I use a Craftsman 10 mm deep-socket. It is a pretty close fit, it works fine and it is less expensive than the special tool.

When you buy the valve stem seals, try to get the little plastic installation covers that slip over the ends of the valve stem to protect the inner sealing surface of the seal. Not everybody will have these, but if you find them, get them.

Most installation covers are too long to use as-is, but you can trim them back enough that once the valve stem seal is in place, the installation cover can be removed. The installation cover sometimes seems more fragile than the seal itself, so after the seal is past the keeper grooves, take the installation cover off so it does not get damaged. You usually get only a couple of these, and they have to last through eight seal installations.

When you buy Viton seals, be sure they are green, and be sure they are made by Goetze. There are similar compounds with a reddish-brown color that are sometimes called Viton. Insist on the green Viton seals.

Followers

The valve adjustment method on the Volkswagen is another great example of a compromise. Instead of requiring a screwdriver and a wrench so that anybody could set his or her own valves, it requires a spring depressor, special pliers and a whole lot of shims—and that adds up to a lot of money.

Lash caps for use with solid-top followers. The one on the left has been ground to fit. Eurorace

Viton valve guide seals. Eurorace

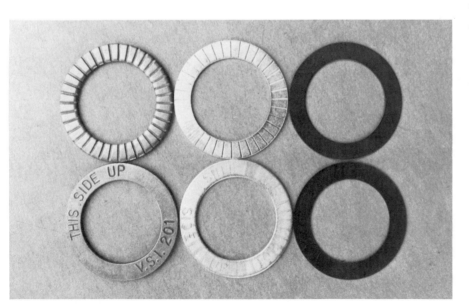

Valve spring shims in various thicknesses are available at most auto parts outlets.

Valve spring retainer cut to allow spring height measurements. Eurorace

However, by using shims the valves really stay adjusted. At the normal 15,000 mile interval, it is unusual to have to adjust more than two or three valves if they have previously been properly adjusted. That is about as maintenance free as you get without using hydraulic adjusters.

The stock followers and shims are rugged enough for most applications, but they do fall short when you are using a very high lift race cam. Once the difference between the base circle and the tip of the lobe gets too great, the camshaft lobe has a tendency to strip the shims out of the pockets and (sometimes) hit the head next to the lifter bore.

To overcome this, you can change over to a camshaft follower with a larger top. One setup that many people use is the 35 mm solid-top follower. To adjust these you have to have the camshaft installed. Using feeler gauges, make measurements on all the camshaft lobes. From this measurement subtract the amount of clearance you are running. The number you get will be the thickness of the lash cap you will need to install on the end of the valve stem underneath the camshaft follower. Remove the camshaft and fit the caps, then reinstall the camshaft and double-check all your measurements.

This can be time-consuming, but it is the only way to run a big cam. A quicker way to do this same job would be to use the Pad Saver, as you could get all your measurements without having to install

the camshaft, and it would be much faster to determine the actual distances involved.

For racing, these followers are not the only way to make a big camshaft work, they are also lighter than the stock shim-and-bucket setup. The stock setup weighs about seventy-one grams. The solid-top followers and lash caps come to about forty-three grams. This substantial weight savings will make it possible to increase the redline further without getting into valve float.

If you cannot bring yourself to give up the convenience of the stock Volkswagen adjuster, or if you have damaged the camshaft follower bores, or if you need to clearance the head anyway before

you can swing that big camshaft around, you can enlarge the camshaft follower bores to 37 mm and use Fiat camshaft followers. These look almost identical to the Volkswagen-style camshaft follower except that the shim is 33 mm across instead of 31 mm. Of course, then you have to buy shims from your local Fiat dealership instead of from Volkswagen or your normal aftermarket supplier. Super Vees use 37 mm and 39 mm Alfa Romeo one-piece cam followers, both of which necessitate the use of lash caps.

Again, none of these alternative types of camshaft follower are necessary in a street motor. When used in a race motor, increasing the bore for the oversized followers has the added advantage of simul-

From left to right are stock solid adjuster, stock hydraulic adjuster, Eurorace solid-top follower and 35 mm Alfa follower. Eurorace

Welding an old valve to the valve seat . . . Eurorace

. . . allows you to knock the seat out from behind. Eurorace

taneously clearancing the cylinder head so the toe of the camshaft can swing by without hitting.

Adjusting the valves

If you turn the engine over by hand (as opposed to using a remote starter switch), it is easier to be methodical about the order in which you adjust the valves. If you do use a remote starter, buy a grease pencil from an art or welding supply store. After checking or adjusting each follower, touch the grease pencil to the gasket sealing surface of the hot cylinder head. Always adjust the valves with the engine hot unless the engine is not in running condition. If you adjust the valves with the engine cold, remember that the clearances are slightly less: 0.006 to 0.010 inch on the intake side, and 0.014 to 0.018 inch on the exhaust.

As said earlier, the valves generally do not go very far out of adjustment. If they do, you will need a special lever to depress the camshaft follower bucket, special pliers to remove the current shim and a set of replacement shims.

The procedure for adjusting the valves can be found in the shop manual. In addition, here are a couple of tips: First, the shims sometimes do not want to come out of the camshaft follower buckets. If this happens to you, examine the camshaft follower bucket depressor lever to make sure it is not interfering

with the shim. If it is, grind it down, making certain you leave enough of the lever surface to press down on the camshaft follower bucket.

Even if the lever is not hitting, the shim still may not come out easily. This can be partly because of the suction that develops between the two parts (the motor oil creates a seal), and partly because of interference between the shim and the bucket. Many nonfactory shims are just a little larger in outside diameter than the factory shims, and they can get really stuck in the camshaft follower buckets.

One thing that often breaks loose a stuck shim is air pressure. Put a rag over the head so you do not blow oil everywhere, and direct the airflow from a high-pressure air nozzle at and around the shim. Sometimes you will get the best results from pointing the stream of air between the shim and the heel of the cam. This creates a venturi effect with low-pressure air that can suck the shim out. Sometimes, aiming the air stream at the edge of the shim will allow some air to get underneath the shim and lift it out. When a shim gets stuck like this, you may have to try a couple of different techniques.

When you are buying replacement shims, make sure that the shims are stock factory shims or from a company called Metelli. Cadmium-plated shims can shed their coating. Buy the best shims, because if a shim goes bad it takes the camshaft lobe with it.

After you have checked and adjusted all the valves, the grease pencil markings will wipe right off the gasket surface. If you have not yet bought your oil deflector, this is the time to do so. Install the new seals (the red one at the sprocket end, and the blue one at the transmission end), and then fit the valve cover gasket. The gasket will seal fine without any sealant. Tighten down the valve cover, and you are done.

Lubrication

Most people have met (or heard about) someone who drove his or her old Chevy 120,000 miles and never changed the oil or did a lick of work on the engine. Do not try duplicating this accomplishment unless you harbor a secret desire either to buy a new car or to enrich your mechanic beyond his or her wildest dreams.

As important as it is, oil is a complex subject. You can read all about what oil is supposed to do, and what is supposed to go into good oil, and you can talk to friends, neighbors and mechanics about the stuff, but when it comes right down to it most of us buy oil because somebody says on national TV that he uses it in his tractor down on the farm.

Fortunately, just about any major brand-name oil is passably good these days, which has not always been true about motor oils. This does not mean that there are no poor-quality oils. I have tried many of the oils on the market, and

This is a basic oil cooler setup, with a sandwich plate adapter and braided hose. The do-it-yourself ends allow you to run the oil lines where you want them to go.

A cut-away view of the installed-height measurement. Do not try this at home. Eurorace

most seemed about the same, with two exceptions.

The first is Castrol motor oil. Castrol has been reported to destroy new camshafts. If you have sworn to use Castrol to your dying day, I suggest you cheat a little when you put in that new camshaft or assemble that fresh motor. You can safely go back to using Castrol after your motor's break-in period.

The rest of the Castrol products, especially the LMA brake fluid, are just fine—the February 1987 *Consumer Reports* oil comparison test shows that Castrol GTX is one of the few nationally advertised oils that do not shear down in use. Perhaps when they formulated Castrol GTX, they traded some of the extreme pressure additives in favor of viscosity improvers, which do not lubricate.

Other than this isolated instance, all *conventional* motor oils seem to be just about identical as far as performance and protection go. Change them early and often, and you should not have a problem.

Notice that I specify conventional oils. There are also several synthetics on the market, and although some are selling well they cannot yet be classifed as conventional. The only three I would use in my own car are Amsoil, Mobile 1 and Blueprinted Synthoil. Amsoil is an ester-based lubricant, Mobil 1 is a mixture of polyalphaolefins and polyol esters (with some kind of binder to keep these otherwise unfriendly components together), and Synthoil is a highly refined petroleum product with a special (and very expensive) polymer package. Synthoil is not a true synthetic, but with all the extra processing and ingredients it is not really a conventional oil, either.

Of these three, the only one I have extensive experience with is Synthoil, and I have accumulated hundreds of thousands of miles on my own and friends' cars with not a single problem. Many racers say that Synthoil works well for them too. And in seven years, I have not heard of one engine failure with Synthoil. I would recommend Synthoil without hesitation to anyone who cares about his or her engine. That makes Synthoil the second exception I mentioned earlier.

In a pinch, Synthoil can be mixed with any conventional oil, although you would lose the benefits of using a pure, high-quality oil. In theory, Amsoil and Mobil 1 are supposed to be miscible with conventional oils, although I would not recommend it except in "limp home" situations.

Oil pumps

Starting with the 1985 cars, Volkswagen began using a high-volume oil pump (compared with its earlier pump). Some aftermarket firms started selling the high-volume pumps, as high-performance pieces for pre-1985 cars, but no one has yet demonstrated why it is better to circulate oil through the engine faster. provide adequate oil pressure not only when the motor is new, but after there is some wear in the bearings. Therefore, the stock early oil pump is fine for the early cars. The reason for the bigger pump? The hydraulic lifters require more oil, necessitating a larger oil pump. If you have an engine with hydraulic lifters, you need the late-model pump.

Volkswagen again increased the size of the oil pump with the introduction of the 16V motor. With twice the number of hydraulic lifters, and the crankcase oil jets (see the section on the block for details) squirting oil on the underside of the piston crowns, there is also a bigger demand for oil. If you have a 16V, you will need the bigger oil pump. Otherwise, the smaller pump should work just fine—even in your two-liter.

If you choose to replace your oil pump, be cautious of non-brand-name pumps. Some Brazilian pumps, for example, are not made with tolerances as close as they need to be. Good German pumps are made by Melling and Febi.

To be on the safe side, always check your oil pump tolerances, whether the pump is old or new. The procedure and specifications are shown in the Bentley manual, but for high-performance work you want your pump clearances to be on the low side of the specs. For example, the backlash should be closer to 0.05

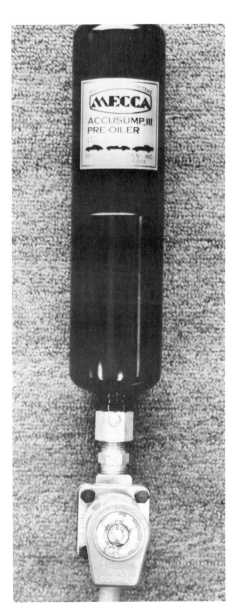

The Mecca Accusump III is a spring-loaded reservoir that stores oil under pressure, both for prelubrication and for low-pressure situations while the motor is running. *Autotech*

The System 1 filter has more filter area than the Oberg, but otherwise works on the same principle.

mm than to 0.20 mm, and the further the axial clearance is under 0.15 mm, the better.

Oil pans

Considering how hard your motor works, the early factory oil pan with 3.7 quart capacity looks like a great expression of minimalist design. Lots of cars came with them, however, as the factory did not change over to the 4.7 quart design until 1981. Even before the factory enlarged the oil pan, the aftermarket was offering a variety of different sumps.

Extended oil pans

Although you lose a minor amount of ground clearance with an extended oil pan, you gain several benefits if you can manage to keep it off the pavement. First, the greater mass of oil requires more calories (heat) to get it warm and keep it that way. This means your engine runs cooler. Second, the greater amount of oil will trap and hold more contaminants, keeping them away from your expensive engine parts.

If you have a pre-1981 car, consider exchanging your 3.7 quart oil pan for the stock 4.7 quart pan found on the 1.7 liter cars. One good deal is to buy a Dasher oil pan, as it is virtually identical to the pan on the late motors.

Baffled oil pans

Installing baffles in the oil pan is usually done for one of two reasons. First, the baffles may direct the hot oil past a cooling area in the pan before allowing it to feed into the oil pump pickup point.

More commonly, however, baffling will be done to prevent the oil pump pickup from being left high and dry during hard acceleration, lateral or otherwise.

How important is this? Essential.

The factory 3.7 quart pan had a built-in oil pocket at the bottom, so although baffles were difficult to install they also were not as necessary. With the introduction of the 4.7 quart pan (and other extended-capacity oil pans) it became much easier for the oil to get out from under the oil pump pickup in high-g maneuvers. Late-model factory oil pump pickups started coming with plastic oil baffles to help prevent oil pump cavitation during cornering. This is a halfway measure, however. For best results, a baffled oil pan is required.

One special baffled oil pan is the European Dasher oil pan, a few of which have made their way into the United

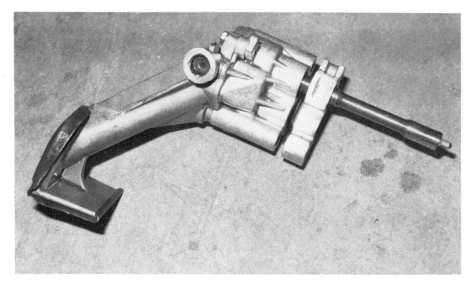

Because of the extra depth of the Oettinger wet sump you must use this extended oil pump. Note the turned-down shaft and the spacer. Techtonics

An exploded view of the two-piece Oettinger wet sump. At the top is the windage tray; at the bottom is the baffling. Techtonics

The Oettinger oil pan looks good and works well, but ground clearance is somewhat reduced; it is expensive. James Sly

States. The European Dasher pan is very distinctive in finned aluminum with a protrusion to each side of the pan for additional capacity and cooling. When you install this pan in a Rabbit, Scirocco, Jetta and so on, the protrusions stick out in front and in back instead of to either side, and the cooling fins run across the airflow instead of along with it.

None of this matters as much as the fact that this pan must be used only to gain extra oil cooling. The inside of the pan presents a maze to the oil. This maze makes sure that the oil travels to one of the cooler regions of the pan before being returned to the oil pump pickup point, but it also guarantees that the last place the oil is going to be is under the oil pump, where you will need it in a corner. This is not a high-performance oil pan.

Windage trays

It may be hard to believe that oil can slow your car down, but it sometimes can. Under hard running, the crankshaft may trail long fans of oil, or worse, it may splash around in hot, frothy oil. In either instance, a windage tray is the answer.

The windage tray sits between the crankshaft and the sump, as close to the crankshaft as possible without hitting it (many of the baffled oil pans have windage trays built in). As the crankshaft swings by the windage tray, the tray scrapes off the excess oil, eliminating the tiny amount of drag the oil has on the crank.

This also reduces the tendency of the oil to foam or froth, first because the crankshaft does not whip oil around in the pan, and second because as the oil drains down through the holes in the windage tray the Coriolis force separates the air bubbles from the oil. At high rpm, you can appreciate the importance of pumping only deaerated oil to your engine, especially considering that your oil pump does not pump air nearly as well as it pumps oil. If you are running a high-rpm, high-compression engine and are finding a lot of oil in your air cleaner or spill tank, consider a windage tray for part of the solution.

Although you could buy a pan that had only one of the preceding characteristics, it is just as easy to buy one that has them all. An extended, baffled oil pan with a windage tray can solve just about all your problems at once. If you choose to go with a cast-aluminum oil pan such as those offered by Volkswagen Motorsport or Oettinger, be aware that they will crack instead of bend if you smack them on something. And they are expensive.

If an aluminum pan is not to your liking, there are many fine steel pans available, such as the very nice Drake unit. The stamped-steel pans are fairly durable, but they too can be bent only so far before they split.

A sump guard is the ticket for oil pan protection. Just make sure the guard you buy will fit around your extended oil

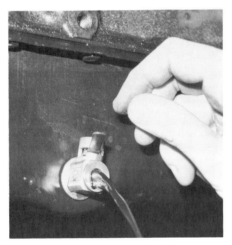

The oil drain valve makes oil changes quicker, easier and less messy.

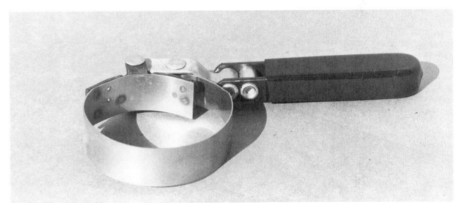

This oil filter wrench design seems to work best in the VW.

Oil filter comparison

	Particle size	Oberg 900	System 1	Well-known paper element
	10 microns	11%	14%	18%
Percentage	20 microns	14%	17%	70%
of filtration	40 microns	20%	40%	94%
	90 microns	29%	48%	90%
Tested at 16.5 gallons per minute *with 250 milligrams per liter of A-C fine test dust as per SAE test HS-J806B*				
Max. contaminants		2.26 grams	6 grams	60 grams
Time until by-pass valve opens		3.5 minutes	9.5 minutes	110 minutes
All filters were tested until the pressure differential stabilized, indicating that the by-pass valve was fully open.				

Although the screen-type filters are popular among some of the racers, a paper element filter is going to work better in just about every VW application, especially considering the low by-pass valve setting of the screen filters.

pan. Most of the aftermarket pans are patterned after the late-model stock unit, and the sump guard is a Volkswagen piece, too, so you are pretty safe there.

There are some steel oil pans to avoid, too. Do not buy an oil pan with chrome on it unless you show your car instead of driving it. Chrome does not dissipate heat nearly as well as the thin coat of flat-black paint that Volkswagen uses on the stock pan. Some aftermarket oil pans are made of very thin steel, and some will not even bolt up to the block without either alteration or separating the engine from the transmission. None of this is necessary, so if you find yourself confronted with such a pan, consider sending it back in favor of a properly engineered piece.

Dry sump

For the ultimate racing machine, a dry sump is the only way to go. It is called a dry sump because the pan underneath the crankshaft is not used to store the oil. That task falls to a separate reservoir located elsewhere in the car. With the possible exception of a Ferrari, the only modern production car that comes with a dry sump is the Porsche 911.

A dry-sump system requires five things:

• A dry-sump reservoir to hold the oil
• An oil pump to supply pressurized oil to the motor for lubrication
• An oil pump to scavenge the oil from the oil pan and send it to the oil reservoir (multiple pumps are often used, with separate pickups in different parts of the oil pan)
• An oil pan to direct the oil to the oil pickup, keeping the oil off the rotating parts
• Oil lines to and from the reservoir, pumps and engine

This system provides more effective and thorough lubrication under extreme conditions, and allows better oil cooling. It also reduces the amount of oil in the sump; the less oil there is, the less it will be able to aerate or cling to the crankshaft. In addition, the reduced height of the oil pan allows the motor to be moved closer to the ground for a better center of gravity.

Most racing motors that use dry sumps run stacked pumps. One belt drives all the oil pumps (one for pressure and the others for scavenge) and the fuel pump for the mechanical injection. One benefit of using this setup (besides not having to have separate drives for everything) is that if the belt breaks, robbing the engine of lubrication, the motor instantly runs out of fuel, too.

Magnetic drain plugs

Magnetic drain plugs have been available for transmissions for years, and were even a stock item with some air-cooled transmissions. But they never quite made it over to the water-cooled engines, even though these engines have a lot more ferrous metal than do air-cooled engines.

If you do not plan on running an oil drain valve or a Preluber, using a magnetic drain plug is an inexpensive way of keeping an eye on what is wearing off inside your engine. The plug also traps and holds particles that would otherwise cause trouble.

Oil drain valves

The more often you change your oil, the more you will appreciate this little item. Instead of using a wrench to drain your oil, you simply lift and turn the handle on the valve. The oil comes out a little slower, but that does not matter because you can spend the time inspecting the rest of the car.

The oil drain valve comes with a crush washer that will accept quite a bit of compression. This allows you to tighten the valve until it is straight up and down, and therefore easiest to use. Even though it opens easily, there is no chance of it popping open by itself.

Prelubrication

As you go through the sections on installing a new camshaft and starting a rebuilt motor, you might get the idea that in addition to everything else you do when cranking over a fresh engine, you also cross your fingers and hold your breath, hoping against hope that everything will go all right. It wouldn't hurt to do that *every* time you start the motor, even after it is broken in.

Studies show that a lot of engine wear occurs during start-up. When a hot engine is shut off, the heat-thinned oil

The Mecca oil filter.

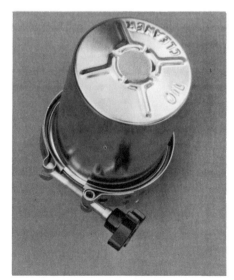

The Frantz by-pass oil filter.

drains off the parts into the sump. When it comes time to start the engine, the oil is all in the bottom of your engine, doing no good whatsoever. In the long seconds that it takes for that oil to completely pressurize the oil galleys and start protecting your engine, a lot of damage has been done.

The Preluber from Lubrication Research and Accusump III from Mecca help eliminate start-up damage by pressurizing the oil galleys to 50 psi before the starter motor is engaged. This means that as soon as the crankshaft and camshaft start rotating, they ride up on a cushion of oil instead of scraping on the bearings.

The Preluber is designed around a small motor that powers a separate oil pump. The Accusump III is a straight-ahead mechanical device, using a spring-loaded piston to pressurize the oil. After the Accusump III provides start-up lubrication it resets itself using normal engine oil pressure, so it is always ready to go.

For racing use, the Accusump III can be triggered by low oil pressure to provide emergency oil pressure on a temporary basis. The Preluber, on the other hand, could be called upon to provide oil pressure in the event of an oil pump failure (not a very likely happenstance, but possible). The only problem with either system is finding the space to put it. Neither is what you would classify as dainty.

Filtration

The key to maintaining oil protection is keeping the oil clean. If you change your oil every 700 miles, it is not going to make much difference which filter you use. The rest of us have to worry about filter quality, especially those of us using long-drain-interval synthetics.

Proper oil filtration means that all the primary wear particles—tiny pieces of metal (that have worn off the inside of the motor), sand (from when the engine was cast), grit (that comes in through the air cleaner) and carbon (from imperfect combustion)—are removed from the oil before they have the opportunity to do any damage. If these contaminants are not caught they act as abrasives, wearing away the motor.

These new contaminants are called secondary wear particles. They join their friends, the primary wear particles, and create more friends, the tertiary wear particles. Then they create more friends, and *they* create more friends and so on.

With the flat-bottom factory oil pan, the stock oil pump needed these baffles for oil control. Eurorace

A European Dasher pan looks impressive with its deep, cast fins and front-and-back protrusions . . . Eurorace

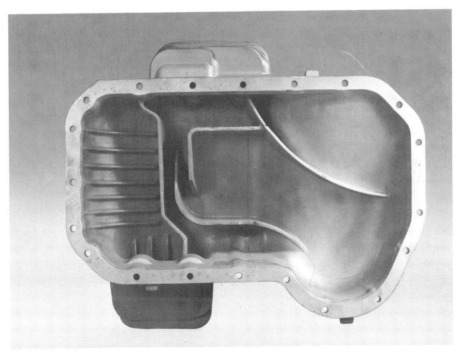

. . . Inside, however, the baffles are for cooling, not for oil control during high-g maneuvers. Eurorace

You can thus appreciate how important it is to catch those first wear particles immediately.

To trap these contaminants, there are two basic types of oil filter: full flow and by-pass. There are different ways of constructing and plumbing both of these types, but the principle of operation remains the same for all.

Full-flow filters

The oil filter that comes on the Volkswagen is a full-flow filter. It is so called because in theory all oil supplied to the engine must pass through the filter first. This can be very important when a catastrophic engine failure threatens to send thousands of metal particles to every corner of your motor, including the hard-to-clean oil cooler. A full-flow filter is the only type that has a chance at minimizing the effects of an engine disaster.

Because all the oil in a full-flow system passes through the filter, inside the filter is a by-pass valve in case the filter element or elements clog, collapse or just plain fail. This ensures that the motor will also continue to get lubrication when the oil is too cold to flow easily through the filter element.

In most cars, the by-pass valve is the filter's worst enemy because it spends a lot of time in the open position, allowing unfiltered oil to circulate through the engine. This is not the case with the Volkswagen.

The Volkswagen OEM (original equipment manufacturer) oil filter by-pass valve is set to open at around 32 psi of pressure differential (the difference in pressure between the oil coming from the oil pump and the oil going to the motor), according to the Volkswagen factory specification. This is in contrast with the by-pass valves on many American car filters, which are set to open at between 7 and 9 psi of pressure differential.

A small malfunction can create the 7 to 9 psi differential required to open the by-pass valve in an American car, but there must be something seriously wrong for the stock Volkswagen by-pass to open at 32 psi of differential. However, the whole system is designed with this by-pass valve in mind, just as other systems are designed with their lower-pressure by-pass valves in mind. Because of this, always make sure that your oil filter has a 32 psi by-pass valve. The Mann filters used by the factory meet this specification, as do the better aftermarket filters like the Fram PH2870A.

By-pass filters

Now regarded by many as a curiosity, a by-pass filter is in some ways a mirror image of the full-flow filter in the sense that the strong points of the by-pass filter are the weak points of the full-flow filter, and vice versa. The by-pass filter is so called because it taps into the oil system and bleeds off oil a little at a time. Working in this way, it takes several minutes for most of the oil in the system to pass through the by-pass filter at least once.

The main disadvantage to the by-pass filter is that it offers no protection against catastrophic engine failure. If a bearing were to disintegrate, metallic particles would be pumped through the engine, impregnating the good bearings with shrapnel and scoring the crankshaft, camshaft and other vital engine components. The by-pass filter would have caught only a small percentage of the particles by the time the damage was done.

In other areas, the by-pass filter excels. Whereas unrestricted oil flow is paramount with a full-flow filter, oil flow is of almost no concern with a by-pass fil-

Early stock oil pan. Angled sides forced oil toward the oil pickup. Eurorace

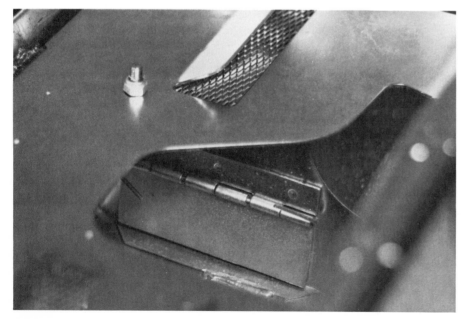

One-way doors trap oil around the oil pump pickup. Eurorace

ter. As long as oil flows through it, it will filter. When the element becomes clogged the filtering action stops, but there is no danger of oil starvation to the engine as a result. In fact, while a full-flow filter performs worse as it fills up with contaminants, the by-pass filter actually filters better. Because pressure differential is not a factor in the performance of the by-pass filter, it can use restrictive elements that filter much finer contaminants than a full-flow filter element. It is its ability to filter superfine particulates from the oil that makes the by-pass filter worth the investment.

By-pass filters can also be much easier to service. This is because low flow, cavitation, aeration and other factors that are detrimental to the operation of a full-flow filter are of secondary or no importance with the by-pass filters; therefore, they can be mounted for convenience sake. Unlike with a full-flow filter, air in the oil lines of a by-pass filter does not mean the motor is running dry.

One concern with the by-pass filter is its source of oil. Because it bleeds oil off a high-pressure oil galley, it appears to the engine that there is an oil leak. The "leak" in this case drips back into the crankcase, but still, pressure is lost. The Society of Automotive Engineers recognized this problem and developed a specification for by-pass filter feed lines. All oil going to the by-pass filter must pass through a 0.062 inch restrictor. This prevents the by-pass filter from bleeding off too much oil from the main pressure circuit.

Filter elements

Both full-flow and by-pass filters must have some sort of filtration material (the element). There are many types of filtration material, but they can be broken down into two categories: surface and depth.

Surface elements are the most common. They are usually resin-coated pleated paper through which the oil passes. The resin coating adds strength and integrity to the material used in the element. The advantages of the pleated paper filter are its low cost, large surface area and moderate restrictiveness. It is, however, susceptible to blow-out if subjected to high pressure or to too much water in the oil system.

Another type of surface filter is the stainless steel screen. The screen is separate from the housing, allowing the screen to be cleaned and returned to duty indefinitely. As with other types of elements, as the screen fills up it starts catching smaller and smaller chunks of contamination. Screen-type elements offer very low initial restriction, and are often used where it is important to be able to inspect the element to see what contaminants are in the oil.

The weave of the steel threads and the opening size of the weave determine the maximum-size particle that can pass through. The common screen size is sixty microns, which is pretty large for a dirt particle in your engine. The screen can trap smaller particles with irregular shapes, although it can also miss long, skinny chunks if they thread their way through the mesh.

The size of the weave of the screen also determines how much pressure drop there will be across the filter element. Typically, a sixty-micron screen-type filter, as found in the System 1 or Oberg, will have between 2.5 and 3.5 psi of pressure drop. Finer screens would generate unacceptably high pressure differentials, and so are not commonly used (although they are available).

Both the Oberg and the System 1 require far less differential pressure than the stock paper-element filter (7 psi or higher) before going into by-pass. This is because they were not designed for the Volkswagen engine, but for the typical American filter application.

One area in which the screen-element filters do excel is in initial flow character-

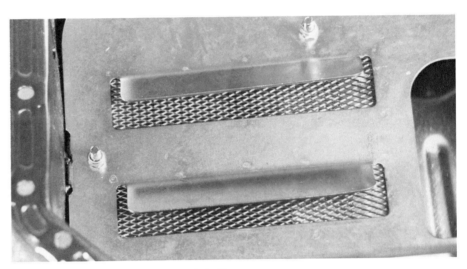

Angled flaps catch oil off the crankshaft. Screen de-aerates the oil before it gets to the sump. Eurorace

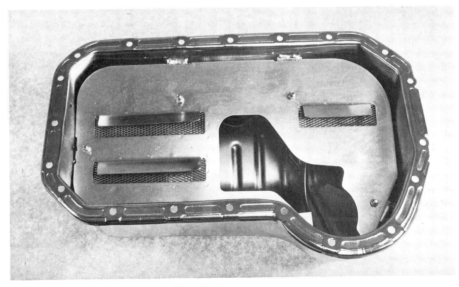

A typical aftermarket oil pan with built-in windage tray and baffles. Eurorace

istics (the amount the filter will flow when clean). This sounds good on paper, but in reality it is unimportant. Just about any filter element with a few square inches of element will have a higher initial flow characteristic than the nipple that holds the filter to the filter mount. Having the capability for more flow is nice, but it is not needed.

Another plus for the screen-element filters is that they are readily disassembled for inspection. Some racers like this because they no longer have to carry around cases of oil filters.

In other areas, the screen elements do not fare so well. One of the worst features of the screen element is that it has poor single-pass efficiency. This means that oil must pass through the element several times before the particles are removed. It is vitally important to your engine that the filter have good single-pass efficiency so it will trap and hold as many of the contaminants as it can the very first time the oil passes it, and every subsequent time.

Screen-element filters also have smaller filter elements than the normal spin-on filter. The Oberg is the worst in this case, with only sixty-four square inches of filter media in its nine-inch filter (its largest). The System 1 is far better with 136 square inches, but neither is close to a good-quality paper-element filter like the Fram PH2870A filter, with nearly 300 square inches of filter media.

Depth elements come in many varieties, but all offer the same basic thing: thicker element material. They do this with a penalty, however, and that is usually higher resistance. For this reason, depth filtration is popular on by-pass filters, which can have much more tolerance to flow restriction than can full-flow filters.

Because of its relatively large pressure drop, toilet paper (as used in several filters now on the market) makes a poor full-flow element. It performs reasonably well as a depth-type by-pass element, however, and the price is certainly right. Oil is fed into the end of the roll, making it easy to scan a used element for debris. Because of the amount of paper in a roll of toilet paper, it also has a fair capacity for trapping water, although water will channel between the layers, reducing the effectiveness of the filter. Even this tendency can be mitigated through the use of tight rolls of toilet paper, as opposed to the "extra fluffy" brands.

Amsoil designed an elaborate line of individual filter elements that are guaranteed to be nonchanneling. This sophistication adds to the cost of the element, but it does work much better than a roll of toilet paper under a wide range of conditions.

One state-of-the-art depth element can be found in the Mecca line of oil filters. Mecca elements feature its exclusive synthetic depth element—and no pressure valve. These filters are able to run without the pressure valve required in almost every other full-flow filter because they give only a one-half-pound drop, they can flow over fifteen gallons per minute, and their element can trap and hold a lot of particulates without loosing effectiveness.

If you are nervous about not having a pressure relief valve in your filter, Mecca also sells a differential pressure gauge that will tell you exactly when to change the filter. Even though the Mecca element is supposed to be good for up to

The piston oil jets in a 16V block. Techtonics

For stock-size oil pans this sump guard provides a lot of protection. Autotech

10,000 to 15,000 miles of street use, the differential gauge is a good idea.

Filter housing shape and mounting

The housing shape? Yes, the housing shape. The stock Volkswagen oil filter hangs from the filter mount. This allows heavy particles to drop to the bottom of the housing and (with any luck) stay there. Any spin-on-type filter will benefit from this, so the only problems you will have are with the Oberg (which cannot be mounted to take advantage of this phenomenon) or with oddly shaped or mounted by-pass filters.

Selecting a filtration system

When it comes to figuring out how well each filter will do its job, you get conflicting stories from all sides. According to Frantz, fifty-eight percent of engine wear particles are ten microns or less in diameter. Fram, on the other hand, claims that its dyno tests prove the most damaging contaminants lie in the twenty- to forty-micron range.

Naturally, the manufacturer of each type of filter claims that its is the best. The biggest push comes from Oberg and System 1 with their screen-element filters. They claim particulate filtration down to five microns, but their claims are not borne out in oil filtration tests conducted to the SAE HS-J806B standard. At a flow of 16.5 gallons per minute (just over five times the flow rate of the Volkswagen motor), both the screen-type filters filled up quickly and failed to trap high percentages of particulates, as stated in their sales literature. Of course, neither of these filters has the proper by-pass valve for the Volkswagen application.

Mecca claims eight microns for its element. James Sly has conducted an impromptu test of the Mecca filter. A turbocharger bearing in his motor unexpectedly disintegrated, creating enough scrap metal to clog the Mecca filter. He was alerted to this fact by the dual oil pressure sender that comes on the 1984–and-later Volkswagens. Subsequent examination of the motor revealed no damage!

Without having to go to the effort of sorting out the claims, you can conclude that for maximum filtration you would use a high-quality full-flow filter like the Fram (or the Mecca), with a by-pass filter like the Frantz or Amsoil. With a dual-mode setup like this, the extra cost of the filters is more than made up by the savings in engine wear.

If inspecting the filter element for wear particles is important to you, buy a case of spin-on filters (to get a volume discount) and purchase an inexpensive 3½ inch tubing cutter. Then if you do not feel like taking apart your spin-on, you don't have to. With the Mecca and the screen-element filters, you do not have that choice.

Even if the performance of all the different types of full-flow filter were the same, I would still use the traditional paper-element spin-on filters; I do not enjoy washing filters out, and I prefer filters with seams that do not leak.

Oil additives

There are nearly as many oil additives available as there are oils to put them in. Most of these additives are friction modifiers, viscosity modifiers, or "boosters" that replenish the detergents and dispersants in the oil to extend oil life.

Of the friction modifiers, the three most common are molybdenum compounds, graphite and polytetrafluoroethylene (PTFE), better known as Teflon.

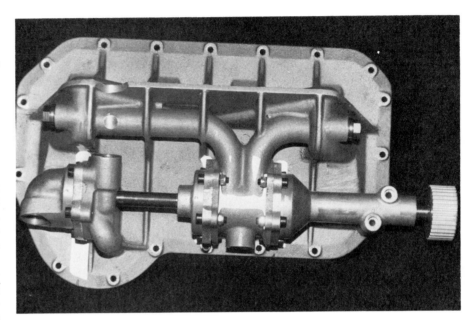

The inner workings of an Oettinger dry-sump oil pan. The windage tray bolts between this piece and the block. James Sly

This Pulsar Racing windage tray integrates with the stock oil pan. James Sly

Molybdenum, as explained in chapter 2, has a high affinity for metal. Moly is also attracted to hot spots in the engine. Once the moly attaches itself to the metal it is very difficult to remove, so even though it is not oil it is an excellent lubricant.

Graphite once played a starring role in Arco Graphite, but since then it has lost some status as an oil additive. Graphite is quite slippery but it does not have the same metal affinity as moly, and thus has fallen by the wayside.

Teflon, from Du Pont Chemical, is also well-known as the slippery coating in frying pans, but like graphite it has no natural affinity for metal. To get Teflon to stick to metal, the metal first must be painstakingly cleaned, and that is not going to spontaneously happen in your motor. Du Pont was not satisfied that its product would perform as advertised, so it forbade the use of the trademarked Teflon name, even though it still sells it as PTFE.

Viscosity improvers make your oil thicker, and are usually the same consistency as cold honey. This is just about the last thing you want to put in your motor.

Detergency packages claim to replenish the additive package that most oils come with from the refinery. Typical of this type of product are claims to boost the TBN (total base number) of the oil. Boosting the TBN is no problem. However, the TBN of the oil is not the only thing that determines good lubrication. In fact, none of the detergents or dispersant additives, as important as they are, are lubricants. And after a point, too much of these nonoil components does you no good, if indeed the additives are not detrimental (which in some cases they are).

Keep in mind that most of the current additive technology (both from the refinery and from the aftermarket) is keyed around petroleum base stocks. Ten years ago, synthetic oil manufacturers were having a tough time figuring out what additives to use, how much of them to put in and how to keep them in solution. The situation has improved a lot in the last few years, but if you are using a synthetic and considering an additive, first make certain that the additive will work with your synthetic. If not, you will merely contaminate your expensive oil without seeing any gain from the additive.

The best thing to do is to use a good oil, keep it clean and change it on an appropriate schedule. If you want to use an additive, try moly. The rest you can live without.

Oil analysis

One way of keeping tabs on the condition of your oil, and monitoring engine wear in the process, is to have your oil analyzed. The analysis itself is conducted in special laboratories. In return for an oil sample and a few dollars, the lab will send you a sheet telling you how much of each element it found in the sample, along with an explanation of what it all means.

Although you could wait until you suspect something is wrong in your motor before you send that first sample in for testing, it is far better to put yourself on a schedule and then stick to it. That way, you will have a better idea of the rate of wear on various components. For best results, also send in a sample of clean, fresh oil of the type you use. The lab probably has a fair idea about what is in clean oil, but it would not hurt to make sure it has a good base line for your car.

I use oil analysis mostly to find out what engine components are shedding metal, and for this it seems to work well. If you are building race engines or doing maintenance on a fleet of cars and you need to know ahead of time when an engine is going to have a problem, oil analysis can be a good tool. Oil analysis can also be good for those using extended-drain-interval synthetics. For most people, however, changing the oil and filter regularly costs about the same amount and is less trouble.

Assembly

As you assemble the motor, constantly be on the lookout for anything that will cause the engine to self-destruct once it is all together, even if this means cleaning parts you *know* are clean and double-checking measurements you *know* are right.

In addition to making sure all clearances and procedures are correct, you will need to lubricate many of the parts so that the initial start-up procedure does not ruin them. For bearings, use a good grade of motor oil, with a little moly paste mixed in if you wish. If you use a heavy grease, paste or oil, you will not be able to feel if a clearance is too loose. Also, grease or paste will not move out of the way fast enough to let oil into the bearings once the motor is running.

For cam lobes and the tops of the cam followers, use moly cam lube, usually available in little tins. Here it is okay to use paste, because these parts are splash oiled. The moly lube is to be applied *only* to the top of the cam follower and to the camshaft lobe. Do not coat the cam follower skirts with moly lube, grease or anything else except motor oil. Heavy grease might prevent the cam follower from rotating, leading to extreme wear or failure of the shim, the camshaft lobe or both.

For cylinder walls, use a light coat of WD–40. This will allow the rings to seat

Late-style stock oil pan. Note the relative flatness of the bottom of the pan. Eurorace

quickly and without galling. The only problem with using WD-40 is that it does not stay on the cylinder walls very long, so start the motor as soon after assembly as possible.

If you will not be starting your motor soon after you assemble it, use something a little heavier than WD-40 on the cylinder walls, such as a thin coat of motor oil. Motor oil will not drain off as fast and will thus protect longer than the thinner WD-40.

With the engine on an angle the way it is, it can be a real trick to get the block, the head gasket and the cylinder head all lined up when it comes time to bolt everything together. The block dowel pins you see advertised are one way of addressing this problem. Or you can take a couple of old head bolts and saw an inch or so off the threaded end to use as guides. To make it easier to get them out after the head is on, cut a slot in the top to fit a screwdriver blade. They may not be as elegant as dowel pins, but they work just as well and are reusable.

Before attempting to put the head on the block, screw these guides into two of the rear cylinder head holes. A couple of turns will do. Then slip on the head gasket and ask a passerby to help gently lift the head into place.

After centering the head and getting a couple of head bolts started, slip a screwdriver down the hole, unscrew the line-up studs and then fish them out with a magnet.

The most difficult part of this procedure is sawing the head bolts. Plan on going through a couple of hacksaw blades if you do this job by hand; a cutoff saw would work well here. Do not be dissuaded by the prospect of hard labor, however. This is a very important step in the life of your motor.

Before you put the head back on, you must remove all traces of dirt, grease and especially water from the cylinder head bolt holes. The only thing you want between the cylinder head bolt and the threads in the block is a light coat of motor oil.

One last thing to be on the lookout for when tightening the head bolts is the way they feel. It is fine to trust the torque wrench, but sometimes a head bolt will start to fail as you torque it down. One clue that this is happening is that you will have to turn the head of that bolt more than the others. If you suspect something is odd, stop and replace the head bolt with a new one of the same type (there are many different types of head bolt, so do not mix them).

Speaking of torquing head bolts, the pattern for future instructions seems to be to specify an initial low torque setting and then a certain number of degrees to turn the fastener beyond that point. This is important because the engineer knows the pitch of the bolt, knows how much stretch should be in the bolt and can precisely calculate how much the bolt has to be turned to get that stretch. These instructions will allow you to avoid dealing with the frictional and tolerance differences among head bolts and block threads, to say nothing of the calibration of the torque wrench.

The only problem is that a special tool is required to gauge the number of degrees the bolt has been turned. This tool is available in Germany for nearly $150, but Snap-On will soon be marketing a similar device that will retail for around $40. The prediction is that by the early 1990s most important torque specifications will be expressed in terms of this low initial torque/additional number of degrees method.

Start-up

Again, most engine damage occurs on start-up, before the lubricant can circulate to protect the engine. Just imagine what happens when you start a brand-new engine! Fortunately, there are several things you can do to make the initial start-up less traumatic for your motor.

The very best thing you can do is to fill the oil galleys with pressurized oil before you turn the key. If you have access to a cutoff saw, cut about eight inches of ⅜ inch bar stock and notch the end of it to fit over the drive tang of the oil pump (with the distributor removed). You can then chuck up the bar stock in a drill motor and manually prime the oil galleys using the oil pump. Hold on tight to the drill motor, however, because when the oil is at room temperature and the oil pressurizes, you will run into strong resistance. This method is so effective that Darrell Vittone ships one of these tools with each motor he sells. Remember that you must have the flywheel bolts in place in the crankshaft before you pressurize the oil system, or oil will pour out of the bolt holes.

Also remember to *never* crank the motor over until the oil pressure builds up by itself. When the motor cranks over without oil pressure, all your new parts rub against each other at relatively slow speeds, and without lubrication.

The best approach is to prelube the engine as described earlier, and make

sure that the ignition and fuel delivery are both ready to go so that when you hit the starter the engine fires right off.

Now a word about the break-in oil, the oil you have been working so hard to get into the engine before you engage the starter motor for the first time. In the past, the practice was to use a poor-quality oil, such as something with a rating of SB, for the break-in period. (The B in SB does not mean that the oil is for break-in use. It just happens to be the

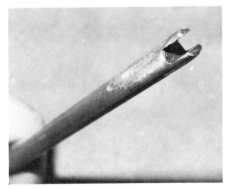

⅜ inch bar stock with a slot in the end makes the perfect pre-oiler for a new engine. Techtonics

Priming the engine before that all-important first start-up. Even on a warm day, 80 psi is not unusual using this method. Techtonics

rating of the oil.) Low-grade oil like this does allow the engine to break in, but you will have greater success with normal SE- or SF-rated motor oil, with two exceptions.

First, do not use a synthetic during the break-in period. Synthoil, for example, is far too slippery to let the rings seat against the cylinder walls. Second, Castrol has a poor reputation as a break-in oil.

Once the engine is running, do not let it idle. Run it up to about 2000 rpm and run it for about twenty minutes. This will allow plenty of time for the parts to get to know one another. After twenty minutes, shut it down and recheck everything to make sure that nothing has wandered out of spec. If you are worried that the cam followers are not rotating, shut the motor off after about five minutes and check them for unusual wear patterns. Otherwise, let the motor go the full twenty minutes.

On the off-chance that your rings do not seal, there is a trick you can use to help them along. Find an empty stretch of road and shift into third at the appropriate speed. Accelerate hard from about 1200 rpm to about 4500 rpm, and then let the car coast down against the motor's compression until you reach 1200 rpm again. Then do the whole procedure over. After a few runs (no more than ten) your rings should be seated—and a good thing, too, consider-ing how badly the car has been smoking! If not, you did something wrong somewhere along the line, and it is time to think about tearing down the engine to fix it.

Front and side motor mounts

Not only do the stock motor mounts (pre–1985) take a pretty good pounding from all the vibration of the motor, they are a little soft for high-performance use. There is a wealth of heavy-duty motor mounts out there, all the way from hardened rubber to polymer to solid metal. In the pre–1985 cars, the stock front motor mount was a little too loose to allow the use of tube headers, and even the cast-iron European header had a problem now and again as a result of all the flex the stock motor mounts will allow.

Even if you have a ball joint type of exhaust, you should switch up to a heavy-duty front motor mount to reduce wheel hop and improve traction during hard launches. The Techtonics front mount is made of the same material as the stock mount, but with a different cross-section so it fits the cup better. This gives you the benefits of a stiffer mount without an undue amount of extra vibration. Harder front mounts will chatter your teeth out.

The side motor mounts can be checked by sliding a floor jack under the motor and lifting up a little. If the mount is worn-out, the motor will move a lot before it is caught by whatever is left of the motor mount. If your side motor mount is worn-out and you have not replaced your front motor mount, do so. A better front motor mount will take some of the load off the side motor mount.

Sawed-off cylinder head bolts are handy for aligning the head gasket when reinstalling the cylinder head.

Hollow dowel pins for locating the head gasket on assembly. Techtonics

The dowel pins go in the rear oil return holes. Techtonics

Air and fuel

3

It is critically important to get the right air and fuel mixture delivered to the cylinder. The stoichiometric ratio (the ratio at which combustion is most efficient) takes place when there is a 14:1 air-to-fuel ratio, but maximum power is obtained with up to ten percent less air, although economy suffers. For best economy the mixture should have ten percent excess air, but at that point you lose some power and engine temperatures will be higher because of the slower rate of combustion. The best idle is obtained with thirty to forty percent less air.

Therefore, the best fuel delivery system is one that runs slightly fat at idle, slightly lean at part-throttle and a smidge rich under acceleration.

When working with either carburetors or fuel injection, a vacuum leak will throw everything off. Even small air leaks can radically alter the behavior of a motor. Keep all vacuum lines connected and in good repair (you can use the new silicone vacuum line in place of the fabric-covered rubber), and periodically check to see that there is no unwanted air

leaking in at manifold joints, through vacuum advance or retard canisters, or through other vacuum-operated accessories.

Tools and techniques

In the old days, good mechanics could listen to the motor, spit on the exhaust manifolds and tell you how to adjust the carbs. These are difficult skills to develop, however, which is why the rest of us rely on the wide range of tools we have at our disposal.

Infrared gas analyzer

The simplest of the high-quality diagnostic machines is the two-gas analyzer. This sniffs the exhaust and tells you how many hydrocarbons (HC) there are, and the percentage of carbon monoxide (CO).

High HC means that the fuel is not being burned. This could be because one of the spark plugs is not firing or because the valve overlap is so great that the fresh air/fuel mixture is being blown right out the tailpipe. High CO means that the mixture is running rich.

Probably the most popular two-gas analyzer is the Sun EPA-75. With the

stiffening of air pollution laws, two-gas analyzers are being replaced by four-gas analyzers. In addition to HC and CO, the four-gas analyzers measure oxides of nitrogen and carbon dioxide.

Computer diagnostic analyzers

The next step beyond the four-gas analyzer is a computer diagnostic analyzer, such as the Sun Interrogator 2. As mentioned in chapter 1, the Interrogator 2 and similar machines keep track of virtually everything of any importance that is going on in the motor, and then give you a print-out of what was found.

Neither the computer analyzer nor an infrared gas analyzer is likely to be within your budget, but if you cannot determine what is wrong with the way your car is running, spending a few minutes with one of these machines can be very revealing.

Colortune

Now we reach a more affordable level of diagnostic aid. The Gunsen Colortune is an inexpensive device that allows you to set the fuel mixture by sight. The principle behind the Colortune 500 is quite simple. If you have ever seen gas

The Uni-Syn is one of the best-known carburetor synchronizing tools around.

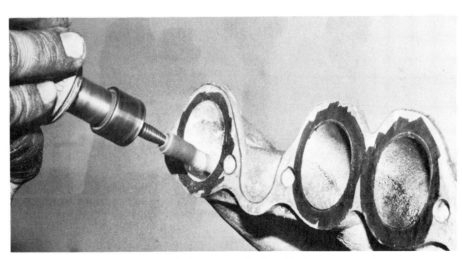

To match port the intake manifold to the cylinder head, use the intake gasket as a template and grind both the manifold and the head to the same exact opening. James Sly

burning (any gas), you no doubt noticed the different hues present. The color differences correspond to the percentages of air and fuel in the combustible mixture. The perfect mixture burns "bunsen" blue. Richer mixtures burn more yellow, and leaner mixtures burn white-blue. If there is oil present in the mixture, a purple tinge will show up in the flame.

Because combustion occurs inside your automobile engine while it is running, it too produces colors, albeit not commonly seen. The Colortune 500 allows you to temporarily see into your combustion chamber so you can adjust the air/fuel mixture while observing the color of the combustion.

It does this by means of a clear "spark plug" that runs in place of any (or all) of your normal spark plugs. By peering through the Colortune spark plug, you can see into your engine.

The Colortune kit contains adapters that allow it to be used with just about anything that uses a spark plug for ignition. Engines with single carburetors or fuel-injected cars with one throttle plate can get by with one Colortune. Multiple carburetors are most often adjusted with one Colortune for each carburetor. Troubleshooting uneven cylinder balance is easily accomplished with one Colortune per cylinder.

The basic Colortune kit comes complete with a standard 14 mm clear spark plug, a high-tension lead to connect the clear plug to the plug wire, a viewscope, cleaning fluid and brush, copper gaskets, full directions and a diagnosis chart.

Exhaust gas temperature readings

EGT (exhaust gas temperature) readings can give you a very accurate picture of what is occurring during combustion, but because it is difficult to connect the sensors, not many people take the time to do it.

For best accuracy, the thermocouple should be as close to the exhaust port of the head as you can get it. Ideally you would have one thermocouple per port in a carbureted application, with either four gauges (one for each cylinder) or one gauge that can be switched to read the temperature in selected cylinders.

A CIS-equipped car will run quite evenly across the cylinders, so one thermocouple should work fine unless you are running at the ragged edge and are losing pistons or valves to heat. Because the thermocouple could break off, on turbo motors you should run the thermocouple *downstream* of the turbine. This location will throw your numbers off to the low side, but this is better than running pieces of metal through your turbine.

If you have a Lambda-equipped car with the exhaust emission test pipe (the one with the light blue silicone plug on the top), putting the thermocouple where the test pipe normally mounts will save you some drilling. If the thermocouple threads do not match the threads for the test pipe, make an adapter for the test pipe before you drill and tap the hole for the thermocouple, so you can reinstall the test pipe later.

Whichever method you choose, the EGT should stay between 1,300 and 1,400 degrees Fahrenheit for hard running (idle temperature will be right around 625 degrees Fahrenheit). This is best checked on the dyno, where you can run the engine at full throttle under load. It does not matter if your car is carbureted, fuel injected, turbocharged or supercharged; the EGT should be within this range whenever you are running gasoline. Colder temperatures mean the mixture is too rich, hotter temperatures mean the mixture is too lean. This includes engines that have had the combustion chamber surfaces coated with zirconium oxide or moly.

Fuel additives

There is something you can do for your fuel injection (or carburetor) that does not improve the performance (as far as I know) but that does help keep it

This two-liter Oettinger motor with the dual-sidedraft Solexes put out 185 hp by the time Techtonics was through with it.

That's enough power to take you 0-60 in 7.0 seconds, or through a quarter-mile in 15.06 at 94.57 mph. James Sly

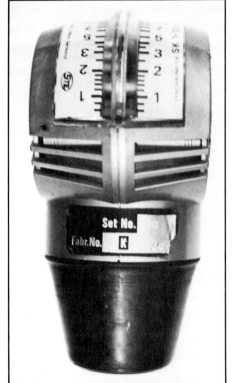

The Synchro Meter is a newer design than the Uni-Syn, is easier to use, and does not affect the airflow into the carb as much as the Uni-Syn.

alive, and that is to regularly use Swepco 503 Fuel Improver. It is one of the few fuel additives condoned by Bosch, so it must be safe, and it will help clean the system of moisture and fuel deposits. Adding a bottle of this at every oil change is sufficient to do the job. It is not available in most retail stores, but a few performance shops carry it, and it is worth looking for.

Another additive that helps keep things clean is called Z-Power. Z-Power is made of organic esters and is just about safe enough to eat, so it should be okay in your gas tank. Z-Power provides upper cylinder lubrication, cuts down on pollution (by surrounding the sulphur and nitrogen molecules, and preventing them from forming sulphuric acid and oxides of nitrogen), encourages more complete combustion (again lowering pollution) and cleans the inside of the combustion chamber.

Carburetors

Tools and techniques

If you are going to be running multiple carburetors, purchase a flow meter so you can synchronize the carbs to each other. There are two basic designs, the Uni-Syn and the Synchro Meter. Both work well, but each fits onto the carburetor differently, so make sure you buy one that fits your carburetor or you will have to use adapters.

It is no secret that the Volkswagen Zenith carburetor is not a high-performance piece. If you are having trouble with yours, however, be sure to check all the basics before spending your money

on a replacement carburetor. If you fail to do this, you could easily have the same problems with the new setup.

Check the distributor to make sure it is advancing and retarding properly, and that the vacuum canister is not leaking vacuum. Another source of air leaks is the phenolic EGR piece at the base of the carburetor. Make sure also that you have enough compression and that the leakdown is not abnormally high. Finally, check to see that the carburetor ground strap is connected so the electric idle jet can function properly.

Selection

With carburetors available in every size and style, choosing a carburetor can

be a challenge. The best place to start is to find out what others are buying (*not* necessarily what the parts supply houses are *selling*), and see what their experience has been. Failing that, you will have to make an educated guess based on what the parts supply houses tell you and on the information found in the following section on estimating carb size.

There are progressive carburetors and nonprogressives, downdrafts and sidedrafts. A progressive carburetor has a primary and a secondary throttle butterfly. Most of the time the primary will be the only butterfly open. When you accelerate hard, the secondary will open up as well. In a nonprogressive carbure-

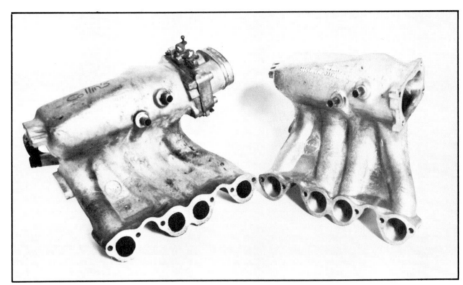

The intake manifold on the left has been ported to eliminate the air restriction in the runners found in the stock manifold next to it. This is a very time-consuming procedure. Techtonics

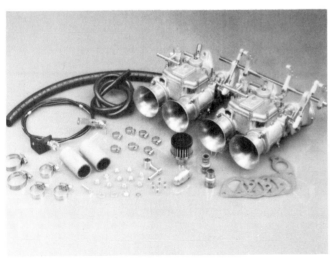

Mikuni also offers sidedrafts for the VW in both 40 and 44 mm sizes.

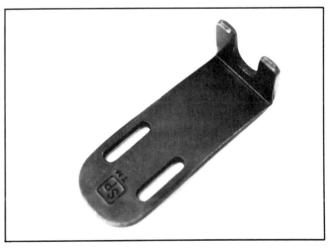

This injector remover makes it easy to overcome the resistance of hardened injector O-rings.

tor, one throttle butterfly covers the entire driving range.

The difference between a downdraft carburetor and a sidedraft carburetor is nothing more than the direction of airflow through the carburetor.

Downdraft carburetors

The carburetor that came on the 1975 and 1976 Volkswagens was a progressive downdraft carburetor. If you are planning to replace the stock carburetor, do not spend too much time agonizing over the horsepower claims of the various units; dyno tests show that all the replacement carburetors are pretty close to one another in terms of power output. The real differences show up in features, drivability and fuel economy. The limiting factor seems to be the intake manifold, but if you are searching for more horsepower you should change to sidedrafts rather than go through the trouble and expense of porting the manifold.

Features include items such as type of choke (water, manual, electric), vacuum ports (EGR, manifold) and electric idle jets.

Drivability is difficult to guess with a carburetor. There is no substitute for experience here. The chart shows, for example, that the Claude's Buggies carburetor was down on horsepower compared with the others, but with its tiny venturis is was the nicest to drive. The Brosol, on the other hand, when properly tuned made a significantly higher amount of power than the other four. Getting it tuned that way was a real problem, however, so for most of the time your drivability would be off.

Currently available progressive downdrafts for the Volkswagen include the Weber DFEV and the Solex XE. I prefer the Solex XE for a couple of reasons.

First, unlike the DFEV, it was designed for the transverse engine. It is a more recent design than the DFEV and is constantly being updated. It has centrally located jet stacks for good performance when accelerating, decelerating and cornering. The float chamber surrounds the main throttle bore, as well. In the DFEV, the jet stacks are offset, which is more appropriate for this carburetor's original application (with a longitudinal engine).

Second, the XE has ports on both the manifold side and the air filter side of the throttle butterfly. The DFEV has ported vacuum only. The XE has two adjustments on the choke unloader, and the DFEV has only one.

Both carburetors can be bought with water or electric chokes and with electric idle jets, and both have mechanical secondaries instead of the vacuum-operated secondaries that come on the stock carburetor.

There is a nonprogressive downdraft carburetor that some use in high-performance applications. The Weber IDF is typically found in specialized equipment such as desert racers and dune buggies, and is not recommended for other uses. Usually you can get more power from a pair of sidedraft carburetors (see the following section), although with no limitations on manifold length the downdrafts will gain the upper hand. It is also easier to shock mount the IDFs with a flexible manifold if that is what

Stock replacement downdraft carburetors

RPM	Brosol	Claudes	Holley/Weber	Weber DGV
2000	81.9	77.2	81.4	79.8
2500	84.0	81.9	84.0	76.2
3000	91.4	92.4	91.4	90.3
3500	95.1	95.6	94.0	94.5
4000	93.5	92.4	91.9	90.9
4500	87.7	89.3	87.2	88.2
5000	83.5	81.9	80.9	79.8
5500	74.6	73.5	73.0	74.6

Although there are small variations in their dyno figures, these carburetors perform roughly the same on the car.

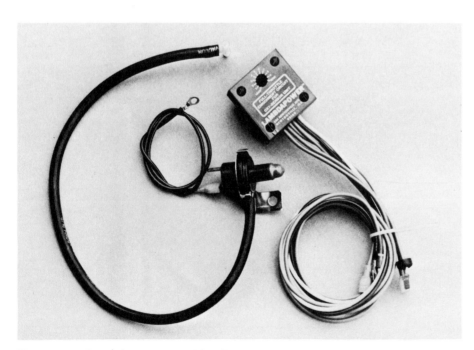

The Lambda Power improves the drivability of pre-1985 Volkswagens.

This tool allows you to remove and replace the Lambda sensor.

you need. Because of their installed height, these carburetors will not fit under the hood of your car.

Sidedraft carburetors

For performance applications, you must consider nonprogressive sidedraft carburetors. Sidedrafts can be configured either in singles or as duals. Single sidedrafts are more expensive than progressive downdrafts, and make only a little more power, if any. There are only two manifolds available for single sidedrafts, one from Lynx and the other from Eurorace. Still, there are those who swear by the Weber DCOE with a fourteen-gram float for off-road use. If your application is different, read on.

Dual sidedrafts are the ultimate carburetors for the Volkswagen motor. They offer good economy, good performance and good drivability. There are three brands of sidedraft available: Dell'Orto, Solex and Weber. In terms of flow and basic construction, the Dell'Orto and Solex are virtually identical. The Weber flows a little differently but not much, and certainly not enough to base a purchasing decision on.

The three brands all seem to run about the same, but the Dell'Orto and Solex have a more modern design. Both of these carburetors have two-piece auxiliary venturis, while the Weber offers only a one-piece auxiliary venturi. For most applications, the outer piece of the Dell'Orto or Solex two-piece auxiliary venturi is left out, although it can be easily installed any time to help cure the rare drivability problem.

In the Weber, the auxiliary venturi is held in place by the velocity stack. If you want to mount air filters, you will need to pick up a set of Eurorace's O-rings so you can eliminate the velocity stacks

without leaving your auxiliary venturis to float around and get into trouble.

Estimating carb size

The best way to check carburetor selection and jetting is on a dyno. However, if you do not have a dyno and you need to take a guess at a carb for your application, there is a formula:

$$cfm = \frac{D \times rpm \times E}{56,634}$$

In this formula, cfm is cubic feet of air per minute, or the rating of how much air will flow through the carburetor. D is the displacement of the motor in cubic centimeters. rpm is the highest rpm at which you will be running the motor. E is the volumetric efficiency of the engine, or how completely the cylinder fills with the air/fuel mixture on the intake stroke.

The dispacement value you use will be different if you use a two-carburetor setup instead of a single carb, because each carb in a dual setup feeds half of the motor. The rpm value you select should be realistic. If you will be taking your engine to 8000 rpm once, and then driv-

ing it daily on the street at 5000 rpm and under, do not size the carburetor for the 8000 rpm figure.

The value you use for the volumetric efficiency of the motor will be the toughest to figure out. For a stock engine, the value would be in the neighborhood of 0.75 to 0.80, while for a strong-running street performer the value would be closer to 0.85. If you are going all out, the value will be in the neighborhood of 0.95.

The volumetric efficiency of the motor depends on compression ratio, cam and head work, and is difficult to calculate without some (here it is again!) dyno time. However, by using the preceding formula, playing with the figures and looking to see what is available, you should be able to arrive at a reasonable estimate.

Fuel injection

The K-Jetronic fuel injection is a simple design. All air entering the engine is metered as it pushes past the airflow sensor plate. The more air that enters the

Sidedraft carburetors

Size	Dell'Orto	Solex	Weber	Mikuni
40	40 DHLA	40 ADDHE	40 DCOE	40
42			42 DCOE	
44				44
45	45 DHLA	45 ADDHE	45 DCOE	
48	48 DHLA	48 ADDHE	48 DCO*	
*NOTE: The DCO carburetor uses a different manifold.				

This chart lists the available sidedraft carburetors.

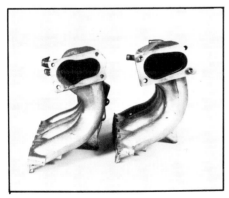

Bolting on a throttle body using an adapter is an almost complete waste of money. To see any benefits at all you must match port the intake manifold to the throttle body, as shown on the right. Techtonics

The Weber Big Throat (on the left) and the Audi 5000 progressive throttle body.

engine, the more that air pushes up on the plate. The plate is connected to a fuel-metering rod with laser-cut orifices on it.

As the rod is pushed higher in the fuel distributor, more of the orifice is uncovered, and more fuel is sent out the fuel lines to the injectors. The warm-up regulator applies a counterforce (called control pressure) to the top of the fuel-metering rod. The shape of the cone through which the air must pass as it

The Colortune lets you see into the combustion chamber through a special clear spark plug.

pushes around the air sensor plate, along with the control pressure from the warm-up regulator, determines how high up the fuel-metering rod can rise, thus controlling the amount of fuel (the air/fuel mixture) that enters the engine.

For cold starts, the warm-up regulator temporarily reduces the amount of control pressure so the fuel-metering rod can rise higher in the fuel distributor for the same amount of air intake, richening the mixture. Also during cold starts, an auxiliary air valve allows more air to enter the engine by by-passing the throttle, increasing the idle.

The controlling systems of the Lambda sensor and KE-Jetronic injections are somewhat more sophisticated, but the basic principle is the same in that the fuel is metered in relation to the flow of air past the air sensor plate.

Tools and techniques

The CIS fuel injection has two major adjustments: idle speed and idle mixture. Everything else is pretty much automatic. Because of the simplicity of the system, the adjustment does not wander around much (on the later cars the idle mixture adjustment hole is sealed up!), so you will find that the most workout these adjustments get is when you are trying to troubleshoot a problem. On the early cars with EGR, you need a two-

or four-gas analyzer to set the fuel injection adjustment; on the later-model cars with the Lambda sensor you can get close with a dwell meter.

Locate the small two-connector plug (it is a white plastic male plug with two female connectors in it) near the right front strut mount inside the engine compartment. One wire will be brown and the other should be light blue or gray with a white stripe. You will need a dwell meter (for example, a Snap-On MT-926) for this procedure.

The ground lead for the dwell meter is clipped to the brown wire, and the other lead from the dwell meter is clipped to the light blue or gray wire. You can make a special plug-in adapter that will allow you to make this connection easily, or cut off a couple inches of an old Audi 100LS shift cable, which is the exact size needed for a tight fit in the female connectors. Then connect the dwell meter to these exposed leads.

Select the four-cylinder setting on your dwell meter. When the car is cold, the dwell reading should be forty-five degrees. You can calibrate your dwell meter by unplugging the Lambda sensor momentarily, since forty-five degrees is the system's default setting. There should be no variation in this reading.

As the motor warms up, the dwell reading should drop to around twenty degrees. This is the enrichment kicking in to give you a smooth idle until the engine is up to full operating temperature.

With the motor hot, the reading should be in the neighborhood of forty-five degrees, with seven degrees of leeway on either side. Forty degrees translates to about one percent carbon mon-

By running the velocity stacks on these Weber 45s through the firewall, the engine gets cooler intake air for a better air charge. R+A Applied Arts

The downdraft Solex makes a nice replacement carburetor if your factory Zenith dies. Eurorace

oxide, which is right where the car should be run. Higher percentages of CO mean the car is running richer; lower concentrations mean the car is running leaner.

To make the adjustment you will need a long 3 mm Allen wrench. The mixture adjustment access hole is located on the air sensor housing, between the air sensor plate opening and the fuel distributor. If you have a later car on which this hole has an aluminum plug or a wedged-in ball bearing, you will need to open up the access hole before you can make the adjustment. Unfasten the air sensor housing and turn it wrong-side up. With a small punch, knock the plug or ball bearing upward (away from where the air filter would be). It should pop right out.

Screwing the mixture adjustment screw clockwise richens the mixture; counterclockwise leans it out. Always adjust from lean to rich and work in small steps, allowing the system to stabilize before making further adjustments.

Do not rev the motor with the adjustment wrench in the adjustment hole.

There are several different procedures for adjusting the fuel injection on different-year cars. Consult the Bentley manual for the correct procedure for your car. After making the adjustment, seal the adjustment access hole so air and dirt cannot get in.

If everything is working right, this should do it. Because this adjustment does not often wander too far off the original setting, think twice before making any major changes. If you get completely out of the ballpark, unplug the Lambda sensor and the idle stabilizer (if you have one), and lean out the mixture until the car stumbles, then richen it back up until it runs smoothly. If your car is in good shape, you will hear the difference. Then go back and plug everything in and try again. If you still cannot get it, you may have one or more bad components, and it is time to consult your mechanic.

One technique that might save you a few hours of time is bleeding the air from your fuel injection system. If you have any of the fuel lines apart for any reason, the system may not be able to prime itself once you get everything back together. To purge the air from the system you will need to bridge the fuel pump relay using a jumper wire. With the fuel pump running, reach underneath the airflow housing (you will have to unclip the air filter housing to do this) and push up on the air sensor plate until

you hear gasoline squeaking from the injectors.

Do not get too carried away with this, as you can flood the motor. You need do it only long enough to get the fuel into the injector lines. After that, the fuel injection should be able to clear itself. In a pinch, you can even use this to get your car running again if it vapor locks in the heat.

The two styles of fuel distributor shims.

These dual-sidedraft Solexes look nice and work great. Eurorace

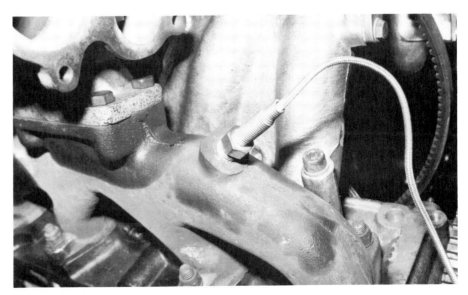

Use the emissions sniffer port for the EGT probe. Techtonics

93

Tweaks

The CIS fuel injection system is so elegant that there is not much you can do to optimize it. The airflow cone is essentially a mechanical computer, and it does a pretty good job of handling fuel delivery for such a simple piece. The best results come from watching what Volkswagen does and then figuring out why. Be suspicious of quick fixes—the K- and KE-Jetronic systems are pretty well dialed in.

If you are more familiar with carburetors than with fuel injection you might want to richen up the mixture to get more gas into the system. This looks simple enough to do: Insert a 3 mm wrench into the CO adjustment access hole and crank away. The only problem is that this adjustment predominantly regulates the idle mixture. The running mixture is governed by the profile of the cone that the airflow sensor plate rides up and down in, as mentioned earlier.

For a while, the rage was shimming the fuel distributor to get the system pressure as high as possible, while using an Audi 5000 warm-up regulator to get the control pressure as low as possible. I spent hours tracking down shims (there are two different styles), installing warm-up regulators and shimming fuel distributors. When I was all done we could only bench race the new setup because we did not have a dyno at our disposal. If we had dyno tested these changes (as Darrell Vittone later did), we would have found that there was no measurable difference between the stock setup and the trick setup. As it was, with the absence of factual information, it was not very difficult to convince ourselves that the car ran faster!

One tweak does seem to work, but it applies only to 1985-and-later cars with the new fuel injection (the one without the warm-up regulator). I stumbled across this on a pair of brand-new cars that Paul and Karl Hacker were racing. The Hackers are extremely competitive and manage to come home winners fairly often, so when they complained that their cars were down on horsepower at high rpm I knew they were not simply making excuses. I went over those cars with a fine-toothed digital voltmeter and a fuel pressure gauge, and found absolutely nothing wrong.

The Hackers finally discovered that in addition to the regular CO adjustment, there was another basic adjustment to the fuel distributor: control plunger height. The only problem is that it is difficult to get to and adjusting it is a cut-and-try procedure.

Here is how it works: Adjust the CO percentage as you normally would. Remove the fuel distributor and measure the distance between the tops of the seating pads (where the fuel distributor sits) and the roller on the airflow sensor plate lever. The distance should be within 0.1 mm of 19 mm.

If it is not, adjust the height by turning the CO percentage adjusting screw until it is. Reinstall the fuel distributor and check to see how much sensor plate clearance (upward movement before the lever contacts the fuel distributor plunger) there is. If the clearance is okay, readjust the CO and idle, and check to see if this has solved your problem. If the clearance is not okay, remove the fuel distributor.

On the bottom of the plunger of the fuel distributor is a slot into which a screwdriver will fit. This is the stop screw of the control plunger. Turning the stop screw clockwise increases the clearance, turning it counterclockwise decreases the clearance. A quarter-turn results in about a 1.3 mm difference in sensor plate position.

Reassemble, readjust the CO percentage and idle speed, and recheck the performance.

Even when this adjustment is perfect, you could still experience poor response. Now, however, you know where to tinker with the adjustments to approach the problem. For example, for lean running you might set the sensor plate at the lower limit in the housing, and set the sensor plate basic adjustment at the tight end of the adjustment to get the control plunger as high into the fuel distributor as possible.

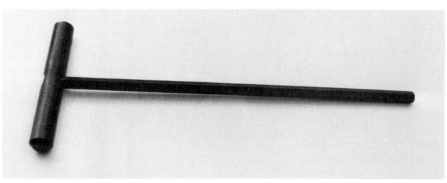

CIS mixture-adjusting wrench.

This throttle body comes pretapped for microswitches.

Another tip for those of you who race is to drill out the screen in the banjo bolt on the inlet side of the fuel distributor (next to the differential pressure regulator). VW Sports recommends that you drive the car for 1,000 miles before you do this, however, and I would not recommend this for any street car.

Throttle bodies

As was covered in the chapter on bolt-on performance, the throttle body works best in combination with other modifications that free up the breathing of the engine. This is because the throttle body is not the source of restriction in the intake tract. In 1985-and-later cars, the stock throttle body is the same as the high-performance or Audi 5000 throttle body. For these cars, the intake manifold was also changed, with longer runners of different shape; the exhaust manifold has over one square inch more area at the outlet end than the previous champ, the Euro GTI exhaust manifold; and the head porting is improved and mated with good-sized valves.

Also note that Volkswagen did not use the single-butterfly throttle body. This was the first aftermarket throttle body for the Volkswagen, but its poor drivability has since proved its undoing.

The proper way of mounting throttle bodies is directly to the intake manifold, but they do not bolt up directly so most are sold with an adapter plate. Unfortunately, with the adapter plate the throttle body will flow only about one percent more air than a stock unit.

This means that to see any improvement you have to remove your intake manifold and match the inlet of the manifold to the outlet of the throttle body. On some manifolds the aluminum is not thick enough to allow the manifold to be hogged out, making it necessary to weld additional metal in the appropriate places.

After all this work, the throttle body will flow between one and two percent more air than the stock unit (at full lift in a big-valve head with a 0.425 inch camshaft). If you are looking for the one big change that will turn your stock car into a road-mauling tire burner, this is not it. If you have exhausted all other possibilities and are looking for incremental gains of any magnitude, read on.

If you are mounting the throttle body on a pre-Lambda car, you will have to disconnect and plug the EGR vacuum line. If you are not sure if your car has EGR or not, look into the throat of the throttle body. If there is a 20 mm restrict-

or on the small side of the throttle body, you have EGR. The restrictor is there to increase the vacuum available to run the EGR system. Later cars without the EGR system did not need this extra vacuum, and the restrictor was eliminated.

If you have a throttle body with a restrictor and want to see if there is anything to be gained by removing the restrictor, there is a trick to removing it. The restrictor is held in by the EGR vacuum port. If you grab the vacuum port with a pair of pliers, you will crush the restrictor. Find a nail that just fits inside the port and insert it before grabbing on with the pliers. This allows you to remove and replace the port without ruining the restrictor. Once you get the

A single-sidedraft carburetor and manifold. Eurorace

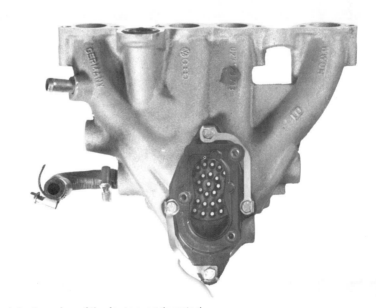

The latest version of the factory carbureted manifold. Note the posts in the plenum area. Eurorace

restrictor out, replace the port and put a rubber vacuum plug over the end to prevent leaks.

When you mount the intake manifold back to the head, be sure you clean all traces of the old gasket from the head. Use gasket remover if you have to. Any vacuum leaks anywhere in the intake tract will rob you of horsepower. If the leak is big enough, the car will not run properly at idle, if at all.

Install the throttle body using the new gaskets that are usually provided with the kit. Connect the throttle linkage with a little slack in it, and ask a friend to push the accelerator fully to the floor while you watch to see that the throttle body is opening up all the way. If it is not opening all the way, tighten the throttle cable. If it is opening all the way but the accelerator is not all the way down, the cable is too tight and must be loosened.

Check to see that all your microswitches (if any) are being properly actuated, and then reconnect everything else. When tightening down the clamps that secure the black plastic intake ducting, remember that the ducting will collapse if you crank down too hard. Take it easy, and only tighten the clamps as far as they need to go. Now set the idle, and you are ready to go.

Intake manifolds
Two-valve manifolds

As just mentioned, the 1985-and-later fuel injection manifolds are of completely different design than the earlier manifolds. On the earlier manifolds the runners can be the most restrictive part of the intake system. This was not discovered for several years, until Darrell Vittone noticed that after a point you could saw the intake manifold plenum in two and the flow would not improve. Provided with this clue, intake manifold porting was born.

The difficulty of intake manifold porting is reflected in the prices that tuners charge for it. The benefits that accrue from manifold porting vary from engine to engine, so you might want to think twice about how much you need those few extra horsepower before deciding to

The Solex found on the 1.8 liter engines is not much better than the old Zenith for high-performance use. Eurorace

The stock 1975-76 Zenith carburetor, vacuum-operated secondaries and all. Eurorace

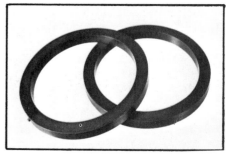

These adapter rings hold the auxiliary venturis in the Webers when velocity stocks can't be used. Eurorace

Injector O-rings must periodically be replaced when they stop sealing effectively.

have your intake manifold opened up. For a ported and polished head with GTI valves and a 0.425 inch camshaft, Darrell found you can expect roughly ten percent more flow through the manifold using the stock throttle body, with roughly five percent more airflow available on top of that when a match-ported aftermarket throttle body is bolted up.

Four-valve manifolds

Although the 16V motor has just been introduced, the press package that accompanied it holds an interesting tidbit of information. Six months before the car was to first appear in the United States, Germany sent Volkswagen of America some samples of the new motor. Volkswagen of America took one look at the dyno sheets and spotted a major problem: The horsepower peak was somewhere between 6500 and 7000 rpm. This might have been great for the Autobahn but it was next to useless in the United States.

To change the torque curve to more closely resemble that of a drivable engine, Volkswagen reduced the size of the intake runners from 50 mm to 40 mm. This picked up the velocity and the low-end torque at the expense of ultimate top-end horsepower.

If you have a 16V motor and have already changed to the European exhaust system and exhaust camshaft, and you still do not have a peaky enough motor, there might be something to gain from bolting up the intake manifold from a non-catalyst-equipped Euro car, as they still use the 50 mm runners for that application.

Air sensor housings

One thing we have learned from Volkswagen is that the small-plate airflow sensors are not the hot tip for pre–1985 high-performance motors. This is something that we have also verified on the dyno. The small airflow sensor housing has a 60 mm plate in place of the 80 mm plate used in the other Volkswagens, so it is easy to see the difference at a glance. If you have a small-plate airflow unit, switch over to a unit with the bigger plate for better results.

Of the big-plate units used in the United States, there are two different versions with slight differences between the two. On the dyno, Darrell Vittone found that the unit with the thinner (3.2 mm) lip around the top made more horsepower in a normally aspirated motor than the unit with the thicker (6.35 mm) lip.

You usually have to remove the air boot to make the identification, although many of the thick-lip units also have a black sticker on the outside that reads "67 K." The thick-lip air sensor plate housing runs a little richer than the thin-lip version, making it a better choice for supercharged motors that need a bit more fuel.

In further tests, Darrell found that even at full chat (full throttle) on the dyno the air sensor plate is not at the maximum height it could be. In other words, the stock injection is good to nearly 170 hp in a normally aspirated motor (Callaway Turbosystems feels safe using the stock CIS injection to only 130 hp in a turbo application). You can check

The threads of the injector housing must be sealed to prevent air leaks.

Intake air for the GTI 16V comes from behind the right headlight.

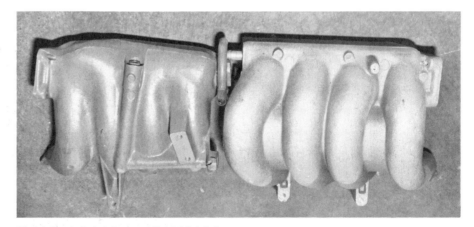

The late-style intake manifold (right) has larger runners compared to earlier units. Autotech

this yourself the same way Darrell did—cut a section out of the boot and replace it with a sturdy piece of clear plastic. This does not necessarily mean there is a lot more fuel waiting to be used. At the extreme end of actuator arm travel there is proportionately less additional fuel available, owing to the geometry of the arm itself.

The early European GTIs had a completely different airflow housing, with steeper walls. This has led some tuners to speculate that it might be possible to develop an inexpensive slip-in plastic insert that would change the fuel flow characteristics for the better. Another possibility is to use a housing from another similar car to get more fuel. An early 924 fuel distributor and airflow housing, for example, is sized to feed a 1.9 liter motor.

Air filters

Some tuners sell low-restriction air filters with the claim that they increase horsepower. Theoretically, this sounds good. If you are considering one, do some back-to-back time/speed runs, first with a paper-element air filter installed and next with the element removed completely. (Do this in an area that is not dusty.) If you find enough of a difference to justify the expense, go for it. However, the results of numerous tests with stock motors, big-displacement motors and turbo motors show no increase in performance with the air filter completely removed, let alone with a different type of filter element in place.

Fuel filters

It is much more critical that you change your fuel filter with fuel injection than with carburetors. The reason lies with the difference in fuel pump output pressure. When the fuel filter in your carbureted car fills up, the engine will starve for fuel and simply stop running. At 4 to 5 psi of fuel pressure, not much will be forced through the dirt-clogged filter.

When the filter in a fuel injection system fills up enough to restrict fuel flow, the pressure differential across the filter can far exceed the total pressure of a carbureted fuel pump's output. This is why you sometimes find trash in the fuel injectors and fuel distributor in spite of the four-micron rating of the Bosch fuel filter.

Unfortunately, there is no way of telling when the fuel filter is full, and it takes only one contaminated tank of gas to fill it up. About the only thing to do is play

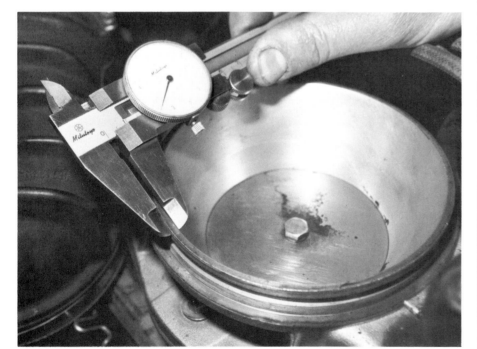

A thick-rim 80 mm fuel distributor. Note the "67 K" decal. Techtonics

A thin-rim 80 mm fuel distributor. Techtonics

The stock 60 mm fuel distributor. Autotech

the odds and change the filter at the 15,000 mile service.

Hot-start problems

All CIS-injected cars can fall prey to the dreaded "hot-start" syndrome. It usually happens on a hot day, and the symptom is that you cannot restart your car twenty to thirty minutes after shutting it off. You can crank and crank and crank, but the car simply needs to cool down before it will go again. If your car was built before 1980, the chances are very good that you have experienced this.

There are several ways of approaching this problem. If you need only an ad hoc solution, you could activate the fuel pump and manually raise the air sensor plate until you hear the fuel squeaking out of the injectors. For more permanent solutions, you can look at both prevention and cures for this problem.

One preventive measure involves lowering the underhood temperatures so the fuel does not cook out of the fuel lines in the first place. This might involve installing a cooler fan switch and an oil cooler. I did both of these on my Scirocco and still had a problem, until I changed to Blueprinted Synthoil 100, at which time the problem was almost totally eliminated.

Curative measures include performing a comprehensive CIS test and fixing whatever you find to be wrong. If everything tests out okay and your car was built before 1980, change over to the Volkswagen part number 431.133.441C fuel accumulator and the injectors to match. (The late-model fuel accumulator holds a higher pressure, and can cause the early-style injectors to leak down. You have to replace both at the same time.) The injectors you are looking for have production numbers higher than 829.

A CIS test of your system after you have installed these parts should reveal a ten-minute leakdown residual pressure of 2.6 bar, and a twenty-minute leakdown residual pressure of 2.4 bar.

If this fails, you can install a hot-start pulse relay kit, available from your Volkswagen dealer. This kit automatically pulses the cold-start injector upon starting to purge the system of fuel vapors. If you have a late-model car and are experiencing starting difficulties, this relay should be checked along with the rest of the CIS system.

A quick alternative would be to wire up an additional ground wire for the cold-start valve, so you could activate the cold-start valve with a button in the passenger compartment whenever you wanted. However, if you elect to cure your hot-start problem this way you may often flood the engine, something that is extremely difficult to do with the stock fuel injection.

Fuel injectors

For best performance, test a batch of injectors for spray pattern and use the ones that have the best misting action. This can take a while because even new-out-of-the-box, many injectors will squirt a stream out of one side of the orifice instead of evenly atomizing the fuel. I am not aware of anyone checking the difference this makes on a dyno, but it is no secret that properly atomized fuel burns much better than liquid fuel droplets.

This is the reason Volkswagen went to the air-shrouded injectors in 1985. By adding another air port behind the injector, it was able to get better mixing of the fuel with the incoming air charge. Unfortunately, the way Volkswagen implemented this change makes it just about impossible to retrofit to an early-model head, and whatever gains there are cannot be worth the cost of changing heads.

Without air-shrouded injectors your motor will run just fine. For that last little bit of performance, however, check the spray pattern and the opening pressure on the injectors you are using. If they look sick (for example, if they are dribbling or streaming), test several new Bosch injectors to get four that all open and close at the same pressures and have nice spray patterns.

If your car has some miles on it, there is a good chance that the fuel injector O-rings have become hardened, and they may be leaking vacuum. This will be noticeable only at idle (and when you are trying to adjust the mixture!), but it must be attended to.

The injector O-rings fit into plastic or metal inserts that are threaded into the head. Remove the inserts, clean them up and replace them with a little sealant on the threads. The old O-rings can become so hardened that you will have to cut them off with side-cutters, but the new ones will slide right on with a little push. The Bentley manual recommends soaking new O-rings in gasoline for a few minutes before installation.

Repairs

The Bosch CIS injection requires special troubleshooting tools and techniques that are beyond the budget of all but the most serious enthusiast. For repairs, then, you often will be dealing with a mechanic.

Not all mechanics were raised on fuel injection, and some do not have the proper tools to work on it. If neither you nor your mechanic can figure out what is going on with your Bosch fuel-injected motor, help is at hand. Bosch has now

In spite of their outward similarities, the Solex on the right is a much newer design than the Weber next to it. Eurorace

established a network of authorized service centers across the United States. The centers must meet minimum requirements for fuel injection test equipment and product knowledge, and can replace components under warranty when needed.

If your car is equipped with Volkswagen's Digijet or Digifant system, go to the dealership for help with repairs.

Converting fuel injection to carburetors

If, for whatever reason, you need to convert from fuel injection to carburetors, there are three main things you must do. The first thing is to replace the fuel pump. The fuel pump for the injected motor puts out over twenty times more pressure than your carburetors will tolerate. Next, get a fuel pressure regulator to keep your carburetor-type fuel pump honest; carburetors are very touchy about the amount of fuel pressure they get. Third, take off all the fuel injection components except the injectors themselves. Leave the injectors in to plug the holes in the head, and make sure you check them for air leaks after you get the carburetors hooked up.

After everything is converted over, keep an eye on the fuel filter. If your fuel injection was contaminated, the junk will still be floating around in the system. Change the filter often enough to keep it clean.

Special fuels and fuel additives

With all the talk about the poor quality of fuel these days, it is not surprising that the market is flooded with octane boosters of every type. Save your money; none of them show any improvement on the dyno.

If you want real gas, you can always drop by the airport and get a load of 100 octane low-lead Avgas. It is expensive and it has lead in it, but if you do not have an oxygen sensor or a catalytic converter, and are running enough compression to make a difference, it is kind of fun to fill up with Avgas on your way to the weekend drag races.

Always buy a name-brand product from a busy station. Most people with fuel contamination problems have, coincidentally, always bought the cheapest gas they could find.

Forced induction

4

When discussing forced induction, many of the experts disagree, sometimes on minor points, sometimes on major ones. And the sparks really fly when a turbocharger expert is in on the same conversation with a supercharger expert.

Forced induction is not necessarily the answer to the question of how to get higher performance, but turbochargers have become very popular. In spite of this, or maybe because of it, there are also some exciting developments in superchargers. Most students of automobile history will recognize this trend as another of a long series of pendulum swings, but it is difficult not to get caught up in the excitement of the moment.

Theory

As air is drawn into the engine by the pressure differential between atmospheric pressure and the vacuum created in the wake of the receding piston, it encounters many impediments such as throttle butterflies, valve guides, valve stems and so on. The air itself also drags along the walls of the intake tract. All of this adds up to a system that is not 100 percent efficient. In some race motors, 100 percent efficiency can be had over a narrow rpm range, but a race motor would be a real handful to coax into a parking space, and rush hour would be very dramatic.

In the effort to improve the volumetric efficiency of the stock motor (the ability of the motor to completely fill the cylinder with air), the traditional hot rod approach is to port and "polish" everything in sight, install a big cam, stick in big valves, bump up the compression and stand back.

If, however, instead of depending on the difference between the ambient air pressure (14.7 psi at sea level, less as altitude increases) and the slight vacuum created by the piston to *suck* air into the cylinder, we were to *shove* air into the motor, it would be less critical to port, polish, cam or valve the engine to get the volumetric efficiency up to where we wanted it.

Supercharging is the generic term used to describe this forced induction of air into the combustion chamber. Forced induction is accomplished with one of two devices, one called a mechanical supercharger and one called an exhaust gas turbocharger. Both of these devices require energy from the motor to run. The increase in horsepower comes because the increased efficiency of the motor more than makes up for the small horsepower loss.

Although forcing more air into the cylinder raises the compression ratio of the motor, this is not the only reason forced induction makes horsepower. In a typical high-compression motor, the piston compresses the air/fuel mixture into the relatively small combustion chamber for ignition. Force-fed motors typically run with lower compression to start with, meaning that when the piston comes up to compress the air/fuel mix-ture it does so into a larger volume. In theory, a low-compression engine, therefore, is a perfect candidate for forced induction because the supercharger will create a high-compression mixture in the larger combustion chamber volume. With more air and fuel to burn, the power stroke will be longer and will make more horsepower than it would with a smaller, equally dense air/fuel mixture in a high-compression motor.

In practice, motors built this way tend to be very peaky in their response. The Porsche 930 is one example. With its low compression and big turbo, low-end response seems nonexistent, but hang onto your hat when the tachometer hits 3500 rpm.

Both forced-induction devices also cause the engine to run hotter. Although there are several reasons for this, the main one is that compressing air also heats it. The more air is compressed the

The G-lader. The inner scroll is on the left at the bottom, the two halves of the outer scroll are at the top, and the twin eccentrics are at the bottom right.

101

hotter it gets, whether you compress it with a turbocharger, a mechanical supercharger or a trash compactor.

You can calculate the approximate theoretical temperature rise before starting if you know in advance how much boost you plan to run. For example, consider a system with six pounds of boost.

The first thing to calculate is the pressure ratio. This is found by adding the amount of boost to the ambient air pressure, and dividing by the ambient air pressure. (For the ambient air pressure at altitudes other than sea level, refer to the chart.)

In this example, taken at sea level, you come up with

$$\frac{14.7 + 6}{14.7} = 1.408$$

With the pressure ratio, you can calculate the temperature increase constant, which is expressed as $r^{0.283}-1$ (the pressure ratio raised to the 0.283 power, minus 1). This gives a temperature increase constant of 0.100.

You also need to know the ambient air temperature in Rankine. Rankine is another temperature scale similar to centigrade and Fahrenheit, only in Rankine water freezes at 491.69 degrees. Fortunately, one degree of temperature change in Rankine is the same as one degree of temperature change in Fahrenheit, so to convert Fahrenheit to Rankine you simply add 459.69 to the temperature in Fahrenheit (it is okay to round it off to 460).

With an ambient air temperature of seventy degrees Fahrenheit, the temperature in Rankine would be 530. Now multiply the ambient temperature by the temperature increase constant to get the approximate theoretical temperature increase:

$$530 \times 0.100 = 53 \text{ degrees Fahrenheit}$$

Notice that the result comes out in degrees Fahrenheit. This means that the outlet temperature of the sample system running six pounds of boost will be fifty-three degrees warmer than when it went in, for a total temperature of 123 degrees Fahrenheit.

You are not done yet, however, because this is the temperature increase under perfect conditions—in other words, with a compressor that is 100 percent efficient. To approximate the temperature rise under real-world conditions, divide the theoretical temperature increase by the compressor efficiency. Using a sixty-five-percent-efficient turbocharger as an example, you get

$$\frac{53}{0.65} = 81.4$$

The calculated real-world increase in temperature is therefore 81.4 degrees, for a calculated real-world outlet temperature of 151.4 degrees. As this example shows, the trend is to higher outlet temperatures as the efficiency of the supercharger decreases.

There are three main reasons why the increase in intake charge temperature is so important. First, a hotter intake charge requires higher octane or a special ignition system to combat detonation. Second, the higher the intake charge the hotter the engine runs, which not only can cook the motor but can also contribute to detonation and preignition. Third,

This is the intercooled Callaway setup for the 1985-and-later model cars.

The IHI (Ishikawajima-Harima Heavy Industries) turbo for the VW has a built-in wastegate.

the hotter the intake charge the lower the density of the air charge—and the whole reason for using forced induction was to have a denser intake charge. Cooling the intake charge is primarily the job of an intercooler, as discussed later.

Turbochargers

Turbochargers utilize exhaust gas to spin a turbine wheel. This turbine wheel connects with a shaft that is connected to a compressor wheel that forces air into the motor. Turbochargers are not the most efficient form of forced induction, but they are near the top with ratings of sixty-five to seventy percent.

Contrary to popular belief, turbochargers do not make free horsepower. To develop boost in a street application, you will see about 2.5 psi of backpressure for every psi of boost. At 6 psi of boost, the backpressure would be 15 psi. If you try to run that much backpressure on a normally aspirated motor, it will choke and die. The turbocharger does not provide free horsepower, but it does manage to overcome its own drive losses.

Turbochargers fall into a class of force inducer called centrifugal compressors. With a centrifugal compressor, the delivery air volume increases as the square of the rotational speed of the impeller. At lower turbine speeds the turbo will make relatively little boost, but at higher turbine speeds it can easily

develop too much. This explains why turbos must be carefully sized to the motor and the application. The lack of boost at lower rpm is sometimes referred to as turbo lag, although this term more properly refers to the amount of time between when the accelerator is opened and when the turbo can pressurize the intake system.

Three factors determine the amount of boost delay in a turbo system. First, it takes a few seconds for the turbine to spin up to speed. And because of the relationship between boost and turbine speed, low speeds mean low boost. Second, when the engine is at idle or low rpm there is not much energy in the exhaust. The velocity is down and the

EGT is low. You may have lots of high-energy exhaust at high rpm, but you sometimes have to wait for the turbo to get to that point. Third, the bigger the pressure drop between the throttle valve and the air-metering unit, the longer the delay. When the throttle is opened suddenly, a pressure wave is created in that area of the intake tract. Until that pressure wave reaches the air-metering unit and everything becomes equalized, the turbo does not know what to do.

If that were the least of a turbocharger's problems, we would all own one. In spite of what anybody tells you, turbochargers, with their peaky adiabatic efficiency graph, are not well suited for automobile use. For example, sup-

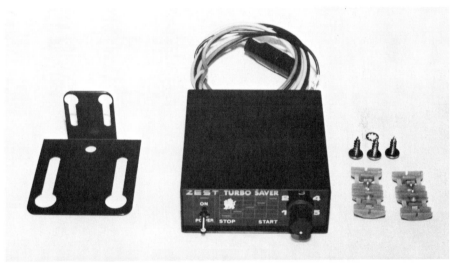

The Zest Turbo Saver is easy to connect, and can be set to keep the engine running up to five minutes to maintain oil flow through the turbo bearings while the housing cools, preventing premature turbo failure.

This is the intercooled Callaway setup for pre-1985 cars.

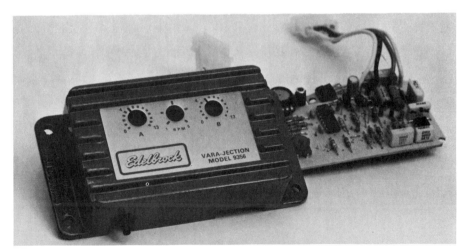

The Edelbrock Vara-Jection water injection has controls for manifold vacuum set point, rpm set point and liquid delivery.

103

pose a turbocharged motor running at 3000 rpm is getting just the right amount of air it needs and the turbine is spinning at X rpm. On accelerating up to 6000 rpm, assume that the turbine speed doubles as well, to 2X rpm. The motor needs twice as much air as it did at 3000 rpm, but the turbine is supplying four times as much air!

These numbers are purely hypothetical, but they are indicative of what happens. There will be rpm ranges when the turbo is supplying too little air, times when it is supplying too much air and times when it supplies the right amount of air. When there is too little air or just the right amount, there is not much that can be (or needs to be) done. When too much air is supplied, the turbo system needs to vent off some of the boost through a safety valve called a wastegate.

A wastegate is installed in all modern street turbo systems to limit the amount of boost to a reasonable level. The wastegate is needed because until someone perfects a variable inlet turbine, all the exhaust gas has to flow through one hole after it leaves the cylinder head and tries to get into the turbocharger housing. The size of that hole is critical to the performance of the turbocharger. If the hole is too large, the exhaust gas velocity will be low and boost will come in only at a higher rpm (as it does in the Porsche 930). The opposite happens if the hole is too small; the boost will come in sooner, but it will run out sooner as well.

Turbo systems are usually designed with the hole a little on the small side. When the backpressure builds up beyond a certain point the wastegate opens, venting much of the heat energy and exhaust gas velocity we hoped the turbo would make use of.

Turbocharger sizing is also a problem. Because of the peakiness of its adiabatic graph, you can size the turbo smaller and get a more linear response (as the rpm climb from low to high) at the expense of ultimate high-rpm power, or you can size the turbo bigger and give up some of your low-rpm drivability. For a street motor, a fair compromise seems to be to run a higher compression to keep the low-rpm response up, and run a big turbocharger timed to deliver maximum flow at the engine's torque peak to augment the high-rpm power.

A variable-inlet turbine housing would address these problems the correct way, letting us get away from the wasteful

The NOS fogger nozzle mounts in a sandwich plate downstream of the throttle body. One of the feed lines is nitrous, the other gasoline. Autotech

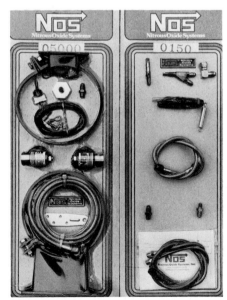

The NOS kit contains all the pieces you need to add 50 hp to your car. Autotech

The extra fuel for the fogger nozzle comes from a tap off the fuel distributor. Autotech

wastegate. Another solution that so far has not been applied to a Volkswagen turbo system is the twin-scroll turbocharger. Although not as efficient as a variable-inlet turbine, it does a much better job of matching the exhaust flow to the needs of the turbine than does a single-scroll unit, and it is much more simple to design than a variable-inlet turbine.

Another problem with turbochargers involves the conditions under which they run. One half of the turbocharger works in the hot exhaust gas stream, while the other half works in the relatively cool intake air stream. With turbine speeds up to and over 100,000 rpm, it is no wonder that turbo bearings and oil seals are prone to failure.

To minimize the negative aspects of exhaust heat, some turbocharger housings incorporate water jackets through which coolant runs. In sophisticated applications, there is even a separate water pump to circulate coolant through the turbo water jacket after the motor has been turned off. Keeping the housing cool goes a long way toward eliminating heat soak, the term used to describe what happens when a red-hot turbo is shut off and the heat cooks the lubricant in the turbo bearing into a dry, hard compound called coke. Coke-covered bearings, oil feed lines and oil drain lines restrict the flow of lubricant vital to the turbo bearing, and turbo failure is quick to follow.

Another key to longevity in a turbo involves cooling the motor off after use. The simplest way is to let the engine sit at idle for five minutes before turning off the key. At idle the exhaust temperature is greatly reduced, giving the turbo housing, the turbo bearing and the engine oil time to stabilize and cool down.

However, few people will spend the five minutes sitting there waiting for the car to cool down. The Zest Turbo Saver is a device that allows the car to idle for a preset period of time, freeing the driver to go on his or her way. Another handy item is the Turboluber, sibling of the Preluber mentioned in the chapter on engines. The Turboluber can be preset to pump engine oil through the turbo for several minutes after the key is turned off, as well as to provide prelubrication on start-up.

The issue of heat is not confined to the turbocharger and the oil. Heads with the exhaust and intake manifolds on the same side are not ideal for turbocharging. Heat from the turbocharger will soak into the head, the valve guides, the valves and the intake manifold on both sides, and nothing can be done about it. (Maybe this is one of the reasons Volkswagen gave up on turbochargers and switched over to mechanical superchargers.)

One final oiling consideration on the turbocharger unit is that the Volkswagen motor can produce extreme oil pressure when started on a cold morning with thick oil in the crankcase. This high pressure can and will blow out turbocharger oil seals. The feed line to the turbocharger must have a properly sized restrictor in it to prevent this from happening.

The placement of the turbocharger is pretty much fixed in the Volkswagen because of space and other considerations. A custom exhaust manifold allows it and the wastegate to hang off the back of the motor. This turns out to be a good location, as the turbo response is best when the turbo is close to the source of the hot, fast-moving exhaust gases that spin the turbine.

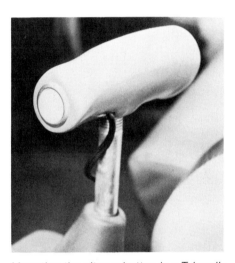

Mounting the nitrous button in a T-handle like this makes it very convenient to squeeze in a little more horsepower. Autotech

A boost gauge does more than keep you entertained while you drive. Problems with idle vacuum or boost leaks are immediately indicated, saving troubleshooting time. Autotech

The poly-V belt that Autotech uses on its supercharger not only provides positive drive to the blower, it also makes it easier to vary the blower drive ratio than with a cogged belt and sprocket. Autotech

The tricky part is plumbing the pressure side of the turbocharger. When running an intercooler and all of its associated piping, the engine compartment can become crowded.

Superchargers

Mechanical superchargers pressurize air to gain the same effect as the turbocharger, but there are some big differences between the two.

Mechanical superchargers (also known as blowers) utilize direct drive to spin their impellers, usually in the form of a belt run off the crankshaft or camshaft. There are many more types of mechanical supercharger than there are turbocharger, with three different types available for the Volkswagen.

All positive-displacement mechanical superchargers deliver roughly the same amount of air per engine revolution. This makes it relatively easy to size the blower to the needs of the motor with-

out having to rely on a wastegate. Another aid to correct sizing is that once you are close, you can vary the ratio between the drive sprocket and the driven sprocket. As a side benefit to this correct sizing, throttle response across the rpm range is far more linear than with a turbocharged motor.

The poly-V belt. Autotech

The nitrous oxide system can also be set to turn on automatically at a preset rpm in racing applications. Autotech

The Autotech supercharger installed, with the added touch of an NOS system. Autotech

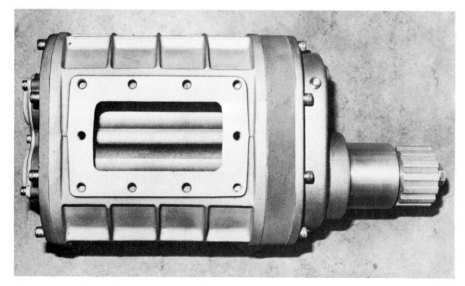

A close-up of the Magnacharger with an early-style cogged gear. Autotech

Although I have not yet heard of one being used in a Volkswagen, this AiResearch turbo has a water cooling jacket to cut down on turbo bearing failures.

Blown motors will benefit from head flow work and from free-flow exhaust systems. Stay away from radical camshafts, however, as a long overlap period will allow the blower to push the incoming air/fuel mixture right out the exhaust valve without waiting for it to be burned. The Volkswagen supercharger (discussed later) uses a camshaft with far less overlap than you will find in a normally aspirated motor. (A more complete discussion of supercharger camshafts can be found in chapter 2.)

All the mechanical superchargers available for the Volkswagen are positive-displacement types, meaning that in theory the same amount of air is delivered to the engine per revolution regardless of speed. The most common type of mechanical supercharger is the Roots design, which runs thirty-five to sixty percent efficient. The Magnacharger unit used in the Autotech supercharger is an example of this type.

One ramification of this design is that at higher altitudes a supercharger will not produce as much boost as a turbocharger. A supercharger provides the same percentage of boost; a turbocharger provides the same amount of boost, plus it benefits from the lower density of the ambient air.

To illustrate, David Singer of General Motors found that when a supercharger and a turbocharger were both calibrated to a pressure ratio of 1.4 and were taken to an altitude of 3,650 feet, (at Warren, Michigan), the supercharger maintained its forty-three percent pressure increase. The turbocharger pressure increase climbed to seventy-one percent. However, running more boost hastened the onset of detonation.

The Roots blower has two- or three-lobe straight or curved impellers to shove the air into the motor. (The Autotech blower uses three straight-lobe rotors.) Because of its design, even if a Roots blower were as efficient as a turbocharger, it would still heat the air more. How is this possible?

A Roots blower is a constant-volume supercharger. Air enters the Roots blower at atmospheric presure. The lobes carry the air around the inside of the blower housing and deposit it in the intake manifold *without* changing the air pressure. Air compression starts only when the "new arrivals" find out there is too much air in the intake tract already.

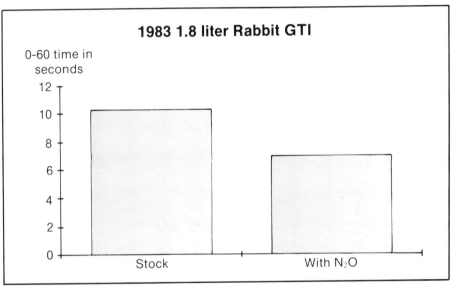

Adding nitrous to an engine can drastically improve your acceleration.

Pressure ratio	Turbocharger			Compressor efficiency					
	40	50	55	60	65	70	75	80	85
1.00	70	70	70	70	70	70	70	70	70
1.05	88.4	84.7	83.4	82.3	81.3	80.5	79.8	79.2	78.7
1.10	106.2	99.0	96.3	94.1	92.3	90.7	89.3	88.1	87.0
1.15	123.4	112.7	108.9	105.6	102.9	100.5	98.5	96.7	95.1
1.20	140.1	126.1	121.0	116.7	113.2	110.1	107.4	105.1	103.0
1.25	156.3	139.1	132.8	127.5	123.1	119.3	116.0	113.2	110.6
1.30	172.1	151.7	144.2	138.0	132.8	128.3	124.4	121.0	118.0
1.35	187.4	163.9	155.4	148.3	142.2	137.1	132.6	128.7	125.2
1.40	202.3	175.8	166.2	158.2	151.4	145.6	140.6	136.1	132.3
1.45	216.8	187.5	176.8	167.9	160.4	153.9	148.3	143.4	139.1
1.50	231.0	198.8	187.1	177.3	169.1	162.0	155.9	150.5	145.8
1.55	244.9	209.9	197.2	186.6	177.6	169.9	163.3	157.4	152.3
1.60	258.4	220.7	207.0	195.6	185.9	177.7	170.5	164.2	158.7
1.65	271.6	231.3	216.6	204.4	194.1	185.2	177.5	170.8	164.9
1.70	284.6	241.7	226.0	213.0	202.0	192.6	184.4	177.3	171.0
1.75	297.2	251.8	235.3	221.5	209.8	199.9	191.2	183.6	176.9
1.80	309.7	261.7	244.3	229.8	217.5	206.9	197.8	189.8	182.8
1.85	321.8	271.5	253.1	237.9	225.0	213.9	204.3	195.9	188.5
1.90	333.8	281.0	261.8	245.8	232.3	220.7	210.7	201.9	194.1
1.95	345.5	290.4	270.4	253.7	239.5	227.4	216.9	207.7	199.6
2.00	357.0	299.6	278.7	261.3	246.6	234.0	223.1	213.5	205.1

This chart shows the calculated temperature of the intake charge for a turbocharger when the ambient temperature is 70 degrees Fahrenheit. As you can see, the intake charge temperature is more sensitive to compressor efficiency than it is to pressure ratio, so doubling the efficiency of the turbocharger means you can double the boost pressure and get less temperature gain.

Parameter	Supercharger	Turbocharger
Performance	=	=
Octane requirement	=	=
Emissions	✓	
Response	✓	
Exhaust temperature	✓	
Fuel economy	=	=
Altitude performance		✓

Superchargers are inherently better for a street-driven gasoline engine than for a turbocharger. One factor not shown here is wear. A Magnacharger is a low-wear device, and the G-lader reportedly is extremely wear-free. Turbos don't wear out too much, but with the heat they generate they do break. Turbos do make more boost at altitude, but this is not necessarily a plus.

The high-pressure air in the intake tract constantly tries to escape back out the way it came in, past the rotors that are dumping in ever more unpressurized air. As a result, the air in the intake tract is beaten back and forth by the rotors, creating additional heat. Instead of the temperature increase constant being $r^{0.283}-1$, it is closer to $r^{0.4}-1$ (remember that r is the pressure ratio, as described earlier).

This higher temperature increase constant was derived in tests done years ago with straight two-lobe rotors; there appears to have been little testing of modern Roots designs utilizing better materials and construction techniques, and three-lobe rotors. However, this temperature increase constant can be used to illustrate the point. As the accompanying chart shows, a difference in the temperature increase constant makes a difference in the amount of heat in the intake air charge.

In theory, the positive-displacement blower delivers the same amount of air to the engine for each revolution. This is not completely true, because as the speed of the blower increases from 2000 rpm to 10,000 rpm, the *volumetric* efficiency rises from about forty percent to about sixty percent as a result of gains from moving the air at a higher velocity. So even though you have some boost at 1500 rpm the instant you put your foot down, you still see maximum boost at maximum rpm.

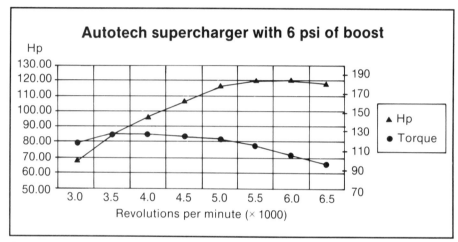

Shown here is the horsepower and torque curve for the 1.8 liter Autotech supercharged Golf, with 6 psi of boost.

Pressure ratio	Supercharger			Compressor efficiency					
	40	50	55	60	65	70	75	80	85
1.00	70.0	70.0	70.0	70.0	70.0	70.0	70.0	70.0	70.0
1.05	96.1	90.9	89.0	87.4	86.1	84.9	83.9	83.0	82.3
1.10	121.5	111.2	107.4	104.3	101.7	99.4	97.4	95.7	94.2
1.15	146.1	130.9	125.4	120.8	116.9	113.5	110.6	108.1	105.8
1.20	170.2	150.1	142.9	136.8	131.7	127.2	123.4	120.1	117.1
1.25	193.6	168.9	159.9	152.4	146.1	140.6	135.9	131.8	128.2
1.30	216.5	187.2	176.6	167.7	160.2	153.7	148.1	143.3	139.0
1.35	238.9	205.1	192.8	182.6	173.9	166.5	160.1	154.4	149.5
1.40	260.8	222.6	208.7	197.2	187.4	179.0	171.7	165.4	159.8
1.45	282.2	239.8	224.3	211.5	200.6	191.3	183.2	176.1	169.9
1.50	303.2	256.5	239.6	225.4	213.5	203.2	194.4	186.6	179.7
1.55	323.7	273.0	254.5	239.2	226.1	215.0	205.3	196.9	189.4
1.60	343.9	289.1	269.2	252.6	238.6	226.5	216.1	206.9	198.9
1.65	363.7	305.0	283.6	265.8	250.7	237.8	226.6	216.8	208.2
1.70	383.1	320.5	297.7	278.7	262.7	248.9	237.0	226.6	217.4
1.75	402.2	335.8	311.6	291.5	274.4	259.8	247.2	236.1	226.3
1.80	421.0	350.8	325.3	304.0	286.0	270.6	257.2	245.5	235.2
1.85	439.5	365.6	338.7	316.3	297.4	281.1	267.0	254.7	243.9
1.90	457.6	380.1	351.9	328.4	308.5	291.5	276.7	263.8	252.4
1.95	475.5	394.4	364.9	340.3	319.5	301.7	286.3	272.7	260.8
2.00	493.1	408.5	377.7	352.1	330.4	311.8	295.7	281.6	269.1

Here is shown the calculated temperature of the intake charge for a supercharger when the ambient temperature is 70 degrees Fahrenheit. Although these figures were arrived at using a two-lobe straight Roots blower, virtually any compressor that does not have internal compression will create more heat in the intake charge than one that does.

This instantaneous boost is what makes blowers so nice to drive. Volkswagen did a study in which two engines of equal displacement were compared. One was equipped with a turbocharger and the other with a supercharger. Both engines made 88 hp at 6000 rpm and 110 lb-ft of torque at 3700 rpm, but the supercharger-equipped engine produced 96 lb-ft of torque at 2000 rpm while the turbocharged engine produced only 70 lb-ft of torque. This test showed that the supercharger-equipped engine responded to abrupt full-throttle acceleration in one-third of the time taken by the turbocharged engine. The study also showed that at least ninety percent of maximum torque was available from 2500 to 6000 rpm.

Another benefit of blowers is that the exhaust tract is essentially untouched, and there is no extra backpressure to deal with. This may not be a cause for much concern for individual hot rodders, but for a manufacturer like Volkswagen it means that existing emissions technology will work with only minor modifications.

The lack of backpressure in a supercharged motor brings up another plus: Positive work is carried out on the piston during the intake cycle. As the air is forced into the motor it both relieves the piston of the job of pulling in the fresh air/fuel charge and helps push the piston along. This phenomenon is not as strong with a turbocharger, which is why the supercharger is said to have a positive gas exchange loop while the turbocharger has a negative gas exchange loop.

If superchargers are so good, why aren't they used in more forms of racing? There are three answers to that. First, when building a street machine we are not necessarily concerned with what is done in a race machine, because there are lots of techniques racers use that simply do not work in a street rod.

For the second reason, consider a Formula 1 engine needing 43 psi of boost. A Roots blower is not going to do the trick because in spite of its flat adiabatic graph with respect to speed, as boost pressure increases, efficiency plummets. The limit appears to be approximately 14 psi of boost, however, which is more than enough for a street machine. That is why Formula 1 engines make use of special turbochargers that develop 1 psi of boost for every 0.75 psi of backpressure. You will never see a turbocharger that efficient on a street vehicle.

The third reason has to do with heat. A turbocharger dumps a lot of heat into the oil, and a supercharger does not. In a motor that is run continuously for most of its life, this heat can be dealt with. A street car does not run continuously, and when the motor is shut down that heat must be allowed to escape. Race motors

Altitude in ft	Altitude in mi	HP
0	0.00	100
328.1	0.06	99.00
656.2	0.12	98.01
984.2	0.19	97.03
1312.3	0.25	96.06
1640.4	0.31	95.10
1968.5	0.37	94.15
2296.6	0.43	93.21
2624.6	0.50	92.27
2952.7	0.56	91.35
3280.8	0.62	90.44
3608.9	0.68	89.53
3937.0	0.75	88.64
4265.0	0.81	87.75
4593.1	0.87	86.87
4921.2	0.93	86.01
5249.3	0.99	85.15
5577.4	1.06	84.29

For every 300 feet in altitude you lose one percent of your horsepower.

Altitude in feet	Air pressure in PSI	Altitude in meters
0	14.7	0
656	14.3	200
1000	14.2	305
1641	13.9	500
2000	13.7	610
3000	13.2	914
3281	13.0	1000
4000	12.7	1219
5000	12.2	1524
6000	11.8	1829
6562	11.5	2000
7000	11.3	2134

As you go up in altitude, the air pressure drops. If it drops too much you might feel you need forced induction for day-to-day driving, let alone high performance.

Pressure ratio	Turbocharger factor	Supercharger factor
1.10	0.027	0.039
1.15	0.040	0.057
1.20	0.053	0.076
1.25	0.065	0.093
1.30	0.077	0.111
1.35	0.089	0.128
1.40	0.100	0.144
1.45	0.111	0.160
1.50	0.122	0.176
1.55	0.132	0.192
1.60	0.142	0.207
1.65	0.152	0.222
1.70	0.162	0.236
1.75	0.172	0.251
1.80	0.181	0.265
1.85	0.190	0.279
1.90	0.199	0.293
1.95	0.208	0.306
2.00	0.217	0.320

Assuming the theoretical factors are accurate, you can see the difference in the intake charge temperature multiplier between a compressor with internal compression and one without.

This is the setup for some serious breathing: a supercharger atop a 10.0:1 16V Scirocco motor. With 6 psi of boost this car makes close to 180 hp and runs to 60 mph in the low seven-second range. Bellevue Motor Sports

	3.0	3.5	4.0	4.5	5.0	5.5	6.0	6.5
Torque	117	127	127	124	122	115	105	95
HP	66.86	84.67	96.76	106.29	116.19	120.48	120.00	117.62

Here is a comparison between horsepower and torque of a 1983-84 GTI 1.8 with an Autotech supercharger with 6 psi of boost.

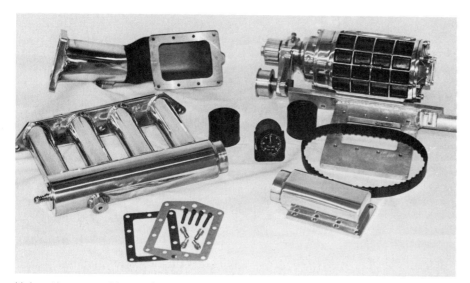

Using the same Magnacharger blower found in Autotech's kit, Dennis Bryden fabricated the rest of the pieces to fit the 16V induction system. Bellevue Motor Sports

It looks complicated but the kit goes together very quickly. Autotech

are also rebuilt much more often than street motors, so longevity must be taken into consideration as well.

The Autotech supercharger

The Autotech supercharger works just the way you would expect a supercharger to work—as it should considering how much time and effort Autotech has invested in putting together its kit. Unlike blowers for many American cars, the Autotech blower runs dry (in other words, it pumps only air instead of air and fuel). This gives it eight to eleven percent better power because fuel increases the density of the air, creating drag within the compressor housing. The Autotech blower also uses hollow rotors for lower rotational inertia. This blower requires so little horsepower at full boost that the small Woodruff keys holding the cam belt sprockets to the crankshaft and camshaft in the early cars are strong enough to drive the blower without shearing off.

Autotech now uses a poly-V belt instead of the cogged belt found in its early kits. This allows more leeway in sizing the driven pulley on the supercharger to set the boost pressure. The stock system comes with a 1.4:1 pulley setup that makes 8 psi of boost, and replacement pulleys are available up to 1.6:1 to make 12 psi of boost. Although Autotech recommends running low compression (8.5:1) with its blower, Griffin Motor Werke in Berkeley uses the Autotech blower setup with 16V motors running 10.0:1 compression.

One nice feature of the Magnason blower Autotech uses is that of all the mechanical supercharger designs, it is

The sneeze valve as installed on Autotech's blower manifold.

the best autorotator. In other words, when the blower is not making boost, the engine vacuum is enough to cause the rotors to rotate on their own. This reduces the load on the blower bearings, the drive belt and other components. Autorotation helps because even the heaviest lead-foot is going to be in boost only ten percent of the time or less. The other 90 percent of the time you are not using the blower.

The Magnacharger's straight lobes may be noisier, but its design is efficient enough at autorotating that the car can be driven with the belt off (although performance would suffer).

The Volkswagen G-lader

The G-lader blower design is slated to appear in the next generation of Volkswagens (scheduled for release in 1989). The G is for the shape of the unit, and *lader* is the German word for blower. The G-lader (or G-charger, as it is also called) is based on a steam engine design that was patented in 1906. As a steam engine it never succeeded, but as a supercharger it does quite well.

While G-lader is the generic name, the actual article comes in different sizes. The version that is fitted to the Polo in Europe is called the G-40. This stands for a G-lader with a 40 mm scroll. The G-60 unit expected in the United States by 1989 is the same G shape with 60 mm deep scrolls.

These scrolls do the same job as the lobed rotors found in the Roots blower. The inner scroll is moved relative to the outer scroll by means of a dual eccentric drive. The motion described by the inner scroll alternately uncovers the intake port to take in air at atmospheric pressure and then uncovers the outlet port for the discharge cycle.

Because the air feed is essentially constant, only weak pulsations occur on the intake of the supercharger, thus keeping noise to a minimum. The soft openings and closings also eliminate heavy pulsations in the intake tract. Because of the shortness of the scrolls, the G-lader has no internal compression. This makes the G-lader a high-volume, low-pressure device.

Still, the G-lader can make 0.8 bar of boost, and it does so fairly efficiently. When working at 0.5 bar of boost, efficiency is rated at sixty-five percent. This is further enhanced by the intercooler that drops the intake charge temperature 131 degrees Fahrenheit.

The G-lader currently runs seventy-two percent overdrive, for a supercharger speed of just over 10,000 rpm at an engine redline of 6000 rpm. Maximum speed for the G-lader is 13,000 rpm.

Extended testing by Volkswagen showed that the internal engine components were adequate for the fifty percent additional power. For reasons of reliability, however, the supercharged engine uses special top piston rings and sodium-filled exhaust valves. The basic compression ratio is set at 8.0:1. European versions use the Heron head.

As an autorotator, the G-lader is quite poor. Volkswagen designed around this

For the early cars with warm-up regulators, Autotech fools the Audi Turbo unit on the left into supplying the extra fuel the motor needs.

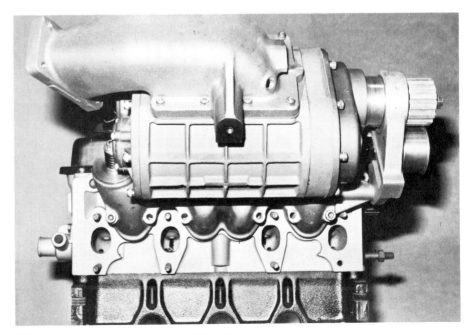

Off comes the stock intake manifold, on goes the blower. This is almost easy enough to be classified as a bolt-on. Autotech

by including a feedback loop that returns the output of the G-lader back to the inlet side when there is no demand for the extra power. This does reduce the power demand from the engine, but it also gives the intake air charge more time to pick up heat from the compressor.

The Sprintex/Lysholm blower

One exciting development in mechanical superchargers is the appearance of the Sprintex supercharger. The Sprintex (also a positive-displacement device) is based on the old Lysholm compressor that is capable of very high efficiency operation. The main problem with the Lysholm design has been that until now machining and manufacturing the unit were so expensive that it was impractical for automotive use.

The rotors used in the Lysholm compressor are complex. The male rotor has four lobes on it, and the female rotor has six flutes. The rotors are twisted so that as the lobes and flutes mesh, the intake air is gradually squeezed into a smaller and smaller volume.

Sprintex developed a method for machining the rotors in two minutes instead of forty-five minutes, and at a lower cost as well. Like the turbocharger, the Sprintex features internal compression. In other words, unlike in a Roots blower or G-lader, the air begins to be pressurized in the unit itself rather than in the intake manifold only.

The Sprintex S82 is a compact unit, measuring 11×7×5 inches, with the air intake on the end of the housing for easy mounting. One characteristic of the Lysholm compressor is that higher efficiencies come with larger units. The specifications sheet on the Model S82 shows that it is just under fifty percent efficient at a pressure ratio of 1.6, and just over fifty percent efficient at a pressure ratio of 2.0. This puts it between the Roots and the G-lader in terms of efficiency. It is, however, a miserable autorotator, so it will also need some kind of by-pass. Owing to the internal compression of the Sprintex, the heat gain from recirculating the air is more of a factor than with the G-lader.

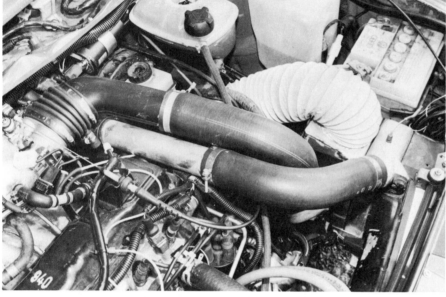

For a while, VW was experimenting with turbocharging, but then scrapped the project in favor of supercharging.

The European 1.3 liter Polo with the 40 mm G-lader supercharger.

Fuel enrichment

Under boost, the supercharged motor needs a lot more fuel than a normally aspirated motor. The CIS injection supplies adequate fuel for the additional horsepower a blower demands up to about 130 hp, but it can run short in a higher-performance motor. Back in the early days we rigged up switches in parallel with the cold-start enrichment system, but this was crude and experimental.

When using K- and KE-Jetronic injection, it is virtually impossible to add on an auxiliary fuel injector that works properly. The Callaway Microfueler, for example, provides more of an approximation of what the engine needs than an exactly metered fuel charge. This might sound inefficient, but it seems to work well enough for most street rod applications.

Autotech has gone a different path with its fuel enrichment system by tricking the injection into supplying the fuel through the stock injectors. If fuel enrichment is ever going to be done right, this is certainly a good start. The turbocharged Porsches and Audis do not use supplementary fuel enrichment devices, relying instead on the built-in ability of the CIS to deliver the fuel. Although the Autotech system is neither as sophisticated nor as costly as the factory setup, it does get the fuel into the engine.

For the K-Jetronic blower kit, Autotech uses an Audi 5000 Turbo warm-up regulator, which it has plumbed to produce rapid response to changes in manifold vacuum and pressure. For the KE-Jetronic, Autotech has developed an add-in circuit board and pressure sensor for continuously variable modification of the control pressure through the differential pressure regulator. This unit is also available from Autotech for other forced-induction systems needing fuel enrichment.

One unit that looks promising is the Arkay Turbo unit. This unit suffers from the same problem as the Callaway Microfueler in terms of approximating the fuel needs of the motor, but it has the additional capability to control a water injection unit, and it also controls boost retard electronically.

With any system, it is difficult to provide proper fuel enrichment. If you are putting together your own system or if you run into problems, you will need to dyno test and take EGT readings to get everything straightened out, and even then you might not find a solution.

Things are not as bleak as they seem, however. Although you can easily run a motor into meltdown on the dyno by keeping it in boost for several minutes, in real life you will be lucky to stay in boost more than a few seconds at a time. This is one reason why fuel enrichment systems that seem all wrong theoretically can provide a sufficient margin of safety for street applications.

One rumor about supercharged CIS motors is that the CIS cannot supply the fuel needed by the motor because the fuel pressure to the injectors is kept at a constant, while the boost pressure rises. The example usually given is that if you had 6 psi of fuel pressure and 6 psi of boost the pressure differential across the injector would be zero, so you would get no flow. Although this is an extreme example, if it were true it would mean that the fuel injection's ability to operate gets worse at the precise time the motor needs fuel the most.

As it turns out, this is not the case. The dynamics of injecting a fluid into a gas are fairly complex, but suffice to say that because air is compressible and fuel is not, the injectors will work fine at any boost level you are likely to see.

A basic rule of thumb for figuring this out is as follows:

$$\frac{\text{Manifold pressure}}{\text{fuel pressure}} < 0.5$$

For this formula to work, both manifold pressure and fuel pressure must be expressed in terms of absolute pressure (psia), or the measured pressure plus the

For a while, GMP was marketing a Roots supercharger setup. Included in the price of the kit was a complete engine rework for reliability.

Callaway offers its Stage 1 turbocharger without an intercooler, which makes a very trim package when installed.

The GMP kit includes an intercooler. The special fuel distributor is at the bottom of the photo, and the piece at the lower right is a by-pass valve . . . a very advanced setup in early 1986.

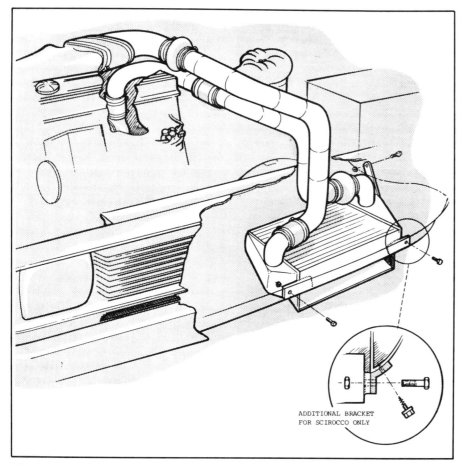

ADDITIONAL BRACKET FOR SCIROCCO ONLY

The Callaway intercooler for turbo cars with air conditioning.

atmospheric pressure. At sea level, the atmospheric pressure is 14.7 psi, so if you have a boost (manifold) pressure of 7 psi, adding 14.7 psi gives you 20.7 psia. For fuel pressure, CIS runs at a minimum of 68 psi. Adding 14.7 psi gives you 82.7 psia. This works out to

$$\frac{21.7}{82.7} = 0.26$$

This is well under the 0.5 limit. As long as you keep the boost-pressure-to-fuel-pressure ratio under 0.5, the amount of boost will have no appreciable effect on fuel delivery. Above 0.5, the relationship is not linear, so this formula will no longer approximate the effect of a lower pressure differential across the injector.

In the example with 6 psi of fuel pressure and 6 psi of boost, the formula tells you that the ratio is 1, meaning no flow. In real life the injector would still work, although less efficiently. Playing with the numbers a little, you can determine that the stock CIS fuel injection is good to 27 psi of boost in this respect. Of course, with that much boost you have lots of other things to consider.

While on the subject of fuel delivery, one thing to watch out for on fuel-injected cars with superchargers of any kind is that the fuel injectors are held in the heads by nothing more than the friction of the rubber fuel injector O-ring. Under lots of boost or during a backfire, the injectors can be popped out of their holders. With the resulting massive air leak, the car will run very poorly at low rpm, although it sometimes will smooth out at higher rpm as the percentage of air leaking into the system becomes small compared with the overall volume of air. If your car exhibits poor running at low rpm (such as at idle), check to see that the injectors are fully seated. (See the discussion on fuel injector O-rings in chapter 3.)

Ignition

Even if you are running a low-compression engine and do not get carried away with the boost, you must have some way of backing down the ignition advance under boost. Force-inducted motors can melt down in minutes from detonation.

The easiest way to control the advance is to route your vacuum hoses so that under boost the ignition timing progressively becomes more retarded. This is accomplished by connecting a manifold port to the advance side of the distributor vacuum can (the vacuum can must also have a retard side port so it can breathe). When the supercharger is not producing boost, you will have some vacuum advance. As you roll into boost the advance will gradually go away, eventually being replaced by retard.

Make sure you use hose clamps on all vacuum fittings, or the boost will blow them right off.

Intercoolers

If you are pumping 6 psi of boost or less into a motor with less than 8.5:1 compression, you can get by without an intercooler. Those of you with more boost or more compression, read on.

An intercooler sits between the turbo or supercharger and the cylinder head, and cools the intake charge. There is a price for this feature, and it is called pressure drop. Proper intercooler sizing and construction will minimize pressure drop.

Intercoolers also have efficiency ratings, just like everything else. If you used an eighty percent efficient intercooler in the turbo system in the preceding example, the intercooler would remove eighty percent of the heat above ambient temperature from the system. The calculations look like this:

$$(151.4 - 70) \times 0.8 = 81.4 \times 0.8 = 65.12$$
$$151.4 - 65.12 = 86.28 \text{ degrees Fahrenheit}$$

This works out to a substantial drop in intake charge temperature due to the intercooler. An intercooler must be at least seventy percent efficient and have a pressure drop of less than 2.5 psi to be worth the trouble of mounting it. Otherwise, your car will be just as fast or faster without it.

The mathematics that prove this are involved, but basically they show that in a typical street turbocharger system, for each additional psi of boost you will add roughly eighteen degrees Fahrenheit to the intake air temperature. If you lose 3 psi of pressure and you need 6 psi in the intake, you will have to make 9 psi of boost at the turbo outlet.

That 3 psi of extra boost is going to cost you fifty-four degrees Fahrenheit of additional temperature in the intake charge. If the intercooler is less than seventy percent efficient, it will not be able to remove enough of that additional heat

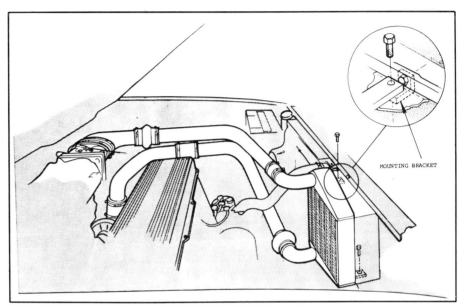

The Callaway intercooler for turbo cars without air conditioning.

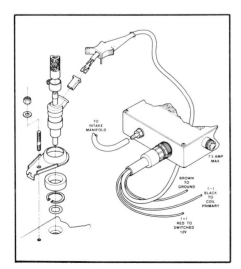

Callaway's fuel enrichment device, the Microfueler.

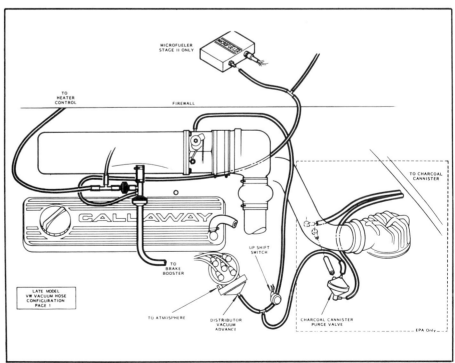

The routing of the vacuum lines for the Callaway turbocharger kit.

to keep the charge density from being thinner than it would be on a system that has less restriction, and thus less heat, in the intake tract to begin with. However, since superchargers do not have this problem with backpressure, even an inefficient intercooler is better than nothing. You just have to find room to put one.

The simplest intercooler to plumb in is the air-to-air intercooler, in which ambient air carries the heat away from the intercooler as the heat is picked up from the intake charge.

Cartech in Texas has had some interesting experiences with air-to-water intercoolers, in which a separate cooling system is used instead of air to cool the intercooler. An air-to-water intercooler

Too much boost with too little octane. The top ring was completely gone. Techtonics

is much more complex to install, but because of the superior thermal reserve of the water the unit can be much smaller. The water has a far greater ability to transfer heat away from the intercooler surface than does air, leading to increased intercooler efficiencies.

One fallacy about intercoolers used with turbochargers is that if there is a loss across the intercooler, you can make up for it with more boost. This is not the way it works. For every pound of boost, your backpressure must increase by 2 to 2.5 psi. This is known as fighting a losing battle. It helps to not have the loss in the first place.

Water injection

Water injection is an idea that never really caught on because of the maintenance it requires.

Here is how it works: The water that enters the combustion chamber acts to boost octane because it does not burn. (Remember that octane is the rating of a fuel's ability to resist compressive detonation. That's why EGR increases octane, too.) It also expands when turned to steam by the heat of the gasoline being ignited, which helps force the piston downward. As it changes from water to steam, it absorbs heat out of the combustion chamber, which helps lower the temperature there. And it will help clean the combustion chamber of carbon buildup and then keep it clean.

Water injection is so effective that you will get more power from it than you would from injecting an equal amount

of extra gasoline. If you inject too much water, however, it will cool the combustion process too much, robbing you of power.

The correct way to connect water injection (so it works under periods of low vacuum) is to have a pressure-sensitive switch controlling a water pump and an rpm sensor to tell the water injection how much water is needed. When the switch detects that the manifold vacuum has risen to a certain level, it should turn on the pump.

As mentioned earlier, water injection does have a couple of drawbacks. Unlike an intercooler, water injection requires that you keep water in the tank. The better units have a water level warning control, but you still have to stop and fill up. Also unlike an intercooler, water injection puts a lot of extra water into the motor. Some of this water can find its way into the crankcase (accelerating sludge formation); some of it can attack the rings, valves, valve seats and exhaust system (hot metal oxidizes faster than metal at ambient temperature); and some of it can attack the aluminum of the head.

To my knowledge there is only one company making a water injection unit that addresses these and other questions, and that is Edelbrock.

Nitrous oxide

Nitrous oxide, or N_2O, is also used to increase the density of the intake air charge, only in a radically different way. N_2O provides an instant, neck-snapping acceleration. A conservative nitrous oxide system that can be operated in complete

The guts of a turbocharger. The compressor side is on the left, turbine on the right. This one got too hot, and the turbine-side bearing was damaged. Techtonics

Oil return line from the turbocharger. Eurorace

safety (as far as the engine components are concerned) will add 50 to 60 hp on a 100 hp engine.

N_2O is sold bottled under high pressure. As it is released into the intake system, the nitrous oxide expands. In the process of expanding, there is a pronounced cooling effect due to the latent heat of vaporization as the nitrous changes states from liquid to vapor. This in turn rapidly cools the intake charge, making it much denser. In a normally aspirated motor, the temperature drop is around fifty degrees Fahrenheit. In a supercharged motor, the temperature drop can be up to 100 degrees Fahrenheit.

The purpose of injecting nitrous oxide is not to get more fuel into the cylinder. What you are after with nitrous is the oxygen. As you may remember from science class, combustion that involves pure oxygen is extremely violent. The nitrogen in nitrous oxide acts as a buffer, releasing the oxygen at a more gradual rate. Therefore, nitrous oxide is actually better for our purposes than pure oxygen.

With all this extra oxygen, you also need to augment the amount of fuel entering the motor. It is critical that the motor *never* be allowed to go lean when using N_2O. Not ever. Not even for a little while (The pistons and piston rings would melt in the resultant detonation!).

The traditional method of introducing nitrous into the engine utilizes a plate that bolts up between the throttle body and the intake manifold. The plate holds two tubes, one that meters nitrous into the intake and one that meters gasoline to keep the motor from going lean.

This is a great way to melt down the number 3 and 4 pistons on an early car. The Volkswagen intake manifold is described in the parts list as an "air distributor." This manifold was never meant to carry fuel. When you hit the nitrous button, the air mixture rushing into the manifold suddenly has to share its limited space with the nitrous and the gasoline.

On top of that, the gasoline molecules are heavier than the air or the nitrous molecules, so their momentum tends to carry them toward the end of the intake plenum that feeds the number 1 and 2 cylinders. The air and nitrous turn the corner into cylinders 3 and 4, but the gasoline does not. This creates a lean condition on cylinders 3 and 4, and that melts pistons. It also puts a combustible mixture into the intake manifold, and if this ignites it can blow the intake boot off the fuel distributor so hard it can dent the hood and curl back the edges of the air sensor plate.

Autotech mounted an NOS (Nitrous Oxide Systems) nitrous system on its blown Project Golf using a sandwich plate with what is called a fogger nozzle instead of a twin-tube setup. The fogger nozzle is the new high-tech way of getting nitrous into the manifold.

The effect of using nitrous oxide on a normally aspirated motor is stunning. On the Autotech blown Project Golf the boost is still evident, but the kick is nowhere near as strong. The combination of the blower and the nitrous oxide injection results in a very smooth torque curve, and the speedometer needle swings around much faster than with the blown motor without nitrous. Autotech gives up a little blower efficiency by running a wet mixture through the rotors, but the nitrous gets it all back and then some.

Because of the relatively short duration of N_2O injection into the motor, the stock crankshaft, rods, pistons and so on are more than equal to the additional stresses involved, even though horsepower output far exceeds stock levels.

The correct way to introduce nitrous into the Volkswagen motor would be through individual fogger nozzles at each cylinder, the same way the fuel is delivered. Nobody has yet done this, but it should not prove too difficult. The jetting on the fogger nozzle would have to be changed, but NOS offers a wide range of drop-in jets for just such occasions. It has been estimated that a well-thought-out four-injector nitrous oxide setup would double the output of a 100 hp engine. Without the individual fogger nozzles for each cylinder, you risk getting uneven fuel distribution, which will lead to engine meltdown.

An old-style nitrous sandwich plate. Stay away from these. Techtonics

Exhaust system

5

For racing or off-road use or for use with leaded fuels, the catalytic converter is often replaced with a straight pipe. Paul Hacker

For racing, the rear muffler is also replaced with a straight pipe. The angle cut on the pipe reduces the strength of the reflected pulse. Paul Hacker

Following the theory that the engine is an air pump, and that the more efficiently it pumps air the more horsepower it will make, the exhaust becomes a key part of the overall picture of boosting the horsepower. However, there is more to a great exhaust setup than sheer size, especially in Volkswagens with oxygen sensors.

Because pollution control equipment and vehicle inspections are so prevalent, a good way to start understanding exhaust systems is by looking at some of the factory air pollution controls.

Pollution control equipment

Generally, as the engine is run leaner, CO and HC are gradually reduced but

The best (and the most expensive) tube header for the 1974-84 VW is the Super-Sprint. Always use improved motor mounts with any high-performance exhaust. Electrodyne

oxides of nitrogen are increased. As the mixture richens, oxides of nitrogen are increased slightly, then fall off somewhat. This means that mixture control does not provide the total answer to pollution reduction. Volkswagen has tried various pollution-reducing schemes over the years, but the current cars are by far the most dialed in.

Exhaust gas recirculation

With exhaust gas recirculation (EGR), a portion of the exhaust gas is fed back into the intake manifold, where it acts to reduce the peak combustion temperature, and thus the oxides of nitrogen. With air injection, atmospheric oxygen is injected into the exhaust, where it serves to oxidize any unburnt fuel. The reason the unburnt fuel is there in the first place is because the timing is run slightly retarded, allowing combustion to continue taking place after the exhaust valve opens. Without the EGR, the HC and CO values would be far too high, so the engine is tuned to eliminate oxides of nitrogen at the expense of the other two emissions, which the EGR takes care of afterwards.

EGR was used in the early Volkswagens. Because EGR makes the engine less efficient it will often run rougher, and horsepower and mileage suffer. In addition, the air pump found in the carbureted cars draws horsepower from the motor while operating.

Catalytic converter

In a catalytic coverter, heat and chemical reactions combine to reduce pollutants. There are different internal designs for catalytic converters. The one used by Volkswagen creates relatively little back-pressure. It was soon found that the catalytic converter would work much better in a closed-loop system, or in a system in which the mixture was constantly being adjusted over a narrow range. This discovery led to the Lambda sensor.

Lambda sensor

With the introduction of the oxygen sensor and the Lambda closed-loop control, Volkswagen was able to get away from the EGR system. The oxygen sensor continually tests the exhaust gas to determine the amount of oxygen remaining in the mixture. If there is too much oxygen the car runs lean, and the oxygen sensor tells the fuel injection to richen the mixture. If there is too little oxygen the car runs rich, and the fuel injection is instructed to trim the fuel allotment.

With the three-way catalyst and a Lambda closed-loop control, CO and HC are at a minimum when the air/fuel mixture is just slightly more lean than stoichiometric. Oxides of nitrogen are

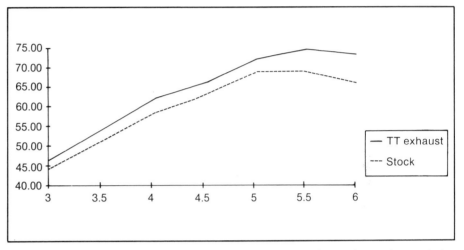

On a 1600 cc motor, replacing the exhaust improved horsepower across the board. On a 1983 or 1984 GTI, the improvement would be even better due to the restrictive nature of the stock exhaust system. Techtonics

The Borla stainless steel exhaust is very distinctive from the rear. It costs more than other systems, but it offers good performance and great longevity.

If you really want to get carried away you can even port your exhaust manifold (top). Techtonics

virtually eliminated when the air/fuel ratio is slightly richer than stoichiometric. By maintaining the air/fuel mixture within a hair's breadth of stoichiometric, the combination of the three-way catalyst and the oxygen sensor can almost totally eliminate pollution. It is a little like having a mechanic under your hood constantly tinkering with the mixture adjustment so it will always be just right.

High-performance exhausts

Just as with the intake manifold, the size of the exhaust is critical. Too small an exhaust will be restrictive, too large an exhaust will lose too much energy and thus horsepower.

The length of the exhaust is also critical. Exhaust pulses have a frequency, meaning that as with sound waves there are areas of compression and areas of rarefication. When the exhaust design causes an area of rarefication to help "suck" out the area of compression that follows it, the design is referred to as tuned. Because the frequency of the pulse changes in proportion with the change in rpm, exhaust tuning works best over a narrow range of rpm.

Finding an exhaust system that flows well and is fairly well tuned is not much of a problem. The trick is in either trying to get a free-flow exhaust that incorporates the catalytic converter, or mixing and matching the various years and styles of exhaust components, usually done in an effort to retain the converter.

Removing the catalytic converter gains horsepower and reduces exhaust temperature. It is also illegal in many states, and doing so contributes to pollution. If for any reason you do remove your catalytic converter, replacing it with a center resonator will cure the "raspberries" that occur at certain rpm.

Headers

It was once common practice to remove everything from the head back, bolt on a short-tube header and free-flow exhaust, and feel as if you had some real horsepower. In fact, some of the stock manifolds are better than a short-tube header and will make more horsepower.

Headers are constructed of tubing instead of cast iron, which in addition to making them lighter also makes it easier to play around with diameters and lengths. Unfortunately, the thinness of the material used in headers makes them far less resistant to cracking than are cast-iron manifolds. With the amount of flex in the Volkswagen motor mounts, this means trouble.

Headers can be either short-tube or long-tube four-into-one style or tri-y. In the four-into-one design, the header runs from the cylinder head to a common collector, where the tubes are arranged so that the exhaust pulses will be next to each other in the circle. Thus, starting at the tube for cylinder number 1, the tube next to it would be the tube for cylinder number 3. Next to that, and diametrically across from the tube for cylinder number 1, would be the tube for cylinder number 4. Between this tube and the number 1 tube would be the tube for cylinder number 2.

Cast iron is tough to work with, but you can see how much larger the port area is. This manifold is off a very strong running car that uses every bit of that extra area. Techtonics

The Techtonics exhaust is a real price leader, and the performance is close to that of the best of them. Note the front motor mount that is included with the system.

Short-tube headers make power at higher rpm than long-tube headers. As an example, a Super Vee motor uses headers twenty-five to twenty-eight inches long. For a street car, a short-tube header is less than ideal because the length helps neither the high end nor the low end. The long-tube header is a little better, with the understanding that it will not flex enough to prevent cracking.

At one time, antireversionary headers were available for the Volkswagen. This design features an exaggerated mismatch in port openings, so that a smaller port empties into a larger one. This makes it more difficult for the pulse to be sucked back into the motor, as it then has to move from a larger port to a smaller port. Unfortunately, the antireversionary header was prone to cracking because of the elaborateness of the design. Also, even with theory on its side, the antireversionary headers were never as efficient as the tri-y design.

The tri-y design can also be referred to as a four-into-two-into-one exhaust. Each exhaust port has its own tube, but is paired with one other cylinder. Cylinders 1 and 4 share a collctor, as do cylinders 2 and 3. These two collector tubes then merge into one tube. The distances from the cylinder head to the first collector and from the first collector to the second collector are selected to tune the exhaust to the desired rpm range of the engine.

Cast-iron manifolds

The factory exhausts all use a cast-iron manifold. With the exception of the 1982 Scirocco and all the 1983 and 1984 US cars, the factory manifolds work well. The 1983–84 manifold is easy to identify, as it was the first manifold that used clips instead of threaded fasteners to hold the downpipe.

Clips or not, the 1982 Scirocco and the 1983 and 1984 Rabbit, Scirocco and Jetta manifolds are just about as bad as you can get, so if you have one of these cars by all means replace the manifold. The most popular replacement has been either an earlier manifold (for example, from a 1982 Jetta) or a Euro GTI manifold. The two are internally identical, the difference being that the Euro version has a heavier flange where the downpipe attaches. You will also need the matching downpipe. The European-style manifold and downpipe will give you ten percent more horsepower than the stock setup.

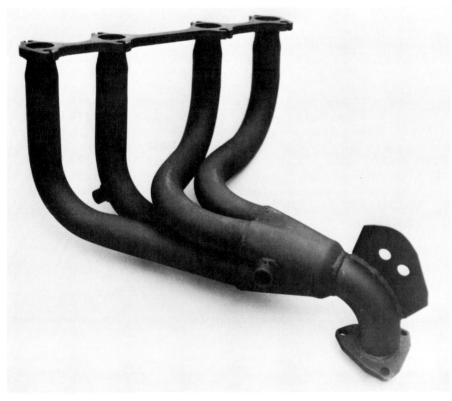

The famous four-into-one header. Autotech

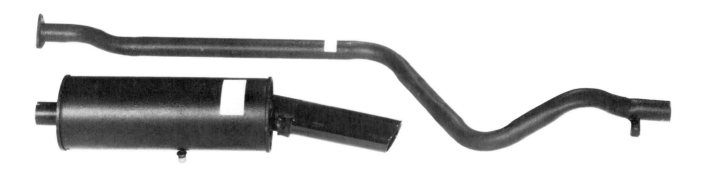

The Leistritz exhaust. The oversize 944-style tip sometimes requires that the body be clearanced before it will fit. Autotech

For the 1985 and 1986 cars, the exhaust manifold for cars with 100 hp and less looks similar to the 1983–84 manifold except that it has a piece of metal bisecting the large opening. This manifold flows well, but it has so far proved difficult to find a good exhaust system to go with it.

For the 102 hp engines, there is a very exotic looking manifold with a flange similar to that on the Euro GTI. The downpipe for this system features ball pivots and all kinds of other trick-looking stuff. It flows okay, but the cost is very high.

There are many good exhaust systems available, including the Leistritz, the Gillet and the Borla. All are made with good-quality materials, make good horsepower and with one exception fit well. That one exception is the Leistritz, which has a 944 style tip that requires minor clearancing of the body. This is not difficult, but it does encourage rust.

Techtonics offers a budget version of the Euro GTI exhaust system with two-inch pipes instead of the 1¾ inch stock pipes. It is made of thinner material and will not last as long as the factory setup (or as long as the Leistritz, Gillet or Borla), but it is also far less expensive, and it makes good horsepower.

Porting and gaskets

Again, as with the intake manifold, you want to match port the exhaust manifold with the exhaust ports on the cylinder head. If you have opened up the exhaust ports, you will need to either port the entire manifold (in the case of a cast-iron manifold) or blend it in. Porting cast iron is very time-consuming, so you will probably want to blend the ports together. Do your blending at least one inch into the exhaust manifold.

There are three types of exhaust manifold gasket, and one hot tip. The first type is the well-known stock gasket. The next is the very expensive turbo gasket, which incorporates more metal and is thus more resistant to blowing out under

A European header can be drilled and tapped for an oxygen sensor... Techtonics

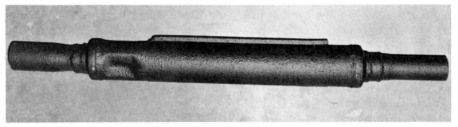

After removing the catalytic converter you may need to use this resonator pipe to reduce "raspberries." Autotech

... Just make sure the hole goes through to both ports so the sensor gets an accurate reading. Techtonics

From left to right are a stock exhaust gasket, a heavy-duty turbo gasket and a special gasket for ported heads. Room temperature vulcanizing (RTV) silicone sealer is cheaper, easier to use and works just as well. Abt

122

the heat and pressure created in turbo applications. The third is a very narrow gasket, designed to allow the maximum porting of the cylinder head and still allow a gasket to seal.

All of these gaskets work, after a fashion, but the hot tip is to use High Temp RTV silicone sealer—"blue silicone." This stuff works. Use it without a gasket, but be careful around Lambda sensors because the silicone will neutralize the ceramic, making it necessary to buy a new sensor.

Flex couplings and motor mounts

As mentioned earlier, one problem with the transverse engine is that the motion of the engine can put a lot of stress on an exhaust system. (This is different from the normal vibration that is caused by having a straight four—which is much smoother in a longitudinal position—placed in a traverse position.)

To combat this, Volkswagen has tried a variety of different flexible couplings. The aftermarket has been busy on this problem, too, with the result being the development of the exhaust ball joint. Different exhaust systems require different flex couplings, so find out what you need when you buy your system. You will definitely need a flex coupling, however, if you hope to get the maximum life from your system.

The Techtonics exhaust system takes a slightly different approach to this problem. Darrell crimps his downpipe flange in such a way that it takes more flex than the 1976-84 European GTI setup.

One thing that really helps cut down on exhaust flex in the pre-1985 cars is to replace the front motor mount, as described in chapter 2.

The dreaded 1983-84 exhaust manifold. Techtonics

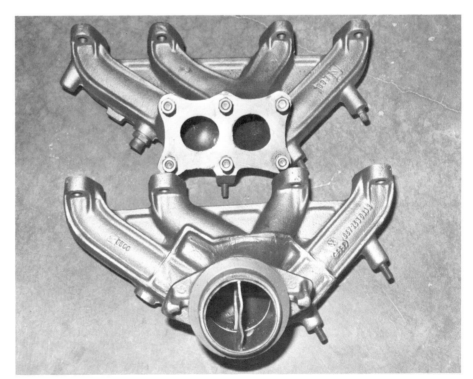

The European manifold (top) compared with the slightly larger late-model US manifold. Flow is about the same, although the European manifold has more aftermarket bolt-ons available for the time being. Autotech

Cooling system

6

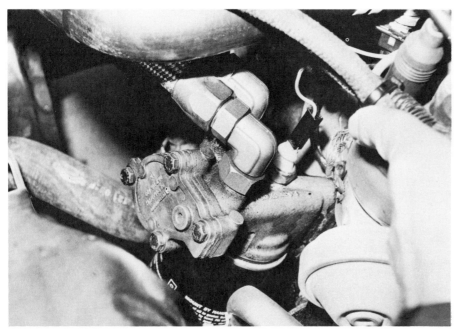

Here is a European thermostatic oil filter mount drilled for American fittings. Compare the restrictive right angles of these fittings to the curved hoses on the factory setup.

Many feel that the Volkswagen engine runs hotter than is prudent. The reason Volkswagen designs the car to run that hot is to help meet fuel emissions and economy standards.

That is fine for a car that has to pass federal inspection, but for the car in your garage—the one you want to keep for several trouble-free years—too much heat means reduced longevity and more problems along the way. Seals dry up and blow away, oil bakes out to a thick sludge, heads warp and close fits lose tolerance. For these and other reasons, many choose to give up some of the fuel economy of the hotter motor in favor of long-term savings in engine repairs.

This does not mean you should run your engine as cold as it will go. After a point, the colder the engine is the worse it runs. In some cases, oil for example,

Here is a typical oil cooler mount in a Golf. Sturdy brackets such as these go a long way toward minimizing vibration and failure. Autotech

The wax-element oil thermostat from the Porsche 911 will fit into the European oil cooler filter housing and opens earlier than the Volkswagen element.

the engine must be hot enough for it to work properly.

What you are aiming for, then, is the right balance between longevity and usability.

Water cooling

Fan switches

The stock fan switch turns the radiator-mounted electric cooling fan on at 194 to 199 degrees Fahrenheit. A better setup seems to be a fan switch one step colder, one that turns on at around 180 degrees Fahrenheit. If you go too cold with the fan switch, your fan will run all the time, even after you turn off the motor. This will create a drain on the electrical system that will ultimately cause the battery to go dead (and your fan will wear out).

Thermostats

The only problem I ever have with the thermostat occurs when refilling the cooling system after it has been drained. My guess is that an air pocket develops around the thermostat so it does not get warm enough to open. As you might expect, the motor gets extremely hot when this happens. If this happens in your car, keep adding coolant, making sure that the coolant level is right up to the top of the filler neck. This allows coolant to get to both sides of the thermostat through the small tube at the top of the radiator, breaking the air pocket.

Once the thermostat opens, set the coolant level as you normally would.

The thermostat is just about the last thing you should need to replace in a hot rod Volkswagen. With a good oil cooler, a slightly lower fan switch and synthetic oil (if necessary), you should not have any heat problems.

If you do everything and still have a heating problem, as might be the case in a turbo motor, check your EGT before changing the thermostat (see chapter 3 for a discussion of using exhaust gas temperature as a tuning aid). If your EGT is too high, changing the thermostat is not going to help.

Radiators

The stock radiator is aluminum with plastic end caps. It works fine in every conceivable street application, but it is somewhat fragile. Many aftermarket radiators are available that are 100 percent steel in construction. You give up a little in weight and gain a little in strength, usually at a lower cost. The diesel cars have a copper radiator that is very nice and that is also unnecessary for anything putting out less than 200 hp.

The 16V Golf and Scirocco do have available a heavy-duty cooling package that includes a different radiator and hoses. If you are going to be racing one of these cars or you live where it gets really hot, check this out.

If you are racing, also go to the hardware store and buy some metal screen like that used in screen doors to put in front of your radiator. This extra layer of protection helps keep rocks from putting holes in your radiator.

Water pumps

The stock water pump works fine right out of the box, which is good considering there are no aftermarket high-performance pumps available. If your engine is suffering from overheating at speed but is cooling okay at idle, and the coolant seems to be circulating through the radiator when you look into the filler neck, the impeller vane may be no longer solidly attached to the pump shaft. At low rpm it will go along for the ride, but when it is asked to do some real work it simply spins on the shaft. This does not happen very often, but it can.

Special coolants

We all know that a mixture of ethylene glycol (also known as *antifreeze*) and water is used because it freezes at a lower

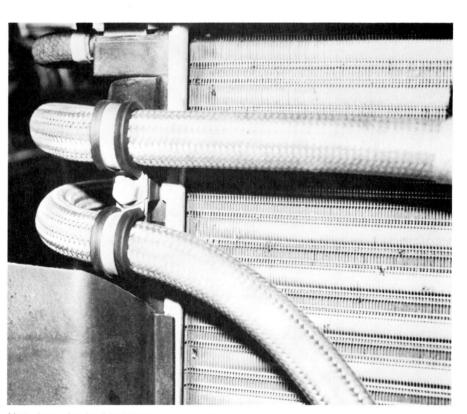

Here's an interesting place for an oil cooler in a GTI. One little bump, though, and you're on foot.

Note how the braided lines are securely fastened on the right side of the radiator with hose clamps. Autotech

temperature and boils at a higher temperature than straight water, and the standard cooling system is pressurized to further raise the boiling point. Ethylene glycol also protects the engine from the corrosive combination of water and heat, and there are special coolants formulated for engines with aluminum components. As the coolant protects the engine parts, some of its additives become depleted, making it necessary to change the antifreeze every year or two to maintain protection.

As well as this system has worked over the years, there is another type of coolant coming to the market that is significantly different.

First a review. For the purposes of this comparison, consider the characteristics of the coolant when the engine is up to operating temperature. Boiling occurs locally in all circulating-liquid engine cooling systems at critical areas where the heat flux is greatest, such as around the exhaust valves in the cylinder head. The vapor that is created must then be condensed into the surrounding bulk liquid.

The problem with water-based coolants is that the vapor generated is primarily water vapor; the ethylene glycol (or whatever additive is being used) remains a liquid. Under high ambient temperatures with heavy loads, the bulk of the coolant can be so close to the boiling point of water that the vapor will not readily condense. Conventional cooling systems catastrophically fail when the bulk coolant temperature cannot be maintained below the boiling point of water for the pressure of the system (250 degrees Fahrenheit with a 15 psi cap). In other words, the whole system gets so hot that the water remains vaporized, forming large vapor pockets that become hot spots.

Enter anhydrous propylene glycol (*anhydrous* means no water is added). Propylene glycol is a substance so low in toxicity that it is an ingredient in some foods. Its boiling point is 369 degrees Fahrenheit and it has a pour point of minus seventy-one degrees Fahrenheit.

Propylene glycol coolant, with the additives required for automotive use, has been developed by Dow Chemical but is not available for general use. Industrial-grade propylene glycol is okay for experimentation, but it is not recommended for long-term use. Do *not* use the propylene glycol sold by recreational vehicle dealers, which is intended for mixing with water—it has the wrong additives. The technology of propylene glycol coolant is very promising, and the automobile manufacturers and aftermarket are sure to develop this product.

A patented engine-cooling process, invented by Jack Evans, president of Mecca Development and marketed by National Technologies, takes advantage of the characteristics of anhydrous propylene glycol. Because the boiling point of propylene glycol is so high and most coolant is maintained far below this boiling point, Evans' "hybrid engine cooling process" avoids the creation of hot spots by preventing pockets of vapor from lingering. Any vapor that is generated locally immediately condenses into the surrounding coolant. Thus, the propylene glycol continues to cool the engine even when the motor is turned off.

The system is "hybrid" in the sense that it combines features of boiling-liquid systems (the Model T Ford, for example, used a straight-vapor system, relying on the heat lost through boiling the water to cool the system) and circulating-liquid cooling systems (found in modern cars). The coolant jacket is not pressurized, but rather vented through a condenser system to the atmosphere. The cooling system, not bound by the limitations of water, can function up to and beyond 300 degrees Fahrenheit without failure.

Water has served us long and well because it has the largest latent heat of vaporization (calories/gram) of any substance. Evans identified, however, that the heat of vaporization must be viewed on a molar basis (calories/mole) rather than on a mass basis (calories/gram) to be of significance. The problem in the cooling system is due to the volume occupied by vapor, not to the mass of the vapor. On a molar basis, propylene glycol has a heat of vaporization twenty-five percent greater than water.

Critics point out that propylene glycol has a much lower thermal conductivity than water, and a lower specific heat. Evans' studies show that at critical areas the mechanism of heat transfer is by boil-

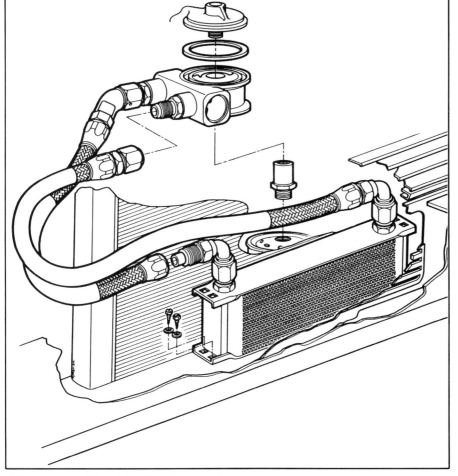

This is the traditional location for the oil cooler in cars without air conditioning.

ing, not by conduction. Although propylene glycol is less effective at transferring heat from itself to the radiator, the bigger problem has always been the transfer of heat from the radiator to the air.

Specific heat refers to the amount of heat needed to raise a given quantity of the liquid one degree Celsius. Comparing specific heats, if water has a value of 100, then propylene glycol rates a seventy-three. In other words, it requires less heat to increase the temperature of the propylene glycol. However, cooling systems using a fifty/fifty mix of ethylene glycol and water rate an eighty-eight on this scale, making propylene glycol's value an eighty-three compared with fifty/fifty ethylene glycol and water. This fifteen percent disadvantage is more than made up by the benefits of using propylene glycol.

The bad news is that ideally, the cooling system should be modified to realize the full benefits of propylene glycol. Evans' favorite configuration is to reverse the coolant flow direction so that the coolant enters the cylinder head first. The head runs cooler, and as the coolant flows into the block it gives up some of its heat, reducing the demand on the radiator. When used this way, it is also possible to run the motor much hotter for better efficiency and lower emissions. With the coolant running hotter, radiator efficiency is also improved because the difference in temperature between the radiator and the ambient air is greater.

The good news is that propylene glycol also can be used as a coolant in conventional flow systems. Either way it is important that the coolant jacket not be pressurized. Engine temperatures are a function of the boiling point of the coolant (unless vapor pockets form). Propylene glycol already has a high boiling point, and pressurization would drive it too high. The conventional flow direction is a compromise because some pressurization (by action of the coolant pump) is unavoidable.

The Volkswagen cooling system requires very little modification to be adopted for use with propylene glycol because the by-pass-type thermostat is located at the input side of the pump. There is no restriction at the outlet from the top of the engine to the radiator. A recovery condenser, vented to the atmosphere, must be added to communicate with the top of the radiator or expansion tank. This prevents the system from becoming pressurized, and allows the

creation and condensation of vapor without losing coolant.

You will be hearing a lot more about propylene glycol technology.

Coatings

The reason the Volkswagen owners manual recommends that you change your coolant periodically is that coolant changes chemically as it ages. Eventually, it starts attacking the metal parts in the cooling system, especially aluminum parts. Aluminum does not rust, but it does oxidize in other ways, and the result is the same: The part can become ruined.

G&L Coatings has a resin you can have applied to the water jacket in the cylinder head and block that not only promotes cooling but also protects the metal from oxidizing. This same company can also coat the outside of your motor against corrosion, with the same benefit of added cooling.

Oil cooling

Of the three engine-cooling systems (air, water and oil), oil cooling is the most promising for getting big cooling gains with relatively little effort. Many

Here's one way of mounting a nonfactory oil cooler in the factory position. This engine also has a full Callaway turbo system, so space is at a premium in the engine compartment. James Sly

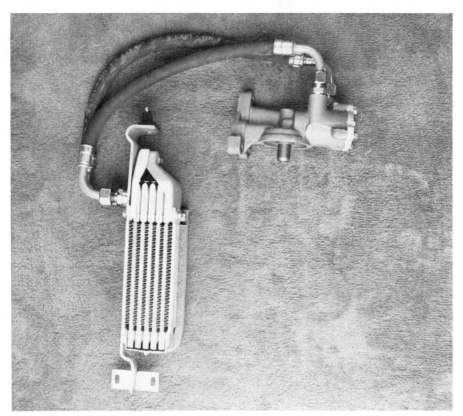

European oil cooler setup for mounting to the right of the radiator. Note the rounded 90 degree adapters, much less restrictive than the sharp 90 degree connectors. Abt

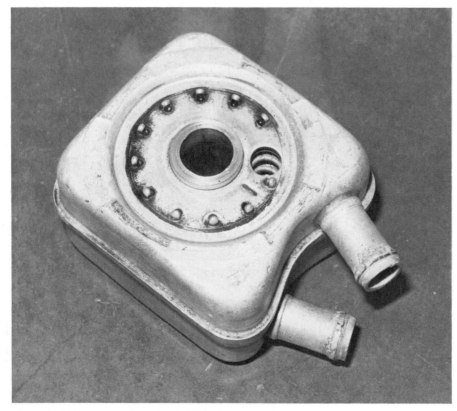

The stock oil-to-water oil cooler. I still don't trust them. Autotech

Volkswagen owners with oil temperature gauges decide to install an oil cooler.

For every eighteen-degree-Fahrenheit increase in temperature, the oxidation rate of oil doubles. In fact, the rate of reaction in any homogeneous system is approximately doubled with each eighteen-degree-Fahrenheit increase in temperature. This does not normally pose a problem for your oil until you hit 200 degrees Fahrenheit or so. This works out well because under normal conditions you want to run the oil between 180 and 212 degrees Fahrenheit. Any colder and the volatile contaminants (fuel, water) that find their way into the oil will not be burned off. Any higher, and the oil will oxidize too fast, seals will get baked out and hot-start problems will begin to crop up.

Unless you live where it is really cold most of the time, consider getting an oil cooler. And unless you live in the tropics, include an oil thermostat in the system. The oil thermostat prevents oil from circulating through the oil cooler until the temperature exceeds a preset temperature.

In addition to helping the motor run cooler, an oil cooler increases the thermal reserve of the cooling system as a whole. With the extra quart of oil and the additional cooling surface, it will take longer for your car to reach meltdown when running under extreme load conditions.

Calibrating the oil temperature gauge

Before you dismiss the idea of purchasing an oil cooler because your oil temperature gauge reads just where you want it to, calibrate your oil temperature gauge so you know it is telling you the truth.

To calibrate your oil temperature gauge, first remove the sender from the motor. You are going to need to drop the sender into boiling water, so arrange that any way that is convenient, and also arrange to have the sender plugged in. You may have to fashion a temporary extension to the oil sender lead to do this. You will also need to ground the sender to the block. You can use a test lead with alligator clips at each end, and make certain that the connectors are secure.

Water boils at 212 degrees Fahrenheit at sea level, lower as altitude increases. When the water boils, note the reading on your gauge. Where the needle falls is 212 degrees Fahrenheit, no matter what the printing on the face of the gauge tells you. Your reading will be more accurate if you do not allow the sender to rest against the hot bottom of the pan in which you are boiling the water.

Types of oil cooler

One of my least favorite oil cooler setups is the factory oil-to-water arrangment. First, I do not trust it. I have seen problems with similar setups in Audi 5000 transmission fluid coolers and Porsche 944 oil coolers that allow coolant to mix with the oil. Second, I do not like the idea of using the same radiator area to get rid of heat from both the coolant and the oil. On the plus side, the oil warms up more quickly than it would normally and it seems to work fine. If you have one, you do not need to replace it, but watch it carefully. Keeping your coolant fresh and ready to combat corrosion makes good sense, too.

On the 1983 and 1984 cars with air conditioning, a cursory examination of the engine compartment will reveal that there is not much room for the oil cooler. The solution is to extend the radiator mounting brackets by welding some extra metal to the end, then drilling new mounting holes one-half or three-quarters of an inch farther back. This leaves plenty of room in front of the radiator for the oil cooler. (Moving the radiator back, when done cleanly, can also be a great source of merriment to your turbocharger installer, who will not be able to figure out why the intercooler plumbing fits with room to spare on everybody else's car except yours.)

For 1985-and-later cars, the European-GTI-style filter mount with the built-in oil thermostat works fine, as it does in the earlier cars. It will not work on the 1983 and 1984 models because the air conditioner brace cuts across right where the filter mount needs to be. The only solution for these cars is to use a sandwich plate adapter.

The Euro GTI setup is very compact, but it comes from the factory with the oil thermostat set to open at 230 degrees Fahrenheit, which is a little warm. However, Darrell Vittone claims that he has no problems with the thermostat opening that late, and that is the temperature at which it is fully open, so there will be some flow before that. If you want to use the Euro GTI mount *and* have the oil thermostat open sooner, the Porsche 911 uses the same size oil thermostat, and it will slip right into the Euro GTI housing. The difference is that it is fully open by 180 degrees Fahrenheit. Autotech sells this oil thermostat with its European oil cooler kit.

Another possible modification of the European GTI mount is to drill and tap the DIN fittings for American-size threads. This is what Autotech does for its oil cooler kits, and it works well as long as you do not overtighten the fittings. Drilling the housing reduces the thickness of the metal in the casting, so caution is advised. With the American fittings, you have available a wealth of different shapes, sizes and efficiencies of oil cooler. You also will have available a wealth of fittings. Bear in mind that a ninety-degree-angle fitting is as restrictive as ten feet of hose. Use bent-tube right-angles if you can find them.

When you buy your oil cooler kit, you may be offered the choice of rubber hose or braided stainless hose. The braided stainless lines are more popular because they do not give as many problems as rubber hose, but a commercial-grade heavy-duty rubber hose should give you no problem. Make sure the rubber hose you get is rated to at least 150 psi, as the Volkswagen motor when cold can develop very high oil pressure. If you lose a hose while driving and do not notice it, your motor will be history in a hurry.

If your motor does blow up when you are running an oil cooler, the cooler must be thoroughly cleaned of all the garbage that is in it. If you do not get the scrap metal out, it will come out later after you put your motor back together again, ruining everything.

Most shops simply flush the oil cooler with solvent for hours on end, shaking it and swishing it around to try to dislodge as many of the pieces as possible. While this may work, the best way to clean the cooler is with an ultrasonic cleaner. Because you probably do not have an ultrasonic cleaner, you will have to find someplace that performs this service. The alternative is to set that cooler aside and buy a new, clean one.

Transmission and drivetrain

Clutches

As motor size has increased, Volkswagen has increased the size of the clutch. This makes sense until you find out that the spring pressure of the pressure plate has not been boosted that much. In other words, the same amount of spring pressure is being distributed over a larger area, for a lower psi.

This was done because Volkswagen did not make the clutches bigger to handle more power, but to improve the longevity of the clutch. This is why the Sachs 190 mm sport clutch was for a while considered to be the hot tip for high-output motors. With a thirty percent stiffer spring and a relatively small surface area, it resisted slip quite well.

The 210 mm clutches hold up to 180 hp with no problems, so the best bet is to use whatever-size sport clutch is easiest for you. When purchasing your sport clutch, make sure you get all the right pieces; don't mix and match them. If you do not get all sport clutch pieces, you might as well get stock components.

When you are buying clutch parts, also make sure that you get the right pieces to fit your car. The 210 mm clutch for the 16V transmission will not exchange for the earlier 210 mm clutch, and the new-style Volkswagen clutches that are rumored to be coming on the new motor will not retrofit to the current batch of engines and transmissions.

For race use there are four-puck clutches, so called because instead of continuous friction material they use metallic pucks. These are extremely unpleasant to drive on the street, but for racing they really hold on.

Reinforcing the transmission

Unless you are hard on transmissions, this may be an area in which you can save some money. People with high-performance Volkswagens have gone both ways with street machine transmissions, fully prepped and totally stock, with equal results. You may feel better about putting 180 hp through a transmission that has been thoroughly massaged, but in my experience the stock box works great. Some racers set the box up "loosely" (at maximum tolerance), but many others do not bother.

If you need the strongest box available to handle serious horsepower, you will need to start out with the 16V transmission. It has a stronger input shaft and larger clutch splines.

As with any other machined part, gears have a wealth of stress risers that can lead to failure. The fillets at the roots of the teeth are especially prone to cracking, and therefore would be strengthened by shot peening. In addition to the normal benefits of shot peening, the indentations caused by the peening process create reservoirs that hold gear lube for

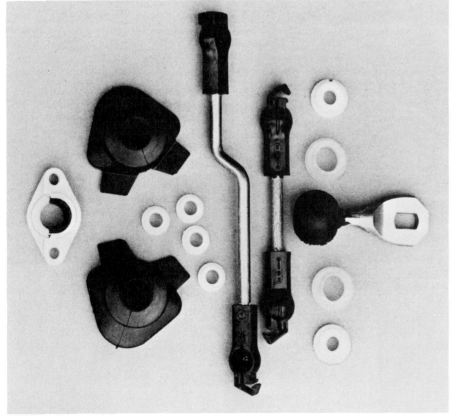

If you like the stock shifter but it is starting to feel sloppy, a factory bushing kit such as this one will do the trick for you.

With your stock drain plug, a magnet from Radio Shack and some epoxy you can make your own magnetic transmission drain plug. Stuttgart Automotive

better lubrication. If you want shot peening and smooth gear teeth, the gears can be lapped after shot peening, as long as no more than ten percent of the surface depth is removed.

If you want gears that are stronger to begin with, special heat-treated gears in limited ratios are available from Abt Motorsports. For racers, straight-cut gears can be had, as well. The noise makes these unacceptable for street use, but they are stronger.

Transmission swap: five speeds in place of four

One thing you should consider on an early car with the four-speed transmission is swapping it for a five-speed. Whereas the four-speed just barely seems to cover the bases, the five-speed gives you just about as much latitude as you can use in terms of gear ratios. With the five-speed, for example, you can have four close-ratio gears on the bottom for racing, and an overdrive fifth gear for cruising. Or, you could make first just low enough so you do not stall it coming off the line, and have four close-ratio gears up top.

The point is that there are possibilities with the five speed, and it is not difficult at all to install one. You should be able to find a good used five-speed at your local wrecking yard for a reasonable fee. Make sure you get the clutch pushrod that goes with the transmission; the five-speed pushrod is different from the four-speed pushrod. Also try to get the mounts that go with it, and if you are really lucky you may even get the linkage, too. If these three items do not come with the transmission, you can get the pushrod from a dealer, and some aftermarket tuners have kits that include the mounts and all the linkage pieces you will need for the conversion.

Examine the pushrod before you install it. A bent or damaged pushrod should never be used, as it will hang up and alter the clutch engagement. If you suspect it, or if your clutch is giving problems, replace it with a new one from the dealer.

Shift points

Matching your gear ratios to your motor

So there you are with your 2021 cc sixteen-valve turbo motor. You spent every waking hour for the last seven months working on it, and just about every spare nickel as well. You are obviously interested in acceleration, but do you know when you should upshift to maximize the power that your engine is putting out?

For maximum acceleration, you want to upshift when the torque available at the driving wheels is going to be greater in the next higher gear than it is in the gear you are using. If you shift too late, you will be under utilizing the power available in the next lower gear. If you shift too early, you will be running in an rpm range at which the engine is not making full power.

Gear ratio	Final drive ratio				
	3.67	3.89	3.90	3.94	4.17
3.45	12.66	13.42	13.46	13.59	14.39
2.12	7.78	8.25	8.27	8.35	8.84
1.94	7.12	7.55	7.57	7.64	8.09
1.75	6.42	6.81	6.83	6.90	7.30
1.44	5.28	5.60	5.62	5.67	6.00
1.37	5.03	5.33	5.34	5.40	5.71
1.29	4.73	5.02	5.03	5.08	5.38
1.13	4.15	4.40	4.41	4.45	4.71
1.06	3.89	4.12	4.13	4.18	4.42
1.03	3.78	4.01	4.02	4.06	4.30
0.97	3.56	3.77	3.78	3.82	4.04
0.91	3.34	3.54	3.55	3.59	3.79
0.89	3.27	3.46	3.47	3.51	3.71
0.76	2.79	2.96	2.96	2.99	3.17
0.75	2.75	2.92	2.93	2.96	3.13

Number of turns on the input shaft for one turn of the output shaft

One way of estimating gear ratios of a mystery transmission is to count the number of times you have to turn the input shaft to get one turn of the drive flange. Make sure both flanges are turning freely while you do your counting. If the angle is too close to tell, take the input shaft for another spin or two so the discrepancy between the two numbers can accumulate.

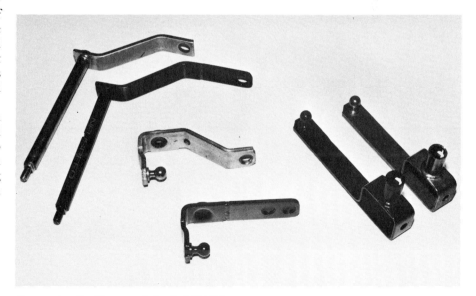

Comparing the Neuspeed short-shift kit (in black) to the stock parts you can see that there are some major changes in the lengths of the arms. APS

131

There are two ways of determining what you transmission ratios should be. (Note: If you have not changed gear ratios, you should still do these calculations, as they will tell you what the proper shift points are for maximum acceleration.) Neither method takes into account drivetrain losses, air resistance or other subtleties, but even so you can get pretty close.

For now, assume that you are interested in maximum acceleration. If you are road racing on different circuits and can mix and match gear ratios to each circuit, you will find some pointers later in this section.

Before you do anything else, get your engine's torque curve from your engine builder. If you are running a stock engine, you can use the factory-supplied charts; they will be close enough.

Method 1

The first method uses gear charts to figure out either where your shift points should be or what gears you should be using. This method will appeal to those of you without a computer. If you have a computer or have access to one, use it. Calculating shift points with gear charts is possible, but only barely.

Because gear charts for the Volkswagen are difficult to obtain, you may want to make your own. You will need a few large pieces of graph paper and a straightedge. If you have access to a pocket calculator or a slide rule, things will go much faster.

Consult the list of available gear ratios, and look up the height of the tires you are using from the chart. Also consult the list of final drive ratios, and pick one to start with. You will need to make a separate chart for each final drive and tire diameter you are considering using.

The formula you will be using is

$$mph = \frac{rpm \times tire\ diameter \times \pi}{final\ drive\ ratio \times gear\ ratio \times 1056}$$

You already know the tire diameter in inches, the value of π and the final drive ratio, so you can make things go much quicker by choosing an rpm point (5000, for example), and doing all your calculations from that rpm. You will then have one data point for each gear. Instead of calculating another data point for each gear, make sure your chart starts out at zero rpm/mph. At zero engine rpm, the car will not be moving so you have an automatic and highly accurate second data point for all the rear ratios, and you do not have to do any calculations. When you draw your gear lines on the chart, you do not have to stop at 5000 rpm. Extend the line up far enough to cover whatever redline you are using for your shift point analysis.

The calculations will go quicker still if you multiply the three values on top,

The plastic rod ends must be unclipped and then pried off their pivots. APS

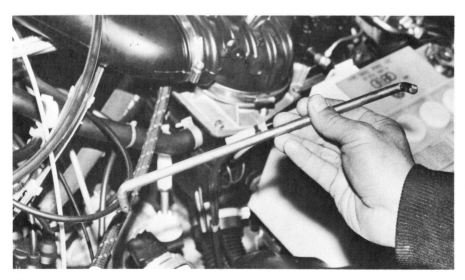

Remove the relay shaft rod. When reinstalling, note that the 90 degree bend goes with the relay shaft. The 95 degree bend goes with the selector shaft. APS

Remove the selector lever. Be on the lookout for any other worn or broken parts so you can replace them at the same time. APS

multiply the final drive ratio by 1056 on the bottom and then divide the value on top by the value you just got for the bottom. Then all you have to do to get the mph with any gear ratio is to divide this subtotal by the gear ratio, and you will get the speed in that gear at the rpm you have chosen. With a 5000 rpm redline, a tire diameter of 22.76 inches and a 3.90 final drive, this works out to

$$mph = \frac{5000 \times 22.76 \times 3.14}{3.90 \times gear \times 1056}$$

which reduces to

$$mph = \frac{35,7512.9}{4118.4 \times gear} = \frac{86.8}{gear}$$

To get your upper data points, divide 86.8 by the gear ratio.

Once you have all your data points, label the Y-axis (on the side of the chart) rpm and label the X-axis (at the bottom of the chart) mph. The bigger the piece of graph paper you start with, the more accurate you will be able to make your chart. The most important thing is to have the axes cross at the zero point. Now take the values you calculated for each gear and graph them on your paper.

Get out your dyno sheet. If it does not have horsepower figures on it, you will have to calculate the horsepower from the torque figures, using the formula

$$hp = \frac{torque \times rpm}{5250}$$

On a separate piece of graph paper, draw a representation of your horsepower curve. Then make photocopies of it; this allows you to mark all over your horsepower curve drawing without ruining the original. You are now ready to calculate your shift points.

Read across the side of the gear chart until you come to the highest rpm your car can attain. Follow this line across. There will be several gear lines crossing it, but you are looking for the one that crosses nearest to the horsepower peak of the engine. A little under is fine, and so is a little over as long as it is not above your redline. The gear ratio line that crosses at that point is your ideal high-performance fifth gear.

In selecting the rest of the gears, you will get to mark up your horsepower curve drawings. What you are looking for is the maximum area under the curve. You do not want to shift at the horsepower peak. To visualize what happens when you shift to the next higher gear, take one copy of your horsepower graph and draw a vertical line straight down from the horsepower peak, and extend it until it touches the X-axis.

When you upshift, the rpm in the higher gear is less than the rpm in the lower gear. Suppose your rpm falls off by 1800 rpm when you upshift. Subtract 1800 rpm from 6500 rpm, and draw another vertical line downward from 4700 rpm. The area on your graph that is surrounded by the two vertical lines, the X-axis and the horsepower curve is called the *area under the curve*, or the power you have available when you shift at this rpm.

Now assume you hold off shifting until the rpm reach 7500. Draw a vertical line downward from 7500 on your graph.

At this higher rpm, you will have more of an rpm drop when you shift—for example, 2000 rpm. Subtract 2000 rpm from 7500 rpm, and draw a vertical line downward from 5500 rpm. There is much more area under the curve now than in the first example, so it will be better to shift on the other side of the horsepower curve than right at the horsepower peak.

Lubricate the selector shaft from the short-shift kit with moly grease and put it into position. APS

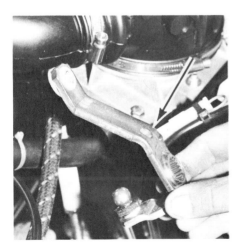

Replace the stock selector shaft with the one from the kit. APS

Install the relay shaft that came in the short-shift kit. APS

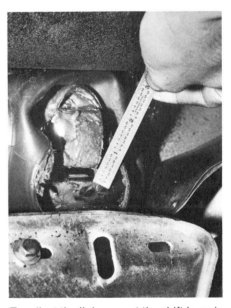

To adjust the linkage, put the shift lever in neutral, aligned with the 3-4 gate. There should be ½ inch of clearance. If not, rotate the shift rod on the selector lever until there is. Don't get frustrated; shift linkage adjustment always seems to work backward from the way you expect it to. APS

If you next want to explore the differences it would make to change final drives, you have to make up another whole gear chart with all new numbers and lines. If you do not drive your car all winter anyway, and you need a project to work on while you are waiting for spring, you can figure out the proper transmission ratios using gear charts. Otherwise, check out method 2.

Method 2

This method uses a computer, so if you neither have a computer nor have access to one, the first method will have to do. The program demonstrated here is written in BASIC. It has been run on a personal computer using GW-BASIC under MS-DOS as is, and on a NOVA-compatible minicomputer using Business BASIC under IRIS with the CLS statements changed to PRINT 'CS'. With a few changes, you should be able to run it on any computer.

This program was written by Jack Broomall, who is now an engineer with Chrysler. Instead of a gear chart it makes use of one additional equation that calculates the torque available at the drive wheels:

Front wheel torque = engine torque × gear ratio × final drive ratio

```
100 REM SHIFTPOINT OPTIM-
    IZER PROGRAM
105 REM Jack Broomall Racing
110 CLS
115 DIM R(30)
120 DIM T(30)
125 PRINT "Shift Point Optimizer
    Program"
130 FOR A=1 TO 1000
135 NEXT A
140 CLS
145 GOTO 195
150 CLS
155 PRINT "Note: It will be necessary
    to re-enter all data points."
160 FOR W=1 TO 30
165 R(W)=0
170 T(W)=0
175 NEXT W
180 PRINT
185 PRINT
190 GOTO 200
195 CLS
200 PRINT "Input Torque vs. RPM
    Information from Dyno Testing"
205 PRINT "++++++++++++++++++
    ++++++++++++++++++++++++++++"
210 N=1
215 PRINT "Data Point "N
220 PRINT
225 INPUT "Engine Speed
    (RPM):";R(N)
230 PRINT
235 INPUT "Engine Torque
    (ft/lb.):";T(N)
240 PRINT
245 CLS
250 PRINT "If you wish to enter
    another data point enter 1"
255 PRINT
260 PRINT "If you wish to run the
    program enter 2"
265 INPUT "1 or 2";I
270 IF I>1 THEN 295
275 N=N+1
280 CLS
285 GOTO 215
290 CLS
295 CLS
300 PRINT "Please check that tor-
    que/RPM data points are correct"
305 PRINT
310 PRINT
315 PRINT "Data points entered this
    run:"
320 PRINT
325 PRINT "Data", "RPM","Torque"
330 PRINT "Point",,"(Ft/lb)"
335 PRINT "------------------------"
340 FOR J=1 TO N
345 PRINT J,R(J),T(J)
350 NEXT J
355 FOR A=1 TO 1000
360 NEXT A
365 PRINT
370 PRINT
375 PRINT "If data is correct as
    displayed, enter 1 to continue"
380 PRINT "If data is incorrect enter
    2 to make corrections"
385 INPUT "1 or 2";I
```

The Quaife torque biasing differential has relatively few parts and is simple of design. Autotech

The Sachs Sport 215 mm clutch disc and pressure plate.

```
390 IF I>1 THEN 150
395 CLS
400 GOTO 420
405 CLS
410 PRINT "Note: It will be necessary
    to re-enter all gearing & tire info."
415 PRINT
420 PRINT "Input Transmission Ratio
    Information"
425 PRINT "------------------------------"
430 PRINT
435 PRINT "Please enter information
    as requested."
440 PRINT
445 INPUT "Number of forward
    gears:";G
450 FOR T=1 TO G
455 IF T=1 THEN 475
460 IF T=2 THEN 495
465 IF T=3 THEN 515
470 IF T>3 THEN 535
475 PRINT
480 PRINT "First gear ratio:"
485 INPUT G(1)
490 GOTO 550
495 PRINT
500 PRINT "Second gear ratio:"
505 INPUT G(2)
510 GOTO 550
515 PRINT
520 PRINT "Third gear ratio:"
525 INPUT G(3)
530 GOTO 550
535 PRINT
540 PRINT T "th gear ratio:"
545 INPUT G(T)
550 NEXT T
555 CLS
560 PRINT "Input differential ratio"
565 PRINT "----------------------"
570 PRINT
575 PRINT "Differential ratio:"
580 INPUT D
585 CLS
590 PRINT "Input tire diameter"
595 PRINT "------------------"
600 PRINT
605 PRINT "Tire diameter (inches):"
610 INPUT T1
615 CLS
620 PRINT "Please check that the
    following input data is entered
    correctly."
625 FOR A=1 TO 1000
630 NEXT A
635 PRINT
640 PRINT
645 FOR B=1 TO G
650 PRINT "Gear" B "is" "G(B)":"1"
655 PRINT
660 NEXT B
665 PRINT "Differential ratio is"
    D:"1"
670 PRINT
675 PRINT "Tire diameter is" T1
    "inches"
680 PRINT
685 FOR A=1 TO 1000
690 NEXT A
695 PRINT "If data is correct as dis-
    played, enter 1 to continue"
700 PRINT "If data is incorrect, enter
    2 to make corrections."
705 INPUT "1 or 2";1
710 IF I>1 THEN 405
715 CLS
720 PRINT "For maximum torque at
    front wheels, make upshifts as
    follows:"
725 PRINT "-------------------------------------
    -----------------"
730 PRINT
735 FOR F=1 TO (G-1)
740 G1=G(F)
745 G2=G(F+1)
750 FOR U=R(1) TO R(N) STEP 20
755 FOR C=1 TO (N-1)
760 IF U>=R(C) AND U<R(C+1)
    THEN 770
765 NEXT C
770 T2=T(C)+(T(C+1)-T(C))*
    ((U-R(C))/(R(C+1)-R(C)))
775 T3=T2*G1*D
780 U2=U*(G(F+1)/G(F))
785 IF U2<R(1) THEN 840
790 FOR K=1 TO (N-1)
795 IF U2>=R(K) AND U2<R(K+1)
    THEN 805
800 NEXT K
805 T5=T(K)+(T(K+1))*
    ((U2-R(K))/(R(K+1)-R(K)))
810 T4=T5*G2*D
815 IF T3<T4 THEN 825
820 GOTO 850
825 PRINT "Make" F "-"(F+1)" shift
    at "U" rpm."
830 PRINT
835 GOTO 860
840 NEXT U
845 U=U-20
850 IF U=R(N) THEN 825
855 GOTO 840
860 NEXT F
865 PRINT
870 PRINT "END OF OUTPUT"
875 END
```

Torque is transmitted from one side of the differential to the other via the ten smaller planetary gears. Autotech

These ten fasteners are all that hold it together. No special tools are required. Autotech

This program not only tests for proper shift points at the rpm and torque figures that you enter, but it calculates what the torque and road speed will be at rpm in between the given data.

To test the program, start off with some known quantities. Plugging in the torque figures for a stock 1983 GTI, along with the stock gear and final drive ratios, this is what you should get:

```
NUMBER OF GEARS: 5
GEAR 1:3.45
GEAR 2:2.12
GEAR 3:1.44
GEAR 4:1.13
GEAR 5:0.91
DIFFERENTIAL RATIO: 3.90
TIRE DIAMETER: 22.76 INCHES
```

For maximum torque at the front wheels make upshifts as follows:

```
MAKE 1–2 SHIFT AT 6500 RPM
MAKE 2–3 SHIFT AT 6300 RPM
MAKE 3–4 SHIFT AT 5940 RPM
MAKE 4–5 SHIFT AT 5880 RPM
```

From looking at the output you might divine that the factory did things pretty well with the exception of first gear, which is at redline. Otherwise, each upshift matches the torque in the next higher gear with the torque in the lower gear for a smooth acceleration curve throughout the speed range. This is probably one reason you bought a Volkswagen.

Now "build up" the motor and try those same ratios again. Taking the stock torque figures, add 5 lb-ft to each number and plug them into the program. Your results should be as follows:

For maximum torque at the front wheels make upshifts as follows:

```
MAKE 1–2 SHIFT AT 6500 RPM
MAKE 2–3 SHIFT AT 6380 RPM
MAKE 3–4 SHIFT AT 6000 RPM
MAKE 4–5 SHIFT AT 5940 RPM
```

The gearbox works better with the built-up motor as long as the torque curve follows the factory curve. As the GTI and 16V became more powerful, they were able to use the same gearbox because Volkswagen concentrated on preserving the low-end torque. The more powerful motor also allowed Volkswagen to eventually use the overdrive 0.89 fifth gear.

Now test the program with a difficult example: a strong-running turbo motor with a torque peak at 4000 rpm and a horsepower peak at 7000 rpm. Remember that you are still running this motor with the stock gearbox, as many people do. Turn on the computer, load the program and plug in the numbers. You should see the following:

For maximum torque at the front wheels make upshifts as follows:

```
MAKE 1–2 SHIFT AT 7500 RPM
MAKE 2–3 SHIFT AT 7500 RPM
MAKE 3–4 SHIFT AT 7500 RPM
MAKE 4–5 SHIFT AT 7500 RPM
```

Clearly, something undesirable is happening here. Each shift is at redline, leaving you to guess what is going on. Now you miss the manual gear chart that tells what the rpm drop is, and whether or not the transmission is working for you or against you.

One way around this limitation is to use the formulas with a spreadsheet program or a database program (if it can perform calculations) to generate charts from which you can pick out the information you need. It is less accurate than the BASIC program at picking shift points, but either the spreadsheet or the database can, with very little programming, approximate the actual shift point while showing some of the things missed by abandoning the manual gear charts.

Setting up a spreadsheet to do these calculations is easy. Setting up a database program is a little more difficult, but not much. Here is a quick and dirty example of a dBASE II command file that will generate some numbers for you to examine. If you wanted to get fancy, you could convert the BASIC program into your database language and have the best of both worlds!

```
Set talk off
Erase
Use GEARSHIFT
Input "First gear ratio:" to first
Input "Second gear ratio:" to second
Input "Third gear ratio:" to third
Input "Fourth gear ratio:" to fourth
Input "Fifth gear ratio:" to fifth
Input "Final drive ratio:" to final
Input "Tire diameter:" to tire
Store tire *3.14159 to a
Store final*1056 to b
Store first*final to tf1
Store second*final to tf2
Store third*final to tf3
Store fourth*final to tf4
Store fifth*final to tf5
```

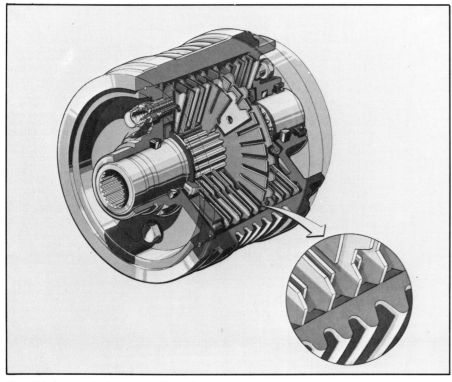

The VW viscous limited-slip differential.

go top
?"Calculating speed in first"
Replace all speed 1 with
   (rpm*a)/(first*b)
?"Calculating speed in second"
Replace all speed2 with
   (rpm*a)/(second*b)
?"Calculating speed in third"
Replace all speed3 with
   (rpm*a)/(third*b)
?"Calculating speed in fourth"
Replace all speed4 with
   (rpm*a)/(fourth*b)
?"Calculating speed in fifth"
Replace all speed5 with
   (rpm*a)/(fifth*b)
?"Calculating torque in first"
Replace all tq1 with tq*tf1
?"Calculating torque in second"
Replace all tq2 with tq*tf2
?"Calculating torque in third"
Replace all tq3 with tq*tf3
?"Calculating torque in fourth"
Replace all tq4 with tq*tf4
?"Calculating torque in fifth"
Replace all tq5 with tq*tf5
?"Rpm   First   Second   Third
   Fourth   Fifth"
?"   mph fwt   mph fwt   mph
   fwt   mph fwt   mph fwt"
list rpm, speed1, tq1, speed2, tq2,
   speed3, tq3, speed4, tq4, speed5,
   tq5
off

The database for this program is called GEARSHFT.DBF, and it looks like this:

STRUCTURE FOR FILE:
   GEARSHFT.DBF
NUMBER OF RECORDS: 00010
DATE OF LAST UPDATE:
   09/17/87
PRIMARY USE DATABASE

FLD	NAME	TYPE	WIDTH	DEC
001	RPM	N	004	
002	TQ	N	006	002
003	SPEED1	N	005	
004	SPEED2	N	005	
005	SPEED3	N	005	
006	SPEED4	N	005	
007	SPEED5	N	005	
008	TQ1	N	005	
009	TQ2	N	005	
010	TQ3	N	005	
011	TQ4	N	005	
012	TQ5	N	005	
TOTAL			00061	

This dBASE program has no rounding algorithm, and the memory variables are not saved so they have to be reentered each time. The horsepower and torque figures can be retained for later examination by copying the database to another name, and then changing the USE statement to pick up the file you want.

Spreadsheet programs like Excel have more flexibility and slightly better accuracy than databases. If you run the same numbers with Excel that you ran with the BASIC program, starting off with the stock motor, you should get the following data on front wheel torque.

Rpm	First MPH	First FWT	Second MPH	Second FWT	Third MPH	Third FWT	Fourth MPH	Fourth FWT	Fifth MPH	Fifth FWT
2000	10	1278	16	785	24	534	31	419	38	337
2500	13	1359	20	835	30	567	38	445	48	358
3000	15	1386	25	852	36	578	46	454	57	366
3500	18	1372	29	843	42	573	54	450	67	362
4000	20	1319	33	810	48	550	61	432	76	348
4500	23	1292	37	794	54	539	69	423	86	341
5000	25	1251	41	769	60	522	77	410	95	330
5500	28	1157	45	711	66	483	85	379	105	305
6000	30	982	49	604	72	410	92	322	114	259
6500	33	821	53	504	78	343	100	269	124	216

This program gives two pieces of information that the BASIC program did not tell you: the rough rpm drop at the shift point (2500) and the speed at each shift point.

Here is round 2, with the additional 5 lb-ft at each torque point. The figures confirm that the car *is* quicker and that everything else has stayed right in line the way you wanted it.

Rpm	First MPH	First FWT	Second MPH	Second FWT	Third MPH	Third FWT	Fourth MPH	Fourth FWT	Fifth MPH	Fifth FWT
2000	10	1346	16	827	24	562	31	441	38	355
2500	13	1426	20	876	30	595	38	467	48	376
3000	15	1453	25	893	36	607	46	476	57	383
3500	18	1440	29	885	42	601	54	472	67	380
4000	20	1386	33	852	48	578	61	454	76	366
4500	23	1359	37	835	54	567	69	445	86	358
5000	25	1319	41	810	60	550	77	432	95	348
5500	28	1224	45	752	66	511	85	401	105	323
6000	30	1049	49	645	72	438	92	344	114	277
6500	33	888	53	546	78	371	100	291	124	234

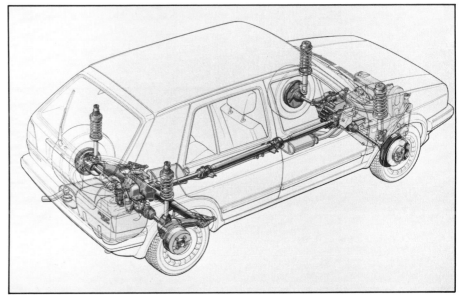

A phantom view of the Golf Syncro.

What about the turbo motor? With the stock gearbox it looks something like this:

	First		Second		Third		Fourth		Fifth	
Rpm	MPH	FWT	MPH	FWT	MPH	FWT	MPH	FWT	MPH	FWT
2000	10	2295	16	1411	24	958	31	752	38	605
2500	13	2543	20	1563	30	1061	38	833	48	671
3000	15	2590	25	1592	36	1081	46	848	57	683
3500	18	2624	29	1612	42	1095	54	859	67	692
4000	20	2560	33	1573	48	1069	61	839	76	675
4500	23	2480	37	1524	54	1035	69	812	86	654
5000	25	2360	41	1450	60	985	77	773	95	622
5500	28	2247	45	1381	66	938	85	736	105	593
6000	30	2178	49	1339	72	909	92	713	114	575
6500	33	2119	53	1302	78	885	100	694	124	559
7000	35	2018	57	1240	84	842	108	661	134	532
7500	38	1790	61	1100	90	747	115	586	143	472

The horsepeak peak at 7000 rpm makes this an inflexible engine for street use. Every time you shift, even at redline, you are losing a lot of torque. (Most people would not even miss it with this much power, but in spite of the fact that the car is fast you are throwing away horsepower you spent good money for because the transmission will never let you fully exploit it.) And with over 2000 lb-ft of torque being transmitted to the front tires all the way from 2000 rpm to 7000 rpm, you will be lucky to keep the car on the ground.

To get the most from this motor, you would need to build up a transmission using gears that do not yet exist. Just for fun, I have "constructed" a gearbox using an available first gear and final drive, and arranged the other gear ratios to allow full use of the acceleration latent in this engine. The results of this exercise are as follows:

FIRST	2.50	FOURTH	1.60
SECOND	2.16	FIFTH	1.38
THIRD	1.86	FINAL	3.00

	First		Second		Third		Fourth		Fifth	
Rpm	MPH	FWT	MPH	FWT	MPH	FWT	MPH	FWT	MPH	FWT
2000	18	1280	21	1105	24	952	28	819	33	706
2500	23	1418	26	1225	30	1055	35	907	41	782
3000	27	1444	31	1247	36	1074	42	924	49	797
3500	32	1463	37	1264	42	1088	49	936	57	807
4000	36	1427	42	1233	49	1062	56	913	65	788
4500	41	1382	47	1194	55	1028	63	885	74	763
5000	45	1316	52	1137	61	979	71	842	82	726
5500	50	1253	57	1082	67	932	78	802	90	691
6000	54	1214	63	1049	73	903	85	777	98	670
6500	59	1181	68	1021	79	879	92	756	106	652
7000	63	1125	73	972	85	837	99	720	114	621
7500	68	998	78	862	91	742	106	638	123	551

Notice that the final drive ratio has been dropped from 3.90 to 3.00, and the first gear has been changed from 3.45 to 2.50. This has brought the front wheel torque more down to earth; with the stock box, there was more front wheel torque available in second gear than this box has in first. This combination of first gear and final drive gives about the same front wheel torque as the improved GTI motor in the second example. From second gear on up, however, the turbo motor keeps charging while the GTI motor starts falling off.

This is a true close-ratio box, as the 1000 rpm drop at redline will attest. The top end suffers, however, and freeway cruising at 3500 rpm in fifth gear is bound to be a little buzzy. When these figures are run through the BASIC program, you get 7400 rpm as the shift point for all gears.

This may all be discouraging for those of you who had your hearts set on a high-revving motor without considering the role played by the transmission. On the other hand, those of you who have not yet started your project rocket will be better able to plan what tradeoffs you can live with until someone starts manufacturing all those in-between gear ratios that the factory has no use for.

Selecting gear ratios for the track

In his book *Tune to Win*, Carroll Smith gives a complete explanation of how to gear a transmission to any given track. The digested version of his information is this: Fifth gear is selected so that the top speed you will see at the track corresponds with your horsepower peak, and second gear is chosen such that the motor is just coming up on the torque peak of the motor at the slowest point of the course. Third and fourth are chosen to best span the in-between area. First gear is used only to start the car from a dead stop, so neither the ratio nor the torque drop between first and second is of critical importance.

Another factor to consider for the track, where your top speed will be fairly high, is that air resistance increases sharply as speed rises above 60 mph. You would therefore want to make your shift points a little closer together on top to compensate. You should do this when setting up a street transmission, too, but with the low maximum speed limit in the United States, acceleration is a bigger consideration than top-speed performance.

Factory gear ratio selection

Volkswagen does some sophisticated modeling when selecting gear ratios. It makes use of a computer program that factors in air resistance and drivetrain losses, among other things, although it is limited to using the same ratios that are available to us through the aftermarket.

Volkswagen approaches gear selection a little differently than Carroll Smith recommends. Its concern is with *engine elasticity*, which has to do with the car's performance in passing gear. *Passing gear* is defined as the gear one below top gear. In a five-speed box, that would be fourth gear.

Volkswagen looks for the best passing time (the time it takes for the car to accelerate from 40 mph to 60 mph) while maintaining some semblance of fuel economy. This choice is tempered by the gear ratios that are available for fourth, as well as by the need to match shift points both to and from fourth.

Fifth-gear conversion

In the GTI transmission chart, the 0.91 gear has a different spacing than the rest of the gears, hence the lower shift point. Volkswagen did this because with the 55 mph legal speed limit in the United States when these cars were introduced, top-end speed was not nearly as important as passing speed. The 0.91 and 0.89 fifth gears deliver enough torque to the front wheels that often you do not need to shift down to pass or go up grades.

There is a stock Volkswagen factory fifth gear that has the "right" spacing for the GTI gearbox. This 0.76 fifth gear predated the 0.91 fifth gear in the earlier Formula E cars because of the great fuel economy it gave. If you plan to do a lot of upshifting into fifth at 100 mph, this is the gear for you.

For the rest of us, the 0.76 gear presents too big of a hole between fourth and fifth. With the 0.91 gear there is between 60 to 80 lb-ft of front wheel torque lost shifting from fourth to fifth at 55 mph, roughly half of the loss of torque for that same shift using the 0.76 fifth gear. Along those same lines, the even taller 0.71 fifth gear is too tall for all but the stoutest motors.

Overdrive fifth gear

rpm	Fourth mph	FWT	Fifth mph	FWT
2000	31	419	46	282
2500	38	445	57	299
3000	46	454	69	305
3500	54	450	80	302
4000	61	432	91	290
4500	69	423	103	285
5000	77	410	114	276
5500	85	379	126	255
6000	92	322	137	216
6500	100	269	148	181

This does not mean that the 0.76 gear is worthless, however. If you know you will be driving more than 25,000 miles in fifth gear over the life of your car, a 0.76 gear will save you money based on fuel costs alone. As a bonus, you will also get reduced engine wear (the motor will not have to turn as many rpm to get you where you are going) and a quieter car. The BASIC program for optimum shift points shows that the shift from fourth to fifth should be made at 6340 rpm for maximum acceleration.

Installing an overdrive fifth gear

If you have a 1983-or-later five-speed GTI, Scirocco or GLI and you want to exchange your sporting fifth gear for an overdrive fifth gear, with the help of the Bentley manual you can perform a fifth-gear swap yourself without taking the transmission out of the car. It will be much easier if the car is up off the ground, however, where you can get a good look at things.

Before you start there are two things you should know. First, you will need to

This is the fifth-gear conversion kit as it comes from Autotech, complete with gasket, special tool and all the parts you need.

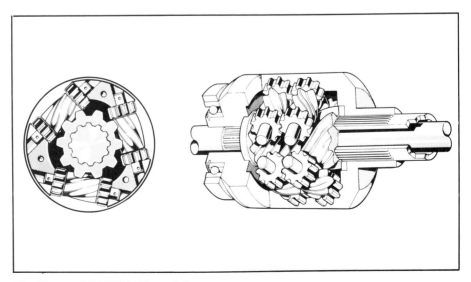

The Gleason TORSEN differential.

be able to refill your transmission with gear lube. (See the note on disposing of used gear lube in the "About safety" section in the introduction of this book.)

Second, this job requires a little finesse. In some steps, if you make a mistake you will have to take your transmission out of the car and all the way apart to put things right. If you do not feel comfortable with this responsibility, seek out someone who understands these transmissions.

In addition to the gear lube, finesse and the usual set of tools, you will need a twelve-point wrench the same size and style as that used for the head bolts.

If you buy your fifth-gear conversion from an aftermarket supplier, you will usually get a gear set, a nose cone gasket, instructions, a list of tools you will need, and a special tool or two to help things along. If you save money by buying the gears from the Volkswagen dealer, you are on your own. At least make sure you get a new gasket.

Fifth gear in the Rabbit sits in the nose cone that is farthest away from the engine. The nose cone is the piece of the transmission that has the round green plug in it. It is relatively easy to drop that

end of the transmission a little to clear the inner fender and make the change.

Put the transmission in neutral and get the car safely in the air so you can get beneath it. Ask a friend to operate the brake pedal to keep the axle from turn-

With the nose cone off, fifth gear is exposed. Do not allow the selector rod to come out of the transmission.

ing while you remove the CV (constant-velocity) joint bolts at the transmission on the left side of the car. Put a jack under the transmission and remove the transmission mount. When you lower the jack, the transmission nose cone should lower with it. If not, check to see if there is anything holding it up.

You can now remove the nose cone. With the nose cone off, the fifth gear and selector rod are exposed.

Do *not* allow the selector rod to come out of the transmission. Inside the transmission housing there are pieces that use the selector rod to locate themselves. If the selector rod is removed, these pieces will relocate themselves until the transmission is dismantled so they can be repositioned.

Measure the shift fork adjustment before you take it apart, so you will be able to return it to the correct position upon reassembly. Lock the gears from turning as described in the instructions you got with your gear set. Then use the twelve-point wrench to remove the bolt that holds on the fifth gear.

Disconnect the CV joints in preparation to lower the transmission. Have a friend step on the brakes to help hold the axle from turning.

Measure the shift fork adjustment before dismantling. This allows you to set the shift fork accurately upon reassembly.

Pry up the lock-tab on the late-style transmissions. The early-style lock requires minor grinding.

Remove the transmission mount to allow the nose cone to drop down for easier access.

Remove the bolt on the end of the main shaft with the same 12 point wrench used for cylinder head bolts.

The special tool is now needed to remove the threaded sleeve that retains the fifth-gear shift fork.

Before the fifth gear will come off, you will have to disengage the shift fork from the shift rod. On the early transmissions you will have to grind some metal, as shown in the Bentley manual. On the later transmissions, you will be able to bend up the tabs.

This is when you need the special tool. The tool slides over the end of the selector rod and engages the special threaded sleeve that holds the fifth-gear shift fork to the shift rod. This can be done with regular or locking pliers, but it is very difficult, and the threaded sleeve will not look like much when you are done, even if you do it well.

You are now ready to begin taking pieces off. Watch which way they fit so you can put them back the same way. With the fifth-gear shift fork free you can remove the fork, the dogs and the operating sleeve. Next slide the fork, synchro, gear hub and fifth gear off the main shaft. Use circlip pliers to remove the retainer for the pinion shaft side of the fifth gear, and remove that half of the gear set.

Install the new pinion side of the gear set with the groove facing outward, just as it was with the original gear. Reinstall the snap ring, remembering that the sharp edge of the ring always faces outward. Preassemble the thrust washer, gear, synchro, hub and operating sleeve, and reinstall them all together, along with the shift fork.

Again using the special tool, reinstall the threaded sleeve to the exact same height as the old one you measured. If you have an early transmission, you will have to peen the fork to retain it. If you have a later transmission, you can simply bend the tabs back into place.

Remove any remaining nose cone gasket and wipe the mating surface clean. Install the nose cone with the new gasket, and tighten the bolts. Before you button everything up, raise the transmission back up with the jack and test shift it. If everything seems good so far, refasten the transmission mount bolt and the CV joint bolts. Do not forget to refill the transmission with gear lube.

Limited-slip differentials

Back in the days of 70 hp Volkswagens it was not necessary to worry too much about getting the "power" to the ground. Nowadays, however, it seems fairly commonplace to come across a Volkswagen with 140, 150 or 160 hp, and in a front-wheel-drive car this much horsepower can prove to be a real handful, especially in a corner.

Weight transfer works against good traction. Under acceleration, the weight transfer is to the rear (off the front wheels), and in a corner the weight transfer loads one side greater than the other. This means that one of the front wheels has very little weight on it, making it easier for that wheel to spin when torque is applied.

Previous solutions included detent-type locking differentials and friction plate limited slips (we have yet to see a viscous limited slip in a Volkswagen, although it must be undergoing testing somewhere else besides Ford in Europe). The detent locking differentials were great for building up pectorals and biceps, and because they work in an on/off

Remove the circlip for the pinion-shaft half of fifth gear. Note the indicator groove on this gear faces outward.

Preassemble the thrust washer, gear, synchro, hub and operating sleeve before reinstallation.

Slide the old fifth gear, synchro and gear hub off the main shaft (the operating sleeve, fork and dogs have already been removed).

Given 200 hp and bad shifting habits, you can break these transmissions, but it is the exception rather than the rule. Techtonics

manner (they are either locked or spinning) they are very hard to drive. The friction-type limited slips were only marginally easier to muscle around, but because of their construction they tend to wear out in use, losing effectiveness.

A four-puck racing clutch disc. Eurorace

Changing the ring and pinion alters overall ratio but leaves gear spacing the same. Abt

GTI "mini-slip"

When the GTI first came out in 1983, one of the first things we noticed was that when the car was up on the hoist, turning one of the front wheels caused the other to turn in the same direction—just as if there were a limited slip in the transmission. The transmission drive flanges were different, too, and upon pulling them off we discovered that there were springs behind them applying preload. In all the excitement we figured that this was a secret limited slip.

As it turns out, Volkswagen did this not to provide a limited slip but to eliminate a problem it was having with vibrations in the drivetrain. If you have one in your car, great. If you do not have one, you need not bother to get the pieces and install them.

Torque biasing

A couple years ago, Gleason introduced a new type of limited slip differential that had automotive writers the world over scratching their heads for a way of explaining its operation. But as complex as the Gleason design is, it works. The whole idea is that gears inside the Gleason allow the differential to apply torque proportionally to wheels that are spinning at different speeds, or to one wheel even when the wheel on the other side of the car has lost traction. Thus the name, TORSEN for Torque Sensing. (TORSEN is a registered trademark of Gleason Power Systems.)

The Gleason has one main drawback, however. Gleason only sells to original equipment manufacturers, not to the aftermarket. A small firm in England, however, has come up with a torque biasing differential for the Volkswagen that is available to the enthusiast, the Quaife. The Quaife differential uses helical cut gears as opposed to the Invex cut gears in the Gleason.

On either side of the differential, each stub axle connects to its own large helical gear. There is no direct connection between these two large helical gears. Each of the two large helical gears drives five smaller-diameter helical gears (for a total of ten). The smaller gears from one side of the differential mesh with their counterparts from the other side of the differential.

In a corner, the outside wheel must turn faster than the inside wheel. The Quaife (and the Gleason, for that matter, as they both work essentially the same) allows this speed differential. But because the axles are connected through the smaller planetary gears, both axles receive the proper amount of torque.

In practice, the Quaife differential does increase the steering effort slightly in low-speed maneuvers. This stiffness is the result of the application of torque to both wheels. NOT because of any loss of differential action. And unlike detent, viscous, friction plate, and other limited slips, the Quaife limited slip does not "snatch" (slip a little and then catch). This not only makes it more pleasant to drive, it is also easier on tires and other drive train components. In fact, a Formula 1 car equipped with a limited slip of the same design was able to run an entire race on the same tires, an impressive testimony to the smoothness of this differential.

The design is the result of five years of development, with "test vehicles" provided by various police agencies and ambulance firms. Under these conditions, the differentials have gone over 100,000 miles without wearing out. Either of these two torque sensing differentials can be used with ABS, which is not true for detent or locking differentials.

As of the middle of 1987, the price of the Quaife differential is projected to be between $650 and $700, not counting the labor involved to install it. This would mean that the Quaife differential would appeal mostly to those at the high end of the performance spectrum. However, if you are running a Volkswagen with over 150 hp, this might prove to be the icing that lets you enjoy your cake.

Detent

Here is a truly unpleasant unit to live with, although it is fairly easy to set up. And back when it was one of the few units around, you either put up with it or did without. It is different from the torque biasing unit in that it is either locked or unlocked. There is no "slip" per se. The percentage of lock is determined by the number of spring-loaded detents you install. With just a few detents there is a little bit of locking power; with the differential fully loaded with detents, you have a substantial percentage of lock.

Friction clutch

This is a traditional construction for a differential. An arrangement of plates (some with a smooth finish, some with a friction surface) are interleaved to obtain the desired amount of slip. Unlike a torque biasing differential, the friction clutch has the amount of torque transfer preset (for example, at forty percent) so that when one drive wheel breaks loose, a preset amount of the otherwise lost torque is applied to the other wheel. Like most things that rely on friction to operate, the clutches wear out, necessitating replacement.

In addition to replacing the clutch disks every 10,000 to 25,000 miles, you can vary the amount of slip by using shims of different thicknesses. The harder you set the differential and the harder you run it, the more often you will have to replace the clutch disks.

Shimming valves for friction clutches		
Setting	Load in Nm	Shims used
Mild street	180 Nm	1.9 mm + 1.9 mm + 1.9 mm
Sport	230 Nm	2.0 mm + 2.0 mm + 2.0 mm
Rally	270 Nm	2.0 mm + 2.0 mm + 2.1 mm
Race	310 Nm	2.0 mm + 2.1 mm + 2.1 mm

Steel synchros (left) are heavier duty than the stock brass version, but they tend to accelerate wear on other components. Abt

Stick with helical-cut gears for street use. Straight-cut gears are stronger but make a lot more noise. Helical gears can be either shot peened or heat treated if additional strength is needed. Abt

If you have one of these differentials and it is making noise, it may be the gear lube you are using, as the friction plates are somewhat finicky about what you feed them. A quick fix is drain a little of the gear lube out and add some General Motors Limited Slip Differential Lubricant Additive, part number 1052358.

Viscous

The viscous differential also has interleaved plates, and in fact works because of the viscosity (internal friction) of the silicone fluid that fills the gaps between the plates. The plates therefore do not actually touch one another. The percentage of torque transfer varies with the difference in speed between the two wheels, partly as a result of the plate design and spacing, and partly because of a physical property of silicone fluid that it experiences virtually no change in viscosity when heated. If one wheel is rotating only a little faster than the other, only a little torque transfer occurs. When there is a big difference between the speeds of the two wheels, the viscous differential will transfer up to ninety-five percent of the torque to the wheel with traction.

Because of the difficulties in handling the silicone fluid, servicing a viscous differential can be accomplished only with special equipment. The silicone fluid is under pressure, and there is an air bubble of known (and controlled) volume included in the differential casing. Any deviation from the correct amount of pressure or air bubble volume can radically change the characteristics of the differential.

Antislip

The antislip system is tied in closely with antilock brake systems. It is an in-between system that allows you to use the big horsepower in a front-wheel-drive car without having to go to the expense of a torque biasing differential. The catch is that the car must have ABS and electronic throttle control.

Here is how it works: On acceleration, a computer measures relative wheel speed, just as it does when braking. If one wheel starts spinning, the computer will sense this and will then tell the ABS to apply braking force to that wheel. This slows down the wheel, but it also transfers the excess torque over to the wheel with traction. If neither wheel has traction, the computer will send out a signal to the throttle to cut back on engine power until traction is achieved.

How does it back off the throttle? The throttle is not connected to the accelerator pedal. The accelerator pedal is connected to a potentiometer. As you depress the accelerator pedal, the potentiometer sends a signal to the computer to open the throttle. No throttle cable! With the physical connection between the accelerator pedal and the throttle butterfly eliminated, the computer can then adjust the throttle to its liking.

Because of the complexity and cost of this system, probably few people will be retrofitting this to their cars. Besides, why go to that much trouble and then not even be able to smoke the tires once in a while?

Lubrication and maintenance

Transmission lube in some ways has it easy compared with motor oil, because there are no combustion by-products to contend with. But gears and bearings still wear, creating millions of little pieces of garbage for the gear lube to contend with—and thus far, changing gear lube has proven easier than rigging a filtering setup.

Transmission lube also is subjected to shear forces that are far in excess of those found in a motor. You can prove this by draining the gear lube and replacing it with motor oil for a couple days. The motor oil will shear down, and shifting will become progressively more difficult. Do not put transmission lube in your motor, though, as the extreme-pressure additives tend to attack bearings.

In addition to conventional gear lubes, there are fine synthetic gear lubes available from Amsoil and Synthoil. Mobil also has a synthetic gear lube available (but I have no experience with it).

Magnetic drain plug

In the Beetle, Volkswagen was careful to use magnetic drain plugs to trap at least the ferrous wear particles in the transmission. With the water-cooled generation, this practice seems to have been dropped. I recommend that you use a magnetic drain plug in your transmission. Although you can use two magnetic plugs (one for the drain and one for the fill), you need only one.

When you take out your drain plug, you will see a little hole on the inside where the magnet is supposed to go. You can clean the drain plug and epoxy a magnet to it, or just buy a magnetic drain plug ready to go.

Constant-velocity joints

Volkswagen constant-velocity joints are not a problem as long as they are kept clean and lubricated. Inspect your CV boots early and often, and immediately replace any torn or leaking boots. The factory uses metal bands to retain the boots; everybody else uses big tie-wraps, and they work great.

If you have never disassembled and reassembled a CV joint, be very careful. They go back together two ways. One way is the correct way. The other way causes the joint to lock up tight, and you may not be able to get it unlocked. If in doubt, mark the inner and outer pieces so you can get them back together the same way they came apart. The Bentley manual contains an illustration showing the correct orientation of the pieces.

When you buy a new CV joint, it comes with a new boot, a new boot clip and a little blue bottle of CV joint grease. This grease appears to be the same brand used as the factory fill, and I do not trust it. In every CV joint I have ever taken apart, the grease is runny and uninspiring. I recommend repacking your CV joints with either Swepco moly grease or Synthoil grease, although many of the better moly greases work well. Never attempt to run your car without the CV joint stub axle firmly in place in the front wheel bearing.

Wheel bearings

Wheel bearings rarely fail, but it has been known to happen. The Hacker Brothers used to have problems with front wheel bearings until they started repacking them with Synthoil grease. This requires a special bearing packer that they made themselves, but they have had no bearing failures in years of racing with Synthoil.

First find (or fashion) a bearing packer for these bearings. Then use a blunt screwdriver to carefully pop out both seals on both sides of the bearing. Set these aside for later; you are going to reinstall the same seals. Force the new grease into the bearing until the old grease (the factory grease is a clear white color) has been pushed out the other side and you can see the new grease coming in behind it. Replace the seals the same way they came out, and you are done.

For street use, this is all you should need to do. For racing, it is a good idea to carry an extra set of bearings and repack them periodically just to be on the safe side.

Rear wheel bearings should be treated to the same routine maintenance required by any open roller bearing.

Front hubs

For street use, the front hubs will work just fine and never wear out. For racing, they seem to break right at the shoulder where the hub emerges from the wheel bearing. This is the only part in the drivetrain that tends to fail under race conditions. That tendency argues eloquently in favor of proper CV joint maintenance, which most racers perform religiously.

Under race conditions, hubs can reach a ninety percent failure rate, but some racers do have a cure. After tightening the stub axle bolt to the proper specifica-tion, they get a big wrench and add as much extra torque as they have people available to stand on the wrench handle. I shudder to think what the final torque reading must be, and removal is a chore, but the failure rate drops to less than twenty percent. Follow this procedure at your own risk.

Linkage

If you have ever examined the shifter linkage, you may have wondered how in the world it works with all those levers and rods running hither and yon.

It works okay, as long as all the bushings are in good shape, although some may find the shift throw to be excessive—I often find myself shifting into fifth

To repack the front wheel bearings, first carefully remove the outer seal . . .

With some scrap aluminum, a bolt and some Zerk fittings, you can make your own front wheel bearing packer. Paul Hacker

. . . Then clamp on the bearing packer and force in the new grease until you can see that all the stock (white) grease has been displaced.

. . . Then the inner seal . . .

After curing a front wheel bearing problem by using Synthoil grease, the Hacker Brothers found the next weak link in the front suspension was the hubs, which would fail at this high-stress point.

when I really wanted third. But there is a solution to this.

The short-shift kit changes the fulcrum points and lever lengths of the shift linkage to reduce shifter throw. The disadvantage of this alternative is that the effort required to make a shift is increased. Yet even with half the shifter throw, the effort is not so bad that I would steer anyone clear of a short-shift kit.

Both Abt Motorsport and Automotive Performance Systems (APS) offer short-shift kits. The Abt kit comes from Volkswagen Motorsport's rally program and offers a straightforward fifty percent reduction in shifter throw. The APS kit gives you a choice of either thirty percent reduction or fifty percent reduction. I have not tried the thirty percent reduction, but the fifty percent reduction is enough to make it seem that there is little motion involved in shifting gears.

8

Suspension and steering

Tools and techniques

There is good news and bad news about the Volkswagen suspension. The bad news is that many things cannot be adjusted—things that it would be nice to be able to adjust for ultimate performance.

The good news is that with fewer adjustments, fewer things can go wrong. Most people will not spend the hours of testing it takes to dial in a suspension, but they will crawl under the car with a wrench and crank in some more roll stiffness, without knowing if the car needed more roll stiffness, or even without knowing what roll stiffness is!

This does not mean nothing can be done with the Volkswagen suspension. One just has to approach it a little differently than a race car that has adjustable everything.

It is beyond the scope of this book to describe slalom testing, but you might be able to do some skid pad testing. Skid pad testing tells you only the car's ability to corner on a flat surface at a constant speed, so it is not indicative of the way the car will ultimately handle or ride. However, it is one aspect that can be measured, pondered and improved upon if you so desire.

The first thing you need is a skid pad. The pad area should be level and as free from irregularities as possible. The best size for a skid pad is 200 feet in diameter. This is big enough to make the steering angle less significant and small enough to avoid involving aerodynamics during the test.

When running a skid pad test, run both clockwise and counterclockwise, and take the average of the two times.

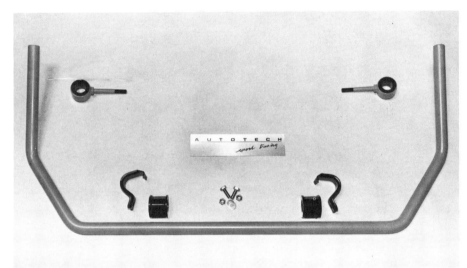

The Autotech rear antiroll bar has sliding ends that eliminate binding but still provide reinforcement against trailing arm deflection.

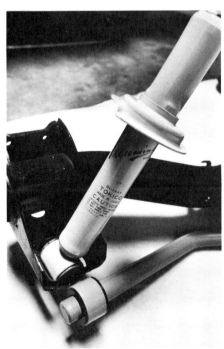

A close-up fo the Autotech sliding rear anti-roll bar mount.

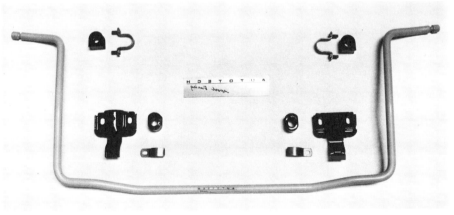

A typical front antiroll bar setup to mount in the stock location using polyurethane bushings.

Your counterclockwise times will always be better than your clockwise times, because the weight of the driver is on the inside of the car.

Winding the spring with the coils closer together at one end makes the spring rate progressive.

Pulsar Racing's front strut housing lowers the car while maintaining suspension travel.

APS antiroll bars feature Heim joints at the ends for adjustability.

You will also need an accurate way of measuring the time it takes to drive around the skid pad. After you have run around the pad both directions and have an average number, the formula you use is

$$\frac{1.226 \times r}{t^2} = g$$

In this formula, r is the radius of the skid pad, t is the time you measured and g is the g-rating of the car. Driving around the skid pad, you can see that only rarely, if ever, will you reach your car's maximum lateral acceleration while driving on the street. Still, skid pad testing can give you a feel for your car, and for what it will do at and beyond the limit of tire adhesion.

Shocks

To understand why gas shocks evolved in the first place, look at what happens in a hydraulic shock, the type your car probably came with from the factory.

Dozens of makes of hydraulic shocks exist, including Koni, Boge and Sachs. Although it is called a shock *absorber*, that duty is really carried out by the spring. The thing we call a shock absorber is actually a *damper*—it damps excessive spring reactions to driving surface irregularities. Rather than rock the

Prematched suspension components make it easier to buy the parts you need. This is a Bilstein kit.

boat, however, I will refer to them as shocks.

Shocks are filled with a fluid, usually oil. As the suspension is compressed and extended, this oil is forced through metered holes (valves) in a piston attached to the end of the piston rod. The oil slows the movement of the piston, and thus damps the otherwise uncontrolled spring action of the suspension springs. Some hydraulic shocks incorporate another set of valves at the bottom of the shock that serve to make the shock react progressively. This can improve both ride comfort and handling, because a progressively valved shock will provide a good ride when the piston velocity is low (such as when you are riding over a smooth freeway or traveling at low speeds), and it will also provide good handling when the piston velocity is high (such as would be the case over rough roads or at high speeds).

As the piston travels through the oil, two things happen. First, heat is generated by the friction of the oil passing quickly through the valves. Heat can cause the oil to boil or give off gaseous by-products. When this happens, the shock absorber's response characteristics start to change rapidly, and handling will become unpredictable. Second, the piston leaves a wave in the oil, similar to the way a boat leaves a wake in the water as it passes. A mild amount of turbulence creates a harshness in the shock absorber, and excessive turbulence will lead to cavitation, even more harshness and loss of controlled damping. Although the undemanding driver might never notice the effect heat and turbulence make in shock response, the enthusiast would—and thus was born the gas shock.

The first gas shock design to successfully attack both problems was the de Carbon, which surfaced in 1950. This system, employed by Bilstein, is also referred to as a high-pressure gas shock because nearly 300 psi of nitrogen gas (N_2) is sealed inside the shock absorber housing. The effect of the nitrogen gas on the oil is to raise the temperature at which the oil will boil, much as a pressure cooker does. It also eliminates air pockets, where hot, foamy oil might cause problems in a regular shock. More important than that, the de Carbon system stops cavitation, so erratic handling is much reduced.

This does not mean the de Carbon system is perfect. Because of its construction, a de Carbon shock has only one set of valves. A de Carbon shock absorber might be a comfort shock or a performance-valved shock, but not both.

Because the gas chamber is put at one end of the shock absorber, a de Carbon shock will have less travel than a conventional shock of the same dimensions. Finally, there is the matter of the gas pressure. If all the gas pressure were only on one side of the piston, the shock would be very stiff, as it would have 300 psi of preload pushing the piston to its full extension. Therefore, the gas pressure must act on both sides of the piston.

But one side of the piston must connect to the piston rod, and this reduces the surface area of the piston by the radius of the piston multiplied by π. Because the area of the piston on the side opposite the piston rod will always be more than that of the side with the piston rod, there will be more area for the gas pressure to push against on one side of the piston. This causes the piston to slowly grow to full extension when relieved of outside compression. It also means that the piston rod is normally of a smaller diameter than the piston rod on an equivalent hydraulic shock.

In most cars, this is no problem, but in the Volkswagen it is, because these cars incorporate MacPherson struts in the front suspension. In a MacPherson strut suspension, the shock absorber (which is called the strut in this application) is subjected to many types of side loading not found in other suspension geometries. With a reduced piston rod diameter, many feel that the de Carbon-style shock absorber is at a disadvantage. Even so, the positives outweigh the negatives, and until recently the de Carbon system was considered the best possible way to go.

Modern advances in shock absorber technology have resulted in designs that retain the advantages offered by the de Carbon system, while eliminating the disadvantages. This new generation of shocks, developed by Tokico, is referred to as low-pressure gas shocks. They feature a state-of-the-art pressure seal that allows more latitude in designing the internal components and damping characteristics than with a high-pressure

Although there isn't much room to lower the VW for street applications, the car will handle better when the center of gravity is closer to the ground.

This APS rear antiroll bar has an adjustable link that allows you to remove (or dial in) preload.

With the many variations in engine compartments over the years, upper stress bars also come in a wide assortment.

shock. They offer shock travel, piston rod diameter and valving equivalent to those of a hydraulic shock, and the cavitation and foaming control of a de Carbon shock. Since they were first introduced to the US aftermarket in 1981, low-pressure gas shocks have made quite an impression on the shock absorber industry, and now nearly every serious shock manufacturer is offering a low-pressure gas shock.

If you change both your shocks and your springs at the same time, and the resultant ride is too harsh, the normal reaction is to blame the springs. My experience with the Volkswagen is that the shocks have more of an effect on the ride of a street car than do the springs.

Therefore, be very careful about the shocks you choose, staying either with original equipment replacement shocks or with the Tokico low-pressure gas shocks. The regular nonadjustable Tokicos are very nice, and for a lot more money the adjustable ones are, too. Unlike earlier adjustable shocks that would compensate only for wear, the Tokicos adjust both bounce and rebound. If you get the adjustable Tokicos, do not get carried away. The Hacker Brothers set theirs at number 2 in the front and number 1 in the rear in their race cars.

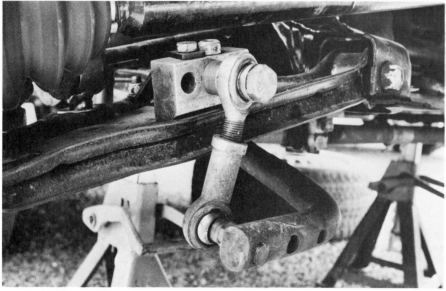

This racing front antiroll bar has both an adjustable link for preload and multiple settings to change the rate of the bar. For all but the most specialized applications, the antiroll bar should have no preload. Paul Hacker

The Koni gas shocks are externally adjustable, unlike their hydraulic counterparts.

Tokico started the trend toward low-pressure gas technology. This five-way adjustable Illumina is Tokico's top-of-the-line shock.

A typical lower stress bar with some adjustability built in. Forward-mounted antiroll bar is less effective than other designs because of front end flex.

One last word on shocks. The amount of stiffness you can put up with in your suspension is not only a function of your mindset, it is also determined by the roads you must normally travel. A stiff suspension that feels perfect in California, Tennessee or Texas may be very uncomfortable in Ohio, Arkansas or New York. Rather than try to do everything with the shocks, use softer shocks and springs, and heavier antiroll bars.

Springs

The stock Volkswagen up to 1984 has just under four inches of suspension travel before it bottoms out, which is why most aftermarket springs lower the car about an inch or so. Any more than that and you will run out of suspension just about anywhere you drive, causing the shocks to blow out. Stock suspension travel was increased in 1985 to five inches, but the principle remains the same. Because of this it is difficult to lower the center of gravity a significant amount for a street vehicle.

Springs can be either single-rate or progressive-rate, depending on their construction. A single-rate spring offers linear response across all levels of compression. A progressive-rate spring becomes more stiff as it is compressed more. This allows the spring to deliver a good ride for normal street use and then stiffen up when the going gets rough.

Early Volkswagens had single-rate springs. The 1977 Scirocco had a trick taper-ground progressive-rate spring. The taper-ground spring is a nice way to go, but in the United States, taper grinding of spring wire is expensive.

An alternative to using taper-ground wire is to wind the springs with different spacing between the coils (for example, closer together at the top than at the bottom) or with a different diameter at one end than at the other.

With lowered springs and reduced ground clearance, you need more spring rate to keep your car from bottoming out. With a single-rate spring this objective is easy to achieve, but at the expense of ride comfort. With a progressive-rate spring you can preserve at least a little of the ride comfort, and still keep your oil pan off the ground in a dip.

Most of the better aftermarket springs are now made of chrome silicon that has been cold wound. These are far superior to the mandrel-bent, oil-tempered steel springs we used to have to put up with.

With all the good chassis springs around, it is not necessary to butcher a set of stock springs, either by heating and bending or by cutting off coils. Heating and bending will not give you a predictable spring rate, and cutting off a

The suspension on the 1985-and-later VW is much different from that on the earlier cars. Note the large subframe and the redesigned A-arm, for example. A-arm bushings for this suspension minimize unwanted suspension geometry changes without sacrificing the ride characteristics.

The 1985-and-later VW also sports a much different rear torsion beam setup, including special bushings for better tracking.

The adjustment on the rear Tokico Illumina shock.

coil makes the spring stiffer, and far from progressive.

Another problem with shortening chassis springs is that when the suspension is at full droop (that is, when the suspension is as far down as it can be), you want the springs to be still touching both the bottom and the top spring perches. If the spring is not touching the top perch, spring action becomes unpredictable.

If you wish to lower your car more than an inch for racing, you will need to either find a shortened shock absorber (good luck!) or extend your shock towers upward. Extending your stock towers allows you to retain the full suspension travel while moving the chassis (and center of gravity) closer to the ground. Another benefit of extending the shock towers is that you can give yourself some camber adjustment up top, instead of at the bottom of the strut only. You do need to use special small-OD springs with this setup, and the top of the strut is metal-to-metal with the chassis as I said, race only.

Remember to have your headlights realigned any time you change the ride height of your car.

Kits

Springs are often sold in kit form, so you do not have to figure out what rates and heights are going to work on your car. Although many kits come with just the springs, there are kits available that include fully assembled front struts as well. The cost is higher, but you do not need a spring compressor to install them; you unbolt your current springs and shocks, and bolt in the new parts. If your shocks are due for replacement when you upgrade your springs, a preassembled kit will make your job much easier.

Just remember that any time you take apart your front suspension, you will need to have it realigned. One nearly new set of Comp T/A radials wore down to the belts in 700 miles because the owner did not have the car aligned after lowering his car.

Front suspension

After toying with different front suspension settings (some literally by accident!), I have found that the stock settings work the best. The difference really shows up when you put some torque through your front end. James Sly's 180 hp turbo Rabbit at one point was almost too "squirrelly" to drive hard, in spite of three alignments. I finally set it back to stock, and the problem disappeared.

For racing, the best setting is about ⅛ inch of toe-out and up to 2.5 degrees of camber. This much negative camber helps control understeer and improve turn-in response. Tire wear with these settings will be high. Camber can also be asymmetrical (for racing only) to better match the course. For example, at Riverside where all the important turns are right-handers, the Volkswagen racers run two degrees of camber on the left side and one degree of camber on the right side.

You can get more camber than the stock adjustment will normally give by loosening the adjustment bolts, and having a compatriot pull out at the bottom of the tire and push in at the top of the tire. This gives you the benefit of all the slop inherent around the adjustment bolts. Make sure the adjuster bolt is turned to allow maximum camber. It is harder to get the camber equal from side to side this way, but you can squeeze out a few extra points if you need them.

Those with 1985–and–later cars with the revised suspension who need more front camber than the adjustment will allow can get one degree more camber by changing the top adjustment bolt to Volkswagen part number N 100 766 01. This bolt is the same as the stock bolt everywhere except the shank, which is 1 mm thinner to allow more movement at

The racing auxiliary front antiroll bar runs in metal bushings. The welded-on collars prevent the bar from wandering from side to side under load. Paul Hacker

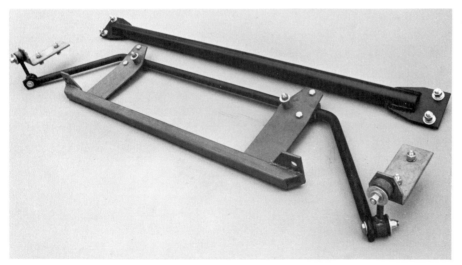

The H&H Specialties front antiroll bar for the pre-1983 cars works in conjunction with the lower stress bar. The rear antiroll bar is hollow and bolts into the triangular corner reinforcements of the torsion beam.

the adjustment point. If you still do not have enough camber, the lower bolt may be changed, too.

To fine-tune your front suspension settings, you will need a tire pyrometer. (For details, see the section on tire temperatures.)

Antiroll bars

Over the years, antiroll bars have been variously called antisway bars, sway bars, roll bars and so on. For the purpose of this book they are called antiroll bars because technically that is what they do—counteract body roll.

The New Dimensions aluminum mount (right) provides positive location of the steering rack.

Some kits come preassembled so you don't need a spring compressor to install them. Autotech

After much deliberation I have come to the conclusion that the best arrangement for the front bar is the factory GTI style. Many aftermarket suppliers have adopted this mounting system as well, so it should not be difficult to find a good set of antiroll bars. If you have a GTI, you can simply unbolt your stock bar and bolt in whatever size bar you desire. Keep in mind that the bigger the bar the harsher the ride will be, although it will not be nearly as harsh as it would be with springs heavy enough to keep the body from rolling.

For racing use, the hot setup is to leave an antiroll bar in the stock location and mount another bar right beneath it. Alternately, the stock front bar is replaced with a 1⅛ inch bar. If you plan to do much exploration into custom antiroll bars, you can make your own bars using stressproof steel (in whatever diameter you choose) and a torch. The stressproof

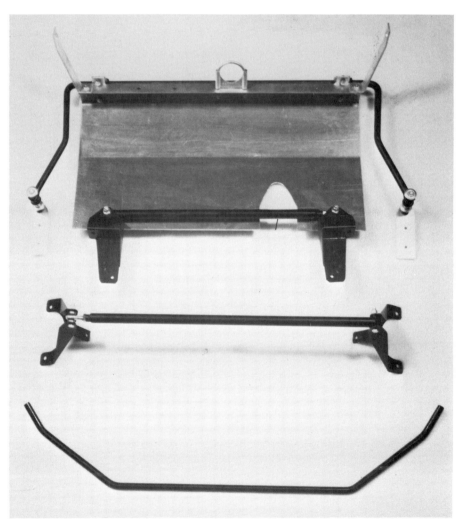

For off-road rallies this setup might not be the ultimate in antiroll bars, but the bash plate can save your motor.

steel can be heated and still retain the properties it needs to act as an antiroll bar. Production bars should all be cold-formed on mandrels.

If you watch much Volkswagen racing (or race yourself), you know that a stock Volkswagen wants to lift its inside rear tire in tight, fast turns. This is the case with most front-wheel-drive cars, because of the inherent understeer that comes from having steering, braking and power all applied at the heavy end of the car.

Understeer is a situation in which increasing the steering input does not change the direction in which the car is traveling. In other words, the car is sliding off the road front-end first. (Oversteer is what happens when the rear end of the car wants to slide while the front of the car can still steer.)

To balance out your car's handling, you can increase or decrease either the understeer or the oversteer. There are many ways to do this.

To reduce understeer (increase oversteer), try one or more of the following:
• Increase weight transfer at rear by increasing rear roll stiffness
• Reduce weight transfer on front by reducing front roll stiffness
• Increase aerodynamic downforce on the front tires
• Reduce aerodynamic downforce on the rear tires
• Use wider front tires
• Use narrower rear tires
• Reduce front spring rate
• Increase rear spring rate
• Use a lighter front antiroll bar
• Use a heavier rear antiroll bar
• Move some weight toward the rear of the car
• Use softer front shocks
• Use harder rear shocks
• Use more negative camber in the front
• Use more positive camber in the rear
• Raise the front tire pressure
• Lower the rear tire pressure
• Make the front track wider
• Make the rear track narrower

To reduce oversteer (increase understeer), try one or more of the following:
• Reduce weight transfer at rear by reducing rear roll stiffness
• Increase weight transfer on front by increasing front roll stiffness
• Reduce aerodynamic downforce on the front tires
• Increase aerodynamic downforce on the rear tires
• Use wider rear tires

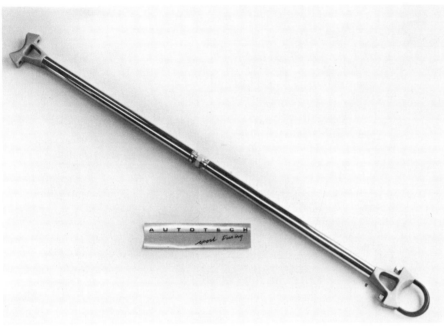

Rear stress bars are not needed as much as front stress bars, but they do lend strength to the chassis. Autotech

This is what the Pulsar Racing strut extender looks like in the car. Note the reinforcement of the rest of the strut tower.

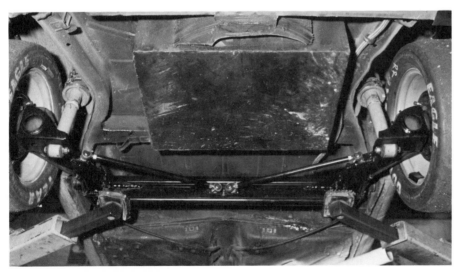

Another Pulsar Racing piece is this setup for preventing rear wheel toe-in under hard cornering. Note the fuel cell.

There are many types of spring compressor for working on MacPherson struts. Do not attempt to disassemble a MacPherson strut without one.

- Use narrow front tires
- Use heavier front springs
- Use lighter rear springs
- Use a heavier front antiroll bar
- Use a lighter rear antiroll bar
- Move some weight forward
- Use softer rear shocks
- Use harder front shocks
- Use more negative camber in the rear
- Use more positive camber in the front
- Lower the front tire pressure
- Raise the rear tire pressure
- Make the rear track wider
- Make the front track narrower

High-performance bushings

Suspension bushings come in stock, hot street and metal-to-metal strengths. For street use, the metal-to-metal versions are much too harsh; these are for race only. Depending on the condition of the roads where you live, the hot street bushings, which are often made of poly instead of the standard-issue rubber, can be a blessing or a curse. When used with very high horsepower applications, high-performance bushings can help you maintain control, although you will have to put up with a harsher ride.

Whether or not you choose to go with high-performance bushings, keep an eye on the front strut bushings. They tend to deteriorate and take the edge off the oth-erwise sharp handling your car is capable of. Replace them when they clunk or get loose.

Boxing the lower A-arms

The idea of boxing (or reinforcing) the lower A-arms is something inherited from the 914 and 924 racers, especially because the 924 front lower-A-arm is so close in design to that of the Volkswagen.

I usually advocate using stronger suspension pieces, but I have not yet seen a big problem with Volkswagen A-arms flexing or completely failing. Boxing the A-arms does increase unsprung weight (which is not good) and provides some wonderful hiding places for corrosion (which is not good either). This modification is not recommended.

Front stress bars

If you have ever looked underneath the front end of your pre–1985 car, you may have been amazed at the way the front of the lower suspension pickup points seems to float in midair. This is not the best setup for hard cornering.

Polyurethane suspension bushings can firm up the handling without destroying the ride. Autotech

When replacing your front struts, check the upper strut bearings, too. If they have been clunking, replace them at the same time. Autotech

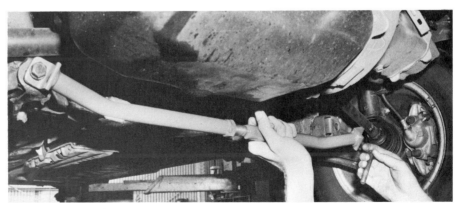

Installing a lower stress bar can be very simple, and the improvement in handling is amazing.

155

The lower stress bar was developed to strengthen this crucial area. If you have enough money to buy only one bolt-on suspension piece, the lower stress bar should be it.

The first lower stress bar was a simple affair: a nearly straight bar attached to the two front mounting points, using the stock pickup point bolt. Now, however, lower stress bars have grown more complex and seem to work even better. There are two styles: one with a built-in provision for mounting the front anti-roll bar, and one with a triangulated mounting scheme. Either one will provide some handling benefits.

One word of caution: Never put a floor jack underneath the stress bar and try to lift the car with it. Eventually, this *will* lift the car, but in the meantime the stress bar will develop a permanent bend, ruining its usefulness and pulling your alignment out of whack. If someone else works on your car, specify to *not* support the car on the stress bar. And be sure to check the lower stress bar before you leave the premises.

Upper stress bars provide less dramatic improvements in feel, but can cut the amount of body flex in the early cars significantly. In 1985, Volkswagen made extensive changes to the chassis that reduce the need for stress bars. Make sure the top stress bar you buy will clear the motor, radiator overflow tank and so on, and still allow the hood to close. There are so many different engine configurations that suppliers have had to develop a multitude of stress bars to accommodate all the cars—just look until you find one that fits.

Rear suspension

Antiroll bars

As shown in the handling lists, changes at one end of the vehicle often produce different handing characteristics at the opposite end of the car. That is why using a stiffer rear bar will not help keep the inside rear tire planted on the ground in a fast corner; this is the job of the front bar.

In the Volkswagen it is more important to have both front tires in contact with the pavement than both rear tires, although the ideal situation would be to

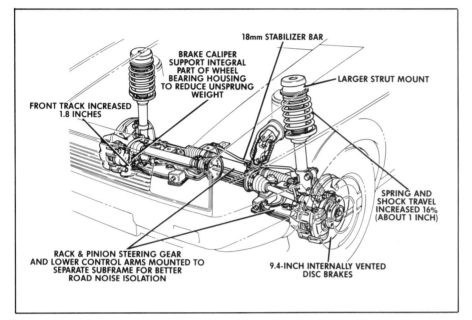

A phantom view of the 1985-and-later front suspension for the GTI, Scirocco and GLI.

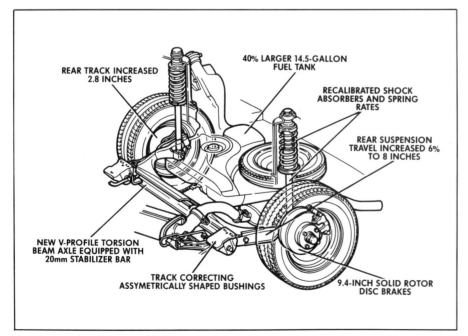

A phantom view of the 1985-and-later rear suspension for the GTI, Scirocco and GLI.

These two bolts can be replaced with bolts having thinner shanks, in order to get more suspension adjustment in the 1985-and-later cars. Paul Hacker

use all four tires all the time. Keeping the front tires on the ground is the job of the rear antiroll bar, which also counteracts the tendency of the Volkswagen to understeer. For the best-balanced handling, you will need both a front and a rear antiroll bar. The 1985-and-later Volkswagens, for example, have a built-in rear antiroll bar to complement the front antiroll bar.

Some rear antiroll bars require that you drill two rather large holes in your rear torsion beam for the bracket bolts. The metal in the beam is tough, so start with small bits and work your way up slowly. Trying to get done too fast will result in burned and dull drill bits, and you may eventually become convinced that you will never get the holes drilled.

When mounting the bar to the torsion beam on some pre-1984 cars (such as the Cabriolet), it is impossible to get the bolt, nut and bracket attached to the torsion beam—there simply is not enough room. The way around this is to temporarily drop the torsion bar down by removing the four pivot bolts (two per side). Be sure you have a jack underneath the torsion beam when you lower it, or it will drop down and hang itself on the brake lines. You will need to lower it only a little bit to get access. Make sure you don't stress the brake lines at any time, and when you are done be sure to snug up the pivot bolts.

Rear stress bars

As in the front, the tops of the shock towers in the rear are separated only by air, and they appear to be prime candidates for reinforcement. However, the rear shock towers do not locate the rear suspension the way the front shock towers locate the front suspension, so any gains from reinforcement probably would be subtle. I am in favor of reducing chassis flex whenever possible, but I would put off installing a rear stress bar until last, if ever.

1985-and-later racing suspensions can make use of this upper strut bearing. Abt

The Bilstein front strut on the left is a little harsh for street use, but it does allow adjustment that is impossible with the stock unit. Abt

The lower control arm bushing can be replaced with this precision bearing (race only). Abt

157

Steering

If the stock-ratio steering rack is not quick enough, you can buy a quick-ratio steering rack. Quick-ratio racks are available both for cars with manual steering and for newer cars with power-assisted steering.

The drawback to the manual quick-ratio steering rack is that steering effort goes up sharply. If you try to combine a quick-ratio rack with a smaller-diameter steering wheel, you will be able to put away your Jane Fonda workout video as long as you commit to driving a few miles each day. A fifteen-inch steering wheel is highly recommended with the quick-ratio manual steering rack.

In racing applications, the power steering reservoir can overflow. The remedy is to provide an overflow bottle so the excess fluid will be automatically recycled back into the system as it cools down, similar to the way a coolant recovery tank works on a radiator.

Weight redistribution

One obvious way to improve the handling of your car is to redistribute the weight so the car isn't so nose heavy. The only component that easily qualifies for relocation is the battery. But, is what you get from moving the battery to the trunk worth the effort of doing it?

Fortunately, you can calculate what the resultant weight differences will be from moving the battery before you make this decision. For this example, assume you are working with a car that has a gross vehicle weight of 2,300 pounds, a front weight bias of sixty-two percent, a rear bias of thirty-eight percent and a battery that weighs forty pounds. (This must be a later-model car, as the early cars weighed just under 2,000 pounds.)

With its 94.5 inch wheelbase, this 2,300 pound Rabbit will have 1,426 pounds on the front axle and 874 on the rear axle. The center of gravity is 35.91 inches behind the front axle, or about where the shifter is.

Moving the forty-pound battery to the trunk, directly over the rear axle, moves the center of gravity back only about 1.9 inches. But the combination of moving the weight *and* the center of gravity at the same time gives you a bigger difference in weight distribution than you might expect. Now, the front axle is supporting 1,380 pounds and the rear axle is supporting 920 pounds.

While all this was going on, the polar moment of inertia has also been changed from its old value of 4,839,124 lb/in to a new, higher value of 4,929,744 lb/in, a difference of 90,620 lb/in. (The polar moment of inertia is calculated by multiplying the weight of the car's components by their distance from the center of gravity.) Raising the polar moment of interia in a car that weighs as much as the Volkswagen is not necessarily a bad thing, and you have transferred forty-six pounds away from the front end, reducing understeer in the process.

If moving the battery sounds better than going on a diet to accomplish a similar end, here is what you will need: a plastic battery box with a top, two battery terminal ends, 250 inches (or so) of 8-gauge wire (or larger) and some cable splices. The plastic battery box should be available at a boating supply store, if you cannot find one elsewhere. Bolt it down so it does not slide around in your trunk. The top is necessary so you can put things in your trunk without subjecting them to battery acid. The heavy-gauge wire can usually be found at a welding supply store. Heavier wire is more difficult to work with and is more expensive, but the greater the diameter of the wire the less voltage drop you will have and the better your electrical system will work. (By the way, if you are planning to put large stereo amplifiers in the trunk, having the battery right there to power them is quite convenient.)

Corner balancing

Corner balancing involves adjusting the weight on each wheel for maximum handling. For example, if the desired weight distribution is fifty-four percent in the front and forty-six percent in the rear, you would raise or lower each end of the car until you achieved this balance. The weight would then be adjusted evenly between the right and left wheels at each end of the car for best all-around handling. Weight balancing is done with the driver in the car, and the maximum difference from side to side should be no more than thirty pounds.

The suspension on the Rabbit is not conducive to easy weight adjustments. Although you can jack weight into the car by preloading the antiroll bars, this is not the correct method for corner balancing the chassis, and the car will handle strangely as a result (this method is better suited for oval-track work).

For true corner balancing, you will need either a bunch of chassis springs that have been precalibrated (so you can swap springs until the weight distribution is correct) or a set of the sophisticated (and expensive) shocks with adjustable spring perches. You will also need a set of special scales for weighing the car corner by corner, and a lot of patience.

Even the hottest street machine usually will not require corner balancing. However, if you are racing your car, consider contacting someone who can help ensure that your car is handling at its maximum potential.

The rear torsion beam pivot can also be upgraded with this solid pivot for racing applications with the later cars. Abt

9

Tires and wheels

Many enthusiasts want to put bigger tires on their Volkswagens but are not sure which sizes will fit and exactly what to expect from bigger tires.

There are two ways to get bigger tires on your car: mount bigger tires on your existing wheels, or mount bigger tires on wheels larger than your existing wheels. The first option is called the Plus option. The second option is known as the Plus 1 option if you increase wheel diameter by one inch, Plus 2 if you increase wheel diameter by two inches and so on.

The Plus concept

The best starting point for demonstrating the Plus concept is the thirteen-inch wheel. The stock tire on this wheel was at one time a 155R13. This is called an 80 series tire, because the measurement of the tire from the bead to the thread is eighty percent of the measurement from sidewall to sidewall (this relationship is referred to as the aspect ratio). This makes it a tall, skinny tire.

To maintain the same tire height in a "bigger" (wider) tire as in a skinny tire, you have to change the aspect ratio. For every increase in tire width (155 mm to 175 mm, 175 mm to 195 mm and so on), you must also decrease the series (80 to 70, 70 to 60 and so on). The rule of thumb is that for every ten percent reduction in series you add 20 mm to the tire size. Thus, a 175/70R13 has roughly the same rolling radius as a 155R13. With the lower aspect ratio, the bigger tire is wider, but retains the same overall diameter.

One misconception is that with a wider tire you achieve better handling because you have more rubber touching the pavement. Not so.

No matter what size tire you have on your car, the *footprint* of the tire will be the same. In other words, a 155R13 tire will have the same amount of rubber touching the ground as does a 195VR-5015. By changing to a wider tire, you are, however, changing the shape of the *contact patch* (where the tire meets the pavement). With a 155R13 tire, the contact patch is long and narrow. With a

This was the first factory alloy available for the VW. There are several versions.

When the American GTIs came out, the factory equipped them with this 14 inch wheel instead of the 13 inch wheel that had been the standard until then. This is the 1986 model year fitment.

These Panasport rims are popular with rally teams because of their light weight and high strength.

195VR5015, the contact patch is short and wide.

In a corner, the 155R13 tire with its tall sidewalls will squirm all over the place in response to side loading. As it pushes out, the tread is pulled away from the pavement, reducing traction and causing the tire to skid. A wider tire, with shorter sidewalls, is not as prone to this, so it is better at maintaining the contact patch.

This all works very well on dry surfaces, but in wet conditions there are other things to consider. As a tire rolls over a wet surface, the first third of the contact patch shoves the water out of the way, the second third squeegees the road surface of excess water and the final third provides the actual grip. With a skinny tire like the 155×13, the long contact patch means that each third of the contact patch has more time to do its job. The 195VR5015, on the other hand, has a much shorter contact patch, leaving each (shorter) third of the contact patch

much less time to get the water out of the way and provide traction. This is one reason wide tires are not as good in the rain as narrow tires, and why they tend to hydroplane (skim along the top of the water instead of forcing through to the road surface) easier.

Therefore, if most of your driving is done in the dry, a wide tire will do you the most good. If you drive in water, snow or ice, a narrower tire would better suit your needs. If you can afford it, consider getting a set of tires for summer use and another set for winter use.

Ronal R-8 spoked wheel.

If you can afford these expensive Ronal RC-2 modular wheels, the Ronal R-10 is a one-piece version that is less expensive, and actually is better suited for day-to-day street use.

One of the many fine Momo road wheels. Note that the gas cap has been cut to match the pattern of the wheel!

A comparison between Yokohama's race-only A-001 (left) and street-going A-008.

The Plus 1 and Plus 2 concepts

Once you have exhausted the possibilities of mounting wider tires on the stock thirteen-inch rims, the next step is to increase the rim size. Wheels are available for the Volkswagen in thirteen-, fourteen-, and fifteen-inch sizes, so if you start with thirteens you can add up to two inches to your wheel diameter, and if you start with fourteens you are

This rim first appeared on the 1987 Scirocco 16V. In spite of the way it looks it is not directional, and it is fairly heavy compared with other available rims.

limited to one additional inch of wheel diameter. Adding one inch (going from a thirteen to a fourteen, or from a fourteen to a fifteen) is referred to as Plus 1. Adding two inches (going from a thirteen to a fifteen) is referred to as Plus 2.

To maintain the overall height of the tire, the aspect ratio must again be reduced when upgrading to a Plus 1 or Plus 2 size. The rule of thumb for the Plus concept usually works here, too, but it is better to consult a tire spec sheet for actual dimensions.

In addition to a wider contact patch, a Plus 1 or Plus 2 tire has the high-performance advantage of a shorter sidewall. Shorter sidewalls flex less, so the tread maintains better contact with the pavement. With a Plus 1 or Plus 2 tire, the wheel extends to where the sidewall of the tire used to be, and the rim is much stiffer than the tire, which also reduces the amount of flex in this area.

Aside from the high cost of a set of Plus 2 wheels and tires, this additional high-performance advantage comes at the expense of wet-weather performance (as previously noted) and ride characteristics.

This brings up the subject of the relative performance of wider tires on stock rims versus a Plus 1 or Plus 2 setup. There are linear relationships for ride, handling, ruggedness and cost. Ride and ruggedness will be best with thirteen-inch rims because of the cushioning

effect of the sidewall. Fifteen-inch tires not only ride worse but do a poorer job of protecting the rim from pothole damage and so on. Handling will be best with the fifteens, however. I prefer the 205/60R13 or the 205/55R14.

Balancing

It seems so simple, and yet it causes so many problems. To be truly balanced, your wheel must have weights both on the inside and on the outside—not just on the inside.

Whenever you have a set of tires mounted, mark the position of the tire relative to the wheel. After 500 to 1,000 miles, check to see if the marks are still aligned. If not, the balance will have to be checked again. This creeping occurs because of the lubricant used to ease the bead over the edge of the rim. It is normal for this to happen, and you may be able to get the shop that balanced your tires to rebalance them at no charge after the bead stops moving.

Rotating

The whole point behind rotating your tires is to squeeze more miles out of tires that are wearing unevenly. It works, too. And I never do it on any of my cars.

I prefer to fix the reason the tires are wearing unevenly. I also prefer replacing the front tires a few months ahead of the

Check tire temperatures with a tire pyrometer.

A rear view of the JJD twin tire. The outside of the rim is a traditional basket-weave pattern.

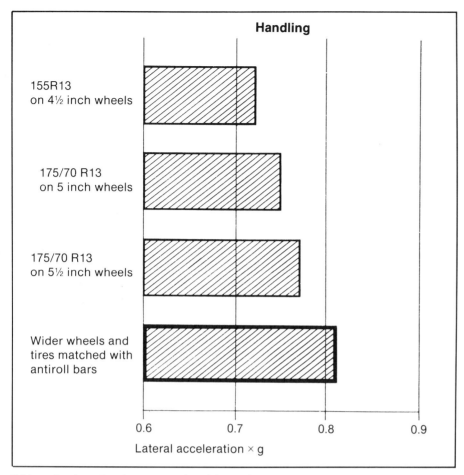

Handling

155R13
on 4½ inch wheels

175/70 R13
on 5 inch wheels

175/70 R13
on 5½ inch wheels

Wider wheels and
tires matched with
antiroll bars

0.6　　　0.7　　　0.8　　　0.9

Lateral acceleration × g

Wider wheels not only support the side-walls better, they also allow you to run wider tires. Match these wider wheels and tires with an antiroll bar, and handling will improve.

The trailer-style stem stays tucked in, out of harm's way. The rim is a lightweight directional 14 incher from Dino.

rears, and reducing the impact on my checking account, rather than replacing all four at once.

If you prefer to rotate your tires, make *sure* you check with the tire manufacturer to see what constitutes an acceptable rotation pattern and what does not. As radial tires evolve, suggested rotation patterns are changing, too.

Tire pressure

In most situations, the factory-recommended tire pressures will be adequate for your driving. As just discussed, the weight of the car remains the same no matter what tire you put on, so you will need only the recommended tire pressure.

If you intend to go racing, give some thought to changing tire pressures. Whereas street tire pressure is checked and adjusted only when the tires are cold, at the track it is adjusted when the tires are at operating temperature. To do this accurately you will need a tire pyrometer in addition to your tire pressure gauge. If you already own a digital multimeter, check to see if there is a temperature probe available for your meter before you buy a pyrometer. You might be able to save some money.

With the tire pyrometer, you can check your suspension adjustments as well. Here is how it works.

• After running the car on the course, bring it in and immediately use the pyrometer to take the temperature of the tires, checking the outside edge, middle and inside edge. After about thirty seconds, the temperature will be too low for an accurate measurement, so hurry.

• Insert the point of the pyrometer just underneath the tread of the tire and wait for the reading to stabilize.

• The tire will be hottest where it is working the hardest. For example, if the inside edge is hotter than the middle or outside, you have too much negative camber. If the middle is hottest, the tire pressure is too high. If the outside is hottest, there is too much positive camber. The opposite works, too. For example, if the middle is cooler, the tire pressure is too low.

	Less		More
Ride	15	▬▬▬▬▬	13
Handling	13	▬▬▬▬▬	15
Ruggedness	15	▬▬▬▬▬	13
Cost	13	▬▬▬▬▬	15

Characteristics of 13 and 15 inch tire and wheel combinations.

162

- You more than likely will be faced with a multitude of different readings, so check and recheck often until you have everything sorted out.

- Do not be surprised if your hot tire pressures are much higher than your cold tire pressures. If you are using your car for both the street and occasional autocrosses, be sure to write down what tire pressures you need for both situations, both hot and cold. This will save you valuable time.

Tire shaving

Shaving refers to the practice of grinding the tread off a tire to prepare it for racing. As opposed to a normal street tire, a shaved tire will have only $^3/_{32}$ to $^6/_{32}$ inch of tread.

As strange as this may sound, shaving the tire actually makes it last longer. With less tread, there is less tread squirm and thus less heat. A full-depth tread on a race tire will lose huge chunks of rubber, throwing the tire out of balance and

shortening its life. For racing use, tire shaving is mandatory.

Usually the tire is shaved evenly across the top. Some racers shave the tread asymmetrically, but the results of this practice seem inconsistent.

Selecting tires

The standard offset of the 4½- and five-inch-wide Volkswagen wheels is 45 mm. With the introduction of the 5½-inch-wide wheels, it changed to 38 mm. The offset is designed into the wheel to complement the negative roll radius built into the front suspension. Negative roll radius causes the car to automatically steer in the direction of a skid caused by unequal front wheel traction, and makes it easier to control the car should you lose pressure in a front tire.

As desirable as it may be to retain the wheel offset (and thus the negative roll radius) the factory intended, with the MacPherson strut front suspension there is little room to fit a wider rim on the inboard side of the wheel; that is where Volkswagen chose to put the strut. After a point, therefore, you cannot make the tire any wider without reducing the offset. Since the wheel offset at which the negative roll radius would be lost is about 31 mm, you should choose a wheel with greater than 31 mm of offset.

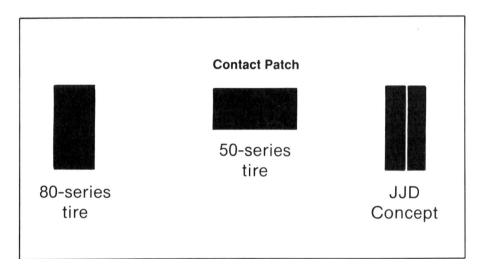

Contact Patch

80-series tire

50-series tire

JJD Concept

In spite of the fact that all these tires have different aspect ratios, they all have the same contact patch.

Tire and Wheel Equivalencies: Plus 1 & Plus 2

Tire height	13	13	13	14	14	15	Rim diameter
Tire size	155R13	175/70 R13	205/60 R13	185/60 R14	205/55 R14	195/50 R15	
Aspect ratio	80	70	60	60	55	50	
Tire designation	P3	P3/70	P6	P600	P600	P7 (P700)	
Cross section*	6.26″	7.13″	8.19″	7.44″	7.87″	7.79″	
Tire diameter	22.76″	22.76″	22.67″	22.76″	22.91″	22.88″	
Revs/mile	917	917	917	917	907	914	

NOTE: All cross section widths measured on 6 inch rim except for the 155 R13, which is measured on a 5 inch rim. Cross section will change by approximately 0.20 inch for every ½ inch change in rim width.

For better handling it is possible to increase the rim size, shorten the sidewall and maintain the same tire diameter making use of the Plus 1 and Plus 2 concepts.

If you need really wide wheels and cannot maintain 31 mm of offset, you need not worry too much about the negative roll radius. The car's handling will be more radically changed by the effects (both positive and negative) of the wider tires than by the loss of the negative roll radius—until you blow a tire.

Most seven-inch-wide wheels have about 33 mm of offset. The change in offset caused by some of these wheels may create wheel bearing problems, but it should not be enough to change the bearing loading to the point of early fail-ure. Even if you go from 45-mm-offset wheels to 31-mm-offset wheels, the total change is only 14 mm.

There exist certain linear relationships among wheel size, tire profile, cost and performance that are easy to remember, and that can make it much easier to decide what combination is right for you. These relationships are shown in the chart.

When using the chart, weigh cost against ride, handling and ruggedness, and make the best decision for your car. James Sly, who for years had one of the hottest Rabbits in southern California, took about a week to change his fifteen-inch tire and wheel combination for a fourteen-inch combination after moving to the Washington, D.C., area.

His is not an unusual case. In the northern regions where frost heaves and potholes are the order of the day, you will want a taller sidewall to help soak up the inevitable jolts. Even in southern California, a combination of fifteen-inch rims and stiff suspension can balloon your strut towers amazingly quickly.

You can get big improvements in handling without going to larger-diameter rims by increasing the width of whatever rim size you want to use. For dry performance, the wider the rim the better the car will handle, as long as everything fits underneath the fender. A good set of 13×6 rims with 205/60 tires will handle quite well, and the stock GTI fourteen-inch rims are also good.

It is difficult to gauge how rugged the rims need to be for your application until you have bent a few. This does become expensive, however. Depending on how rough you are on equipment, you may have to go to extra-heavy-duty rims, like the rally rims made by Panasport.

On the other hand, unless you are desperate for a certain offset, backset or style, stay away from the modulars for street use. Modulars come as either two-

The Work modular wheel. Autotech

The wider wheels such as the eight-inch Abt and these seven-inch Zenders work best when matched with fender flares. GMP

Speed ratings

Letter rating	For sustained speeds up to:
F	50 mph
G	56 mph
J	62 mph
K	68 mph
L	75 mph
M	81 mph
N	87 mph
P	93 mph
Q	100 mph
R	106 mph
S	112 mph
T	118 mph
U	124 mph
H	130 mph
V	130 + mph
Z	150 + mph

Note that a V rated tire is shown as being capable of sustained speeds in excess of 130 mph. This makes the new Z rating superfluous in some respects, but I suppose if you are buying tires for your Porsche 959 you do not want to have to guess whether the tire you are looking at will really do the job or not.

Although we normally deal with S, H or V rated tires, there are lots of other ratings in addition to "unrated" tires.

or three-piece units. In the two-piece versions, the outer rim is one piece and the center is the other. The center is then mounted wherever it is needed, keeping both clearance and offset in mind. In the three-piece versions, the outer rim is made up of two halves. By using different-shaped halves, the manufacturer can vary the clearance and offset while making any diameter or width wheel.

The Ronal modulars seem to be the best, and even they will bend. Ronal also makes one-piece wheels in just about any size you need, so it should not be necessary to go to a more expensive modular.

When running modulars, be aware that some will leak air at the seams, so keep an eye on those tire pressures.

There is only one sixteen-inch tire setup for the Volkswagen, and that is the JJD Concept Tire. Featuring two 105/85VR16 tires on each wheel, this is visually one of the wildest combinations available, as well. With the two thin tires, the JJD Concept is better in the wet than is a traditional wide high-performance tire, but because of the construction of the tires, the contact patch is just as wide as the widest of them.

Having two separate tires on each wheel, you can probably eliminate your spare tire. If one of the two tires loses air, the other will hold the car up for thousands of miles (although handling suffers, of course).

As great as they are, JJD Concept tires are not perfect. They weigh a great deal more than most other tire and wheel combinations, radically increasing your *unsprung weight*. (Unsprung weight includes all the weight *not* supported by the springs.) The greater the unsprung weight, the more difficult it is for the springs and shocks to control wheel movement and deliver the best handling on rough surfaces.

Unsprung weight is important on Volkswagens, which is one reason the relatively light Pirelli P-7 works so well on these cars. The JJD Concept also has a tendency to flex from side to side quite a bit in quick, transient maneuvers. It is expensive compared with traditional tire and wheel combinations, although replacement tires cost less. Tire changing must be done with a European-style changer, which is now becoming available across the United States (Firestone Performance Shops have them, for example).

The JJD Concept skid pad figures are good, however, being only a couple hundredths of a g off from a traditional high-performance tire, so if you need

wet traction you can count on in extreme conditions, you may want to consider the JJD Concept setup.

If you do get the urge to try different wheels and tires but you cannot afford the best of both, skimp on the tires (unfortunately this is not possible with the JJD Concept wheels). You will have to live with the rims for years, so that is where you should spend your money. While you are wearing out your cheap tires, you can be putting aside money to get the ones you always wanted next time around.

When buying high-performance tires, be aware of the hidden cost factor. Tires now come graded as to how they will perform in three areas: temperature, traction and tread life. The tread life rating is the one to be interested in. Most tires that grip the road and thus improve handling have a softer compound and thus a shorter life span, but a low wear rating does not guarantee that a tire will handle well.

Handling aside, the wear rating is your clue to how expensive the tires really are. A low wear rating can make an "inexpensive" set of tires expensive, and an "expensive" set of tires exhorbitant.

Be sure to check the wear rating before you buy, and ask others what kind of life they have been getting from their tires. Also consider alignment and driving habits. Actual experience may confirm or deny the rating that appears on the tire sidewall, but it is the real-world performance you are interested in. The number on the sidewall is generated by the tire company, and at this point there is no agency or committee whose job it is to ensure these numbers are accurate.

Two other numbers appear on the sidewall: traction and temperature. Traction is the tire's ability to maintain grip on a wet surface; temperature is the tire's ability to resist destructive heat build-up. Each of these ratings can score an A, B or C. With ratings this broad, a wide variety of tires have garnered A ratings on both accounts. Do not, then, buy tires solely on their traction and temperature ratings. On the other hand, any high-performance tire you buy should score As in these areas.

Many high-performance tire manufacturers are making race-only versions of the radial tires. As good as they are, these are not the ultimate. That honor falls to specially constructed bias-ply race tires, such as those made by Hoosier and Mickey Thompson. These tires grip very well, turn in extraordinarily well and are often illegal to use in competition. Per-

haps it is just as well; their life spans are measured in hours rather than miles.

Snow performance

Wide, low-profile tires will not do you much good in the mud and snow. The ideal snow tire is tall and skinny, just like the stock tires that come with your car. The skinnier tire pushes down through the snow to give you some traction, although even with the best snow tires there is not much to be had.

High-performance street tires have a closed-tread design to put as much rubber against the ground as possible. In a snow tire, you want an open-block tread. Snow will pack into the voids between the blocks of rubber, and provide extra traction when it sticks to snow on the road.

If you are serious about snow traction—and your state will allow it—studded tires are the way to go, as they will work on ice better than will simple snow tires. Generally, however, you are going to have to take it easier in the snow than on a clean, dry roadway. No matter what you do to improve the snow traction, you will rarely, if ever, see the far side of 0.20 g of lateral acceleration.

If you live in snow country and you have your heart set on steamroller tires for the summer months, keep that set of stock wheels in the garage for when winter rolls around.

Miscellaneous tips and techniques

Replace your old tires before they get too worn-out. If you race, use your old tires for setting up the suspension; if you can get your car to handle well on used-up tires, it will be that much better on new tires.

Also if you are racing, change your stock valve stems for the shorter valve stems used for trailer wheels. This prevents the valve stems from being torn off accidentally if you get too close to a competitor or a wall, and the sudden loss of air pressure that follows. NAPA stores sell these under the description TR412 Valve, part number 90-412.

Directional wheels are a great idea—if they are directional the proper way. Because the normal path for cooling air through the brake rotor is from the inside out, any directional wheel you buy should be mounted to pull air to the outside of the car. This may increase the problem you have with brake dust, but at least your wheels will not be working to reduce brake cooling.

165

Braking system

10

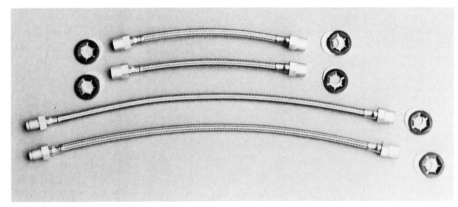

This is a braided stainless brake line set for an early VW. Later sets may require five or six lines to replace all the rubber brake lines. This particular kit is very high quality, with swedged ends and the proper threaded pieces, so that no adapters are required.

Volkswagen is good about supplying brakes adequate for the intended use of the vehicle. As its cars have become more powerful and capable in other respects, so have the brakes improved. But after you install a two-liter kit that Volkswagen did not have in mind when it initially sold you the car, you need more brakes.

Brakes work by converting productive work to useless heat. The heat then dissipates into the air (and the brake caliper, and the brake fluid, and the road wheel, and the wheel bearing, and the axle, and the CV joint). As you may have discovered, metal does not naturally dissipate heat quickly. In fact, it seems to hold heat rather well when the cooling medium is air. For this reason—and because you do *not* want the heat being transferred to the caliper, fluid, wheel, bearing, stub axle or CV joint—additional means must be found to encourage the rotor to accept and dissipate heat properly.

Merely adding metal to the rotor would be one way of creating more of a

Brake Performance

Stopping distance in feet

- 80-0
- - - 70-0

Model year

As the brakes got bigger and better, stopping distances decreased.

The early cars can be upgraded to rear disc brakes using all factory parts, with the addition of a proportioning valve. Autotech

heat sink, but a thick rotor would not heat very evenly, cool very well or be light enough. You sometimes can install more metal, however, by increasing the diameter of the rotor, leaving the thickness the same. This method requires different calipers, and sometimes different road wheels so the whole assembly will fit inside without scraping.

The most common solution is to install vented rotors on cars that have solid rotors. A vented rotor is constructed with air passages radiating out from the center of the disc. As heat builds up on the outer surfaces of the rotor, it is dissipated both from the outside surfaces and through the air channel between the two halves of the rotor. The

natural cooling process is aided by the fact that as the rotor spins, air in the channel is thrown out by centrifugal force, with cool air being sucked in to replace it through the center of the rotor.

Next time you see a race car, note the brake-cooling air ducts feed the center of the rotor instead of blowing on the friction surface of the rotor, for this very

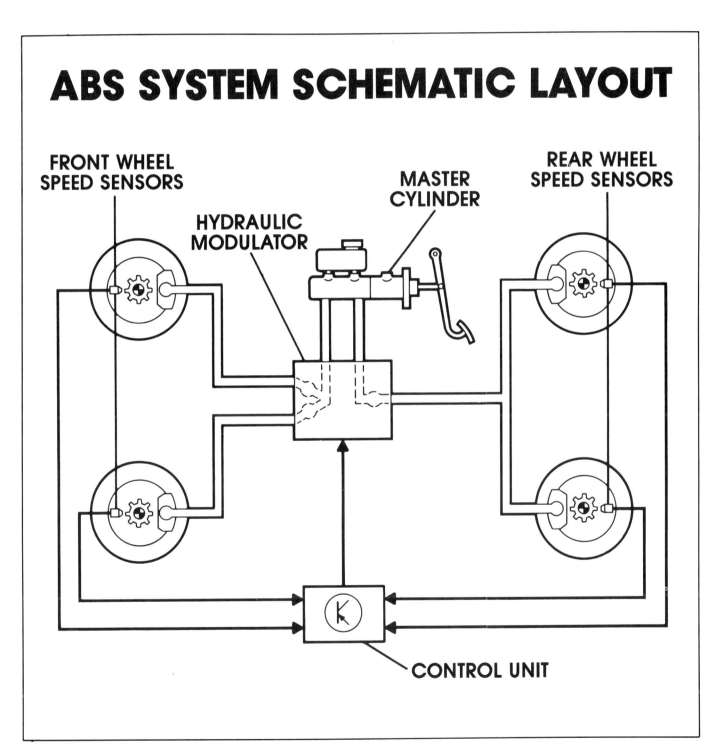

The control unit senses when a wheel locks up and pulses the pressure to that brake so the wheel can turn again.

167

For solid-rotor cars built after the mid-1980, the upgrade to vented rotors is a simple bolt-in that uses thinner pads so you don't have to change calipers, too. Earlier cars can still upgrade, but new calipers are required. This Autotech kit includes Teflon brake lines as well. Greg Brown

reason. Although you probably will never see a car set up with solid rotors and brake-cooling ducts, if you need to do this the center-feed system will not work. To keep from warping the rotor, you must build an air box that distributes the cooling air to both sides of the rotor equally. Unless you are really good at fabrication, consider either foregoing the brake cooling ducts or upgrading to vented rotors.

Weight distribution of the car at rest is heavily biased toward the front. During deceleration, even more weight is transferred to the front, resulting in very little weight in the rear. Therefore, putting a set of force-cooled vented rotors on the rear of the car will not perk up the braking performance by very much. You can check this by keeping track of how fast your rear brake shoes need adjustment or wear out. Typically, you will go through five or more sets of front pads before the rear shoes need attention. Rear rotors will fade less than rear drums, however, making them very handy for those occasional canyon runs, slalom events and road courses.

Another aspect of brake performance that is related to weight distribution is the effect of the proportioning valve that is found on some Volkswagens. This little item, located near the rear axle, senses any decrease in ride height from stock, and then increases the rear brake bias on the assumption that the decrease in ride height is due to a heavy load of cargo in the trunk. If you lower your car, the proportioning valve will be tricked into

This homemade drilled rotor really reduces stopping distances, but it also tends to crack. Techtonics

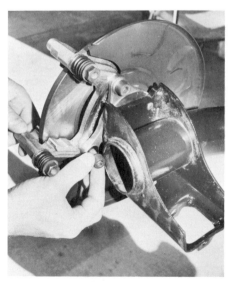

Although it can be expensive when the exchange rate is high, rear disc brakes are an easy bolt-on upgrade. Autotech

thinking that there needs to be more rear brake bias. If you find you are locking up the rear brakes in your lowered car during panic stops, this is the reason.

Brakes

Year	Model	Front	Rear
1974	Dasher	9.4SR	7.9D
1975	Dasher	9.4SR	7.9D
1975	R/S	9.4SR	7.1D
1976	Dasher	9.4SR	7.9D
1977	R/S	9.4SR	7.1D
1977	Dasher	9.4SR	7.9D
1978	R/S	9.4SR	7.1D
1978	Dasher	9.4SR	7.9D
1979	R/S	9.4SR	7.1D
1979	Dasher	9.4SR	7.9D
1980	R/S	9.4SR	7.1D
1980	R/S/J/C	9.4SR	7.1D
1981	Dasher	9.4SR	7.9D
1981	R/S/J/C	9.4SR	7.1D
1982	Quantum	9.4SR	7.9D
1982	R/S/J/C	9.4SR	7.1D
1983	Quantum	9.4SR	7.9D
1983	R/S/J/C	9.4VR	7.1D
1984	Quantum	9.4SR	7.9D
1984	Rabbit	9.4SR	7.1D
1984	S/J/C	9.4VR	7.1D
1985	Golf/Jetta	9.4SR	7.1D
1985	Quantum	9.4SR	7.9D
1985	Quantum Syncro	10.1VR	9.6SR
1985	S/GTI/C	9.4VR	7.1D
1986	Golf/Jetta	9.4SR	7.1D
1986	GTI/16V/GLI	9.4VR	9.4SR
1986	GTI/S/C/GLI	9.4VR	7.1D
1987	Cabriolet	9.4VR	7.1D
1987	Golf/Jetta	9.4SR	7.1D
1987	Quantum	9.4SR	7.9D
1987	Quantum Syncro	10.1VR	9.6SR
1987	Scirocco 16V	10.1VR	9.4SR

Brake pads

The stock brake pads are designed to wear out before the rotors. They are soft and do not squeak much, and if you are lucky they do not make much dust, either. For high-performance use they will do, but there are other options.

The most common choice is the so-called semimetallic pad. These pads are harder than the stock pad and may squeak a little more, but they do last longer and stop better. The drawback is that the harder the pad is the quicker the rotor wears out. Both Ferodo and Repco make excellent replacement pads. Racers also swear by the Ferodo DS11. You can use a harder pad if fade is a problem, but the harder the pad the more time it takes to warm up.

The 10.1 inch vented front rotors from the 16V.

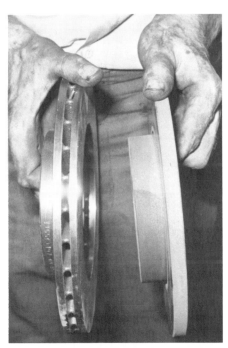

Stock solid rotors and early vented rotors.

Slotting the pads allows brake dust and hot gases to escape from between the pad and rotor for better braking.

169

Brake squeak

Some brake squeak comes from the normal interference between the pad and the disk. There is not much you can do about this. A considerable amount of the noise comes from the backs and sides of the pad, where it touches the caliper.

This noise you can do something about. Use high-temperature moly grease to lightly coat the back and sides of the brake pad backing plate, as well as the mounting hardware, such as the pins and spreaders. This eliminates most of the noise. Perma-Tex and others make special compounds for this use. Whichever you choose, *do not* get any on the pad material.

Slotting the pads

When you apply the brakes, the friction between the pad and the rotor creates heat and brake dust. Some of this dust finds its way between the pad and the rotor, and decreases braking efficiency. Most Porsche pads come with a slot in the middle to allow this dust and heat to escape. Some Volkswagen pads do not have this feature, but it is easy to add with a hacksaw if you cannot locate pads that come already slotted.

Bedding the pads

Brand-new pads (and shoes) need to be broken in before they will work properly. For street use, you might never notice the difference between bedded and unbedded brake linings. For racing, bedding the pads is a *must*. Bedding the pads may also help avoid glazing on the rear pads of newer cars.

The process for bedding brake pads is not new, and a good treatment of the subject can be found in Carroll Smith's *Prepare to Win*. He recommends warming up the pads with a couple of medium-strength stops, then following up with a high-speed "burn-in" conducted someplace where you have enough room both in front (in case the pads do not bed) and behind (to prevent being rear-ended). Visual examination is required to determine if the pads are bedded or not. The top ⅛ to ³⁄₁₆ inch of a properly bedded pad will be a gray-brown, in contrast to the normal gray or black color that new pads come with.

Drilling the rotors

Drilling the rotors is the expensive way to avoid slotting your pads, but it does look trick, and hundreds of racers cannot be all wrong. The holes also provide more surface area for the rotor to promote cooling.

One problem with drilled rotors is that they seem to develop heat cracks. Even on the Porsche rotors that appear to have the holes cast in place, you can sometimes see heat cracks. Drilling the rotor creates stress risers everywhere on an already stressed surface. Heat cracks are inevitable.

Not many people use the drilled rotors, but they are just now becoming readily available through the aftermarket, so the next year or so will tell. If you have a set of drilled rotors that are heat cracked, be sure the cracks do not extend through to the inside of the cooling vent. If the cracks are not that serious, take the wheels off often to check on their progress.

If you decide to drill your own rotors, follow a 3–2–3 pattern, drilling between the webs (if you have vented discs). The holes must be chamfered both for stress reasons and to avoid the cheese grater effect that unchamfered holes have on brake pads.

Remember that the brake rotor is a rotating assembly, so after you remove

Solid rotors drilled in a 3–2–3 pattern. Abt

Vented rotors are drilled so the holes do not penetrate the webs. Abt

metal you will need to get the rotor balanced again. This can be the most difficult part of the operation; it might be a good idea to locate someone who can balance a rotor before you plunge into this project. Also, keep track of your brake wear for the first few thousand miles or so, as the holes cause the pads to wear faster, chamfered or not.

Upgrading the front brakes

There are two stages for upgrading the front brakes. The first stage is to replace the solid rotors with 9.4 inch vented rotors. On cars sold through the middle of 1980 with the small brake pads, you will need to replace your calipers as well. The later cars with the "banana" pads will accept the wider vented rotors fine, although you must use thinner pads. These upgrades can be purchased from the dealer, but it is usually less expensive to buy them as a kit from an aftermarket performance house.

The second stage is for drivers who are serious brake users. This involves trading in your current setup for the 16V rotors and calipers. The 10.1 inch rotors offer nearly twenty-five percent more swept area for braking, and will really stop you in a hurry. The only drawback is that clearance between the caliper and the inside of the wheel may be a problem. The thirteen-inch steel wheels will rub, so you should not use this much brake with that little tire. This is another dealer item that usually can be purchased for less from an aftermarket supplier.

Installing rear disc brakes

With upgraded front rotors and rear drums, your car will stop great—the first couple times. If you are hard on brakes and are experiencing fade, it is time to consider trading in the rear drums and shoes for rotors and pads. Autotech SportTuning, for example, offers a rear disc brake conversion kit, and it has done its homework. The kit comes with the proper brake proportioning valve for your car. Without the proper proportioning valve the rears will lock up before the fronts, putting you wildly out of control as the rear end of the car passes the front of the car on its way to the accident you are about to have.

The price of this kit fluctuates from expensive to very expensive, but it really works.

Braided stainless-covered Teflon brake lines

Stock rubber lines are fine and will last for many years before needing replacement. However, being rubber, and being that the braking system sees pressures on the far side of 300 psi when you apply your foot to the brake pedal smartly, the insides of the lines are going to deflect at least a little, absorbing some of the energy that you are contributing with your foot.

The braided stainless lines use Teflon instead of rubber, and Teflon does not deflect nearly as much as the rubber does. Hence, the energy of your pushing on the brake pedal is transmitted with more fidelity to the calipers. The brake pedal feels firmer, too.

Replacing the front brake lines is easy. The job will be much less messy if you

If you are using 14 inch wheels and solid rotors, you can upgrade your brakes from 240 mm to 260 mm with these VW Motorsport rotors. Abt

When upgrading to rear discs it is critical to get the right brake proportioning valve, such as this one from Autotech.

depress and hold the brake pedal before and during the time you have the brakes lines off. This prevents the brake fluid in the reservoir from running out all over the floor. Always use flare-nut wrenches when working with brake lines.

Replacing the rear lines, especially the right rear line, can be difficult. Be patient, use line wrenches for maximum grip and minimum damage, and if all else fails put the car on jack stands, place a jack beneath the rear torsion beam and remove the four bolts holding the torsion beam to the chassis. *Carefully* lower the torsion beam until you can get to the rear brake lines.

Once you can reach the line itself, you may find that it is still difficult to break the fitting loose. There is little room for two flare wrenches, so if the fitting does not yield easily you will have to take more drastic measures. I do not normally recommend this as a procedure, but you can cut the brake line and use a deep-socket to grab one end of the fitting.

When you are through, thoroughly bleed the brakes until the pedal is firm again. Remember to monitor the brake fluid level in the reservoir while you bleed the brakes; if the reservoir runs dry and you start pumping air through the braking lines, you will have to completely bleed the brake system all over again.

Before you take the car off the jack stands to go for a test drive, wipe all connections dry with a rag, and then ask a friend to apply the brakes steadily while you crawl underneath and look for leaks. It is embarrassing to make a mistake working on your engine. It is deadly to make a mistake working on the brakes.

One thing to watch out for with the braided stainless lines is that they will wear right through whatever they come up against. Route the lines in such a way that they do not interfere with any other components.

There is no DOT (Department-of-Transportation)—approved braided stainless brake line, while the factory rubber lines are DOT approved. However, I have never heard of a braided stainless line coming apart.

Lines made by Westward Hose in Long Beach are finely crafted and have ends that are wedged on. Westward Hose brake lines are available through aftermarket suppliers such as Autotech. Wherever you buy your lines, you should not have to put up with adapter fittings.

Look around until you find brake lines that mount up the same way the factory lines do.

Silicone brake fluid

Silicone brake fluid seems to be the hope of the future. It does not absorb moisture out of the air the way glycol-based fluids do, its boiling point is higher and it is mild on seals. Silicone fluid has been rated DOT 5 by virtue of its physical properties. DOT 5 fluid can be made out of anything that meets the DOT standard, and no other fluid material scores higher than DOT 4.

The higher boiling point is nice, but the really great thing about silicone brake fluid is that it is not hydroscopic, as DOT 3 and DOT 4 fluids are. When water gets into your brake fluid not only does the boiling point plummet, but your internal brake parts are wide open to corrosion.

So silicone brake fluid (DOT 5) is demonstrably better than glycol-based brake fluid, but if ever there was a product aimed narrowly at the enthusiast market, this is it.

Because DOT 5 fluid must be miscible with DOT 3 and DOT 4 fluid by law, you can mix DOT 5 fluid with either of the other types. This is a long way from saying that you can simply pour silicone fluid in on top of your old DOT 3, however. Every drop of DOT 3 or DOT 4 fluid that is left in the system will reduce the positive characteristics of the silicone fluid by that much.

The worst area, and the area for which most people are switching to silicone brake fluid, is the wheel cylinders. Tests conducted by a major automobile manufacturer show that even after a complete flush, there are still pockets of old fluid in the wheel cylinders. Because silicone brake fluid floats on top of glycol-based brake fluid, the remaining glycol-based brake fluid in the system will allow corrosion to continue.

The bottom line is, if you are going to use silicone fluid, you must disassemble everything and thoroughly clean all traces of old fluid before switching over. This includes flushing the brake lines. This can be a real problem because whatever you use to flush with also must be removed. If you use alcohol and then blow out the lines with an air gun, keep in mind that many air tanks and air lines have a lot of moisture in them, so you

could be blowing water back into your nice clean brake lines.

Once you decide to take everything apart, you might as well go to the dealer and purchase all new seals. If you do the job right, this will be the last time the brake system will be apart.

Bleeding a brake system that uses silicone fluid is yet another challenge, but at least you are nearing the end. Silicone brake fluid is more viscous than glycol-based brake fluid, so it will trap and hold air bubbles for a lot longer time. When you decant the silicone brake fluid into your system, exercise extra care not to aerate the fluid. As a precaution, you can carefully pour the silicone fluid through a clean piece of screen to remove air bubbles.

The bleeding process itself should be done slowly to minimize aeration of the silicone fluid. In spite of all your precautions, there is a good possibility that you will be left with a spongy pedal. If so, bleed the brakes again every couple of days until the sponginess is gone—or until you get tired of the whole mess and switch back to glycol-based fluid and yearly maintenance. In some cases it is just not possible to get the air bubbles out of the fluid.

It is things like this for which they invented the category of "trick" stuff. Trick stuff is stuff that works great, but is so expensive or time-consuming that almost nobody will do what it takes to use it.

I doubt that silicone brake fluid will ever be a factory-fill item. The reason is ABS. The Bosch ABS has small fluid passages through which response time is cirtical if the ABS is to function properly. The higher viscosity of silicone fluid is not ideal for this application, and I believe we will see ABS long before we see silicone fluid.

For the near future, automotive engineers are working on a DOT 4+ fluid that will be better than the current DOT 4 while retaining compatibility with ABS. This new fluid might approach DOT 5 in many of the performance areas—and if there is still a problem with moisture absorption, you can always continue bleeding your brakes once a year.

In the meantime, if you are not ready to experiment with silicone fluid, the next best thing is Castrol L.M.A. Just change it every year to keep it fresh, more often if you live in an area that is humid or has frequent rainfall.

11

Body and chassis

From 1975 through 1984, the Volkswagen chassis was pretty much unchanged. In 1985, however, Volkswagen changed not only the chassis, but the method of suspending the engine and transmission, and the front and rear suspensions as well. The chassis was strengthened over the previous version, and a subframe to which the engine mounts was introduced in front.

The suspension mounting points were radically changed, as well. The new version features special bushings with built-in deflection characteristics that make the cars both ride nicer and handle better. Because of this design change, none of the suspension pieces are interchangeable across this dividing line.

Straightening your car after a wreck

With the unibody construction of the new cars, straightening everything back

Full leather seats such as these Recaros can be very comfortable during long-distance drives.

A roll cage should fit tight up against the roof as demonstrated by this Zender cage.

With deep side and seat bolsters, these Scheels are more difficult to get into and out of, but they do provide more lateral support for high-performance cornering.

out after a collision is something not every collision repair shop can handle.

When shopping for a collision repair facility, make sure it has a piece of equipment called a *bench*. With a bench, the car can be precisely measured and pulled back into alignment so it won't drive down the street sideways. If the chassis of your car has been bent in a collision, it is almost impossible to fix it without a bench.

Another consideration when having a major repair done on your car (such as installing a *clip*, when a large piece from another car is used to replace a damaged piece on your car) is that the collison repair shop use MIG (metal inert gas) welding equipment. MIG welding uses an inert gas to flood the spot where the welding is taking place. This inert gas prevents oxygen from getting into the weld and reducing the strength of the joint. Gas welding is not adequate because it is impossible to gas weld and maintain the integrity of the metal. Do not accept a major repair to your vehicle that does not make use of a bench and MIG welding.

For racing and other high-stress use, you will want to strengthen the chassis to reduce body flex. The factory adds inner fender panels on its rally cars, and spot welds (especially on the front shock towers) are fully welded. A properly designed and installed roll cage (such as the one from Safety Systems, Portland, Oregon) will triangulate the chassis from front to rear, making everything stiffer and contributing to better handling. If you need the strength more than you need light weight, find out how the factory stiffened the Cabriolet chassis and follow its example.

Body kits

One of the most difficult things to test properly is a body kit that is to be used on a street vehicle. The changes in performance are usually subtle, the kits can be fairly trying to install properly and to really understand what is happening you need a wind tunnel.

In lieu of a wind tunnel, buying German body kits is the best way of ensuring that you are not ruining the aerodynamics of your car. In Germany, the government certification body TUV tests all kits for several qualities, including one that specifies that the body kit not degrade the fuel economy of the car as delivered from the factory. This does not

This Zender kit displays excellent fit, both between the kit and the car, and among the different pieces of the kit itself. GMP

A low spoiler may improve the look of your Jetta, but a higher one has a better chance of being up in the air stream where it will do some good. Body kit by Kamei. Kamei

This Rabbit spoiler is up in the air stream where it belongs.

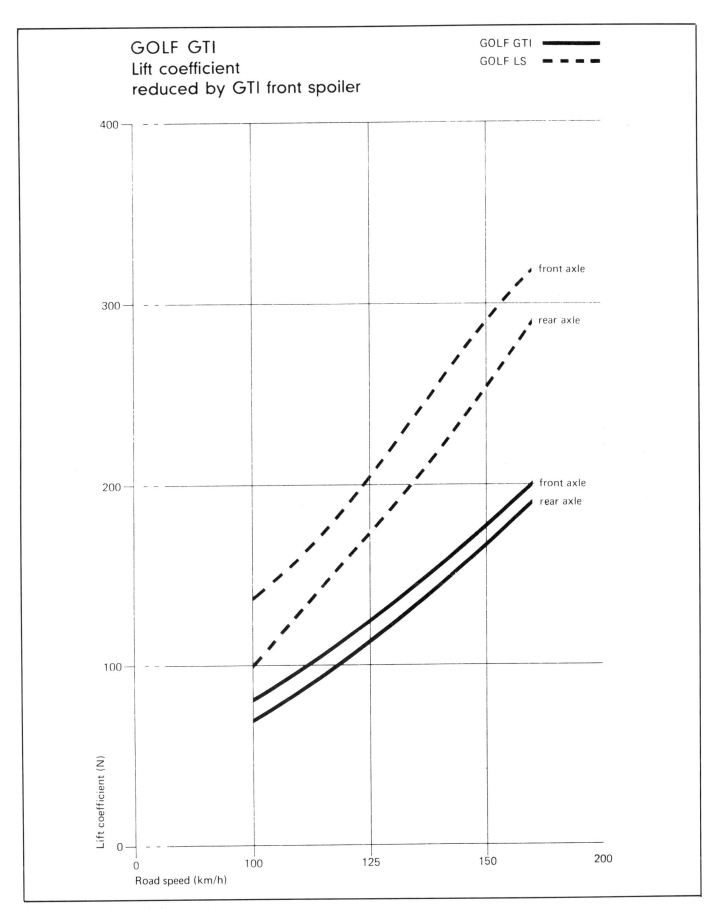

GOLF GTI
Lift coefficient
reduced by GTI front spoiler

GOLF GTI ▬▬▬
GOLF LS ▬ ▬ ▬

front axle
rear axle
front axle
rear axle

400

300

200

100

0

Lift coefficient (N)

0   100   125   150   200
Road speed (km/h)

As speeds get higher it becomes more important to reduce aerodynamic lift. A properly designed front spoiler helps negate lift at both ends of the car.

If you don't need a passenger seat, putting the battery box here is a lot better than putting it in the trunk. Pulsar Racing

mean the kit will help your car, just that it will not hurt it.

If you decide to install body parts, there are a few things to consider. First, between the manufacturing tolerances of your car and the manufacturing tolerances of the body kits, some discrepancies are bound to arise. This means that you should not start installing your full-body kit at four in the afternoon so your car will look sharp for your evening date. Leave yourself plenty of time. This also means that if you start to mount a body panel and it does not seem to fit very well, it is up to you to make it fit. Sending it back for an exchange more than likely will not solve the problem. Be ready to do some fabrication and fitting.

Second, plan ahead. Do not assume that if you buy an air dam today, in six months you will be able to buy front fender flares that integrate beautifully. Some parts are not meant to be used in combination with other parts, even when all the parts are from the same firm. If you want the whole kit, buy the whole kit—or be ready to do some fabrication.

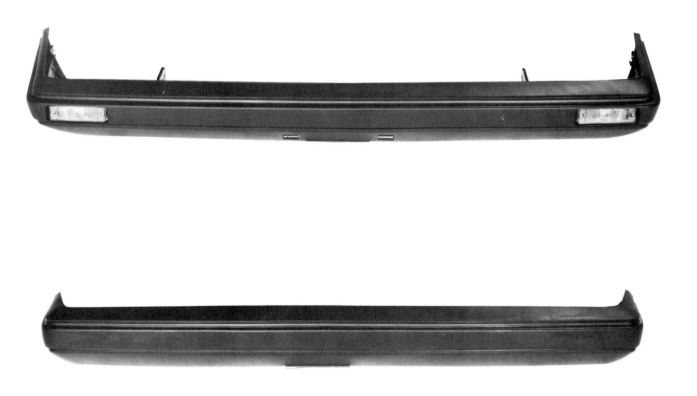

These European front and rear bumpers aren't as crashworthy as the US bumpers, but they are 50 to 70 pounds lighter. Autotech

Third, keep in mind that every time you drill a hole in your sheet metal for a sheet metal screw or a rivet, you are inviting rust to attack your car. If you must drill, clean the inside and outside surfaces of the sheet metal before drilling, and when installing the fastener coat it with silicone caulk (RTV). The silicone will help seal out the moisture and protect against corrosion.

Fourth, prepare yourself for the inevitable wreck. Fiberglass or hard-plastic body panels can be very resilient, but once their stress limit is exceeded they do let go, making it necessary to replace or repair them. If you have a fiberglass body kit, invest in some panel repair items before you need them. Then, when your car gets crunched or a piece gets knocked off, you can repair it immediately.

Air dams

Although the air dam increases the frontal area of the car, it still manages to work as an aerodynamic device because it keeps air from getting underneath the car and creating drag. In fact, some air dams are so effective that brake-cooling ducts must be incorporated into the air dam to prevent the front rotors from cooking to death. Before the introduction of the Golf body style (which features subtle aerodynamic tailoring along the hood mating line), some enthusiasts were also blocking off as much of the front grille as possible to keep air from wandering through the engine compartment and causing trouble. Every little bit helps.

The factory chin spoiler that is common on the early Sciroccos is good for a ten percent increase in gas mileage. The factory duckbill spoiler found on the early GTIs is also very effective, although it will not fit American-built cars after 1978.

The factory Golf GTI spoiler available on the 1986-and-later cars is a very nice piece that incorporates brake-cooling ducts. Because the body style is similar this spoiler will fit the 1985 cars, but it is more difficult to mount it. On the 1986 cars that did not come with this spoiler (such as the Jetta), the sheet metal is formed to accept the spoiler easily, with no body modifications needed.

Wind splits

Wind splits mount on the top edge of the front fenders or on either side of the hood. They work on the principle that directed air is smoother than air that chooses where it wants to go. By providing channels for directing the airflow over the top of the car, wind splits can theoretically help aerodynamics.

A-pillar fairings

A-pillar fairings first appeared on the Formula E (economy) cars, but they can be used on any early car that does not have the flush-mounted windshields and redesigned rain gutters. Those with the later cars can rest assured that Volkswagen did what was necessary to clean up the airflow in this area. On the early cars, however, the A-pillar fairings eliminate a good amount of drag from this problem area.

Rear spoilers

Rear spoilers help the aerodynamics by keeping the airflow over the car attached as long as possible. Without an effective rear spoiler, the airflow wants to detach from the car soon after passing over the rear edge of the roof. This creates a turbulence and thus a drag at the rear of the car.

The problem with some spoilers is that they are so far out of the airflow that they cannot help do anything except make your car look different from someone else's. On a Rabbit, for example, a rear spoiler that is mounted below the rear window is not going to get enough air to make much of a difference to the airflow. A much smaller spoiler above the rear window will be much more effective.

A good example of this can be seen in the factory rear spoilers mounted on the Sciroccos. A small rear spoiler down low would not have done the job, so the factory used a fairly stout spoiler well up in the airflow. (Volkswagen has one of the best wind tunnels around, so it is not a surprise that this design works.) The factory Jetta GLI rear spoiler, although not very big, works because on the sedan there is still some airflow across the rear edge of the trunk.

Side skirts

Side skirts not only make the car look lower, they can also help keep the sides of the car clean by preventing mud from splashing up off the road. As previously mentioned, it is a lot easier to buy the side skirts at the same time you buy the front spoiler and so on, to ensure that everything will fit together and that the overall effect will be what you want.

Electrical systems

12

Once you get used to working with Volkswagen electrical systems you may find that they are not at all unpleasant to deal with. Most German cars conform to the DIN standard for wiring numbers and functions, so in a pinch you might even be able to lend a hand to that Mercedes or BMW owner who finds himself or herself stranded.

It is beyond the scope of this book to explain how to read a wiring diagram, but a few pointers on the descriptions of terminals are included in the following chart.

Terminal	Description
4	High voltage (ignition coil, distributor)
15	Switched positive from battery or ignition switch output
30	Input direct from the battery positive terminal
31	Return direct to battery negative or ground
84	Combination relay contact and relay coil input
85	Relay coil ground
86	Relay coil hot
87	Relay contact, break when activated
88	Relay contact, make when activated
B+	Battery positive terminal
B–	Battery negative terminal
D+	Charging system positive output
D–	Charging system negative or ground
DF	Charging system field terminal

Ignitions

If you are running an early car with a points-condenser-coil ignition, you owe it to yourself to convert to a breakerless ignition whether or not you are interested in high performance.

With an electronic ignition you can set it and forget it, and it will deliver peak performance for thousands and thousands of miles. In contrast, a points ignition begins to deteriorate almost from the moment it is installed.

If you have a points distributor and you do not trust electronic ignitions, at least treat yourself to an ignition that uses the points only as a trigger. This extends the life of the points and gives you some benefits due to improved ignition performance. Some of these systems allow you to revert back to the stock points-condenser-coil-setup in a few minutes.

Most units on the market use points, a photocell or a magnet to trigger the ignition. Here are a few of the more popular setups.

Allison

The Allison ignition completely replaces your points with a photo-optical sensor, and has a black box that mounts outside of the distributor to control the coil. The Allison is a little difficult to install in the Bosch distributor, but once

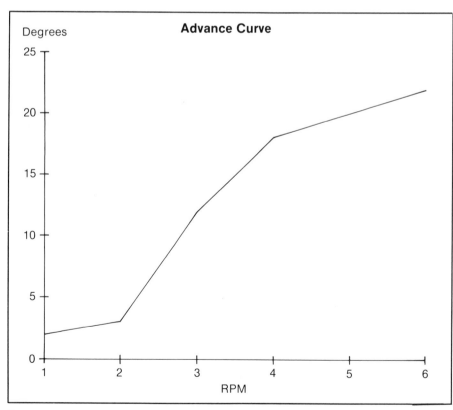

Advance Curve

The advance curve of the mechanical "009" distributor for the VW. With 22 degrees of advance available, the 009 should be set to 14 degrees initial advance (BTDC) for a total of 36 degrees of advance at 6000 rpm.

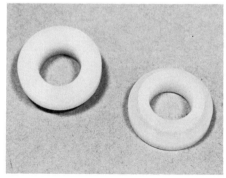

These two-piece Delrin bushings are stronger than the stock rubber item, and they don't melt away so they last longer, too. Stuttgart Automotive

you get it in it is fairly rugged. The Allison uses a red LED (light-emitting diode) as a light source, and it is very hard to get it to misread, even when the inside of the distributor is filthy.

The light beam is interrupted by a control rotor that slides onto the distributor shaft just underneath the distributor rotor. Because of the way the slots are cut in the control rotor, the Allison will tolerate a great deal of wobble in the distributor shaft. If you have a mildly wornout distributor, the Allison might be able to extend its life.

Mount the black box in a cool place (under the cowling is fine) and make sure it is well grounded; you can get a shock from touching it while the motor is running.

Perlux

The Perlux Ignitor is a drop-in component that replaces your points, containing all the necessary electronics inside its black control head. The only clue from the outside of the distributor that something is different is that there are two wires coming out instead of one.

The Ignitor is triggered by a magnetic control rotor, which again slides on underneath the distributor rotor. Perlux includes a nonmagnetic feeler gauge to set the gap between the control head and the control rotor. This gap is somewhat critical, so your distributor has to be in good shape for best operation.

Because it uses the same mounting holes as the points, the Ignitor is very easy to install. If it ever fails, it should be a simple matter to remove the control head and install a set of points and a condenser. You can keep a set in a plastic bag in the glovebox just in case.

If you are suspicious that a piece of electronic equipment could be subjected to the heat inside a distributor and still function perfectly, join the crowd. Perlux has millions of miles of experience with this unit, however, as the US Postal Service utility vehicles all have Audi motors outfitted with Ignitors.

MSD

MSD stands for "multiple spark discharge." The principle behind its operation is that although a capacitive discharge (CD) ignition has a fantastic ability to deliver a high-energy spark to the spark plug, it does so over too short a time. The time is so short that the total area under the curve of a CD spark is less than with other types of ignition systems.

MSD compensates for this lack of area under the curve by triggering the spark plug to fire multiple times at each spark instead of just once.

If this is the way it really worked it would be great, but the multiple spark occurs only at low rpm. By 3000 rpm, the typical street version of the MSD ignition is putting out only one CD-style spark.

MSD does makes same radical units for race use, but they are for race use only and are not recommended for street use.

Factory breakerless

If you have an early car with a point-actuated ignition, a reliable upgrade can be found in your local junkyard in the form of the later-style factory breakerless ignition. This system is more complex than the points-actuated setup but with the shop manual you should be able to muddle through. Dyno tests show that this ignition is good up to 7500 rpm without missing a beat.

Factory knock-sensor ignition

This is currently the hottest ignition you can buy for the Volkswagen. Using a digital "map," the knock-sensor ignition computer knows how much to advance

This stock early Scirocco center console fits early Rabbits with only a little modification and provides space for mounting three gauges. James Sly

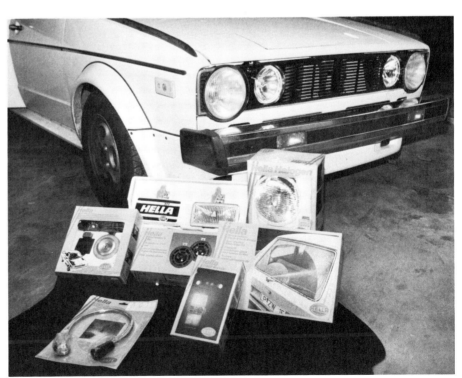

Hella offers many different products for the VW, including map lights, electric horns and, my favorite, the four-light grille for the early Rabbit. James Sly

the spark based on all the engine variables that are fed into it. If it receives a signal from a small piezoelectric crystal that is mounted to the engine, it knows that detonation is taking place and it retards the spark in steps until the detonation disappears. It then constantly checks to see when it is all right to advance the timing again.

This ignition first appeared in 1985 on the GTI, the GLI and the Audi 4000. On the Volkswagen motors it had a checking value of fourteen degrees plus the ignition point at 4300 rpm; Audi used sixteen degrees plus the ignition point at 3000 rpm. With more timing earlier on, the Audis had the edge in horsepower, just as if they had a recurved distributor. On top of this, the Audi rev limiter cut in between 6570 and 6630 rpm, much higher than the Volkswagen limit of 6200 to 6400 rpm. On the spec sheets, the Audi motor made 2 hp more. Because of the different advance curve, however, there was much more than a 2 hp difference in driving feel.

Here is the secret. Both cars used the identical ignition system. Audi felt that with its longitudinal motor it could get away with more spark advance. Volkswagen, with its transverse engine, was not sure it could. The ignition computer used in both cars has two different maps in it. To change your car from the Volkswagen map to the Audi map, pin 11 on the knock-sensor control unit (normally connected to ground) must be disconnected.

Is this safe to do? Apparently so. In 1986, Volkswagen started using the Audi map.

The knock-sensor ignition is available through your dealer, but at a list price of around $1,400 the junkyard is probably the best place to look for one.

If you are running an engine with the same combustion chamber dimensions and the same compression ratio as the factory motor, you will get the most from this ignition. If you are running stock compression you will not see much benefit from this setup, and for the cost and aggravation you should concentrate on other areas in your search for more horsepower.

If you are running anything different you may not see any benefits, either. The ignition map is very precisely tailored to the engine it is mounted on. If you are using a much bigger cylinder bore, the flame front must be started earlier by the spark plug than in a small-bore engine. Thus the knock-sensor ignition might actually be retarded from the position at which it would run best. Unless you cranked in some more lead . . .

On the other hand, if you mounted this ignition on a smaller-bore motor than the motor on which it came stock, the flame front would start too early, giving too much advance and really giving the knock sensor a workout. Unless you cranked in less lead . . .

Bosch, which designed this ignition system, has over 2,000 engineers on the payroll working on nothing but automobile-related stuff, so it's a good bet that most do-it-yourselfers are not going

The stock lighting setup can certainly be improved.

With quartz-halogen lights, the view ahead is remarkably better, side illumination is improved, and light scatter is reduced, as can be seen on the trees in the distance.

to have the sophistication needed to mix-and-match the knock-sensor ignition with various engine configurations.

Distributors

The section on bolt-on horsepower mentioned that a recurved distributor was a good modification for a stock compression engine. Here is why. Advancing the timing improves the torque and helps mileage by fooling the motor into thinking the compression ratio is higher than it is. If the timing is advanced too much, however, detonation will occur. The earlier the spark plug fires the earlier the flame front starts, so the higher the temperature of the combustion process. This increases oxides of nitrogen, which is why the early cars with EGR ran the timing retarded.

Even with the recurve, notice that the vacuum canister is retained. You may have seen advertised distributors for the Volkswagen that are referred to as the "009 version for the Rabbit." These distributors, like their Beetle counterparts, have no vacuum canister, the reason given that you will get more horsepower with a straight mechanical advance distributor. I have not found this to be true. There are a couple of reasons for this.

First, the vacuum retard allows you to set the timing with enough initial lead to get the car off the mark in a hurry and without having to put up with a high idle. The vacuum retard works only when the throttle is closed, so it does not affect performance—and setting the idle on your car without a vacuum retard can sometimes be frustrating.

The vacuum advance comes in only when there is high vacuum in the intake manifold, which means only during part-throttle conditions. This additional advance extends mileage and makes the car run much nicer. When you plant your foot, the manifold vacuum goes away and you are right back to the mechanical advance, so you are not giving up anything.

The mechanical advance distributor is not recommended except for racing use, where it does have a slight advantage over the more complex vacuum-assisted distributor.

If you are running a modified distributor (so the factory specifications do not apply to you), aim for about thirty-six degrees of total advance. With a 009 distributor, this means running about fourteen degrees of initial.

After setting the timing, warm up the engine and try a couple of hard acceleration runs. If you can hear any detonation

The ideal lighting setup; fog lights are low enough to see over but high enough for ground clearance; driving lights are higher for better "throw."

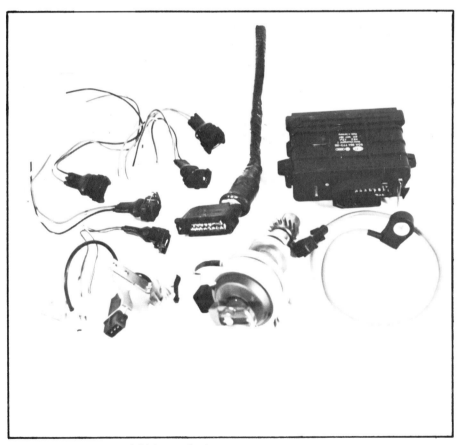

This is the way you might buy a factory knock-sensor ignition from the junkyard. From the dealer, this ignition is expensive. Techtonics

181

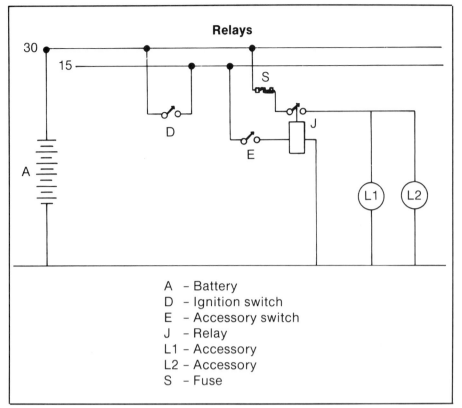

Relays

30
15

S

D

E

J

L1   L2

A

A – Battery
D – Ignition switch
E – Accessory switch
J – Relay
L1 – Accessory
L2 – Accessory
S – Fuse

To make sure your big lights, air horns and stereo gear get the power they need, run them off relays. The wire to the relays should be good and thick, and the distance between the relay and the accessory should be as short as possible.

The Allison ignition uses a slotted control rotor, instead of points, to trigger the photocell.

at all, back the timing off in two-degree increments until it goes away. Listen carefully; detonation can be difficult to hear over the other noises in the car, especially when the pinging is just beginning to come in.

Servicing

It is amazing how many people fail to service their distributors. It is also unfortunate, because they last a lot longer with a little care. All you have to do is pop off the distributor cap and rotor, and put a couple of drops of motor oil on the felt pad. The oil eventually trickles down and keeps the inner shaft free so your timing can advance and retard the way it is supposed to.

If you have a distributor with points in it, never install a set of points without lubricating the points cam with Bosch points grease. It comes in black-and-yellow tubes and can be found just about everywhere. A tube will last forever unless you work on cars for a living, and then you should not expect to get much more than four or five years out of it.

If you perform your own periodic maintenance, it takes only a second to pop the cap and check to see if the points cam is lubed. Your points will stay set longer because the rubbing block won't be wearing away as fast. In some cars, the points cams become so dry that the rubbing block squeaks loudly. Don't let this happen to yours.

Installing

Unless you are swapping your early ignition for one of the later knock-sensor ignitions, it is pretty simple to remove and replace the distributor. A special wrench used to be available from Snap-On (it was meant for a Pinto, but it fit the Volkswagen, too) that made it a much easier job to get to the distributor hold-down bolt. If you plan on doing a lot of work on Volkswagens, bend, weld or fabricate a wrench to the same general dimensions.

Before you remove the distributor, turn the engine to TDC. If you remove the distributor cap, you can watch the rotor. Turn the engine until the rotor points to the mark on the top of the distributor housing.

Remove the points wire or wires, remove the hold-down bolt and clamp, and pull the distributor out. Notice as it comes out that the rotor turns slightly so it no longer points exactly at the mark on the distributor housing. This is normal.

Have your points grease handy if you are working with a distributor that uses points. It takes only a little smear of Bosch grease to radically extend the life of your points rubbing block. Also check the area around the distributor drive hole to see that there is no dirt there waiting to fall into your motor.

Line up the rotor just the way it was after you pulled it out. In other words, it won't be pointing right at the mark on the distributor housing, it will be off to one side. Remember that the gears on the intermediate shaft and the distributor are cut at an angle, so as they mesh the rotor will want to turn.

Normally, you can simply slide the distributor in, and if you have lined up the gears the right way, the rotor will point at the mark on the distributor housing when the distributor is all the way down in the hole. If not, pull the distributor out and try again until it lines up.

Once in a while, the distributor will go down to within about 10 mm of being all the way in and stop. Pull it out, and check to see that the oil pump shaft drive tang is pointed in such a way that it can engage the drive slot in the bottom of the distributor. When the engine is at TDC, the tang should be parallel to the axis of the crankshaft.

When you get the distributor all the way down, check to see that none of your timing marks has moved, and that the rotor is still pointing at the mark in the distributor housing. If so, replace the hold-down clamp and bolt, reconnect all the electrical connections and replace the cap.

Spark plugs

Can you read a spark plug and determine how the engine is running? If so, you are better than most. All those color charts in the shop manuals and spark plug catalogs fail to tell you two important things that you must know before you will be able to read a spark plug.

First, unleaded gas will give you a much more subtle spark plug picture than will leaded gas. Unleaded gas works differently in a motor than leaded gas, and the charts that appear in the shop manuals usually show spark plugs that have been run on leaded. If you are using unleaded gas you are going to have to work harder to read the plugs.

Second, you can't just pull the plugs out any time and look at them. You need to run the engine under load (preferably under the load conditions that are causing you to check the plugs in the first place), then immediately shut it off and coast to the workshop (or pit) area.

Once you learn to read them, though, keeping an eye on the condition of your

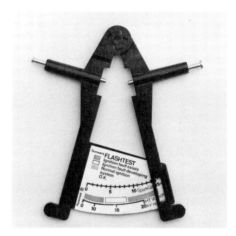

The Flashtest doesn't have the sophistication of a diagnostic scope, but for its small price it tells you a lot about your ignition.

This is the stock Perlux mounting plate. In some distributors the point at the top of the plate hits the vacuum-advance arm.

The ground mounting plate should fit easily without touching the advance arm.

To install the Perlux, first remove the points and check the internal ground strap. The condenser comes off next.

183

A homemade jumper for activating the fuel pump without the relay. I keep one in my toolbox and one in my glovebox.

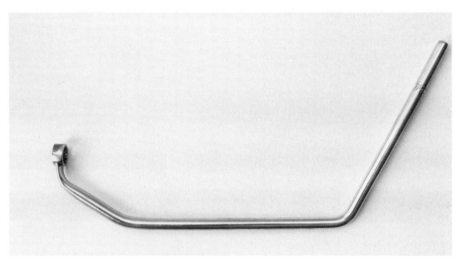

An angled wrench such as this makes it easier to adjust the distributor timing.

The distributor machine shows how much advance there is over the rpm range.

plugs will allow you to anticipate problems.

A normal plug will have a light tan deposit on the insulator nose. Fresh plugs have sharp corners on the center electrode. When those corners get rounded off, it's time for new plugs.

An overheated plug will have blistered or chalky deposits, and there may even be some glue showing between the center electrode and the insulator where it has melted out. The metal in the electrodes may also show heat discoloration.

An oil-fouled plug will have black, wet-looking deposits covering the insulator. The deposits will not easily rub off. This does not mean that your valve guide seals are leaking; your plugs will not show oil fouling even when you are going through a quart of oil every 250 miles. Oil on the plugs may, however, mean a worn guide, or a broken or unseated piston ring.

A fuel-fouled plug will have dry, fluffy black deposits that will wipe off.

Gauges

Volkswagen gauges are for the most part well placed and legible. With all the different trim levels and options over the years, there is no standard equipment in the way of gauges, however. Many Sciroccos have had fairly complete complements of gauges, while the lower-priced Rabbits have only the basics.

Instrument clusters from one Volkswagen will often bolt right into another Volkswagen, as long as the shape of the cluster is the same. For example, on the early Rabbits you can upgrade to the Scirocco instrument cluster (which includes a tachometer) by snapping out the stock unit and snapping in the Scirocco version (along with the necessary extra circuit board). All the wiring is there, ready to go. Likewise, the 120 mph speedometer in the 1984 cars will drop into the 1983 cars with no other changes, and the 140 mph instrument cluster from the 16V will replace the Scirocco instrument cluster. The parts can often be found at the junkyard.

VDO, the manufacturer of all these gauges, also offers an overwhelming assortment of other gauges in many sizes and styles. Several aftermarket suppliers offer three-across gauge panels that make it relatively simple to mount your most-needed gauges.

No two people will agree on what gauges are important, but I like to have a tachometer first, temperature gauges next (oil and exhaust gas) and then electrical (amps and volts). Supercharged motors should have boost pressure gauges.

Beyond that, the choices seem endless, considering the amount of space you have to fit them all into. Outside temperature gauges can be nice in colder climates for predicting the onset of road icing, vacuum gauges can help with engine problem diagnosis and fuel economy, and an engine hour meter will impress your pilot friends.

Although VDO gauges are generally of high quality, it is a good idea to calibrate the gauge when possible. Water and oil temperature gauges can be calibrated by dropping the sender into boiling water while it is connected to the system (remember to rig up a ground wire). Water boils at 212 degrees Fahrenheit at sea level. Voltage gauges can be checked against a test meter, as can ammeters, although a stand-alone ammeter is more difficult to find unless you know someone with an AVR (amp, volt, resistance charging system) tester.

The whole point of having gauges is to get better information for making certain decisions. If the information is wrong, you may make the wrong decisions, so make sure your gauges are accurate.

![Four spark plugs laid on their sides.]

Left to right are Bosch WR5CP (platinum), Bosch W7DCT Super (1986 GTI), Bosch F6DTC (16V) and Champion G-63 (Oettinger). Techtonics

![Distributor on a 16V engine in the engine bay.]

The distributor on the 16V engine is driven off the exhaust camshaft.

Lights

Headlights have two main characteristics: light output and pattern. Output refers to how bright the lamp is; pattern refers to the way the reflector disperses that brightness.

The output of the stock sealed-beam headlight (required on all US cars since the late 1930s) is relatively low, making it easy to outdrive your lights at night. Outdriving your lights occurs when you cannot see far enough ahead to allow yourself time to react at the speed you are driving. Europe has several good-quality kits available to convert to quartz-halogen headlights, but these are illegal in the United States. Fortunately, both GE and Sylvania offer sealed-beam halogens that are legal for use in the United States.

As poor as the traditional sealed beams are in terms of output, they are also wasteful in terms of pattern. The normal sealed-beam pattern sprays light in every direction, further degrading their effectiveness. For halogen headlights, the most popular (and useful) pattern is one with a very sharp horizontal cutoff to keep the light out of other people's eyes and down on the roadway where you need it. Some halogens also have an angled cutoff to the right of the horizon-

These hardened intermediate shaft and distributor drive gears will solve any problems you have with breakage. Abt

185

tal cutoff for better illumination of the roadside.

Headlights are one of the three types of light that can be mounted at the front of the car, the other two being driving lights and fog lights. Each of these is a special-purpose lamp not to be confused with the other.

Driving lights typically have reflectors designed to project the beam a great distance down the road in a long, thin pattern. This is in addition to the greater amount of light they provide.

Fog lights are designed to be mounted low on the car. Having the lights low allows you to look out over the top of your lights, rather than through the light that is being reflected back at you. Fog lights are also lower powered than driving lights, but it is their position you are interested in, not their output. Too bright a fog light will merely add to the amount of reflected light, obscuring your vision as normal headlights do.

A fog light is also available for the rear, in the form of an auxiliary brake light. This is usually a single large light that produces very bright light for better visibility in the fog. You will not make many friends using this in stop-and-go traffic or in the city, however.

Another interesting brake light improvement is to convert the normal brake lights to use quartz bulbs. Automotive Performance Systems sells these, although I would recommend them only in situations where brake light visibility is a real problem.

Whether you opt for the more sedate legal halogens or the quad-bulb flame throwers you found at a Group B rally team's garage sale, you must have them properly aligned. A normal headlight is bad enough when pointing in people's eyes. A misaligned halogen can be deadly. This is true in day-to-day use as well as when you load up the rear of the car with heavy items and alter the ride angle of the car. You must also realign your headlights whenever you change the ride height.

Aside from the legal aspects of using halogen lights, there are other limitations to how much light you can run, based on the electrical system's capacity to provide power. The lights cannot, for example, draw more power than the alternator can produce, without draining the battery.

Generally, you never want to load your charging system to more than eighty percent of its full rated output. Thus, if your alternator is rated at 50 amperes, 40 amperes is the most you should consider drawing out of it for very long. From this eighty percent figure (whatever it turns out to be in your case) you subtract the needs of the car—ignition, running light, radio and so on.

Assume your car needs 5 amperes to run. With a 50 ampere system, you would be left with 45 amperes for your lights. Since watts equal amperes times volts, in a 12 volt system you have 540 watts to play with. If the only other accessory you are running is the lights, this should be no problem—540 watts provides a *lot* of light. Just be careful when you have your dual 50 watt low beams and your dual 100 watt high beams on at the same time you are blasting tunes out of your 200 watt, sixty percent efficient stereo.

Assuming your electrical system can provide the power, if you think the existing wiring might be marginal you should run the lights through relays.

Remote relays

If you are satisfied with the stock lighting and horns, read no further. The stock wiring will power these items quite satisfactorily. When you feel the need for some 100 watt flame throwers, extra driving light or industrial-duty horns, however, you will soon find that the stock wiring is not up to the amperage demands that these devices can place on the electrical system.

The normal electrical pathway starts at the battery, goes back to the dashboard where the switch or button is mounted, and then goes back to the accessory. The factory does it this way for reasons of cost, ease of assembly and reduced complexity, but it makes it more difficult to upgrade the system. The small wires and the long distances involved limit the flow of amperage, possibly leading to overheating and failure.

The way around this problem is to install an electrical relay near the accessory that is drawing a lot of power. By locating the relay close to the accessory and using heavy-duty wire, you can eliminate any overheating problems in the wiring without having to redo your entire wiring harness. The original wiring is used to trigger the relay (tell it when to turn on). The trigger signal is much less than the original use the wires were intended for, so longevity is increased. When triggered, the relay connects the accessory directly to the battery through a much shorter route, and you can use a heavier-gauge wire to ensure that the accessory gets the juice it needs.

If you want the accessory to be off whenever the ignition is off, wire it in. If not, connect the accessory switch to a wire that is always hot (if it is not that way already).

The wire from the battery to the relay and from the relay to the accessory should be heavy-gauge wire. If you are running a lot of current through it, keep the distance as short as possible, too. Although this is usually used for lights and horns, you could also use it to supply power to a big stereo amplifier.

Intermittent wipers

If your car does not have the intermittent wiper option, it can be added anytime. The Volkswagen number for the relay is 191.955.529, and it plugs into the relay board where the jumper is. The only other thing you will need to do then is to break out the small plastic tab underneath the wiper actuator arm, so the arm can move downward to the intermittent wiper position.

Accessories

13

Alarms

Alarms have come a long way since the late seventies when there were only a few companies competing in the automotive security aftermarket. Now you get an alarm at a stereo store, a mobile phone store, a specialty alarm store, a department store and even through the mail.

At the same time, the level of sophistication of the average alarm has risen. In addition to door switches and motion sensors, sound discriminators can "listen" for the sound of the glass being broken (or the squeak of a lug bolt being loosened). Instead of settling for a siren, you can have your alarm yell "Burglar! Burglar!" in a loud, synthesized voice. Alarms are available that will arm themselves automatically after a certain period of time, will lock the door automatically when armed, or will tell you if and why the alarm went off while you were away. Some will do all this and more. There are so many different types of alarm that it would be nearly impossible to cover them all here. There are some general things to look for, however.

The first thing to require in an alarm is that there is no entry delay. If the alarm lets you open the door, sit down and compose yourself before entering the code on a keypad, the thief is going to have that much time, too—and a thief works *fast;* he or she will be gone before your alarm makes its first sound.

The second thing you should do is install the alarm in as remote a location as possible. Try to find the most radically different installation you can think of, because an experienced thief has an advantage in that he or she figures out alarms for a living. If you put yours where everybody else puts theirs, you just wasted your money. This is especially true for alarms installed by professional installers, who usually use a standard alarm layout. If you have an alarm professionally installed, rewire it after you get it home. At the very least, put the siren someplace where it would take Houdini to reach it or the wires leading up to it.

A lot of people put decals on their windows to inform would-be burglars that the car is equipped with an alarm,

This might be a good place to carry a spare extinguisher, but your primary unit should be closer at hand.

F	R									
30	489.7	490.7	491.7	492.7	493.7	494.7	495.7	496.7	497.7	498.7
40	499.7	500.7	501.7	502.7	503.7	504.7	505.7	506.7	507.7	508.7
50	509.7	510.7	511.7	512.7	513.7	514.7	515.7	516.7	517.7	518.7
60	519.7	520.7	521.7	522.7	523.7	524.7	525.7	526.7	527.7	528.7
70	529.7	530.7	531.7	532.7	533.7	534.7	535.7	536.7	537.7	538.7
80	539.7	540.7	541.7	542.7	543.7	544.7	545.7	546.7	547.7	548.7
90	549.7	550.7	551.7	552.7	553.7	554.7	555.7	556.7	557.7	558.7
100	559.7	560.7	561.7	562.7	563.7	564.7	565.7	566.7	567.7	568.7
110	569.7	570.7	571.7	572.7	573.7	574.7	575.7	576.7	577.7	578.7
120	579.7	580.7	581.7	582.7	583.7	584.7	585.7	586.7	587.7	588.7
130	589.7	590.7	591.7	592.7	593.7	594.7	595.7	596.7	597.7	598.7
140	599.7	600.7	601.7	602.7	603.7	604.7	605.7	606.7	607.7	608.7
150	609.7	610.7	611.7	612.7	613.7	614.7	615.7	616.7	617.7	618.7
160	619.7	620.7	621.7	622.7	623.7	624.7	625.7	626.7	627.7	628.7
170	629.7	630.7	631.7	632.7	633.7	634.7	635.7	636.7	637.7	638.7
180	639.7	640.7	641.7	642.7	643.7	644.7	645.7	646.7	647.7	648.7
190	649.7	650.7	651.7	652.7	653.7	654.7	655.7	656.7	657.7	658.7
200	659.7	660.7	661.7	662.7	663.7	664.7	665.7	666.7	667.7	668.7
210	669.7	670.7	671.7	672.7	673.7	674.7	675.7	676.7	677.7	678.7
220	679.7	680.7	681.7	682.7	683.7	684.7	685.7	686.7	687.7	688.7
230	689.7	690.7	691.7	692.7	693.7	694.7	695.7	696.7	697.7	698.7
240	699.7	700.7	701.7	702.7	703.7	704.7	705.7	706.7	707.7	708.7

Fahrenheit to Rankine conversions will be facilitated with this chart.

but there is no evidence that burglars pay any attention to these. Still if you do not mind the look of a decal it may not hurt. The only drawback is that if the decal specifies the type of alarm installed, it can give the thief an idea about what he or she is up against before breaking in. Remember, the thief is the pro, and does not need much of an edge to win at this game.

One way of slowing down the burglar is to install plates around the door handles where burglars usually pry their way in. This is effective, although there is nothing to prevent a thief from breaking a window or slashing your Cabriolet top.

Radio locks

Radio locks are another step in the right direction, although they are difficult to install. The tradeoff is that the burglar may wreak more havoc in the attempt to get at your radio than if you just let him or her take it.

Removable radios are another almost-good idea. For the first week or so you will always take the radio with you when you leave your car. After that, you probably won't, putting you right back where you started—except that the thief will not have to brutalize your dash to steal your radio.

The best alternative lies with the anti-theft radios that are being supplied with many new cars. When it is stolen the radio "forgets" how to work, and it will remember only after the proper code is entered in. Most manufacturers (with Volkswagen being the exception for now) include a warning decal on the window of each vehicle equipped with an antitheft radio. As this is being written, these radios are so new that they are still being stolen out of Volkswagens at a pretty good rate. We will have to wait and see on this one.

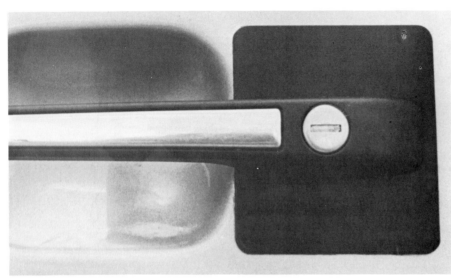

The Armor door plate greatly increases the difficulty of pry-ins.

Wheel locks

Wheel locks are another ploy designed to slow up the thief long enough to make your wheels a less inviting target. If your motion detector is set right, it will detect someone jacking up your car, and sound off before he or she even gets to your tires and wheels. It is still a good idea to use wheel locks, though, because you are not always close enough to hear your alarm and it is doubtful anyone else will respond to the sound of your car alarm.

If the thief is determined to take the whole car, you have a much better chance of foiling him or her.

Vehicle retention

Hanging onto your car can be a real problem in some areas. Volkswagens are nowhere near the top ten on the most stolen list, but that is not much of a consolation when *your* car disappears or is broken into.

Just about anybody with a nice car has at one time or another said those fatalistic words: "If they really want your car they're gonna get it one way or another." Unfortunately, this is true. It is up to you to make it as difficult for them as possible. The thief may do some damage, but it is better to have a slightly tattered car than no car at all.

There are ways of wiring in ignition and fuel pump cutouts so that as long as your alarm is armed, the car cannot be started. Depending on the sophistica-

The Cincinnati Microwave Passport is one of the smallest, best and most expensive radar detectors on the market. It only needs to save you a couple of times, though, to pay for itself.

tion of the setup, these can be very effective.

There are two problems with these setups. The first thing you need to find out about is what happens when the system fails. If there is no way for you to by-pass the system in the event that the whole thing malfunctions, you are going to need to know the number of the local tow service. On reliable systems this may not be much of a concern, but they always seem to quit at the worst possible time.

The second problem is more serious. My good friend Randy Michel recently had his car stolen at gun point. The thief waited until Randy opened the door and then stuck a gun in his face. Taking the keys, the thief invited Randy to crawl under a nearby car, and then drove off. Randy was lucky he did not have an ignition or fuel pump cutoff, because if he had the thief would have found out about it soon enough, and he probably would have wanted to chat with Randy about it.

If this possibility bothers you but you still hate the thought of someone simply driving away in your Volkswagen, find a time-delay ignition or fuel pump cutout. These let the car run for a couple minutes even if you don't push the button to deactivate it. This lets the thief get far enough away so you do not have to deal with him or her on his or her terms if you do not want to.

The hope is that the thief will stall the car right in the middle of an intersection while a police officer looks on. The drawback to this system is that thieves are often quite good at finding hidden switches and buttons. Still, it can be extemely difficult to find a microswitch hidden behind the stock door panel fabric, or back under the rug on the tunnel between the seats. If it sounds as if I am being vague, you are right. If I tell you all my trick hiding places for microswitches, they won't be secrets anymore! You should be able to develop your own secret switch locations with no trouble.

Fortunately, most cars are not taken this way, leaving you with some other methods for making your car just too much trouble to fool with.

One of these methods is to prevent the steering wheel from turning even if the normal steering wheel lock has been disabled. The first devices to do this were called *canes*, in reference to their general shape. They locked the brake or clutch pedal to the steering wheel so neither could be used.

The Vericom Performance Computer will give you read-outs on time to distance, distance to speed and peak g-force. I have found this unit to be extremely valuable for testing.

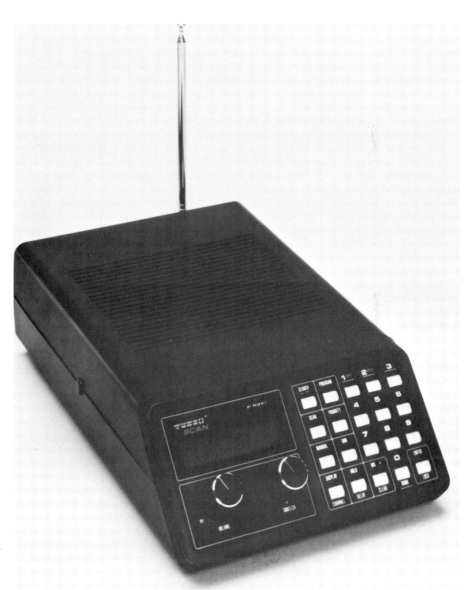

A good-quality scanner such as this Regency Turbo-Scan will allow you to listen to highway patrol broadcasts for clues as to their location.

Year	Code	HP	Torque	Bore	Stroke	CC	Compression ratio
1973 Audi 80 GL		98	89	76.5	80.0	1470.8	9.5:1
1973 Audi 80/L		69	68	75.0	73.4	1297.1	8.5:1
1973 Audi 80S/LS		86	83	76.5	80.0	1470.8	9.5:1
1973 Audi Fox		75	82	76.5	80.0	1470.8	8.2:1
1974 Audi Fox		75	82	76.5	80.0	1470.8	8.2:1
1974 Dasher		75	79	76.5	80.0	1470.8	8.2:1
1975 Dasher		71	80	76.5	80.0	1470.8	8.2:1
1975 Rabbit/Scirocco	FC	71	80	76.5	80.0	1470.8	8.2:1
1976 Audi Fox		79	89	79.5	80.0	1588.5	8.0:1
1976 (with carb)	FN	71	82	79.5	80.0	1588.5	8.2:1
1976 Dasher		79	86	79.5	80.0	1588.5	8.2:1
1976 (with FI)	EE	78	83	79.5	80.0	1588.5	8.2:1
1977 Audi Fox		78	83	79.5	80.0	1588.5	8.2:1
1977 Dasher		78	83	79.5	80.0	1588.5	8.2:1
1977 Rabbit	EE	78	83	79.5	80.0	1588.5	8.2:1
1977 Golf GTI		100		79.5	80.0	1588.5	Europe only
1977 Scirocco		78	83	79.5	80.0	1588.5	8.2:1
1978 Audi Fox		78	84	79.5	80.0	1588.5	8.0:1
1978 Dasher		78	84	79.5	80.0	1588.5	8.0:1
1978 Rabbit/Scirocco	EH	71	73	79.5	73.4	1457.4	Cast crank, 8.0:1
1979 Audi Fox		78	83	79.5	80.0	1588.5	8.0:1
1979 Dasher		78	84	79.5	80.0	1588.5	8.0:1
1979 Rabbit	EH	71	73	79.5	73.4	1457.4	Cast crank
1979 Scirocco	EJ	78	84	79.5	80.0	1588.5	8.0:1
1980 Audi Fox		78	84	79.5	80.0	1588.5	8.0:1
1980 Convertible		76	83	79.5	80.0	1588.5	8.2:1
1980 GTI	EG	110	103	79.5	80.0	1588.5	9.5:1 (European only)
1980 Jetta		76	83	79.5	80.0	1588.5	8.2:1
1980 Pickup		78	84	79.5	80.0	1588.5	8.2:1
1980 Rabbit	FN	75	88	79.5	80.0	1588.5	8.2:1
1981 Convertible		74	90	79.5	86.4	1715.5	8.2:1
1981 Dasher		76	83	79.5	80.0	1588.5	8.2:1
1981 Jetta		74	90	79.5	86.4	1715.5	8.2:1
1981 Pickup		78	88	79.5	86.4	1715.5	8.2:1
1981 Rabbit		74	90	79.5	86.4	1715.5	8.2:1
1981 VW/Audi		74	90	79.5	86.4	1715.5	8.2:1
1982 Quantum		74	90	79.5	86.4	1715.5	8.2:1
1982 VW/Audi		74	90	79.5	86.4	1715.5	8.2:1 (new body style)
1983 GTI		90	105	81.0	86.4	1780.9	8.5:1
1983 Quantum		74	90	79.5	86.4	1715.5	8.2:1
1983 Rabbit carb		65	88	79.5	86.4	1715.5	8.0:1
1983 Rabbit FI		74	90	79.5	86.4	1715.5	8.2:1
1983 Scirocco Wolfsburg		90	100	81.0	86.4	1780.9	8.5:1
1984 Golf carb		75	92	81.0	77.4	1595.4	9.0:1
1984 Golf GLX carb		90	107	81.0	86.4	1780.9	10.0:1
1984 Golf GTI		112	114	81.0	86.4	1780.9	10.0:1
1984 GTI		90	100	81.0	86.4	1780.9	8.5:1
1984 Jetta GLI		90	100	81.0	86.4	1780.9	8.5:1
1984 Rabbit carb		65	88	79.5	86.4	1715.5	8.0:1
1984 Rabbit FI		74	90	79.5	86.4	1715.5	8.2:1
1984 Scirocco		90	100	81.0	86.4	1780.9	8.5:1
1985 Cabriolet		90	100	81.0	86.4	1780.9	8.5:1
1985 Golf		85	98	81.0	86.4	1780.9	8.5:1
1985 GTI	HT	100	105	81.0	86.4	1780.9	10.0:1
1985 Jetta		85	98	81.0	86.4	1780.9	8.5:1
1985 Jetta GLI	HT	100	105	81.0	86.4	1780.9	10.0:1
1985 Quantum Wagon		88	96	81.0	86.4	1780.9	9.0:1
1985 Scirocco		90	100	81.0	86.4	1780.9	8.5:1
1986 Cabriolet		90	100	81.0	86.4	1780.9	8.5:1
1986 Golf		85	96	81.0	86.4	1780.9	9.0:1
1986 GTI	RD	102	110	81.0	86.4	1780.9	10.0:1
1986 Jetta		85	98	81.0	86.4	1780.9	8.5:1
1986 Jetta GLI		102	110	81.0	86.4	1780.9	10.0:1
1986 Scirocco		90	100	81.0	86.4	1780.9	8.5:1
1986 Scirocco 16V		123	120	81.0	86.4	1780.9	10.0:1
1987 Cabriolet		90	100	81.0	86.4	1780.9	8.5:1
1987 Fox		81	93	81.0	86.4	1780.9	9.0:1
1987 Golf GL		85	96	81.0	86.4	1780.9	9.0:1
1987 Golf GT		102	110	81.0	86.4	1780.9	10.1:1
1987 GTI 16V		123	120	81.0	86.4	1780.9	10.1:1
1987 Jetta		85	96	81.0	86.4	1780.9	9.0:1
1987 Jetta GLI		102	110	81.0	86.4	1780.9	10.0:1
1987 Scirocco		90	100	81.0	86.4	1780.9	8.5:1
1987 Scirocco 16V		123	120	81.0	86.4	1780.9	10.1:1

This chart should be very valuable for its comparisons.

The second generation of this idea was a device called The Club. It locked across the steering wheel, extending out from the steering wheel so that the end of The Club interfered with the windshield, the console, the door, your legs and everything else if you tried to turn it.

The Club has three advantages over a cane. First, it is more visible, so it serves as a better deterrent. Second, it is quicker and easier to put on, so you will use it more often than you might use the cane. Third, no amount of bending the steering wheel will allow the thief to remove The Club (a cane can be removed that way).

The Club is not perfect, however, because the steering wheel can still be removed and a different one installed. This falls into the category of "if they really want it," however. How many thieves are going to carry around a spare steering wheel?

When installing either a cane or The Club (or any time you park your car), always point the nose of the car into a corner and then crank the front wheels fully to the left or right. This makes it much more difficult to tow your car without getting into it and defeating the steering lock mechanism.

That brings up the next device: a removable steering wheel. Race cars have these, and now so can you. Again, the chances of a thief having a replacement steering wheel are pretty remote. The drawback is that you have to carry around your steering wheel everywhere you go.

One last thing you can do is immobilize your car so it cannot be towed, pushed or dragged off. This forces the thief to pick all four tires off the ground to move your car. The way to accomplish this is with a brake line lock. This is a device that is plumbed into your brake system. Each time you leave the car, you turn the key on the line lock and push on the brake pedal. The line lock acts as a one-way valve that maintains the pressure in the lines, keeping the discs and drums locked tight. Apparently, this has no adverse effect on the braking system.

Another way to use the line lock is to turn the key without pushing on the brake pedal. The next time the pedal is depressed, the line lock will keep the brakes applied until the key is used to unlock them. This might allow a thief to get to the end of the block before discovering that you were just kidding when you let him or her take the car.

Fire extinguishers

An automotive fire must be dealt with quickly because of the large amount of readily available combustible material involved. That means having your extinguisher mounted close at hand. Under the driver's seat, on the rear seat floor or inside the glovebox are the best locations. Some people prefer a location on the windshield A-pillar, but that blocks the entryway and is a possible safety hazard in a collision. Avoid any trunk

Type of part	Pre-treatment	Priming	Painting		
				Two-step paints	
			Non-metallic	Metallic base	Clear coat
Fiberglas	1. Wash off with hot soap and water	Plasto-flex primer	Paint	Metallic base paint	Clear coat
ABS		Plasto-flex primer	3 paint to 1 flex	Metallic base paint	3 clear to 1 flex
Primed polyurethane	2. Roughen with fine Scotchbrite	Flexprime (if required)	2 paint to 1 flex	9 metallic paint to 1 flex	2 clear to 1 flex
Semi-hard polyurethane foam	3. Rinse	Plasto-flex primer	2 paint to 1 flex	9 metallic paint to 1 flex	2 clear to 1 flex
Soft polyurethane		Plasto-flex primer	2 paint to 1 flex	9 metallic paint to 1 flex	1 clear to 1 flex

This painting table compares various plastic surfaces.

C	F									
0	32.0	33.8	35.6	37.4	39.2	41.0	42.8	44.6	46.4	48.2
10	50.0	51.8	53.6	55.4	57.2	59.0	60.8	62.6	64.4	66.2
20	68.0	69.8	71.6	73.4	75.2	77.0	78.8	80.6	82.4	84.2
30	86.0	87.8	89.6	91.4	93.2	95.0	96.8	98.6	100.4	102.2
40	104.0	105.8	107.6	109.4	111.2	113.0	114.8	116.6	118.4	120.2
50	122.0	123.8	125.6	127.4	129.2	131.0	132.8	134.6	136.4	138.2
60	140.0	141.8	143.6	145.4	147.2	149.0	150.8	152.6	154.4	156.2
70	158.0	159.8	161.6	163.4	165.2	167.0	168.8	170.6	172.4	174.2
80	176.0	177.8	179.6	181.4	183.2	185.0	186.8	188.6	190.4	192.2
90	194.0	195.8	197.6	199.4	201.2	203.0	204.8	206.6	208.4	210.2
100	212.0	213.8	215.6	217.4	219.2	221.0	222.8	224.6	226.4	228.2
110	230.0	231.8	233.6	235.4	237.2	239.0	240.8	242.6	244.4	246.2
120	248.0	249.8	251.6	253.4	255.2	257.0	258.8	260.6	262.4	264.2

Converting from Celsius to Fahrenheit is easy with this chart.

mounting location except for back-up extinguishers; it will take too long to reach in an emergency.

There are different types of fire extinguisher, each of which specializes in a certain type of fire. A car fire extinguisher, for example, has to be safe for use around electrical wiring, oil and gasoline, in addition to the normal flammable materials inside the passenger compartment. In the case of an engine fire, the fire extinguisher must not cause any damage to the engine as it is extinguishing the fire. Dry powders, for example, will get into the motor and ruin piston rings, valve seats and bearings. Some of the other chemical extinguishers will attack hot aluminum and electrical wiring on contact.

Carbon dioxide (CO_2) extinguishers are popular with racetracks because they are a "clean" way to fight fires (leaving no residual gunk) and are relatively inexpensive to recharge. On the other hand, they release a very cold fluid (minus 100 degrees Fahrenheit) that could cause thermal shock to hot underhood components.

The state-of-the-art in automotive fire-fighting equipment is the Halon extinguisher. These release colorless, odorless gases that quickly extinguish fires and evaporate, leaving behind no

mm	inch 0	0.1	0.2	0.3	0.4	0.5	0.6	0.7	0.8	0.9
0	0.000	0.004	0.008	0.012	0.016	0.020	0.024	0.028	0.031	0.035
1	0.039	0.043	0.047	0.051	0.055	0.059	0.063	0.067	0.071	0.075
2	0.079	0.083	0.087	0.091	0.094	0.098	0.102	0.106	0.110	0.114
3	0.118	0.122	0.126	0.130	0.134	0.138	0.142	0.146	0.150	0.154
4	0.157	0.161	0.165	0.169	0.173	0.177	0.181	0.185	0.189	0.193
5	0.197	0.201	0.205	0.209	0.213	0.217	0.220	0.224	0.228	0.232
6	0.236	0.240	0.244	0.248	0.252	0.256	0.260	0.264	0.268	0.272
7	0.276	0.280	0.283	0.287	0.291	0.295	0.299	0.303	0.307	0.311
8	0.315	0.319	0.323	0.327	0.331	0.335	0.339	0.343	0.346	0.350
9	0.354	0.358	0.362	0.366	0.370	0.374	0.378	0.382	0.386	0.390
10	0.394	0.398	0.402	0.406	0.409	0.413	0.417	0.421	0.425	0.429
11	0.433	0.437	0.441	0.445	0.449	0.453	0.457	0.461	0.465	0.469
12	0.472	0.476	0.480	0.484	0.488	0.492	0.496	0.500	0.504	0.508
13	0.512	0.516	0.520	0.524	0.528	0.531	0.535	0.539	0.543	0.547
14	0.551	0.555	0.559	0.563	0.567	0.571	0.575	0.579	0.583	0.587
15	0.591	0.594	0.598	0.602	0.606	0.610	0.614	0.618	0.622	0.626
16	0.630	0.634	0.638	0.642	0.646	0.650	0.654	0.657	0.661	0.665
17	0.669	0.673	0.677	0.681	0.685	0.689	0.693	0.697	0.701	0.705
18	0.709	0.713	0.717	0.720	0.724	0.728	0.732	0.736	0.740	0.744
19	0.748	0.752	0.756	0.760	0.764	0.768	0.772	0.776	0.780	0.783
20	0.787	0.791	0.795	0.799	0.803	0.807	0.811	0.815	0.819	0.823
21	0.827	0.831	0.835	0.839	0.843	0.846	0.850	0.854	0.858	0.862
22	0.866	0.870	0.874	0.878	0.882	0.886	0.890	0.894	0.898	0.902
23	0.906	0.909	0.913	0.917	0.921	0.925	0.929	0.933	0.937	0.941
24	0.945	0.949	0.953	0.957	0.961	0.965	0.969	0.972	0.976	0.980
25	0.984	0.988	0.992	0.996	1.000	1.004	1.008	1.012	1.016	1.020

This conversion chart from millimeters to inches will aid you in your calculations . . .

inch	mm 0	0.001	0.002	0.003	0.004	0.005	0.006	0.007	0.008	0.009
0	0.000	0.025	0.051	0.076	0.102	0.127	0.152	0.178	0.203	0.229
0.01	0.254	0.279	0.305	0.330	0.356	0.381	0.406	0.432	0.457	0.483
0.02	0.508	0.533	0.559	0.584	0.610	0.635	0.660	0.686	0.711	0.737
0.03	0.762	0.787	0.813	0.838	0.864	0.889	0.914	0.940	0.965	0.991
0.04	1.016	1.041	1.067	1.092	1.118	1.143	1.168	1.194	1.219	1.245
0.05	1.270	1.295	1.321	1.346	1.372	1.397	1.422	1.448	1.473	1.499
0.06	1.524	1.549	1.575	1.600	1.626	1.651	1.676	1.702	1.727	1.753
0.07	1.778	1.803	1.829	1.854	1.880	1.905	1.930	1.956	1.981	2.007
0.08	2.032	2.057	2.083	2.108	2.134	2.159	2.184	2.210	2.235	2.261
0.09	2.286	2.311	2.337	2.362	2.388	2.413	2.438	2.464	2.489	2.515
0.10	2.540	2.565	2.591	2.616	2.642	2.667	2.692	2.718	2.743	2.769
0.11	2.794	2.819	2.845	2.870	2.896	2.921	2.946	2.972	2.997	3.023
0.12	3.048	3.073	3.099	3.124	3.150	3.175	3.200	3.226	3.251	3.277
0.13	3.302	3.327	3.353	3.378	3.404	3.429	3.454	3.480	3.505	3.531
0.14	3.556	3.581	3.607	3.632	3.658	3.683	3.708	3.734	3.759	3.785
0.15	3.810	3.835	3.861	3.886	3.912	3.937	3.962	3.988	4.013	4.039
0.16	4.064	4.089	4.115	4.140	4.166	4.191	4.216	4.242	4.267	4.293
0.17	4.318	4.343	4.369	4.394	4.420	4.445	4.470	4.496	4.521	4.547
0.18	4.572	4.597	4.623	4.648	4.674	4.699	4.724	4.750	4.775	4.801
0.19	4.826	4.851	4.877	4.902	4.928	4.953	4.978	5.004	5.029	5.055
0.20	5.080	5.105	5.131	5.156	5.182	5.207	5.232	5.258	5.283	5.309

. . . and going the other way will be just as easy.

corrosive residue, stains or damage. Additionally, gases will reach places within an engine compartment that powders cannot, thereby increasing your fire-fighting effectiveness. The most common type of Halon for automotive use is Halon 1211, which works against fires in three ways.

First, its chilled vapor cools burning cellulose-type material (as might be found in the passenger compartment), but it does not induce the risk of thermal shock as greatly as does CO_2 because Halon releases at a temperature well above zero degrees Fahrenheit. Second, the Halon displaces the fire's life-giving oxygen, thereby stopping additional combustion. Third, it interferes with the method of combustion (by its chemical make-up) to snuff out the blaze.

Halon 1211 is the best choice for an automotive fire extinguisher. It is non-conductive and fully rated for Class A, B and C fires, and leaves no residue. Racers often install a full onboard automatic Halon system, with a central tank feeding several nozzles that are mounted at strategic locations around the car.

Whichever type of extinguisher you choose, make sure it is mounted close at hand and is charged. You hope you never will have to test its effectiveness, but if you do need it, you will need it immediately.

Radar and radio detectors and protectors

Police radar is a major weapon in the law enforcement arsenal to ensure compliance with posted speed limits. Federal, state and local authorities have all aligned themselves on the use of radar for this purpose, with the result being that police departments across the United States use hundreds of radar units every day in the line of duty. This puts the number of radar-equipped police officers you are likely to encounter during a 3,000 mile cross-country trip about equal to the number of fast-food establishments you will see along the way. For long-distance travel, therefore, you may want a radar detector.

About a dozen manufacturers produce radar detectors for sale in the United States. They typically range in price from about $200 to nearly $400, and give different levels of radar detection. Evaluating these devices is beyond the scope of this book, but enthusiast magazines such as *Car and Driver* usually test all the better units nearly once a year. Their in-depth and timely testing

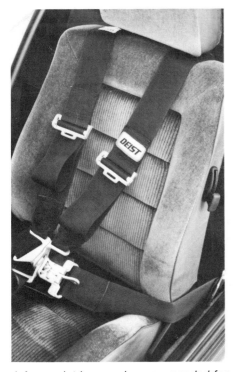

A four-point harness is recommended for racing applications.

If you don't fit the stock seat you should investigate some of the aftermarket seats, such as the Recaro KRX.

F	C									
30	−1.1	−0.6	0.0	0.6	1.1	1.7	2.2	2.8	3.3	3.9
40	4.4	5.0	5.6	6.1	6.7	7.2	7.8	8.3	8.9	9.4
50	10.0	10.6	11.1	11.7	12.2	12.8	13.3	13.9	14.4	15.0
60	15.6	16.1	16.7	17.2	17.8	18.3	18.9	19.4	20.0	20.6
70	21.1	21.7	22.2	22.8	23.3	23.9	24.4	25.0	25.6	26.1
80	26.7	27.2	27.8	28.3	28.9	29.4	30.0	30.6	31.1	31.7
90	32.2	32.8	33.3	33.9	34.4	35.0	35.6	36.1	36.7	37.2
100	37.8	38.3	38.9	39.4	40.0	40.6	41.1	41.7	42.2	42.8
110	43.3	43.9	44.4	45.0	45.6	46.1	46.7	47.2	47.8	48.3
120	48.9	49.4	50.0	50.6	51.1	51.7	52.2	52.8	53.3	53.9
130	54.4	55.0	55.6	56.1	56.7	57.2	57.8	58.3	58.9	59.4
140	60.0	60.6	61.1	61.7	62.2	62.8	63.3	63.9	64.4	65.0
150	65.6	66.1	66.7	67.2	67.8	68.3	68.9	69.4	70.0	70.6
160	71.1	71.7	72.2	72.8	73.3	73.9	74.4	75.0	75.6	76.1
170	76.7	77.2	77.8	78.3	78.9	79.4	80.0	80.6	81.1	81.7
180	82.2	82.8	83.3	83.9	84.4	85.0	85.6	86.1	86.7	87.2
190	87.8	88.3	88.9	89.4	90.0	90.6	91.1	91.7	92.2	92.8
200	93.3	93.9	94.4	95.0	95.6	96.1	96.7	97.2	97.8	98.3
210	98.9	99.4	100.0	100.6	101.1	101.7	102.2	102.8	103.3	103.9
220	104.4	105.0	105.6	106.1	106.7	107.2	107.8	108.3	108.9	109.4
230	110.0	110.6	111.1	111.7	112.2	112.8	113.3	113.9	114.4	115.0
240	115.6	116.1	116.7	117.2	117.8	118.3	118.9	119.4	120.0	120.6

Fahrenheit to Celsius conversions are simple with the help of this table.

makes them required reading if you hope to stay on top of the radar detector market.

There are three types of radar detectors: remote, standard and compact. The remote units are the most covert, and are to be considered if you drive in "radar-prohibited" states, where the police will not only give you a ticket but confiscate your radar detector, as well.

The standard units are single-piece construction (as opposed to the remote units), approximately 5×7 inches in size. The Cincinnati Microwave Escort is one such unit. Although the standard-size units work fine, their larger size makes them more difficult to mount and more easy for the police to spot.

The compact units are the most advanced (and costly) of the three designs, dimensionally about the same as two audio cassette tapes stacked atop one another. The Cincinnati Microwave Passport is an excellent example of the compact detector. The technical sophistication of these units is stunning. The better ones will even discriminate between true radar traps and the almost identical collision avoidance radar.

The police are increasingly turning away from radar and toward repeater

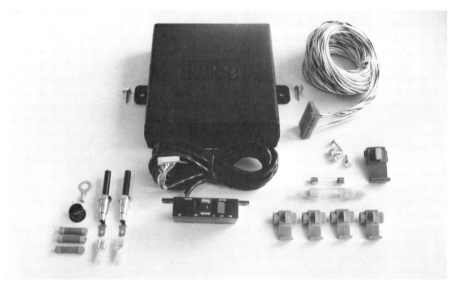

The Ungo Box is one example of a high-quality do-it-yourself alarm system.

When installed, the dead pedal not only is in the perfect place to use as a foot brace, it is also at the right height for using the clutch.

Pressure/Vacuum

PSI	Inches of Hg	Bar
0	0	0
0.50	1.02	0.03
1.00	2.04	0.07
1.50	3.05	0.10
2.00	4.07	0.14
2.50	5.09	0.17
3.00	6.11	0.21
3.50	7.13	0.24
4.00	8.14	0.28
4.50	9.16	0.31
5.00	10.18	0.34
5.50	11.20	0.38
6.00	12.22	0.41
6.50	13.23	0.45
7.00	14.25	0.48
7.50	15.27	0.52
8.00	16.29	0.55
8.50	17.31	0.59
9.00	18.32	0.62
9.50	19.34	0.65
10.00	20.36	0.69
10.50	21.38	0.72
11.00	22.40	0.76
11.50	23.41	0.79
12.00	24.43	0.83
12.50	25.45	0.86
13.00	26.47	0.90
13.50	27.49	0.93
14.00	28.50	0.96
14.50	29.52	1.00
14.70	29.93	1.01
15.00	30.54	1.03
15.50	31.56	1.07
16.00	32.58	1.10
16.50	33.59	1.14
17.00	34.61	1.17
17.50	35.63	1.21
18.00	36.65	1.24
18.50	37.67	1.27
19.00	38.68	1.31
19.50	39.70	1.34
20.00	40.72	1.38
20.50	41.74	1.41
21.00	42.76	1.45
21.50	43.77	1.48
22.00	44.79	1.52
22.50	45.81	1.55
23.00	46.83	1.58
23.50	47.85	1.62
24.00	48.86	1.65
24.50	49.88	1.69
25.00	50.90	1.72
25.50	51.92	1.76
26.00	52.94	1.79
26.50	53.95	1.83

1 PSI = .0689 Bar
1 PSI = 2.03602 inches of Hg
7 PSI = vacuum
14.7 PSI = sea level
20.50 PSI = pressure

Use this conversion chart for pounds per square inch to inches of mercury to bar.

communications systems. One firm has marketed a device called the Chips Detector that is a radio scanner with additional circuitry trained to lock onto repeater signals and alert the driver of their proximity. The range of the Chips Detector is up to five miles, and it works in any area in which the police use repeaters. This means that you will even be alerted when an aircraft is in your vicinity. The Chips Detector comes with a listing of all police frequencies in all the states.

A similar unit is the Regency scanner, which is a glorified police scanner. Like the Chips Detector, it comes with a listing of frequencies. With diligent listening you will be able to track law enforcement, but it does become tiring.

Steering wheels

The small-diameter steering wheels you see in the Formula 1 cars look trick, but they are not the hot tip for a Volkswagen. Although there are many wonderful aftermarket steering wheels out there, I prefer factory wheels for three reasons.

First, the stock wheel affords the best view of the gauges. If you are of average height, you might be able to see the gauges even with a smaller wheel, but it is worth checking out before you buy.

Second, I find that the steering effort is just about right with the stock-diameter wheel. A smaller steering wheel makes the effort too high, and a larger steering wheel (!) makes it seem as if you are driving a tractor or a sixties muscle car.

When the steering effort is just right it is much easier to pass the wheel between your hands, as taught in driving school. This factor is far more critical than the steering ratio in finding the fast way around a turn (or a series of turns).

Third, I enjoy having the horn buttons near the rim of the steering wheel. Having to move a hand to the center of the wheel to actuate the horn button is sometimes not the best way of maintaining control of your automobile.

If you decide to go steering wheel shopping, keep in mind that ergonometric studies have shown that the proper steering wheel does *not* have a smooth, thin rim. A thicker rim with bumps on the back is far less fatiguing to drive. Better still, if you can find one you like, are the sculpted wheels that dictate where you put your hands. They are not for everybody, but once you get used to them they are very nice.

Seating

The stock Volkswagen seat, with the exception of the optional sport seat in the Scirocco, is not designed for maximum lateral support during high-g maneuvers. It is, however, easy to get in and out of. This might be hard to appreciate until you find yourself faced with a million errands to do in one day in a car with high side bolsters.

Even with a wide variety of seating available in the aftermarket, recommendations are difficult to make. Preferences in seating are a personal matter, and the wrong seat can make life miserable.

When you contemplate the purchase of a seat, first check to see that it fits you. Check also to see that the mounting hardware is of high quality. Recaro supplies excellent mounting hardware, and you should expect no less from whatever seat you choose.

One final thing to keep in mind is that the roofline on the Scirocco is lower than on the Rabbit or Jetta. This will make it that much more of an effort to climb over a high bolster, so plan accordingly.

Accelerometers

It is surprising what you can do with a stopwatch or two and some mathematics. The November 1970 *Road & Track* has an interesting article by Ronald F. Brown on just this subject. The article is much too extensive to repeat (or even summarize) here, but if you are interested you can request a copy from your local library.

In chapter 1 is a chart to help you approximate horsepower based on quarter-mile times. This chart has proven itself quite accurate over the years.

Still, with all this you might want more, or you might want the same, only easier. Foruntately, at least two companies now sell accelerometers. An accelerometer works by measuring the acceleration of a known weight. Then, using calculus, it calculates the speed and distance over which this acceleration occurred.

The first of the two units is the G-analyst. Depending on the mode you select, the G-analyst will graphically show you acceleration and deceleration, side-to-side g-forces or all four (using the concept of the friction circle), and provides numbers to go with the graphs.

The second unit is called the Vericom. It is better suited for acceleration and deceleration, although it can be used for lateral acceleration as well. The Vericom has no graphics display, but it will tell you time to speed, distance to speed and peak g-force at the push of a button.

The problem shared by both of these units is that body roll and pitch are also calculated in, unless you trick the accelerometer into ignoring them by entering in a correction factor. But since there is no accurate way to determine the correction factor for a given car, you must guess. Your guess is then the basis for all the high-powered calculations performed by the accelerometer. This renders the results somewhat less than reliable.

Having used both instruments, I prefer the Vericom and a skid pad for ease of setup, even though it is more difficult to get lateral g-force readings with it than with the G-analyst. The G-analyst requires a good-size area in which you can drive like a maniac. This means you must have access to a large parking lot with a smooth surface, or a race track. If you do have such access, and are serious about improving your performance on the friction circle, check out the G-analyst.

Both of these instruments are expensive, but if you have a couple of like-minded friends (or a car club), you could all pitch in and share one.

Windshield wipers

The best wiper setup is the stock Bosch blade and insert. The inserts wear out quickly, but they are not expensive or difficult to change. Many people bend the wiper blade prongs to grip the insert, but this just makes it more difficult to change the insert later on. You can leave them comfortably loose without fear of losing an insert. For best results, orient the insert so that the cutoff end is pointing toward the top of the windshield. Point the other end (the end with the tabs for the thin metal inserts) toward the hood.

I do not recommend the double-wiper systems. If you have the same amount of pressure applied through twice as much surface area, your pressure per unit of surface area is going to be half as much. A double-wiper would therefore work half as well as a single wiper.

If you want to perk up the performance of your windshield wipers, buy some Rain-X and follow the directions. The more it rains, the more you need Rain-X.

Volkswagen part numbers

It can be helpful to understand just what the Volkswagen part number means. Consider this example:

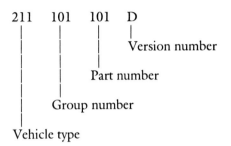

The vehicle type indicates the vehicle (or design project) for which the part was originally designed. This doesn't necessarily mean that this part will be found only on the vehicle for which it was designed, however. The same part (and part number) can sometimes be found on many different Volkswagens, as well as on Porsches and Audis.

The group number indicates what general area of the car the part is used in. Volkswagen has divided the car into ten sections, numbered 1 through 10. The section number serves as the first digit of the group number. For example:

Section 1   Engine
Section 2   Fuel delivery and exhaust
Section 3   Cooling
Section 4   Transmission
Section 5   Suspension and steering
Section 6   Tires, wheels and brakes
Section 7   Linkages
Section 8   Body
Section 9   Electrical
Section 10 Accessories

Engine parts are normally in section 1, so their group numbers are in the 100s. Carburetors and most fuel injection components fall into section 2, so their group numbers are in the 200s, and so on.

The part number is just that—the part number. Part numbers that end in 98 (such as 198, 298 and so on) are kits.

The version number helps keep track of the revisions and improvements to the parts.

There is no number that indicates the vehicle year for which the part was designed. There is also no way of knowing just by looking at the part number if it is the latest or earliest. For that, you

have to refer to the dealer supercedure list.

Two things usually confuse people when referring to Volkswagen part numbers. First, the part number stamped on the part is often not the part number. Confused?

Volkswagen assigns part numbers to everything it does. Therefore, a housing will have a part number all its own without all the things that normally go with it. This number is for internal use only, however, so if you try to order one the parts counterperson will tell you that you do not have a good number. The stamped-in number can sometimes still be used to identify parts for your own information.

The second thing that can confound you is that every once in a while you will find a part for which the part number seems to fall into a "wrong" group. If you are hoping to get a job as a parts counterperson at the Volkswagen dealer, this gives you something to look forward to. For the rest of us, the basics are usually enough to keep us out of trouble and help us sound intelligent when ordering parts from the dealer.

Conversion factors

1 mile = 1.60934 kilometers (km)
1 km = 0.62137 mile

$$\text{Horsepower} = \frac{\text{torque} \times \text{rpm}}{5250}$$

1 Newton/meters (Nm) = 0.7376 pound-feet (lb-ft) = 0.10197 kilo-pond/meters (kpm)
1 kpm = 9.80665 Nm = 7.2334 lb-ft
1 lb-ft = 1.35575 Nm = 0.13825 kpm

1 inch = 25.4 millimeters (mm)
1 mm = 0.03937 inch

1 cubic inch (ci) = 16.3871 cubic centimeters (cc)
1 cc = 0.06102 ci

1 kilogram (kg) = 2.2046 pounds (lb)
1 lb = 0.45359 kg

1 horsepower (hp) = 1.0319 PS = 0.7457 kilowatt (kw)
1 kw = 1.3410 hp = 1.3596 PS
1 PS = 0.98632 hp = 0.7355 kw

$$\text{Celsius} = \frac{5}{9}(\text{Fahrenheit} - 32)$$

Fahrenheit = 1.8 Celsius + 32
Rankine = Fahrenheit + 459.69

1 pound per square inch (psi) = 0.0689 bar = 2.03602 inches of mercury (Hg)

1 bar = 14.5037 psi = 29.5298 inches Hg
1 inch Hg = 0.491237 psi = 0.03386 bar

Skid pad formula:
$$\frac{1.226 \times r}{t^2} = g$$

1 cubic foot per meter (cfm) = 1.6 hp (theoretical) = 1.44 hp (estimate)
1 hp = 0.625 cfm (theoretical) = 0.694 cfm (estimate)

$$\text{Carburetor sizing: cfm} = \frac{D \times rpm \times E}{56{,}634}$$

Suppliers

ABT Tuning
Via Fabricante, G-1
Mission Viejo, CA 92691
  Complete line of engine parts, transmission parts, body kits and accessories

Abt Tuning
Uberwangerstrasse 16
8960 Kempten
Germany
  Complete line of engine parts, transmission parts, body kits and accessories

Addco
103 East Street
Lake Park, FL 33403
  Suspension

Allison Ignition
1613 Flower Avenue
Duarte, CA 91010
  Photo-optic breakerless ignition

ARC
4788 Library Road, Route 88
Bethel Park, PA 15102

Arkay Turbo
2928 Fisk
Redondo Beach, CA 90278

Assenmacher Specialty Tools
5725 Olde Stage Road
Boulder, CO 80302
  Volkswagen special tools

Automotive Performance Systems
1464 Hundley Street
Anaheim, CA 92806
  Complete line of engine parts, transmission parts, body kits and accessories

Autotech SportTuning
1800 North Glassell Street
Orange, CA 92665
  Complete line of engine parts, transmission parts, body kits and accessories

BEL Micro Eye
2422 Dunwin Drive
Mississauga, Ontario Canada L5L 1J9
or
20 Centre Drive
Orchard Park, NY 14127
  Radar detectors

Callaway Turbosystems
6 High Street
Old Lyme, CT 06371
  Turbo systems, suspensions, and accessories

Cincinnati Microwave
One Microwave Plaza
Cincinnati, OH 45296
  Radar detectors

Cobra/Dynascan Corporation
6500 West Cortland Street
Chicago, IL 60635
  Radar detectors

Diest
641 Sonora Avenue
Glendale, CA 91206
  Safety equipment

Drake Performance
2340 West 20th Street
Yuma, AZ 85364
  Complete line of engine parts, transmission parts, body kits and accessories

Edelbrock
411 Coral Circle
El Segundo, CA 90245
  Water injection

Electrodyne
2316 Jefferson Davis Highway
Alexandria, VA 22313
  Parts and accessories

Electrolert
4949 South 25A
Tipp City, OH 45371
  Radar detectors, materials on radar and radar tickets

Euro Rep.
2872 C Walnut Avenue
Tustin, CA 92680

Eurorace
2899 West 190th Street
Redondo Beach, CA 90278
  Engines, engine parts and carburetors

FAT Performance
Glassell
Orange, CA 92665
  Off-road applications

Fox Marketing
4518 Taylorsville Road
Dayton, OH 45424
  Radar detectors

GE Answer Center
800-626-2000
  Product information about Halogen headlights

G&L Coatings
888 Rancheros Drive, #C
San Marcos, CA 92069
  Molybdenum and resin Kal-Gard coatings

GMP, Inc.
P.O. Box 240008
Charlotte, NC 28224
  Complete line of engine parts, transmission parts, body kits and accessories

GTi Engineering
Silverstone Circuit
Towcester, Northants NN 12 8TN
Great Britain
  Full line of performance parts, motors, body kits and accessories

GTI Motorsport
1581 Monrovia Avenue
Newport Beach, CA 92663
  Parts and accessories, complete engines, dyno testing

GUL Industries
23970 Craftsman Road
Calabasas, CA 91302
  Radar detectors

Halo Products
1538 MacArthur Boulevard
Oakland, CA 94602
  By-pass oil filter/cooler

Hofco Alarms
11505 Jefferson Boulevard
Culver City, CA 90230
  Vehicle alarms

Kennedy Engineered Products
10202 Glenoaks Boulevard
Pacoima, CA 91331
  Engine-to-transmission adaptors

K40/American Antenna Corporation
1500 Executive Drive
Elgin, IL 60120
  Radar detectors

Lubrication Research Inc.
2894 Aiello Drive
San Jose, CA 95111
  Preluber and Turboluber

Mecca Development
Route 41
Sharon, CT 06069
  High-performance filters and oiling
systems

M. L. Hill International
P.O. Box 228
Tucson, AZ 85702
  Armor door plates (theft-deterrent door
handle guards)

Motor Guard Laboratories
P.O. Box 814
Matolocking, NJ 08738
  Oil analysis

National Technologies
Route 41 Box 140
Sharon, CT 06069
  Propylene glycol coolant kits

Oberg Filters
12414 Highway 99 South
Everett, WA 98024
  Stainless steel screen oil filter

Per-Lux
1242 East Edna Place
Covina, CA 90032
  Magnetically triggered breakerless
ignition

Porsche Mail Order
135 17th Street
Santa Monica, CA 90402
  Synchro Meter carburetor balancer

R+A Applied Arts, Inc.
555 Gutheil Place
Lyndhurst, NJ 07071
  Installations of high-performance parts
and Callaway turbo systems

Radio Association Defending Airwave
Rights, Inc. (RADAR)
4949 South 25A
Tipp City, OH 45371
  Radar trial video tape

Radio Shack/Tandy Corporation
1800 One Tandy Center
Fort Worth, TX 76102
  Electrical supplies, accessories and radar
detectors (stores everywhere)

Remote Systems
13009 Glenview Drive
Burnsville, MN 55337
  Radar detectors

Rev-Power
268 Cluster
San Bernardino, CA 92408
  Off-road applications

Rimco
520 East Dyer Road
Santa Ana, CA 92702
  Complete machine shop facilities

Ronal Wheel Corporation
15692 Computer Lane
Huntington Beach, CA 92649
  Modular and one-piece road wheels

Suspension Techniques
1853 Belcroft Avenue
South El Monte, CA 91733
  Chassis springs and anitroll bars

Sway-A-Way
7840 Burnet Avenue
Van Nuys, CA 91405
  Suspension components

Synthoil Corporation of California
P.O. Box 6369
Thousand Oaks, CA 91359
  High-performance motor oil, gear lube
and grease

System 1
1822 East Main, Suite A
Visalia, CA 93291
  Stainless steel screen spin-on oil filter

Techtonics
1253 West La Cadena
Riverside, CA 92501
  Complete engine, engine part, fuel
injection, exhaust and dyno services

Tri-Esse Science
622 W. Colorado Street
Glendale, CA 91204
  Burettes

Turbokote Products Industries
P.O. Box 3447
La Habra, CA 90632
  Zirconium oxide coatings

Uniden Corporation
6345 Castleway Court
Indianapolis, IN 46250
  Radar detectors

Valentine Research
10280 Alliance Road
Cincinnati, OH 45242
  G-analyst accelerometer

Valley Werks
209 South 3rd Street
St. Charles, IL 60174

Vericom Corporation
6000 Culligan Way
Minnetonka, MN 55345

VC 200 performance computer

Whistler/Controlonics
P.O. Box 555
Five Lyberty Way
Westford, MA 01886
  Radar detectors

White Eagle Manufacturing
Route 1, Box 279
East Bernstadt, KY 40729
  Colortune and Flashtest test equipment

Winner International
1330 Kimberly Road
Sharon, PA 16146
  The Club antitheft device

Zelenda Machine and Tool Corporation
66–02 Austin Street
Forest Hills, NY 11374
  Volkswagen and Porsche specialty tools

Driving schools

Skip Barber Racing School
Route 7
Canaan, CT 06018

Derek Bell Motorsports
P.O. Box 11912
Ft. Lauderdale, FL 33339

Bondurant
Highways 37 and 121
Sonoma, CA 95476

Bertil Roos
P.O. Box 221
Blakeslee, PA 18610

Brumos Porsche
10246 Atlantic Boulevard
Jacksonville, FL 32211

Jim Russell British School of Motor Racing
22255 Eucalyptus Avenue, Room 2
Riverside, CA 92508
or
P.O. Box 119
Mt. Tremblant
Quebec, Canada J0T 1Z0

Track Time, Inc.
4464 Little John's Place
Youngstown, OH 44511

Index